The Rhetoric of Fiction

The Rhetoric
of Fiction

BY WAYNE C. BOOTH

THE UNIVERSITY OF CHICAGO PRESS

CHICAGO & LONDON

ISBN: 0-226-06577-4 (clothbound); 0-226-06578-2 (paperbound)

Library of Congress Catalog Card Number: 61-14947

THE UNIVERSITY OF CHICAGO PRESS, CHICAGO 60637
The University of Chicago Press, Ltd., London

To Ronald Crane

Preface ⟩

In writing about the rhetoric of fiction, I am not primarily interested in didactic fiction, fiction used for propaganda or instruction. My subject is the technique of non-didactic fiction, viewed as the art of communicating with readers—the rhetorical resources available to the writer of epic, novel, or short story as he tries, consciously or unconsciously, to impose his fictional world upon the reader. Though the problems raised by rhetoric in this sense are found in didactic works like *Gulliver's Travels*, *Pilgrim's Progress*, and *1984*, they are seen more clearly in non-didactic works like *Tom Jones*, *Middlemarch*, and *Light in August*. Is there any defense that can be offered, on aesthetic grounds, for an art full of rhetorical appeals? What kind of art is it that will allow Flaubert to barge into his action to describe Emma as "unaware that now she was eager to yield to the very thing that had made her so indignant," and as "totally unconscious that she was prostituting herself"? Whatever their answers, critics have often been troubled by this kind of overt, distinguishable rhetoric. But it takes no very deep analysis to show that the same problems are raised, though in less obvious form, by the disguised rhetoric of modern fiction; when Henry James says that he has invented a *ficelle* because the reader, not the hero, needs a "friend," the ostensibly dramatic move is still rhetorical; it is dictated by the effort to help the reader grasp the work.

I am aware that in pursuing the author's means of controlling his reader I have arbitrarily isolated technique from all of the social and psychological forces that affect authors and readers. For the most part I have had to rule out different demands made by different audiences in different times—the aspect of the rhetorical relationship treated with great acumen by Q. D. Leavis in *Fiction and the Reading Public*, Richard Altick in *The English Common Reader*, and Ian Watt in *The Rise of the Novel*. I have even more rigorously excluded questions about the psychological qualities in readers that account for the almost universal interest in fiction—the kind of question dealt with by Simon Lesser in *Fiction and the Unconscious*. Finally, I have had to ignore the psychology of the author and the whole question of how it relates to the creative process. I have, in short, ruled out many of the most interesting questions about fiction. My excuse is that only in doing so could I hope to deal adequately with the narrower question of whether rhetoric is compatible with art.

In treating technique as rhetoric, I may seem to have reduced the free and inexplicable processes of the creative imagination to the crafty calculations of commercial entertainers. The whole question of the difference between artists who consciously calculate and artists who simply express themselves with no thought of affecting a reader is an important one, but it must be kept separate from the question of whether an author's work, regardless of its source, communicates itself. The success of an author's rhetoric does not depend on whether he thought about his readers as he wrote; if "mere calculation" cannot insure success, it is equally true that even the most unconscious and Dionysian of writers succeeds only if he makes us join in the dance. By the very nature of my task I cannot do justice to those sources of artistic success which could never be calculatedly tapped, but one can accept this limitation without denying the importance of the incalculable or confining the study to works whose authors thought consciously of their readers.

I could not pursue this study at all without moving far from the secure harbor of my own special training. Careful as I have tried to be, I know that experts in each period or author are sure to find errors of fact or interpretation that no expert would commit. But I hope that my larger argument does not stand or fall on whether the reader agrees with all of my analyses. They are intended as illustrative, not definitive, and though the book includes, I think, some contributions to the reading of individual works, each critical conclusion could have been illustrated with many other works. If there is anything to my case, the experienced reader will be able to supply illustrations to replace those that seem to him faulty. My goal is not to set everyone straight about my favorite novelists but rather to free both readers and novelists from the constraints of abstract rules about what novelists must do, by reminding them in a systematic way of what good novelists have in fact done.

My debts to published criticism are acknowledged as fully as possible in footnotes and bibliography. For more personal help I want to thank Cecile Holvik—always much more than a typist—and those who gave detailed criticism to earlier drafts: Ronald S. Crane, Leigh Gibby, Judith Atwood Guttman, Marcel Gutwirth, Laurence Lerner, John Crowe Ransom, and—draft by draft, year by year—my wife. I am grateful to the John Simon Guggenheim Foundation for the grant which enabled me to complete the first draft, and to Earlham College for the sabbatical leave during which I have completed the last.

Acknowledgments

Thanks are due the following publishers for permission to reprint passages from the works indicated:

Edward Arnold Ltd.: From A Passage to India, by E. M. Forster, copyright, 1924.

Appleton-Century-Crofts, Inc.: From Thomas the Impostor, by Jean Cocteau, trans. Louis Galantière, copyright, 1925.

Jonathan Cape Ltd.: From "The Jilting of Granny Weatherall," by Katherine Anne Porter; from Stephen Hero and A Portrait of the Artist, by James Joyce; and from The House in Paris, by Elizabeth Bowen.

Chapman & Hall Ltd.: From Decline and Fall, by Evelyn Waugh.

Chatto and Windus Ltd.: From "Haircut," by Ring Lardner.

J. M. Dent & Sons Ltd.: From the Decameron, by Boccaccio, trans. J. M. Rigg; and from Nostromo, by Joseph Conrad, with permission of the trustees of the Joseph Conrad Estate.

E. P. Dutton and Co., Inc.: From the Decameron, by Boccaccio, trans. J. M. Rigg, in Everyman's Library.

Farrar, Straus and Cudahy, Inc.: From Epitaph of a Small Winner by Machado de Assis, trans. William L. Grossman. Copyright © 1952 by William L. Grossman. Used by permission of the Noonday Press, a subsidiary of Farrar, Straus and Cudahy, Inc.

Librairie Gallimard: From La Jument Verte, by Marcel Aymé.

Grove Press, Inc.: From Jealousy, by Alain Robbe-Grillet, trans. Richard Howard. Copyright © 1959 by Grove Press, Inc.

Harcourt, Brace & Co.: From A Passage to India, by E. M. Forster.

Acknowledgments

Harper & Brothers: From *The Captive and the Free*, by Joyce Cary.

William Heinemann Ltd.: From *Brighton Rock*, by Graham Greene.

Alfred A. Knopf, Inc.: From *The House in Paris*, by Elizabeth Bowen; from *The Counterfeiters*, by André Gide, trans. Dorothy Bussy; from *The Fall* and *The Stranger*, by Albert Camus, trans. Stuart Gilbert and Justin O'Brien; from *Confessions of Zeno*, by Italo Svevo (Ettore Schmitz), trans. Beryl de Zoete; and from *Mist*, by Unamuno, trans. Warner Fite.

The Macmillan Company: From "Sailing to Byzantium," by William Butler Yeats, copyright, 1929; and from *The Living Novel*, ed. Granville Hicks, copyright, 1957.

New Directions: From *Journey to the End of the Night* by Louis-Ferdinand Céline, trans. John H. P. Marks. Copyright 1934 by Louis-Ferdinand Céline. From *Laughter in the Dark* by Vladimir Nabokov. Copyright 1938 by New Directions. From *Stephen Hero* by James Joyce. Eds.: Theodore Spencer, John J. Slocum and Herbert Cahoon. Copyright 1944 and © 1955 by New Directions.

The New Yorker: From "Seymour: An Introduction," by J. D. Salinger.

Oxford University Press, Inc.: From *The Notebooks of Henry James*, ed. F. O. Matthiessen and K. B. Murdock.

Penguin Books Ltd.: From the *Odyssey* by Homer, trans. E. V. Rieu.

G. P. Putnam's Sons: From *Lolita*, by Vladimir Nabokov.

Random House, Inc.: From *The Brothers Karamazov*, by Dostoevski, trans. Constance Garnett; from "Barn Burning," *Light in August*, *The Sound and the Fury*, and *Intruder in the Dust*, by William Faulkner; and from *Remembrance of Things Past*, by Marcel Proust, trans. C. K. Scott-Moncrieff.

Charles Scribner's Sons: From: *Tender Is the Night* by F. Scott Fitzgerald. Copyright 1933, 1934 Charles Scribner's Sons; renewal copyright © 1961 Frances Scott Fitzgerald Lanahan. Copyright 1948, 1951 Frances Scott Fitzgerald Lanahan. From: *The Great Gatsby* by F. Scott Fitzgerald. Copyright 1925 Charles Scribner's Sons; renewal copyright 1953 Frances Scott Fitzgerald

Acknowledgments

Lanahan. From: *The Art of the Novel: Critical Prefaces* by Henry James. Copyright 1907, 1908, 1909 Henry James; renewal copyright 1935, 1936, 1937. Copyright 1909 Charles Scribner's Sons.

The Viking Press, Inc.: From *Finnegans Wake*, by James Joyce; from *Don Quixote*, by Cervantes, trans. Samuel Putnam.

The Yale Review: From "The Ambiguous Modern Novel," by Earl H. Rovit, copyright Yale University Press.

In addition, thanks are due the following persons for permission to reprint:

Vladimir Nabokov: From *Lolita*.

J. D. Salinger: From "Seymour: An Introduction," and from *The Catcher in the Rye*.

Mrs. William Butler Yeats: From "Sailing to Byzantium," by William Butler Yeats.

Contents

"It is the first necessity of the novelist's position that he make himself pleasant."—Trollope

"My task . . . is to make you see."—Conrad

"Until these things are judged and given each its appointed place in the whole scheme, they have no meaning in the world of art."—Katherine Mansfield, protesting the method of Dorothy Richardson

"The author makes his readers, just as he makes his characters."—Henry James

"I write; let the reader learn to read."—Mark Harris

PART I

Artistic Purity
and the
Rhetoric of Fiction

"Action, and tone, and gesture, the smile of the lover, the frown of the tyrant, the grimace of the buffoon,—all must be told [in the novel], for nothing can be shown. Thus, the very dialogue becomes mixed with the narration; for he must not only tell what the characters actually said, in which his task is the same as that of the dramatic author, but must also describe the tone, the look, the gesture, with which their speech was accompanied,—telling, in short, all which, in the drama, it becomes the province of the actor to express."—SIR WALTER SCOTT

"Authors like Thackeray, or Balzac, say, or H. G. Wells . . . are always *telling* the reader what happened instead of showing them the scene, telling them what to think of the characters rather than letting the reader judge for himself or letting the characters do the telling about one another. I like to distinguish between novelists that *tell* and those [like Henry James] that *show*."—JOSEPH WARREN BEACH

"The only law that binds the novelist throughout, whatever course he is pursuing, is the need to be consistent on *some* plan, to follow the principle he has adopted."—PERCY LUBBOCK

"A novelist can shift his view point if it comes off, and it came off with Dickens and Tolstoy."—E. M. FORSTER

CHAPTER ONE

Telling and Showing

AUTHORITATIVE "TELLING" IN EARLY NARRATION

One of the most obviously artificial devices of the storyteller is the trick of going beneath the surface of the action to obtain a reliable view of a character's mind and heart. Whatever our ideas may be about the natural way to tell a story, artifice is unmistakably present whenever the author tells us what no one in so-called real life could possibly know. In life we never know anyone but ourselves by thoroughly reliable internal signs, and most of us achieve an all too partial view even of ourselves. It is in a way strange, then, that in literature from the very beginning we have been told motives directly and authoritatively without being forced to rely on those shaky inferences about other men which we cannot avoid in our own lives.

"There was a man in the land of Uz, whose name was Job; and that man was perfect and upright, one that feared God, and eschewed evil." With one stroke the unknown author has given us a kind of information never obtained about real people, even about our most intimate friends. Yet it is information that we must accept without question if we are to grasp the story that is to follow. In life if a friend confided his view that *his* friend was "perfect and upright," we would accept the information with qualifications imposed by our knowledge of the speaker's character or of the general fallibility of mankind. We could never trust even the most reliable of witnesses as completely as we trust the author of the opening statement about Job.

We move immediately in Job to two scenes presented with no privileged information whatever: Satan's temptation of God and Job's first losses and lamentations. But we conclude the first section with another judgment which no real event could provide for any observer: "In all this Job sinned not, nor charged God foolishly." How do we know that Job sinned not? Who is to pronounce on such a question? Only God himself could know with certainty whether Job charged God foolishly. Yet the author pronounces judgment, and we accept his judgment without question.

It might at first appear that the author does not require us to rely on his unsupported word, since he gives us the testimonial of God himself, conversing with Satan, to confirm his view of Job's moral perfection. And after Job has been pestered by his three friends and has given his own opinion about his experience, God is brought on stage again to confirm the truth of Job's view. But clearly the reliability of God's statements ultimately depends on the author himself; it is he who names God and assures us that this voice is truly His.

This form of artificial authority has been present in most narrative until recent times. Though Aristotle praises Homer for speaking in his own voice less than other poets, even Homer writes scarcely a page without some kind of direct clarification of motives, of expectations, and of the relative importance of events. And though the gods themselves are often unreliable, Homer—the Homer we know—is not. What he tells us usually goes deeper and is more accurate than anything we are likely to learn about real people and events. In the opening lines of the *Iliad*, for example, we are told, under the half-pretense of an invocation, precisely what the tale is to be about: "the anger of Peleus' son Achilleus and its devastation."[1] We are told directly that we are to care more about the Greeks than the Trojans. We are told that they were "heroes" with

---

[1] Trans. Richmond Lattimore (Chicago, 1951). All quotations are from this translation.

"strong souls." We are told that it was the will of Zeus that they should be "the delicate feasting of dogs." And we learn that the particular conflict between Agamemnon, "the lord of men," and "brilliant" Achilles was set on by Apollo. We could never be sure of any of this information in real life, yet we are sure as we move through the *Iliad* with Homer constantly at our elbow, controlling rigorously our beliefs, our interests, and our sympathies. Though his commentary is generally brief and often disguised as simile, we learn from it the precise quality of every heart; we know who dies innocent and who guilty, who foolish and who wise. And we know, whenever there is any reason for us to know, what the characters are thinking: "the son of Tydeus pondered doubtfully / . . . . Three times in his heart and spirit he pondered turning . . ." (Book VIII, ll. 167–69).

In the *Odyssey* Homer works in the same explicit and systematic way to keep our judgments straight. Though E. V. Rieu is no doubt correct in calling Homer an "impersonal" and "objective" author, in the sense that the life of the real Homer cannot be discovered in his work,[2] Homer "intrudes" deliberately and obviously to insure that our judgment of the "heroic," "resourceful," "admirable," "wise" Odysseus will be sufficiently favorable. "Yet all the gods were sorry for him, except Poseidon, who pursued the heroic Odysseus with relentless malice till the day when he reached his own country."

Indeed, the major justification of the opening scene in the palace of Zeus is not as mere exposition of the facts of Odysseus' plight. What Homer requires of us is sympathetic involvement in that plight, and Athene's opening reply to Zeus provides authoritative judgment on what is to follow. "It is for Odysseus that my heart is wrung—the wise but unlucky Odysseus, who has been parted so long from all his friends and is pining on a lonely island far away in the middle of the seas." To her accusation of neglect, Zeus replies, "How could I ever forget the admirable Odysseus? He is not

---

[2] The *Odyssey*, trans. E. V. Rieu (Penguin ed., 1959), p. 10. The quotations that follow are from Rieu's translation, Books I–IV. Different translations give different emphases to Homer's moral judgments, and some use less forceful epithets than does Rieu. But no translator has been able to portray a neutral Homer.

only the wisest man alive but has been the most generous in his offerings. . . . It is Poseidon . . . who is so implacable towards him. . . ."

When we come to Odysseus' enemies, the poet again does not hesitate either to speak in his own person or to give divine testimony. Penelope's suitors must look bad to us; Telemachus must be admired. Not only does Homer dwell on Athene's approval of Telemachus, he lays on his own direct judgments with bright colors. The "insolent," "swaggering," and "ruffianly" suitors are contrasted to the "wise" (though almost helplessly young) Telemachus and the "good" Mentor. "Telemachus now showed his good judgment." Mentor "showed his good will now by rising to admonish his compatriots." We seldom encounter the suitors without some explicit attack by the poet: "This was their boastful way, though it was they who little guessed how matters really stood." And whenever there might be some doubt about where a character stands, Homer sets us straight: " 'My Queen,' replied Medon, who was by no means a villain . . . ." Hundreds of pages later, when Medon is spared from Odysseus' slaughter, we can hardly be surprised.

The result of all this direct guidance, when it is joined with Athene's divine attestation that the gods "have no quarrel" with Telemachus and have settled that he "shall come home safe," is to leave us, as we enter upon Odysseus' first adventure in Book Five, perfectly clear about what we should hope for and what fear; we are unambiguously sympathetic toward the heroes and contemptuous of the suitors. It need hardly be said that another poet, working with the same episodes but treating them from the suitors' point of view, could easily have led us into the same adventures with radically different hopes and fears.[3]

Direct and authoritative rhetoric of the kind we have seen in Job and in Homer's works has never completely disappeared from fiction. But as we all know, it is not what we are likely to find if we turn to a typical modern novel or short story.

Jim had a great trick that he used to play w'ile he was travelin'. For instance, he'd be ridin' on a train and they'd come to some little

---

[3] Some readers may fear at this point that I am stumbling blindfold into the "affective fallacy." I try to meet their legitimate concern in chaps. iii–v.

town like, well, like, we'll say, like Benton. Jim would look out of
the train window and read the signs on the stores.

For instance, they'd be a sign, "Henry Smith, Dry Goods." Well,
Jim would write down the name and the name of the town and
when he got to wherever he was goin' he'd mail back a postal card
to Henry Smith at Benton and not sign no name to it, but he'd write
on the card, well, somethin' like "Ask your wife about that book
agent that spent the afternoon last week," or "Ask your Missus who
kept her from gettin' lonesome the last time you was in Carterville."
And he'd sign the card, "A Friend."

Of course, he never knew what really come of none of these jokes,
but he could picture what probably happened and that was enough.
. . . Jim was a card.

Most readers of Lardner's "Haircut" (1926) have recognized
that Lardner's opinion of Jim is radically different here from the
speaker's. But no one in the story has said so. Lardner is not present
to say so, not, at least, in the sense that Homer is present in his
epics. Like many other modern authors, he has effaced himself, re-
nounced the privilege of direct intervention, retreated to the wings
and left his characters to work out their own fates upon the stage.

In sleep she knew she was in her bed, but not the bed she had
lain down in a few hours since, and the room was not the same but
it was a room she had known somewhere. Her heart was a stone lying
upon her breast outside of her; her pulses lagged and paused, and
she knew that something strange was going to happen, even as the
early morning winds were cool through the lattice. . . .

Now I must get up and go while they are all quiet. Where are
my things? Things have a will of their own in this place and hide
where they like. . . . Now what horse shall I borrow for this journey
I do not mean to take? . . . Come now, Graylie, she said, taking the
bridle, we must outrun Death and the Devil. . . .

The relation between author and spokesman is more complex
here. Katherine Anne Porter's Miranda ("Pale Horse, Pale Rider"
[1936]) cannot be simply classified, like Lardner's barber, as morally and intellectually deficient; the ironies at work among character, author, and reader are considerably more difficult to describe.
Yet the problem for the reader is essentially the same as in "Haircut." The story is presented without comment, leaving the reader
without the guidance of explicit evaluation.

Since Flaubert, many authors and critics have been convinced that "objective" or "impersonal" or "dramatic" modes of narration are naturally superior to any mode that allows for direct appearances by the author or his reliable spokesman. Sometimes, as we shall see in the next three chapters, the complex issues involved in this shift have been reduced to a convenient distinction between "showing," which is artistic, and "telling," which is inartistic. "I shall not *tell* you anything," says a fine young novelist in defense of his art. "I shall allow you to eavesdrop on my people, and sometimes they will tell the truth and sometimes they will lie, and you must determine for yourself when they are doing which. You do this every day. Your butcher says, 'This is the best,' and you reply, 'That's you saying it.' Shall my people be less the captive of their desires than your butcher? I can *show* much, but show only. . . . You will no more expect the novelist to tell you precisely *how* something is said than you will expect him to stand by your chair and hold your book."[4]

But the changed attitudes toward the author's voice in fiction raise problems that go far deeper than this simplified version of point of view would suggest. Percy Lubbock taught us forty years ago to believe that "the art of fiction does not begin until the novelist thinks of his story as a matter to be *shown*, to be so exhibited that it will tell itself."[5] He may have been in some sense right—but to say so raises more questions than it answers.

Why is it that an episode "told" by Fielding can strike us as more fully realized than many of the scenes scrupulously "shown" by imitators of James or Hemingway? Why does some authorial commentary ruin the work in which it occurs, while the prolonged commentary of *Tristram Shandy* can still enthral us? What, after all, does an author do when he "intrudes" to "tell" us something about his story? Such questions force us to consider closely what happens when an author engages a reader fully with a work of fiction; they lead us to a view of fictional technique which necessarily

---

[4] Mark Harris, "Easy Does It Not," in *The Living Novel*, ed. Granville Hicks (New York, 1957), p. 117.

[5] *The Craft of Fiction* (London, 1921), p. 62.

goes far beyond the reductions that we have sometimes accepted under the concept of "point of view."

Two Stories from the "Decameron"

Our task will be simpler if we begin with some stories written long before anyone worried very much about cleaning out the rhetorical impurities from the house of fiction. The stories in Boccaccio's *Decameron*, for example, seem extremely simple—perhaps even simple-minded and inept—if we ask of them the questions which many modern stories invite us to ask. It is bad enough that the characters are what we call two-dimensional, with no revealed depths of any kind; what is much worse, the "point of view" of the narrator shifts among them with a total disregard for the kind of technical focus or consistency generally admired today. But if we read these stories in their own terms, we soon discover a splendid and complex skill underlying the simplicity of the effect.

The material of the ninth story of the fifth day is in itself conventional and shallow indeed. There was once a young lover, Federigo, who impoverished himself courting a chaste married woman, Monna Giovanna. Rejected, he withdrew to a life of poverty, with only a beloved falcon remaining of all his former possessions. The woman's husband died. Her son, who had grown fond of Federigo's falcon, became seriously ill and asked Monna to obtain the falcon for his comfort. She reluctantly went to Federigo to request the falcon. Federigo was overwhelmed with excitement by her visit, and he was determined, in spite of his poverty, to entertain her properly. But his cupboard was bare, so he killed the falcon and served it to her. They discovered their misunderstanding, and the mother returned empty-handed to her boy, who soon died. But the childless widow, impressed by Federigo's generous gesture in offering his falcon, chose him for her second husband.

Such a story, reduced in this way to a bare outline, could have been made into any number of fully realized plots with radically different effects. It could have been a farce, stressing Federigo's foolish extravagance, his ridiculous antics in trying to think of something to serve his beloved for breakfast, and the absurdity of the surprise ending. It could have been a meditative or a comic piece on the ironical twists of fate, emphasizing the transformation in Monna from proud resistance to quick surrender—something on the order of Christopher Fry's *A Phoenix Too Frequent* as derived from Petronius. It could have been a sardonic tale written from the point of view of the husband and son who, like the falcon, must be killed off, as it were, to make the survivors happy. And so on.

As it is, every stroke is in a direction different from these. The finished tale is designed to give the reader the greatest possible pleasure in the sympathetic comedy of Monna's and Federigo's deserved good fortune, to make the reader delight in this instance of the announced theme for all the tales told on the fifth day: "good fortune befalling lovers after divers direful or disastrous adventures."[6] Though one never views these characters or their "direful or disastrous adventures" in anything like a tragic light, and though, in fact, one laughs at the excesses of Federigo's passion and at his willingness to pursue it even to poverty, our laughter must always be sympathetic. Much as Federigo deserves his disasters, in the finished tale he also deserves the supreme good fortune of winning Monna.

To insure our pleasure in such an outcome—a pleasure which might have been mild indeed considering that there are nine other tales attempting something like the same effect—the two main characters must be established with great precision. First the heroine, Monna Giovanna, must be felt to be thoroughly worthy of Federigo's "extravagant" love. In a longer, different kind of story, this might have been done by showing her in virtuous action; one could take whatever space were required for episodes dramatizing her as worthy of Federigo's fantastic devotion. But here economy is at least as important as precision. And the economical method of imposing her virtues on the reader is for the narrator to *tell* us about them, supporting his telling with some judiciously chosen, and by modern standards very brief and unrealistic, episodes. These can be of two kinds, either in the form of what James was later to call "going behind" to reveal the true workings of the heroine's mind and heart or in the form of overt action. Thus, the narrator

---

6 Trans. J. M. Rigg (Everyman ed., 1930). All quotations are from this edition.

begins by describing her as the "fairest" and "most elegant," and as "no less virtuous than fair." In a simple story of this kind, her beauty and elegance require for validation no more than Federigo's dramatized passion. Our belief in her virtue, however—certainly in Boccaccio a more unlikely gift than beauty and elegance—is supported both by her sustained chastity in the face of his courtship and, far more important, by the quality of what is revealed when-ever we enter her thoughts.

> Whereupon the lady was silent a while, bethinking her what she should do. She knew that Federigo had long loved her, and had never had so much as a single kind look from her: wherefore she said to herself:—How can I send or go to beg of him this falcon, which by what I hear is the best that ever flew, and moreover is his sole com-fort? And how could I be so unfeeling as to seek to deprive a gentle-man of the one solace that is now left him? And so, albeit she very well knew that she might have the falcon for the asking, she was perplexed, and knew not what to say, and gave her son no answer. At length, however, the love she bore the boy carried the day, and she made up her mind, for his contentment . . . to go herself and fetch him the falcon.

The interest in this passage lies of course in the moral choice that it presents and in the effect upon our sentiments that is implicit in that choice. Though the choice is in one respect a relatively trivial one, it is far more important than most choices faced by the char-acters who people Boccaccio's world. Dramatized at greater length, it could in fact have been made into the central episode for the story—though the story that resulted would be a far different one from what we now have. As it is treated here, the choice is given precisely the degree of importance it should have in the whole. Be-cause we experience Monna's thoughts and feelings at first hand, we are forced to agree with the narrator's assessment of her great worth. She is not simply virtuous in conventional matters like chas-tity, but she is also capable of moral delicacy in more fundamental matters: unlike the majority of Boccaccio's women, she is above any casual manipulation of her lover for her own purposes. Even this delicacy, admirable in itself, can be overridden by a more im-portant value, "the love she bore the boy." Yet all this is kept strictly serviceable to our greater interest in Federigo and the falcon; there is never any question of our becoming sidetracked into deep psychological or sentimental involvement with her as a person.

Because the narrator has *told* us what to think of her, and then *shown* her briefly in support of his claims, all the while keeping our sympathy and admiration carefully subordinated to the comic effect of the whole, we can move to the most important episode with our expectations clear and—in their own kind—intense. We can move to Monna's relatively long and wonderfully delicate speech to Federigo requesting the falcon, with our hopes centered clearly on the "good fortune" of their ultimate union.

If all this skilful presentation of the admirable Monna is to succeed, we must see Federigo himself as an equally admirable, though not really heroic, figure. Too much moral stature will spoil the comedy; too little will destroy our desire for his success. It is not enough to show his virtues through his actions; his only admirable act is the gift of the falcon and that might be easily interpreted in itself as a further bit of foolish extravagance. Unless the story is to be lengthened unduly with episodes showing that he is worthy, in spite of his extravagance, the narrator must give us briefly and directly the necessary information about his true character. He is therefore described, unobtrusively but in terms that only an omniscient narrator could use with success, as "gallant," "full of courtesy," "patient," and most important of all, as "more in love than ever before"; the world of *his* desires is thus set off distinctly from the world of many of the other tales, where love is reduced for comic purposes to lust.

These completely straightforward statements of the narrator's opinions are supported by what we see of Federigo's own mind. His comic distress over not having anything to feed his beloved visitor, and his unflinching sacrifice of the bird, are rendered in intimate detail, with frequent—though by modern standards certainly shallow—inside views; his poverty "was brought home to him," he was "distressed beyond measure," he "inwardly" cursed "his evil fortune." "Sorely he longed that the lady might not leave his house altogether unhonoured, and yet to crave help of his own husbandman was more than his pride could brook." All this insures that the wonderful comedy of the breakfast will be the comedy of sympathetic laughter: we are throughout completely in favor of Fede-

rigo's suit. And our favor is heightened by the method of presenting the scene of discovery. "No sooner had Federigo apprehended
what the lady wanted, than, *for grief that 'twas not in his power to
serve her* . . . he fell a-weeping. . . ." At first Monna supposed that
" 'twas only because he was loath to part with the brave falcon that
he wept." We might have made the same mistake but for the author's help provided in the clause I have italicized.

Once we have become assured of his character in this way, Federigo's speeches, like Monna Giovanna's, become the equivalent of
inside views, because we know that everything he says is a trustworthy reflection of his true state of mind. His long speech of explanation about the falcon serves, as a result, to confirm all we have
learned of him; when he concludes, "I doubt I shall never know
peace of mind more," we believe in his sincerity, though of course
we know with complete certainty, and have known from the beginning, that the story is to end with "good fortune."

Having seen this much, we need little more. To make Monna
the heiress as provided in the will, her son must die in a passage
only one or two lines longer than the one or two lines earlier given
to the death of the husband. Her "inward commendation" of Federigo's "magnanimity" leads her to the decision to marry him rather
than a wealthy suitor: "I had rather have a man without wealth
than wealth without a man." Federigo *is* a man, as we know by
now. Though his portrait is conventional, "flat," "two-dimensional," it includes everything we need. We can thus accept without irony the narrator's concluding judgment that married to such
a wife he lived happily to the end of his days. Fiammetta's auditors
all "praised God that He had worthily rewarded Federigo."

If we share in the pleasure of seeing the comic but worthy hero
worthily rewarded, the reason is thus not to be found in any inherent quality of the materials but rather in the skilful construction of
a living plot out of materials that might have been used in many
different ways. The deaths of the husband and son, which in the
finished version are merely conveniences for Federigo's exaltation,
would in any truly impartial account occupy considerably more
space than Federigo's anxiety over not having anything to serve his
mistress. Treated impartially, the boy's death would certainly be

dramatized as fully as the mother's hesitation about troubling Federigo for his falcon. But the demands of this plot are for a technique that wins us to Federigo's side.

Quite obviously this technique cannot be judged by modern standards of consistency; the story could not have been written from a consistent point of view without stretching it to three times its present length and thereby losing its taut comic force. To tell it entirely through Federigo's eyes would require a much longer introductory section, and the comedy of the visit to fetch the falcon would be partially lost if we did not see more of the preparation for it than Federigo can possibly be aware of. Yet since it is primarily Federigo's story, to see it through Monna's eyes would require a great deal of manipulation and extension. Such conjectural emendations are in a way absurd, since they almost certainly would never have occurred to Boccaccio. But they help to make emphatic the great gap that separates Boccaccio's technique from the more obviously rigorous methods we have come to look for. In this story there is no important revelation of truth, no intensity of illusion, no ironic complexity, no prophetic vision, no rich portrayal of moral ambiguities. There is some incidental irony, it is true, but the greatness of the whole resides in unequivocal intensity not of illusion but of comic delight produced in extraordinarily brief compass.

Any temptation we might have to attribute its success to unconscious or accidental primitivism can be dispelled by looking at the radically different experience offered by other tales. Since his different effects are based on different moral codes, Boccaccio can never assume that his readers will hold precisely the correct attitudes as they approach any one story. He certainly does not assume that his readers will approve of the license of his most licentious tales. Even Dioneo, the most lewd of all the ten narrators, must spend a good deal of energy manipulating us into the camp of those who can laugh with a clear conscience at his bawdy and often cruel stories. In the potentially distressing tale of how the holy man, Rustico, debauches the young and innocent Alibech by teaching her how to put the devil in hell (third day, tenth tale), great care is taken with the character and ultimate fate of the simple-minded girl in order to lead us to laugh at conduct that in most worlds, including the world in which Boccaccio lived, would be considered cruel and sacrilegious rather than comic.

If Dioneo, the lusty young courtier, must use care with his rhetoric in a bawdy tale, Fiammetta, the lovely lady, must use even more when she comes to praise infidelity. On the seventh day the subject is "the tricks which, either for love or for their deliverance from peril, ladies have heretofore played their husbands, and whether they were by the said husbands detected, or no." In "The Falcon" Fiammetta worked to build admiration for the virtue of Federigo and Monna Giovanna; she now (fifth tale) employs a different rhetoric. Since her task is to insure our delight in the punishment of a justifiably jealous husband, her commentary tells us directly what is borne out by our views of the husband's mind: he is "a poor creature, and of little sense" who deserves what he gets. More important, she prefaces the story with a little oration, about one-seventh of the length of the whole story, setting our values straight: "For which reason, to sum up, I say that a wife is rather to be commended than censured, if she take her revenge upon a husband that is jealous without cause."

In support of this general argument, the whole tale is manipulated in such a way as to make the reader desire the comic punishment of the husband. Most of it is seen through the eyes of the woman, with great stress on her comic suffering at the hands of the great bullying fool. The climax is his full punishment, in the form of a clever, lashing speech from his wife. Few readers can feel that he has received anything but what he deserves when Fiammetta concludes that the cuckold's wife has now earned her "charter of indulgence."

These extremes by no means exhaust the variety of norms that we are led to accept by the shifting rhetoric as we move through the *Decameron*. The standards of judgment change so radically, in fact, that it is difficult to discern any figure in Boccaccio's carpet.[7]

---

[7] Erich Auerbach, for example, complains that he can find no basic moral attitude and no clear approach to reality lying back of all the tales. So long as he considers what Boccaccio does "for the sake of the comic effect," he has nothing but praise for his "critical sense" of the world, "firm yet elastic in perspective, which, without ab-

I shall try later on to deal with some of the issues raised when an author heightens specific effects at the expense of his general notions of moral truth or reality. What is important here is to recognize the radical inadequacy of the telling-showing distinction in dealing with the practice of this one author. Boccaccio's artistry lies not in adherence to any one supreme manner of narration but rather in his ability to order various forms of telling in the service of various forms of showing.

The Author's Many Voices

In the next three chapters I shall look in detail at some of the more important arguments for authorial objectivity or impersonality. Most of these call for eliminating certain overt signs of the author's presence. As we might expect, however, one man's objectivity is another man's bête noire. If we are to have any degree of clarity as we make our way through attacks on the author's voice, we must have some preliminary notion of the variety of forms that voice can take, both in fiction and in attacks on fiction. What is it, in fact, that we might expunge if we attempted to drive the author from the house of fiction?

First, we must erase all direct addresses to the reader, all commentary in the author's own name. When the author of the *Decameron* speaks to us directly, in both the introduction and conclusion, whatever illusion we may have had that we are dealing immediately with Fiammetta and her friends is shattered. An astonishing number of authors and critics since Flaubert have agreed that such direct, unmediated commentary will not do. And even

---

stract moralizing, allots phenomena their specific, carefully nuanced moral value" (*Mimesis: The Representation of Reality in Western Literature* [Berne, 1946], trans. Willard Trask [Anchor Books ed., 1957], p. 193). It is only on the level of the most general qualities, common to all the stories despite the differing needs of the moment, that Auerbach encounters difficulties and complains of the "vagueness and uncertainty" of Boccaccio's "early humanism" (p. 202). Auerbach's account is invaluable in showing how Boccaccio's style, in so far as it is common to all of the tales, serves as a kind of rhetoric convincing the reader of the reality of his world.

those authors who would allow it have often, like E. M. Forster, forbidden it except on certain limited subjects.[8]

But what, really, is "commentary"? If we agree to eliminate all personal intrusions of the kind used by Fielding, do we then agree to expunge less obtrusive comment? Is Flaubert violating his own principles of impersonality when he allows himself to tell us that in such and such a place one finds the worst Neufchatel cheeses of the entire district, or that Emma was "incapable of understanding what she didn't experience, or of recognizing anything that wasn't expressed in conventional terms"?[9]

Even if we eliminate all such explicit judgments, the author's presence will be obvious on every occasion when he moves into or out of a character's mind—when he "shifts his point of view," as we have come to put it. Flaubert tells us that Emma's little attentions to Charles were "never, as he believed, for his sake . . . but for her own, out of exasperated vanity" (p. 69). It is clearly Flaubert who constructs this juxtaposition of Emma's motive with Charles' belief about the motive, and the same obtrusive "voice" is evident whenever a new mind is introduced. When Emma's father bids farewell to Emma and Charles, he remembers "his own wedding, his own earlier days. . . . He, too, had been very happy. . . . He felt dismal, like a stripped and empty house" (pp. 34–35). This momentary shift to Rouault is Flaubert's way of providing us with an evaluation of the marriage and a sense of what is to come. If we are troubled by all reminders of the author's presence, we shall be troubled here.

But if we are to object to this, why not go the next step and object to all inside views, not simply those that require a shift in point of view. In life such views are not to be had. The act of providing them in fiction is itself an obtrusion by the author.[10]

---

[8] Forster would not allow the author to take "the reader into his confidence about his characters," since "intimacy is gained but at the expense of illusion and nobility." But he allows the author to take the reader into his confidence "about the universe" (*Aspects of the Novel* [London, 1927], pp. 111–12).

[9] *Madame Bovary*, trans. Francis Steegmuller (New York, 1957), p. 80.

[10] Such obtrusions are especially obvious in narration that purports to be historical. And yet intelligent men were until quite recently able to read ostensibly historical ac-

For that matter, we must object to the reliable statements of any dramatized character, not just the author in his own voice, because the act of narration as performed by even the most highly dramatized narrator is itself the author's presentation of a prolonged "inside view" of a character. When Fiammetta says "the love she bore the boy carried the day," she is giving us a reliable inside view of Monna, and she is also giving a view of her own evaluation of events. Both are reminders of the author's controlling hand.

But why stop here? The author is present in every speech given by any character who has had conferred upon him, in whatever manner, the badge of reliability. Once we know that God is God in Job, once we know that Monna speaks only truth in "The Falcon," the authors speak whenever God and Monna speak. Introducing the great Doctor Larivière, Flaubert says:

> He belonged to that great surgical school created by Bichat—that generation, now vanished, of philosopher-practitioners, who cherished their art with fanatical love and applied it with enthusiasm and sagacity. Everyone in his hospital trembled when he was angry; and his students so revered him that the moment they set up for themselves they imitated him as much as they could. . . . Disdainful of decorations . . . hospitable, generous, a father to the poor, practicing Christian virtues although an unbeliever, he might have been thought of as a saint if he hadn't been feared as a devil because of the keenness of his mind [pp. 363–64].

This unambiguous bestowal of authority contributes greatly to the power of the next few pages, in which Larivière judges for us everything that we see. But helpful as he is, he must go—if the author's voice is a fault.

Even here we cannot stop, though many of the critics of the author's voice have stopped here. We can go on and on, purging

counts, like the Bible, packed with such illicit entries into private minds, with no distress whatever. For us it may seem strange that the writers of the Gospels should claim so much knowledge of what Christ is feeling and thinking. "Moved with pity, he stretched out his hand and touched him" (Mark 1:41). "And Jesus, perceiving in himself that power had gone forth from him . . ." (5:30). Who reported to the authors these internal events? Who told them what occurs in the Garden, when everyone but Jesus is asleep? Who reported to them that Christ prays to God to "let this cup pass"? Such questions, like the question of how Moses could have written an account of his own death and burial, may be indispensable in historical criticism, but they can easily be overdone in literary criticism.

the work of every recognizably personal touch, every distinctive literary allusion or colorful metaphor, every pattern of myth or symbol; they all implicitly evaluate. Any discerning reader can recognize that they are imposed by the author.[11]

Finally, we might even follow Jean-Paul Sartre and object, in the name of "durational realism," to all evidences of the author's meddling with the natural sequence, proportion, or duration of events. Earlier authors, Sartre says, tried to justify "the foolish business of storytelling by ceaselessly bringing to the reader's attention, explicitly or by allusion, the existence of an author." The existentialist novels, in contrast, will be "toboggans, forgotten, unnoticed," hurling the reader "into the midst of a universe where there are no witnesses." Novels should "exist in the manner of things, of plants, of events, and not at first like products of man."[12] If this is so, the author must never summarize, never curtail a conversation, never telescope the events of three days into a paragraph. "If I pack six months into a single page, the reader jumps out of the book" (p. 229).

Sartre is certainly right in claiming that all these things are signs of the author's manipulating presence. In *The Brothers Karamazov*, for example, the story of Father Zossima's conversion could logically be placed anywhere. The events of Zossima's story took place long before the novel begins; unless they are to be placed at the beginning, which is out of the question, there is no natural reason for giving them in one place rather than another. Wherever they are placed, they will call attention to the author's selecting presence, just as Homer is glaringly present to us whenever the *Odyssey* takes one of its many leaps back and forth over a nineteen-year period. It is not accident but Dostoevski's careful choice that gives us Zossima's story as the sequel to Ivan's dream of the Grand Inquisitor. It is intended as a judgment on the values implied by

---

[11] Speaking of Joyce's *Ulysses*, Edmund Wilson once complained that as soon as "we are aware of Joyce himself systematically embroidering on his text," packing in puzzles, symbols, and puns, "the illusion of the dream is lost" ("James Joyce," *Axel's Castle* [New York, 1931], p. 235).

[12] "Situation of the Writer in 1947," *What Is Literature?* trans. Bernard Frechtman (London, 1950), p. 169.

that dream, just as everything that happens to Ivan afterward is an explicit criticism of his own ideas. Since the sequence is obviously not dictated by anything other than the author's purposes, it betrays the author's voice, and according to Sartre, it presumably will not do.

But, as Sartre woefully admits (see chap. iii, below), even with all these forms of the author's voice expunged, what we have left will reveal to us a shameful artificiality. Unless the author contents himself with simply retelling The Three Bears or the story of Oedipus in the precise form in which they exist in popular accounts—and even so there must be some choice of *which* popular form to tell—his very choice of what he tells will betray him to the reader. He chooses to tell the tale of Odysseus rather than that of Circe or Polyphemus. He chooses to tell the cheerful tale of Monna and Federigo rather than a pathetic account of Monna's husband and son. He chooses to tell the story of Emma Bovary rather than the potentially heroic tale of Dr. Larivière. The author's voice is as passionately revealed in the decision to write the *Odyssey*, "The Falcon," or *Madame Bovary* as it is in the most obtrusive direct comment of the kind employed by Fielding, Dickens, or George Eliot. Everything he *shows* will serve to *tell*; the line between showing and telling is always to some degree an arbitrary one.

In short, the author's judgment is always present, always evident to anyone who knows how to look for it. Whether its particular forms are harmful or serviceable is always a complex question, a question that cannot be settled by any easy reference to abstract rules. As we begin now to deal with this question, we must never forget that though the author can to some extent choose his disguises, he can never choose to disappear.

"Hard and fast rules, a *priori* restrictions, mere interdictions (you shall not speak of this, you shall not look at that) have surely served their time, and will in the nature of the case never strike an energetic talent as anything but arbitrary. A healthy, living and growing art, full of curiosity and fond of exercise, has an indefeasible mistrust of rigid prohibitions."
—HENRY JAMES

"Since Stephen Crane's time, all serious writers have concentrated on the effort of rendering individual scenes more vividly."—CAROLINE GORDON

"In proportion as in what Fiction offers us we see life *without* rearrangement do we feel that we are touching the truth; in proportion as we see it *with* rearrangement do we feel that we are being put off with a substitute, a compromise and convention."—HENRY JAMES

"There is no such thing as a novel which genuinely portrays the indetermination of human life as we know it."—FRANÇOIS MAURIAC

"The action of my new work takes place at night. It's natural things should not be so clear at night, isn't it now?"—JAMES JOYCE, defending *Finnegans Wake* against Pound's charge that it was "obscure"

CHAPTER TWO

General Rules, I:
"True Novels Must Be Realistic"

FROM JUSTIFIED REVOLT TO CRIPPLING DOGMA

To the first writers who spoke against the old style of authoritative rhetoric, the problem of the author's voice in fiction was extremely complicated. James's Prefaces, for example, those shrewd and indispensable explorations into the writer's craft,[1] offer no easy reduction of technique to a simple dichotomy of telling versus showing, no pat rejection of all but James's own methods. And, in fact, James's own methods were surprisingly varied. The persistent enemy for James was intellectual and artistic sloth, not any particular way of telling or showing a story. It is true that he found himself more and more interested in exploring what could be done with the "scenic art" and less and less satisfied with narrating in his own voice. And he was convinced that he had found a way to perform the traditional rhetorical tasks in an essentially dramatic way, by employing a "center of consciousness" through whom

---

[1] Most easily available in the edition of R. P. Blackmur, *The Art of the Novel* (New York, 1947). For some anticipations of James's emphasis on dramatic, impersonal narration see Richard Stang's *The Theory of the Novel in England, 1850–1870* (New York, 1959).

everything could be seen and felt. What is more, he did talk at times as if he valued his new methods more than all others. But his general emphasis is on the fact that the house of fiction has "not one window, but a million,"[2] that there are, in fact, "five million" ways to tell a story, each of them justified if it provides a "center" for the work.[3] And his catholicity is not confined to technique. In "The Art of Fiction" he explicitly repudiates any effort to say "definitely beforehand what sort of an affair the good novel will be." For him the only absolute requirement is that "it be interesting."[4] He will praise a novel like *Treasure Island* because it succeeds "wonderfully in what it attempts" (p. 605), even though it has very little relation to the kind of realism of subject and manner sought in his own tales.

The same can be said of Flaubert, the other author most frequently referred to by critics interested in the telling-showing distinction. Though he can be quoted to support this or that dogma, he was interested at one time or another in almost every important problem faced by novelists, and he was aware of a real tension between what might be desirable in general and what is possible in the particular case.

It did not take long, however, for these flexible explorations to become schematized. Even in the works of the first critics who attempted to do justice to James, we find the process of reduction already under way. In Percy Lubbock's *Craft of Fiction* (1921), James's treatment of dozens of literary problems—of the author's character, of his method of finding a subject, of the superiority of some subjects over other subjects, of the difficulties in finding credible centers of consciousness, of the methods for disguising one's rhetorical ruses[5]—is reduced to the one thing needful: a novel should be made dramatic. Lubbock's account is clearer and more systematic than James's; he gives us a neat and helpful scheme of

---

[2] *Art of the Novel*, p. 46.

[3] Letter to Mrs. Humphry Ward, July 25, 1899, *Letters*, ed. Percy Lubbock (London, 1920), I, 332–36.

[4] "The Art of Fiction," first published 1888, reprinted widely. My quotations are from *Henry James: Selected Fiction*, ed. Leon Edel (Everyman ed., 1953), p. 591.

[5] See the useful tabulation by Blackmur in his Introduction to *The Art of the Novel*.

relationships among the terms *panorama, picture, drama,* and *scene.* It is a scheme that James can be made to support, but in James's account it is surrounded with important qualifications which in Lubbock are already beginning to be slighted.

Similarly, Joseph Warren Beach is only occasionally dogmatic about the author's commentary. Even while hailing the "exit" of the author as the "most impressive thing about the modern novel," he could still say that "if the author succeeds in presenting his theme effectively . . . we shall not quarrel with his personal appearances. . . . Our main quarrel is with the author who makes his personal appearance a *substitute* for the artistic presentation of his subject, thinking that talking about the subject is equivalent to presenting it."[6] Even when Lubbock and Beach become a bit over-enthusiastic, one feels that they have the legitimate excuse of all champions of a new cause: the old loquacious ways of telling a story had gained the field and needed no defense. It was the "new type of novelist," as Beach wrote two years after James's death, "in the person of its most notable exemplar in English," that was then in need of defense.[7]

But the legitimate defense of the new soon froze into dogma. To Ford Madox Ford, writing in 1930, the battle for truth and light—the battle against a technique which is always in all circumstances bad—had at last been won.

> The novelist must not, by taking sides, exhibit his preferences. . . . He has . . . to render and not to tell. . . .
> On the whole those characteristics which never before characterized the English novel characterize it to-day. No one, that is, would to-day set out to capture the suffrages of either the more instructed or of even the almost altogether naïf with a novel of the type of those written by the followers of Bunyan, Defoe, Fielding. . . . No author would, like Thackeray, to-day intrude his broken nose and myopic spectacles into the middle of the most thrilling scene he ever wrote, in order to tell you that, though his heroine was rather a wrong 'un, his own heart was in his [*sic*] right place.[8]

---

[6] *The Twentieth-Century Novel: Studies in Technique* (New York, 1932), p. 468.

[7] *The Method of Henry James* (2d ed.; Philadelphia, 1954), p. 99.

[8] *The English Novel: From the Earliest Days to the Death of Joseph Conrad* (London, 1930), pp. 121, 122, 137–38. See also p. 77 and *passim*.

Naturally enough, when such rule-making descended further into the hands of unabashed commercial critics, it was simplified to the point of caricature.

> Now consider this bit of writing [Kobold Knight requested of the aspiring young authors of 1936]:
> "I heard many years ago that Grandpa Russell had married again and had had another son, John. . . ."
> While you read through that passage what did you *see?* You saw nothing at all. No picture is presented. . . .
> Now that form of telling is obviously not *dramatic* telling. It is what I call "second-hand" telling. A narrator relates in his own haphazard way something that happened a long time ago. That story . . . is certainly not *telling itself*. As a matter of cold fact that story has not yet even begun to *move.* . . .
> Now notice this:
> "The great car took the hairpin bend on two wheels, and the fugitive cast an agonized glance down the winding mountain road. Far below him but drawing ever closer, was the pillar of yellow dust that was the avenger."
> That *is* dramatic telling. The story *is* telling itself, please note. . . . It is dramatic telling—and it is the only kind of story-telling, speaking broadly, that editors want and will pay for. . . .
> In a word, "The story is *Telling Itself*."[9]

Unfortunately, it was not only in commercial handbooks that technique was reduced to the problem of how to get rid of a commentary that is by definition bad. In serious college textbooks one soon found and still finds the telling-showing distinction presented as a reliable clue to the miraculous superiority of modern fiction. One such text, after deploring certain "inert" passages in Stendhal and treating Poe and Hawthorne primarily as sincere forerunners of the moderns, finally arrives at Joyce's "The Dead." The passage praising this excellent story is worth quoting at length.

> In fact, from the beginning to the end of the story we are never told anything; we are shown everything. We are not told, for example, that the *milieu* of the story is the provincial, middle-class, "cultivated" society of Dublin at the turn of the century; we are not told that Gabriel represents its emotional sterility (as contrasted with the "peasant" richness of his wife Gretta). . . . All this we see

9 Kobold Knight, *A Guide to Fiction-writing* (London, 1936), p. 91.

dramatized; it is all made active. Nothing is given us from the externally omniscient point of view. . . . There is a brief description of Gabriel; but it is not Joyce's description; we see him as Lily sees him—or might see him if she had Joyce's superior command of the whole situation. This, in fact, is the method of "The Dead." From this point on we are never far from Gabriel's physical sight; yet we are constantly looking through his physical eyes at values and insights of which he is incapable. The significance of the *milieu*, the complacency of Gabriel's feeling for his wife, her romantic image of her lover Michael Furey . . . would have been put before us, in the pre-James era, as exposition and commentary through the direct intercession of the author; and it would have remained inert.[10]

Much of our scholarly and critical work of the highest seriousness has, in fact, employed this same dialectical opposition between artful showing and inartistic, merely rhetorical, telling. One scholar, ostensibly defending Trollope's use of "exegesis," finds that he is, indeed, "guilty, and that frequently, of authorial exegesis," that these "intrusions" are "violations of artistry," but that Trollope uses the inartistic device so cleverly that at times he makes "a virtue out of a defect."[11] Another scholar, writing sympathetically of the great eighteenth-century author-commentators, spends much of her time apologizing for their lack of artistry in this regard. Fielding's intrusions are necessarily "defensive," she finds, since the novel was not yet an established form; the century demanded moralizing commentary, with the result that no novelist was able to achieve a "complete fusion between the critic-moralist and the creative artist. . . ."[12] Again, one of the most sensitive authorities on the work of Thomas Hardy describes as a limitation, due to the influence of his times, Hardy's tendency to "intrude upon the narrative to make explicit his philosophy or his judgment of the characters and the events in which they are involved."[13] He makes no effort to distinguish good comments from bad. For him, as for

---

[10] Caroline Gordon and Allen Tate, *The House of Fiction* (New York, 1950), p. 280.
[11] Edd Winfield Parks, "Trollope and the Defense of Exegesis," *Nineteenth-Century Fiction*, VII (March, 1953), 265–71.
[12] Irma Z. Sherwood, "The Novelists as Commentators," in *The Age of Johnson: Essays Presented to Chauncey Brewster Tinker* (New Haven, Conn., 1949), pp. 113–25.
[13] Harvey C. Webster, Introduction to *The Mayor of Casterbridge* (New York, 1948), p. vi.

many others, commentary in itself, especially if there is "too much"—though what is "too much" is usually left unexamined—is simply bad.[14]

One cannot restore telling to critical respect simply by jumping to its defense—not on this field of battle. Its opponents would have most of the effective ammunition. Many novels are seriously flawed by careless intrusions. What is more, it is easy to prove that an episode shown is more effective than the same episode told, so long as we must choose between two and only two technical extremes. And, finally, the novelists and critics who have deplored telling have won for fiction the kind of standing as a major art form which, before Flaubert, was generally denied to it, and they have often shown a seriousness and devotion to their art that in itself carries conviction about their doctrines. Nothing is gained—indeed, everything is lost—if we say to James and Flaubert that we admire their experiments in artistic seriousness, but that we prefer now to relax our standards a little and encourage the novelist to go back to concocting what James called "great fluid puddings." There may be room, in the house of fiction, even for formless puddings—to be read, presumably, in one's slack hours or declining years. But I should not like to find myself defending them as art and on the ground that they are formless.

But are we faced with such a simple and disconcerting choice as the champions of showing have sometimes claimed? Does it, after all, make sense to set up two ways of conveying a story, one all good, the other all bad; one all art and form, the other all clumsiness and irrelevancy; one all showing and rendering and drama and objectivity, the other all telling and subjectivity and preaching and inertness? Allen Tate seems to think that it does. "The action," he says of a passage from *Madame Bovary*—and it is an excellent passage—"the action is not stated from the point of view of the author; it is rendered in terms of situation and scene. To have made this the viable property of the art of fiction was to have virtually made the art of fiction." "It has been through Flaubert that the

---

14 It would be possible to fill a small book with passages of this kind alone. See Bibliography, Sec. II, A.

novel has at last caught up with poetry."[15] This is dramatic, challenging—perhaps it is even the sort of inspiriting program which might yield to a young novelist enough conviction about the importance of what he is doing to get it done. But is it true?

I cannot prove that it is not—given Tate's definitions of "art" and "poetry." But I hope to show that it has been at best misleading, and that the distinction on which it is based is inadequate, not only in dealing with early fiction like the *Decameron* but also in dealing with yesterday's *succès d'estime*.

It will be useful first to look at some of the reasons for the widespread acceptance of the distinction. If we are to conclude that there was after all an art of fiction before Flaubert, and that the art even in the most impersonal fiction does not reside exclusively in the moments of vivid dramatic rendering, why has there been such widespread suspicion of everything but the rendered scene?

FROM DIFFERENTIATED KINDS TO UNIVERSAL QUALITIES

One answer lies in the modern love of generalization about "all novels," or "all literature," or "all art." "All art aspires to the condition of music." "All fiction tries to become poetry." "The *quidditas* of the novel is an interest in the facts." True novels do this, true literature does that. "The one object of *all art* "worthy of the name" is to "carry still a witness to the lost order of the world."[16] For Ortega y Gasset the seven general tendencies that cover *all* essentially *modern works* are "(1) to dehumanize art, (2) to avoid living forms, (3) to see to it that the work of art is nothing but a work of art, (4) to consider art as play and nothing else, (5) to be essentially ironical, (6) to beware of sham and hence to aspire to scrupulous realization, (7) to regard art as a thing of no

---

[15] "Techniques of Fiction," *Sewanee Review*, LII (1944), 210–25; also in *On the Limits of Poetry* (New York, 1948), pp. 143-44, 145.

[16] Denis de Rougemont, "Religion and the Mission of the Artist," in *Spiritual Problems in Contemporary Literature*, ed. Stanley Romaine Hopper (New York, 1952; Harper Torchbook ed., 1957), p. 179. The "music" generalization is of course from Pater and company; "poetry" from Faulkner, Tate, and a host of others; "fact" from Mary McCarthy, "The Fact in Fiction," *Partisan Review*, XXVII (Summer, 1960), 440.

transcending consequence."[17] For Ford Madox Ford the common aim of good modern novelists like James, Crane, Conrad, and himself is "to take the reader, immerse him in an Affair so completely that he was unconscious either of the fact that he was reading or of the identity of the author, so that in the end he might say—and believe: 'I have been [there], I *have* been!' "[18] Now these are all strikingly different programs, though perhaps Ford's is contained in Ortega's sixth point. But they share the effort to find what is common to all works or all good modern works. Ortega says that he is looking for "the most general and most characteristic feature of modern artistic production," and he finds it in the "tendency to dehumanize art" (p. 19). "I am little interested in special directions of modern art and, but for a few exceptions, even less in special works" (p. 18). Caroline Gordon is equally explicit in her search for the "constants" which "all good fiction, from Sophocles and Aeschylus down to a well-constructed nursery tale" will show. Her advice is deliberately kept on the highest possible level of generality: "If one is going to write or read fiction, it is of paramount importance to be able to recognize these 'constants' when one comes upon them, or, if they are not present in a work of fiction, to mark their absence."[19]

This generic search for the constants in all good literature or all good fiction can be useful for some purposes—indeed, some of the most interesting questions about literature and life cannot be answered in any other way. But a criticism that begins with such general definitions is peculiarly tempted to move into value judgments without sufficient care about whether those judgments are based on anything more than the initial arbitrary exclusiveness of the general definition. A careful reading of each of the quotations given above will reveal that already in the formulation normative terms have either crept in or have been deliberately included. After reading Miss Gordon's definition of the constants found in "all

17 *The Dehumanization of Art*, trans. Willard R. Trask (Garden City, N.Y., 1956), p. 13.

18 *Op. cit.*, pp. 138–39.

19 *How To Read a Novel* (New York, 1957), pp. 24–25.

good fiction," we cannot be surprised at her manner of dismissing the works of Aldous Huxley and, indeed, all "novels of ideas."[20] "But why?" asks a young friend of hers who had committed the unforgiveable *faux pas* of expressing interest in Huxley. "Can't there be more than one kind of novel and one kind of novelist? Can't I admire X [a living novelist of whom Miss Gordon approves] and Aldous Huxley, too?" And she is forced by her general principles to reply, "I'm afraid you can't."

But where do her "constants" come from? We need not be ardent defenders of Huxley to recognize that in judging his peculiar kind of satiric fantasia we must appeal to criteria very different from those appropriate to Miss Gordon's own excellent stories— stories which display, one need hardly mention, all of her constants.

It is, after all, a fairly simple logical problem that the critic faces, though the solution to it is far from simple. Having derived a definition of a certain kind of novel, or of "the novel" as a certain kind of literature, or of "literature" as a certain kind of art, how can he use that definition as a standard in passing judgment on a given novel? Only by giving good reasons for believing that this novel fits the definition or *ought* to fit it, whether it does or not. Either my definitions are descriptive or they are normative. If they merely describe, then they give me no basis for condemning a work for not falling under the description. If they are openly normative, then of course I have the problem of giving reasons for my standards in the first place, and for thinking that they should apply to all these things called novels.

One need not read very far in modern criticism to discover how often critics avoid this problem, and how many of them are willing to move happily from vast generalization to particular work as if every schoolboy knew that each poor little novel were trying desperately to come in under the shelter of that comforting generalization. The process is especially deadly in thematic criticism that allows a described theme to become normative. Even careful critics

---

[20] *Ibid.*, pp. 10, 222–24. For defenses of "the novel of ideas," see Lionel Trilling, "Art and Fortune," *The Liberal Imagination* (New York, 1950), and Melvin Seiden, "Characters and Ideas: The Modern Novel," *The Nation*, CLXXXVIII (April 25, 1959), 387–92.

are sometimes overpersuaded by their own definitions. Observe how R. W. B. Lewis, in his valuable book, *The Picaresque Saint*, quickly forgets his own warnings that his definition is not normative. "The aim of this book," Lewis says, "is to identify and to describe a particular generation of novelists in Europe and America."[21] The phrase "representative figures" in his subtitle, he tells us, refers to "figures of speech, to the characteristic metaphors of the generation; as well as to the human figures within the novels and to the figures of the writers themselves. To detect those figures and to describe the world they serve to compose is, as I understand it, a major function of criticism in the present time" (p. 10). Lewis carries out his purpose with admirable diligence and insight, by distinguishing the "human" world of Moravia, Silone, Camus, Faulkner, Graham Greene, and Malraux from the "artistic" world of the earlier generation of Proust, Joyce, and Mann. The "human" quality of the second generation is revealed by its characteristic hero, the saintly rogue who "incarnates" in his "impurity" and even in his "criminality" that "trust in life and that companionship that the contemporary novel so emphasizes" (p. 33).

Lewis' search for illustrations of this general theme is a rewarding one; the reader feels that his view of general trends in contemporary fiction has been enriched. But, as might be expected, recognition of these trends does not yield satisfactory criteria for judging the success of individual works. Despite Lewis' constant effort to "observe and stress important differences" in order to do justice to individual works, it is not surprising that he encounters a conflict between his thesis and his efforts at evaluation. When his judgments are convincing, they spring from particular criteria that relate slightly, if at all, to his general theme: after all, the very worst works as well as the very best can embody the theme of the picaresque saint. His judgments are least convincing when he talks as if novelists *ought* to use the theme he is describing. "Part of the intensity of the contemporary novel is drawn at once from the artist's effort to depict and the created character's effort to become

---

21 *The Picaresque Saint: Representative Figures in Contemporary Fiction* (New York, 1959), p. 9. Lewis' approach is by no means so flagrant an example of these dangers as many one could name.

(as we may put it) both a saint and a sinner, both transcendent and companionable, to embody both the observed truth and the hidden aspiration. The effort [still of both novelist and character?] is by no means always successful, and where successful by no means equally so. It is so easy to 'fall' [both novelist and character?] in the direction of the all too human or the all too saintly: Ike McCaslin no doubt suffers artistically from the latter mistake, and Adriana, Moravia's Roman prostitute, from the former. . . ." So it is, after all, an artistic "fall"; Faulkner and Moravia have failed to make their characters conform to Lewis' general criterion. But on what grounds has he decided that Faulkner's and Moravia's novels are struggling to realize the same general portrait as all the other works he treats? If Faulkner's ends require a more "saintly" character, and if Moravia's require more "sin," how can we say that their portraits suffer artistically from the very success they achieve in doing what is necessary in their respective works? Difficulties of this kind abound in this excellent work; sometimes they are admitted, as when Lewis recognizes that Silone's *Bread and Wine* is a better book than *The Secret of Luca*, even though the latter presents the "best image of sacrificial human heroism that contemporary fiction can offer" (p. 178). Such a judgment can come only from observing something in *Bread and Wine* that the fullest realization of the theme cannot provide. Lewis ascribes it to a preference for the "journey itself" rather than the "spiritual arrival." But it does not require any great search either in the novels themselves or in the history of criticism to discover some rather more helpful, since more specific, criteria.

GENERAL CRITERIA IN EARLIER PERIODS

The search for general criteria was not invented in modern times. Longinus sought the general quality of "the sublime" in all literature; for his purposes such distinctions as that between didactic and imaginative works were unimportant, since all kinds of literature can, at proper moments, achieve that peculiar heightening or ecstasy or transport that he desires.[22] "Instruction and delight" was

[22] See Elder Olson, "The Argument of Longinus on the Sublime," in *Critics and Criticism*, ed. R. S. Crane (Chicago, 1952), pp. 232–59, esp. pp. 235–36. An inter-

at one time found everywhere as a formula for what *all* poetry must achieve. Johnson with his insistence throughout his works that all good poetry is a "just representation of general nature" and Coleridge with his constant reference to the powers of the imagination were at times fully as much practitioners of general criticism as the moderns who insist that the chief test of literature is whether it is vividly convincing, or whether it fuses opposite attitudes into ironic harmony, or whether it suggests an author with the proper objective attitude toward his materials.

It may be that every critic has in his system somewhere, recognized or not, at least one or two constants which he requires of all literature. But what is different about the modern period is the widespread abandonment of the notion of peculiar literary kinds, each with its unique demands that may modify the general standards. While earlier critics did deal with qualities thought to be common to all types of worthwhile literature, some qualities were seen as peculiar to whatever special type was under discussion—to tragedy, comedy, satire, epic, elegy, and so on. Though the types were often defined rather loosely, we can expect, in reading any critic before the Romantic period, a reference sooner or later to the peculiar demands of a more or less precisely defined genre. Fielding, for example, in his famous Preface to *Joseph Andrews*, was aware of general qualities which all successful literature must provide.[23] But his major emphasis is on the peculiar qualities dictated by the kind of work he has sought to create. Having distinguished his novel as comic rather than tragic, as epic rather than dramatic, and as in prose rather than in verse, he goes still further and distinguishes it from romance, on the one hand, and burlesque on the other, both of which might be confused as "comic epics in

---

esting development of Longinus in terms of the modern interest in a universal poetic "language" rather than in distinctive structures or literary kinds is Allen Tate's "Longinus and the 'New Criticism,'" *The Man of Letters in the Modern World* (New York, 1955), esp. pp. 175–92: "Longinus is quite prepared to put his finger directly upon the problem of structure, and by implication to tell us that structure is not in the formal 'type' or genre, a viable body of special conventions, such as the lyric, the ode, or the epic provides, but exists in the language of the poem" (p. 184).

23 "Instruction and entertainment." "Instruction" leads him to the vague defense of the morality of his work, in the fourth from the last paragraph.

prose." It is finally clear that whatever faults or virtues the critic is to find in *Joseph Andrews*, Fielding will think them pertinent only if they apply to the *kind* of work he has carefully prefigured in these many distinctions.

Similarly, when Dryden considers the criteria for judging whether French or English plays are best, he frequently appeals to distinctions of kind: some technical procedures are better for *this* kind of play, some for *that*. Though he does appeal to general qualities required of all plays—suspense, variety, naturalness, unity—he nevertheless is primarily pursuing, in his "Examen of the Silent Woman," the virtues of a comic play and not some other kind of thing. It is significant that, when the effort to achieve the comic threatens verisimilitude, he is willing, within limits, to sacrifice realism to comedy.[24]

Even Coleridge, who shows a great interest in the general qualities of all poetry, is highly flexible in his particular judgments. It is true that he objects to "the mere style of narration" in drama, which betrays "the author himself" with parenthetic thoughts and descriptions; he might thus seem to join the modern attack on telling. But when he comes to deal with a particular problem in *Tom Jones* he asks for more narration, not less—an "additional paragraph, more fully and forcibly unfolding Tom Jones's sense of self-degradation" over the affair with Lady Bellaston.[25]

The abandonment of distinctions of species in the face of demands for universally desired qualities is one of the most interesting events in modern literary history. One aspect of it is the loss of distinctions between levels of style suited to different literary kinds. Auerbach shows in *Mimesis* that this breakdown of levels has occurred in literary history whenever "everyday reality," however defined, has come to be of major importance. It is also clearly related, as M. H. Abrams has shown, to the shift of critical emphasis, during the Romantic period, from poem to poet, from interest in the artistic product to theories of expression dealing with

---

[24] John Dryden, "An Essay of Dramatic Poesy," *Dramatic Essays* (Everyman ed., 1906), pp. 42, 45.

[25] "Notes on *Love's Labour's Lost*," *Essays and Lectures on Shakspeare* (Everyman ed., [1907]), p. 364.

the artistic process. When critics are interested mainly in the author, and in his works largely as they are signs of certain qualities in him, they are likely to look for the same qualities in all works. Objectivity, subjectivity, sincerity, insincerity, inspiration, imagination—these can be looked for and praised or blamed whether an author is writing comedy, tragedy, epic, satire, or lyric.[26]

But the search for general qualities has not been confined to critics interested in everyday reality or in the author's personality. Almost every school of criticism has yielded a program for "The Truest Poetry," as Laurence Lerner called it in the title of his fine recent book. What interest has been shown in describing literary kinds that might, by their specific demands, mediate between universal standards and particular works has often gone into forming very large groupings: the spirit of an age, the qualities of a special school, or, at the most precise, "the figure in the carpet"—the basic pattern informing and summarizing an author's entire work.

For reasons which I hope to make clear as we go along, criticism of fiction has been especially vulnerable to the worst effects of this shift of emphasis. Unassisted by established critical traditions, faced with chaotic diversity among the things called novels, critics of fiction have been driven to invent an order of some kind, even at the expense of being dogmatic. "Great traditions" of innumerable shapes and sizes, based on widely divergent universal qualities, have in consequence been discovered and abandoned with appalling rapidity. *The* novel began, we are told, with Cervantes, with Defoe, with Fielding, with Richardson, with Jane Austen—or was it with Homer? It was killed by Joyce, by Proust, by the rise of symbolism, by the loss of respect for—or was it the excessive absorption with?—hard facts. No, no, it still lives, but only in the work of. . . . Thus, on and on.

---

[26] See Abrams, *The Mirror and the Lamp* (New York, 1953), esp. chap. v, sec. ii. For the effects on criticism of the loss of distinctions among literary kinds, see R. S. Crane's Introduction in *Critics and Criticism*, p. 14. The older criticism, Crane elsewhere points out, mediated between "universal poetry" and "individual poems" by reference to "the various recognized poetic genres." The modern critics are mainly interested in "those large distinctions of poetic quality that can be identified in the poet's handling of words and subjects irrespective of the particular 'forms' his composition takes" (*The Languages of Criticism and the Structure of Poetry* [Toronto, 1953], pp. 95–96).

Occasionally, someone like Northrop Frye attempts a pluralistic classification of genres and warns us against imposing the standards of one kind of fiction on works of another kind.[27] But such attempts are rare, and even when they are made they leave us with the problem described in section two: How can we apply to any one novel the standards appropriate to any one defined type without a divine decree authorizing us to consider *this* novel as of *this* type? Are elements of fantasy inappropriate in "the novel" but acceptable in "the romance"? Very well. I note that *this* novel indulges in fantasy. Shall I call it a botched novel or a successful romance? To do either, I must appeal to standards not derived from within my classification. Again, is commentary inappropriate in the "true novel"? I note that Joyce Cary's posthumous novel is full of it. Shall I call it a "true novel" *manqué* or invent a new category in which commentary is appropriate? Even to do the latter leaves me with the job of deciding—on what grounds?—whether the commentary is done well or badly. Whatever my final judgment on *The Captive and the Free*, it cannot depend on my preconceptions about its large general class.

As we try to find a way out of this maze, it should prove helpful to take a close look at some of the general qualities on the basis of which critics since Flaubert have judged fiction.

THREE SOURCES OF GENERAL CRITERIA

General qualities required in the work itself.—Some critics would require the novel to do justice to reality, to be true to life, to be natural, or real, or intensely alive. Others would cleanse it of impurities, of the inartistic, of the all-too-human. On the one hand, the request is for "dramatic vividness," "conviction," "sincerity,"

---

[27] *The Anatomy of Criticism* (Princeton, N.J., 1957), pp. 302–14. Frye's classification of fiction into four types, novel, romance, confession, and anatomy, with the six possible combinations these four logically yield, reminds us that "a great romancer should be examined in terms of the conventions he chose." Unfortunately, Frye's ten types are of limited use as a basis for judgments on technique, since they give us groups of works still unmanageably large and heterogeneous, groups distinguished from each other less by an induction from their common effects than by a deductive classification of the materials represented (e.g., "The essential difference between novel and romance lies in the conception of characterization"). This is not to deny the perceptiveness and effectiveness of Frye's classification for his special purposes.

"genuineness," "an air of reality," "a full realization of the subject," "intensity of illusion"; on the other, for "dispassionateness," "impersonality," "poetic purity," "pure form." On the one hand, "reality to be experienced," and, on the other, "form to be contemplated." A dialectical history of modern criticism could be written in terms of the warfare between those who think of fiction as something that must above all be real (discussed below in this chapter) and those who ask that it be pure—even if the search for artistic purity should lead to unreality and a "dehumanization of art" (chap. iv).

Attitudes required of the author.—Many take it as axiomatic that the author must be "objective," "detached," "dispassionate," "ironic," "neutral," "impartial," "impersonal." Others—fewer in this century—ask him to be "passionate," "involved," "engagé." And between the two extremes, temperate critics have tried to formulate standards for proper "distance" between author, audience, and fictional world (I discuss the extreme positions in chap. iii, the problem of "distance" in chaps. v and vi).

Attitudes required of the reader.—The terms here tend to duplicate those describing the ideal author. Is the reader able to be "objective" or "ironic" or "detached," or, on the contrary, is he capable of compassion or commitment? On the one hand, a work should provide the reader with questions rather than answers, and he should be prepared to accept inconclusiveness; he should accept the ambiguities of life, rejecting a vision based on "oversimplified blacks and whites." He should use his mind, his critical intelligence, as well as his emotions. As James put one of his general goals, in talking of his plan for "The Figure in the Carpet," "What I most remember of my proper process is the lively impulse . . . to reinstate analytic appreciation, by some ironic or fantastic stroke, so far as possible, in its virtually forfeited rights and dignities."[28]

But, on the other hand, there have been hundreds of pleas for a less cerebral fiction, for more honest confrontation of the basic human emotions. The popular weeklies have frequently demanded a literature that would confront the reader with something more

---

[28] *The Art of the Novel*, ed. R. P. Blackmur (New York, 1947), p. 228. From this point on, all unexplained page references will be to this edition of James's Prefaces.

than the dead kitten, egg shell, and bit of string that Wells once professed to find as the final subject of Henry James's fiction. And, finally, there have been innumerable efforts to rule the audience out of critical consideration. Since these relate closely to demands for "purified" works, I consider them together in chapter iv, examining the rhetorical relation between author and reader as it is affected by the desire for a purified art. In chapter v, I return to the reader from another viewpoint and attempt to broaden the spectrum of human interests that the novelist may "legitimately" play upon— even the novelist who would dwell on Parnassus.

Criteria for works, authors, and readers are closely related—so closely that it is impossible to deal with any one of them for very long without touching on the others. Nevertheless they are, as I think the next chapters will show, clearly distinct. It may be true, as critics sometimes claim, that in a sense the work has no existence in itself; it may also be true, in one sense, that when any good novel is read successfully, the experiences of author and reader are indistinguishable. But critical programs still divide easily, if roughly, according to their emphasis on work, author, or reader.

There are, of course, far more criteria of each kind than one can possibly list, and many of them have little relevance to technical rules. What is more troublesome, many authors show themselves as seeking two or more general qualities; sometimes they are almost torn apart by the recognition that two "absolute" requirements of "all" good art, such as intensity and comprehensiveness, truth to nature and simplicity, artistic purity and truth to life's "impurities," are contradictory. Further, I think it could be shown that all authors are disloyal, at one point or another, to the general standards they profess; they have to be, if they are to take *this* intractable work, caught up as it must be in a multiplicity of base, non-ideal, particular needs, from page one to page the last.

But with all of this said, there is still a good deal to be learned, in the quest for some light on technique as rhetoric, by looking closely at the sacrifices willingly made by some modern authors in the name of one or another of the three types of general criteria.

INTENSITY OF REALISTIC ILLUSION

Perhaps a majority of the attacks on the author's voice have been in the name of making the book seem "real." Consider, for example, Ford's attempt to summarize the practice of "James, Crane, and Conrad" and to hypostatize their aims as "the ambition of the novel" in 1930:

> And the trouble with the English nuvvlist from Fielding to Meredith is that not one of them cares whether you quite believe in their characters or not. If you had told Flaubert or Conrad in the midst of their passionate composings that you were not convinced of the reality of Homais or Tuan Jim, as like as not they would have called you out and shot you, and in similar circumstances Richardson would have showed himself extremely disagreeable. But Fielding, Thackeray, or Meredith would have cared relatively little about that, though any one of them would have knocked you down if they could, supposing you had suggested that he was not a "gentleman."[29]

Ford apparently never lost his faith in the constitution and bylaws of the novel as first formulated, according to his claim, by his own private club. "We evolved then a convention for the novel and one that I think still stands," he wrote in 1935,[30] and he supported his theory with some interesting examples of realistic "rendering" in contrast to mere "telling." "We knew that if we said: 'Mr X was a foul-mouthed reactionary,' you would know very little about him. But if his first words were: 'God damn it, put all filthy Liberals up against a wall, say I, and shoot out their beastly livers . . . ,' that gentleman will make on you an impression that many following pages shall scarcely efface."

More careful critics have put this relation between realistic rendering and authorial reticence in hypothetical rather than categorical form: "If, then, it is dramatic vividness that the novelist wants, the best thing he can do is to find a way of eliminating the narrator entirely and exposing the scene directly to the reader. . . . The frankly omniscient story-teller has well nigh disappeared from

---

[29] *The English Novel*, pp. 89–90. For an excellent survey of demands for realism in criticism immediately before James, see Richard Stang, *The Theory of the Novel in England, 1850–1870* (New York, 1959), chap. iv.

[30] "Techniques," *Southern Review*, I (July, 1935), 33.

modern fiction."[31] But there is almost always in such statements the implication that the author *should* want dramatic vividness and that therefore anything that seems to get in its way is suspect.[32] In one of the best recent books on the novel, Ian Watt's all-pervasive assumption is that "realism of presentation" is a good thing in itself. In fact, Watt sees in what he calls "formal realism" the defining feature of the "novel" as it differs from other forms of fiction.[33] Properly speaking, the novel for him begins only when Defoe and Richardson discover how to give to their characters sufficient particularity and autonomy to make them seem like real people.

In common with all good critics, Watt recognizes that "the accurate transcription of actuality does not necessarily produce a work of any real truth or enduring literary value" (p. 32), and he often disavows the claim that the greater the "formal realism" the better the work. And yet Watt's constant criterion is the achievement of realism. In his treatment of Fielding, for example, despite his repeated demurrer that Fielding's art requires less "formal realism" than Richardson's, it is clear that to sacrifice realism is to sacrifice quality as well. When Fielding narrates his story "in such a way as to deflect our attention from the events themselves to the way that Fielding is handling them and to epic parallels involved" (p. 253), this is a weakness, however necessary it may be for Fielding's different intentions. It tends to "compromise the narrative's general air of literal authenticity by suggesting the manipulated sequences of literature rather than the ordinary processes of life." Similarly, Sophia never really recovers from what Watt calls her "artificial" introduction—that is, she never becomes real for us in the sense that Clarissa is real (p. 254). In short, although Watt is

---

[31] James Weber Linn and Houghton Wells Taylor, *A Foreword to Fiction* (New York, 1935), p. 33.

[32] See, for example, Bernard DeVoto, *The World of Fiction* (New York, 1950), pp. 157–225: ". . . there is one critical absolute. If a reader leaves a novel unfinished, the highest court has issued a decree that cannot be appealed. . . . He will go on reading as long as he is interested, which is to say as long as he believes [that] what is happening on the page is an actual event . . ." (p. 157).

[33] Ian Watt, *The Rise of the Novel* (Berkeley, Calif., 1957).

a far more careful reader than most of the critics quoted earlier, he still finds himself forced to deny Fielding full marks on the sole ground of his deficiency in formal realism. "Few readers would like to be without the prefatory chapters, or Fielding's diverting asides, but they undoubtedly derogate from the reality of the narrative" (p. 286); "such authorial intrusion, of course, tends to diminish the authenticity of the narrative" (p. 285).

"Of course" commentary diminishes authenticity! Everybody knows it, nobody questions it. But the agreement among the critics is, "of course," only superficial. What seems natural in one period or to one school seems artificial in another period or to another school. Each man trusts his own brand of reality, and the seeming agreement about the importance of a natural surface breaks down as soon as we compare doctrines in detail.

For Henry James, "intensity" was "the grace to which the enlightened story-teller will at any time, for his interest, sacrifice if need be all other graces whatever" (p. 318). But intensity of what? Of laughter? Of tears? Perhaps all authors want intensity of one kind or other.[34] For James, it was "intensity of illusion"—most often the illusion of experiencing life as seen by a fine mind subject to realistic human limitations. Like Flaubert, James was constantly concerned with achieving what is "natural," yet he was as much aware as Flaubert of the impossible complexity of reality. "Really, universally, relations stop nowhere, and the exquisite problem of the artist is eternally but to draw, by a geometry of his own, the circle within which they shall happily appear to do so" (p. 5). No action "was ever made historically vivid without a certain factitious compactness. . . . I might produce illusion if I should be able to achieve intensity" (p. 15).

Much as he admired Flaubert, he felt that Flaubert's realism was too superficial. "M. Flaubert's theory as a novelist," he says, "is to begin on the outside. Human life, we may imagine his saying, is before all things a spectacle, an occupation and entertainment for the eyes. What our eyes show us is all that we are sure of; so with

---

34 See Abrams, *The Mirror and the Lamp*, esp. pp. 136, 138, for an account of some of the intensities sought in the Romantic period.

this we will at any rate begin."[35] James began at a different place entirely, with the effort to portray a convincing mind at work on reality. Feeling as he did that the most interesting subject was a fine but "bewildered" mind dealing with life (pp. 63–64, 66, for example), he was disturbed by Flaubert's choice of stupid minds as centers of consciousness "reflecting" events. Emma Bovary as a reflector was for him clearly a mistake, and Frédéric in *The Sentimental Education* represented an almost pathetic failure of insight, even a failure of mind in Flaubert himself. He felt so deeply about this requirement that he even violated at this point his own precept that the critic has no right to reject an author's "subject."[36]

Whether or not his criticism of the man he admired so much is sound, it shows clearly that for him mere "rendering" of surfaces is not enough. The life he hopes to be true to is the life of the mind much more than the life of the objective surface. "The matter comes back again, I fear, but to the author's irrepressible and insatiable, his extravagant and immoral, interest in personal character and in the 'nature' of a mind, of almost any mind . . ." (p. 156). And minds are most interesting, of course, when they are at work on important, interesting subjects, matters of taste, judgment, or morality.

Always loyal to this broad notion of what is real, James tends to seek in each new work the same general quality that was sought in the previous work. Though he is explicitly of that "higher order" of realists whom Maupassant called "illusionists," though more clearly and consistently than Flaubert he seeks "intensity of illusion" rather than the illusory reality itself, he still tends to apply, in his later years, the same test to all of his own works.

The intensity of the illusion, he tells us again and again, is the ultimate test. The mere *illusion* of reality in itself is not enough;

---

[35] Charles de Bernard and Gustave Flaubert, *French Poets and Novelists* (London, 1884), p. 201. The essay is indispensable in understanding James's own realism.

[36] "We must grant the artist his subject, his idea, his *donnée:* our criticism is applied only to what he makes of it" ("The Art of Fiction," p. 599). Critics have sometimes taken this as granting equal value to all subjects. But James never forgets that "there are degrees of merit in subjects" (*Art of the Novel*, p. 309). It is only the critic, not the artist, to whom he denies the right to decide. But in dealing with Flaubert, James seems to be judging the subject itself.

reality is so many things, so many that are not worthy of being conveyed with intensity. On the other hand, *intensity* in itself is not enough, though it is something which the novelist "ruefully envies" the dramatist as a "fortune in itself" (p. 15). Whatever intensity is achieved must be an intensity of the illusion that genuine life has been presented. Limitless, sprawling experience is the beginning; "to give the image and the sense of certain things" is always half the problem. But to give it with intensity, to make the imagined picture of reality glow with more than a dim light, requires the artist's finest compositional powers. And, since any sense of composition or selection falsifies life, all fiction requires an elaborate rhetoric of dissimulation.

Hence it is that most of James's talk about the author's technical choices—what he calls his "form" or "manner," his "doing," his "treatment" as distinct from his "material" or "subject"—is aimed at this twofold goal. His *talk* about rhetoric, in short (as distinct from the actual technique in the works), is for the most part about how to increase in each work the reader's pleasure derived from qualities sought equally in all his works. Each subject requires a slightly different treatment, of course, if it is to yield its "full measure of truth"; but all subjects, if treated properly, yield not such old-fashioned effects as the greatest possible comic or tragic or satiric emotions but generalized, mixed, "natural" effects: it is "for irony, for comedy, for tragedy," he says again and again, all combined in one tale, that we develop our treatment (p. 224). Even such a quality as sympathy, which in older fiction might have been required in order to heighten the tragic emotions, is here required only to make the illusion more intense (p. 12).[37]

His key terms can all be related to this double task. Time must be *foreshortened* to achieve intensity, but in foreshortening the novelist must use *dissimulation* successfully in order to preserve the illusion of reality (pp. 13–14). "The amount of illustration I could allow to the grounds of my young man's disaster," he says of the hero's moral deterioration in *Roderick Hudson*, "was unquestion-

---

[37] For a useful discussion of James's effort to do full justice to both art and life, see René Wellek, "Henry James's Literary Theory and Criticism," *American Literature*, XXX (November, 1958), 293–321, esp. 298–306.

ably meagre, but I might perhaps make it lively; I might produce illusion if I should be able to achieve intensity" (p. 15).

Similarly he is determined to achieve "*composition*"—"unity," "harmony," "synthesis"—and this sometimes sounds like an end in itself. But it is always desired because only through unnatural ordering can art achieve an intensity not to be found in life. Indeed, he will sacrifice order for the illusion; he would rather "have too little architecture than too much—when there's danger of its interfering with my measure of the truth" (p. 43). As one would expect, he is willing to sacrifice both structure and literal truth to an intense illusion of truth (pp. 222–24).

He is deeply interested in *morality*, and there are few tales which do not in some way turn on moral decisions by the main characters. But the moral quality of a work for him depends not on the validity of doctrines; the "moral sense of a work of art" depends completely "on the amount of felt life concerned in producing it" (p. 45). Though he qualifies this statement by including the "kind" and the "quality" of "felt life," he is still unmistakably clear that the morality of the work—that which gives the "enveloping air of the artist's humanity"—comes from the "quality and capacity" of the artist's "prime sensibility."

It is precisely this double goal of "quality and capacity"—yielding in turn the intensity and adequacy of the illusion—that accounts for his attitude toward the *angle of vision* with which he tells his stories. There can be no intensity of illusion if the author is present, constantly reminding us of his unnatural wisdom. Indeed, there can be no illusion of life where there is no bewilderment (p. 66), and the omniscient narrator is obviously not bewildered. The process most like the process of life is that of observing events through a convincing, human mind, not a godlike mind unattached to the human condition. At the same time mere bewildered limitation is not enough; if the experience is to be more intense than our own observations, the mind used as observer must be "the most polished of possible mirrors" (pp. 69–70). It is in this respect, as we have seen, that he finds Flaubert so much at fault: though people like Frédéric and Emma abound in life, their minds can *naturally* reflect to the reader no finer intensity than they are themselves capable of.

On the other hand, the illusion will be sacrificed if the mirror is too highly polished. "Beyond a certain point," he says, such reflectors "are spoiled for us by this carrying of a due light. They may carry too much of it for our credence, for our compassion, for our derision. They may be shown as knowing too much and feeling too much—not certainly for their remaining remarkable [which would serve the end of intensity], but for their remaining 'natural' and typical, for their having the needful communities with our own precious liability to fall into traps and be bewildered" (p. 63). In almost every discussion of "centers of consciousness" and "lucid reflectors," he sets the limits of their lucidity according to what is credible—that is, what will preserve the illusion without destroying the intensity.

Finally, his whole emphasis on the *dramatic*, the *scenic*, an emphasis which relates directly, of course, to the angle of vision, is determined by his desire for intensity. There are times when we might, with Lubbock, think him entirely interested in the dramatic for its own sake, so often does he repeat his formula, "Dramatize, dramatize!" But at the conclusion of his Preface to *The Ambassadors* he confesses that even the dramatic can be sacrificed on the altar of intensity. Commenting on a section of *The Ambassadors* which seems to violate what he has said of its method, a section in which Mamie Pocock is watched, "at an angle of vision as yet untried," during "her single hour of suspense in the hotel salon," he says that the episode is an example of the "representational virtue that insists here and there on being, for the charm of opposition and renewal, other than the scenic. It wouldn't take much to make me further argue that from an equal play of such oppositions the book gathers an intensity that fairly adds to the dramatic—though the latter is supposed to be the sum of all intensities." And he concludes with the claim that it is this very capacity to achieve an intensity more "dramatic" than the dramatic itself that makes the novel the "most independent, most elastic, most prodigious of literary forms" (p. 326).

To point to all this evidence that James was primarily interested in effects common to all good fiction is not to say that his narrative choices are never determined by the unique requirements of particular works. The predominant tone of ironic tragedy in *The Princess Casamassima*, for example, dictates a treatment different from that required by the ironic comedy of *The Sacred Fount*. And he can occasionally talk of heightening particular reactions, like pity, or "the comedy." But if there is conflict between what is required to heighten tragic or comic emotions and what is required for general intensity of illusion, he never hesitates. It is fascinating to observe how even such an essential effect as pity for Maisie in *What Maisie Knew* becomes subordinated to other, more general effects. In the first notebook entry about this story,[38] there is no mention whatever of the girl's feelings; the interest is all in the intricacy of the human situation: the "innocent child" is caught between two indifferent parents who have separated and remarried. She builds a new relationship with each of the new parents, who then develop through her an independent connection. And with this James is off on his exploration of how to produce "suspicion, jealousy, a fresh separation." In the Preface, written of course long after the novel, he does talk of the implied emotional effect of observing the "misfortune of the little victim." But he raises the question of pity only to go beyond it to something that interests him much more. "The business would accordingly be sad enough, yet I am not sure its possibility of interest would so much have appealed to me had I not soon felt that the ugly facts, so stated or conceived, by no means constituted the whole appeal."

In the second notebook entry he is in full chase after "the most ironic effect." Can he not combine the ironic and the *other* interest, "the 'touch of tenderness'—or sweetness—or sympathy or poetry—or whatever the needed thing is . . . ?" Which is to say, may he not achieve what is peculiarly appropriate to this story, the poignancy of Maisie's plight, without sacrificing what he wants from all his stories, the intense illusion of the "full ironic truth"?

[38] *The Notebooks of Henry James*, ed. F. O. Matthiessen and Kenneth B. Murdock (New York, 1947). The excellent index of this edition removes any need for citation of pages in my text. Unless otherwise noted, then, the page numbers I cite will continue to refer to the Prefaces in *The Art of the Novel*.

He seems dimly aware that there might be a conflict between the irony and the sympathy, but he is certainly far from admitting what seemed self-evident even to an enthusiast of irony like Schlegel: "No doubt, wherever the proper tragic enters, every thing like irony immediately ceases."[39] He wants the "full ironic truth," the full illusion, in other words, of justice to the ironies of life itself, and though he expresses the hope that he will not lose the "tenderness" and the "sympathy," it is clear that he is willing to sacrifice some of the poignancy of Maisie, the poor little girl originally seen as "rebounding from racquet to racquet like a shuttlecock," to the "ironic truth" of the whole.

A sign of his willingness in this sacrifice is the ease with which he turns Maisie from helpless victim into a triumphant "central intelligence." It was approximately three years, from November, 1892, to December, 1895, from the time of his first hint of a story to the time of recording the discovery of Maisie's importance as center of consciousness. But once he saw her possibilities in this line, he recognized that her story as originally viewed must be transformed for the sake of her usefulness as a lucid reflector. "At last, accordingly, the residuum, as I have called it, reached, I was in presence of the red dramatic spark that glowed at the core of my vision. . . . This precious particle was the *full* ironic truth—the most interesting item to be read into the child's situation." Not, be it noted, the most poignant or "sweet" or "sad," but the most "interesting." "For satisfaction of the mind," he continues in the Preface, "the small expanding consciousness would have to be saved, have to become presentable as a register of impressions; and saved by the experience of certain advantages, by some enjoyed

---

[39] A. W. von Schlegel, "Shakspeare," from Lecture XXIII, in *Lectures on Dramatic Art and Literature*, trans. John Black (1815), A. J. W. Morrison (1846), p. 370. Reprinted in *Criticism, The Major Texts*, ed. W. J. Bate (New York, 1952), p. 420. There has been too little criticism based on recognizing incompatibilities of different effects. See E. E. Stoll: "The highest tragic effect and a strict psychological probability are ordinarily incompatible; . . . and since the highest effect is the aim and end of this as of every other art, how much better frankly and honestly to adopt a convention, a simplification or short cut, in order to secure it!" (*Shakespeare and Other Masters*, [Cambridge, Mass., 1940], p. 329). See also n. 6, p. 250, below, and Robert Langbaum, *The Poetry of Experience* (London, 1957).

profit and some achieved confidence, rather than coarsened, blurred, sterilised, by ignorance and pain" (p. 142).

The whole process of James's transformations from germ to finished subject is almost as full of suspense as the finished tales themselves; I shall trace it in a different form later on. Nowhere is it more revealing than here, where he explicitly concludes by insisting on his ideal of truth to the moral and emotional complexities of life. "No themes are so human as those that reflect for us, out of the confusion of life, the close connexion of bliss and bale, of the things that help with the things that hurt, so dangling before us for ever that bright hard medal, of so strange an alloy, one face of which is somebody's right and ease and the other somebody's pain and wrong." This ideal is not, we must remember, something that he discovered in the process of writing this story; he believed from the beginning that the most "human" themes are those that reflect the moral ambiguities of life. But in its service he has been led to choices which other ideals, other general qualities, would not demand. In its service the story of "the child" has been determined as necessarily that of a girl: "my light vessel of consciousness, swaying in such a draught, couldn't be with verisimilitude a rude little boy," since "my plan would call, on the part of my protagonist, for 'no end' of sensibility," and little boys have less of it than little girls (pp. 143–44). Most strikingly, in the light of the traditional distinction between comedy and tragedy, it has dictated a change in plan from destruction to salvation for the protagonist. And it has dictated innumerable other transformations and stratagems which would never have occurred to an author who was interested in obtaining the greatest possible tragic, or comic, or epic, or satiric effect.

As the young James had long before said, what the author does is to "make his reader very much as he makes his characters." But James did not then, and he does not in his Prefaces, say that he makes the reader laugh or makes him weep, or hate, or glow with a sense of triumph. "When he makes him ill, that is, makes him indifferent, he does no work; the writer does ill. When he makes him well, that is, makes him interested, *then* the reader does quite half the labor."[40] Thus, from the beginning James's passion for the reader's sense of traveling in a real, though intensified, world dictates a general rhetoric in the service of realism, rather than a particular rhetoric for the most intense experience of distinctive effects.

THE NOVEL AS UNMEDIATED REALITY

James's interest in realism never led him to the notion that all signs of the author's presence are inartistic. Though he might have agreed with Ford that the reader should feel that he has been "really there," he would never have suggested that the reader must entirely forget the guiding presence of the author. His interest is not negative—how to get rid of the author—but positive: how to achieve an intense illusion of reality, including the complexities of mental and moral reality. He can therefore "intrude" into his most rigorously composed works—but only to perform certain very limited tasks (see below, pp. 58–59).

The program of Jean-Paul Sartre is much less flexible. It is not enough for Sartre that an author avoid omniscient commentary altogether. It is not even enough for the author to give the illusion that he is sitting silently behind the scenes, like God objectively surveying his handiwork, as in the theories of Flaubert, James Joyce, and some of the earlier romantics.[41] He must give the illusion that he does not even exist. If we suspect for a moment that he is behind the scenes, controlling the lives of his characters, they will not seem to be free. Objecting to Mauriac's attempt to "play God" with his characters, Sartre accuses him of violating "the most rigorous" of all the "laws" governing "fictional beings": "the novelist may be either their witness or their accomplice, but never both at the same time. The novelist must be either inside or out. Because M. Mauriac does not observe these laws, he does away with his characters' minds."[42]

---

40 "The Novels of George Eliot," *Atlantic Monthly*, October, 1866, p. 485.

41 See Abrams, *op. cit.*, pp. 241–49.

42 "François Mauriac and Freedom," *Literary and Philosophical Essays*, trans. Annette Michelson (London, 1955), p. 16. Originally published as a review of Mauriac's *La fin de la nuit* in *Nouvelle Revue Française* (February, 1939). There are recent signs (January, 1961) that Sartre, like many of his fellows, may be in the process of repudi-

To claim that the novelist must not show any signs of his control, because to do so reveals that he is "playing God," is to condemn, obviously enough, almost all earlier fiction, including that written by the most avid prophets of objectivity. Sartre is aware of this radical break; in fact he seems to revel in it. In his later essays he elaborates his position into a thoroughgoing rejection of the "privileged subjectivity" of all earlier fiction. Taking Joyce as a stepping-off point toward the full glory of the new novel, he calls for an "absolute subjectivity" ("equivalent to absolute objectivity"), an "absolute subjective realism" which will go beyond Joyce's "raw realism of subjectivity without mediation or distance" by achieving at last an absolute conviction that characters are acting freely in time.[43] And he concludes, as we have seen, with a plea for novels that are not viewed as "products of man" but as natural products, like plants or events.

In such novels the author must not allow any suggestion of the ordered world in which he dwells and from which he remembers the events; to imply any ordering will always destroy the reader's sense of real freedom as he faces the absurdity of chaos. An implied order was to some extent excusable in the older fiction; written in an ordered world, it was a fiction in which neither "the author nor the reader runs any risk; there is no surprise to be feared; the event is a thing of the past; it has been catalogued and understood." In that world, narrative technique may quite properly imply "the point of view of the absolute, that is, of order." But in our world where the true chaos of things has at last been realized, only a technique that seems to leave characters genuinely free to face that chaos is tolerable (pp. 102–22).

Sartre concludes by accusing Mauriac of "the sin of pride," a sin which seems to consist, in Sartre's formulation, of denying the complete relativity of all values.

> Like most of our writers, he has tried to ignore the fact that the theory of relativity applies in full to the universe of fiction, that there is no more place for a privileged observer in a real novel than in

---

ating the notions of an engaged literature on which these theories are based. But even if this turns out to be true, his usefulness here as a representative extreme is not affected.
[43] *What Is Literature?* trans. Bernard Frechtman (London, 1950), pp. 228–29.

the world of Einstein, and that it is no more possible to conduct an experiment in a fictional system in order to determine whether the system is in motion or at rest than there is in a physical system. M. Mauriac has put himself first. He has chosen divine omniscience and omnipotence. But novels are written by men and for men. In the eyes of God, Who cuts through appearances and goes beyond them, there is no novel, no art, for art thrives on appearances. God is not an artist. Neither is M. Mauriac [p. 23].

For the true novelist, on the other hand, striving for a complete realism, everything will be appearance and all appearances will be, or at least seem, equally valid. Thus, the *réalisme brut de la sub-jectivité* requires a temporal realism binding the author absolutely to the duration of events as experienced by his characters. He must passively relay to us every detail, however insignificant, that is a genuine part of the experience. He must avoid even the normal abridgments of dialogue. "In a novel, you must either tell all or keep quiet; above all, you must not omit or skip anything" (p. 20). In short, selectivity must be eliminated—or is it simply that all recognizable signs of selection must be eliminated? Sartre is not entirely clear which of these he requires, and he admits that the former interpretation "raises difficulties which nobody has yet resolved, and which, perhaps, are partially insoluble."[44]

In spite of its admitted practical difficulties, this elegant theory is irrefutable, so long as we assume that fiction should seem to be unwritten. But who ever really makes such an assumption? Our entire experience in reading fiction is based, as Jean-Louis Curtis says in his brilliant reply to Sartre,[45] on a tacit contract with the novelist, a contract granting him the right to know what he is writing about. It is this contract which makes fiction possible. To

---

[44] *Ibid.*, n. 11, p. 229. "It is neither possible nor desirable to limit all novels to the story of a single day. . . . Devoting a book to twenty four hours rather than to one, or to an hour rather than to a minute, implies the intervention of the author and a transcendent choice. It will then be necessary to mask this choice by purely aesthetic procedures . . . to lie in order to be true." Amusingly enough, a British moving picture made in 1959 (*The Man Upstairs*) attempted to follow Sartre's principles of realism to the letter; portraying an action that lasts for eighty-eight minutes, the film itself lasts eighty-eight minutes, an awesome instance of devotion to principle. Reviewers seemed singularly ungrateful for the "absolute durational realism."

[45] "Sartre et le roman," *Haute École* (Paris, 1950), p. 181.

deny it would not only destroy all fiction, but all literature, since all art presupposes the artist's choice. "If you destroy the notion of choice it is art that is annihilated."

In all successful reading of fiction, Curtis goes on, the reader spontaneously draws together whatever the novelist presents, scene, gesture, dramatized comment, omniscient judgment, into a single synthesis. "When Balzac bellows into my ears that Vautrin is a 'colosse de ruse' I believe it: Vautrin *is* a *colosse de ruse*. By agreement, I have granted to Balzac an almost unlimited credit" (p. 173).

In short, once I have surrendered to an omniscient narrator, I am no more inclined—except when under the spell of modern rules—to separate the narrator's judgment from the thing or character judged than I am inclined to question James's conventions once I am well into one of his novels. He signs an agreement with me *not* to know everything. He reminds me from time to time that he cannot, in this particular instance, "go behind" because of the convention he has adopted. I accept this, provided it serves larger ends that I can also accept. But in no case do I pretend that I am not reading a novel.

On Discriminating among Realisms

In the general assumption that a novel should seem real, James and Sartre would probably be joined by most novelists from the beginnings of fiction. In the assumption that a realistic effect is worth the sacrifice of most if not all other virtues, they would be joined by many novelists and critics in this century.

Virginia Woolf, for example, saw the novelist as trying to express the elusive reality of character, especially as character is reflected in sensibility.[46] Her judgment of Jane Austen is especially interesting as it reveals how important to her was the novelist's vision of reality. Speculating on how Jane Austen might have de-

---

[46] See her discussion of how the methods of what she calls the Georgians—herself, Forster, Lawrence, Joyce, Eliot—differ in achieving this goal from the methods of the "Edwardians," Bennett, Galsworthy, and Wells ("Mr. Bennett and Mrs. Brown," in *The Hogarth Essays*, ed. Leonard and Virginia Woolf [Garden City, N.Y., 1928], pp. 3–29; also "Modern Fiction," *The Common Reader* [London, 1925; New York, 1953], pp. 154–55).

veloped had she lived longer, she says, "But she would have known more. Her sense of security would have been shaken. Her comedy would have suffered." Of course, since comedy depends on unrealistic exaggerations of various kinds! "She would have trusted less . . . to dialogue and more to reflection to give us a knowledge of her characters." Obviously her purpose, had she matured, would be to "give us a knowledge" rather than to give us comedy. "Those marvellous little speeches which sum up, in a few minutes' chatter, all that we need in order to know an Admiral Croft . . . for ever, that shorthand, hit-or-miss method which contains chapters of analysis and psychology, would have become too crude to hold all that she now perceived of the complexity of human nature. She would have devised a method, clear and composed as ever, but deeper and more suggestive, for conveying not only what people say, but what they leave unsaid; not only what they are, but what life is." In short, "she would have been the forerunner of Henry James and of Proust"—or as David Daiches says, in quoting the same passage, "of Virginia Woolf."[47]

Similarly, Dorothy Richardson defended her endless streams-of-consciousness as a route to "reality"; her method, she said, expressed her first experience of letting "a stranger in the form of contemplated reality" have "its own say."[48] And the youthful Joyce, addressing the Literary and Historical Society in 1899, long before he was to write his much livelier experiments with the same technique, argued that the artist has no interest in making his work religious, moral, beautiful, or ideal; he wants only to make it truthful to fundamental laws.[49] Robert Humphrey summarizes the purpose of all stream-of-consciousness writers as the effort to reveal "the psychic being of the characters," an attempt to "analyze human nature," to present "character more accurately and more realistically."[50] For such writers, Humphrey claims, the distinctive

---

[47] *The Common Reader*, pp. 148–49. *Virginia Woolf* (Norfolk, Conn., 1942), p. 38.

[48] *Pilgrimage* (New York, 1938), I, 10.

[49] Richard Ellmann, *James Joyce* (New York, 1959), p. 74. See epigraphs to this chapter.

[50] *Stream of Consciousness in the Modern Novel* (Berkeley, Calif., 1954), pp. 6, 7.

patterns of individual works are stratagems to give form to what is really formless. The invention of a structure thus becomes a kind of rhetoric to support the illusion, rather than the other way round. "With motive and external action replaced by psychic being and functioning, what is to unify the fiction? What is to replace conventional plot?" The real life of the mind "contains no forms," but the work must be formed if the author "is to communicate." And so the author invents his works as successive devices for "differentiation and variation," "for getting lights and shadows" (p. 88). An extraordinary inversion of the traditional rhetorical problem!

And so we could go on, with superficial variations, through Gide and Proust and Mann, on down to whatever "serious" novelists come into sight between the writing of this sentence and the morning of publication. How are we to make our way through the mass of conflicting claims that we see here clustering about the term "reality"? Short of the major study of realisms that we so badly need, perhaps we can gain some clarity by sorting out these programs into four kinds.

Some realists are most interested in whether the *subject matter* does justice to reality outside the book. For many of the so-called naturalists, no picture could be real unless it did justice to the unpleasant side of life. To others, like Howells, the obvious thought occurred that life is "really" often quite pleasant, and that no realism which overlooks this fact is entitled to the name. Such concentration on what might be called social reality makes no invariable demands on technique or form; the naturalists all felt free to intrude their rhetorical comments whenever necessary.

But when the reality to be reflected begins to leave the visible conditions of life and moves toward metaphysical Truth, invariable technical and formal requirements are likely to be implicated. Many in this century have required that a work reflect adequately the ambiguities of the human condition or even of the universe itself. In objecting to Browning's Pope on the ground that he is "too authoritative," Robert Langbaum, for example, says that it is "certainly a valid criticism of *The Ring and the Book* that good and evil are not sufficiently interfused." A poem "treating different points of view toward the same story" ought to do so impartially, "allowing judgment to arise out of the utmost ambiguity." And what is the reason? "To make poetry rise out of prose and spirituality out of the world's common clay, to meet in other words the conditions for modern intellectual and moral conviction . . . would have to be the aim, I should think, of any genuinely modern literature."[51] In meeting such rigorous conditions, it is hard to see how an author could allow himself to use authoritative narrative techniques.

Others have felt that reality should be sought in an accurate transcription of sensations produced by surfaces rather than in allegiance to any general view of things. This position has recently been carried to almost incredible extremes by the school of "antinovelists" in France, one of whom I shall look at more closely in a moment. And finally—to omit many other programs, economic, psychological, political—there have been many discussions, like Virginia Woolf's, of the precisely correct relation between the reality shown by characters in novels and the reality of their models in "real life." While almost everyone would agree with Arnold Bennett that "you can't put the whole of a character into a book," there is great variety of opinion about how hard you should try to do so.[52]

Most writers who have tried to make their *subjects* real have sooner or later found themselves, like James and Sartre, also seeking a realistic *structure* or shape of events, and wrestling with the question of how to make that shape seem a probable reflection of the shapes into which life itself falls. To some it has seemed unrealistic to show chance at work in the fictional world; to others a careful chain of cause and effect is forbidden, since in real life chance plays an obviously great role. Some have deplored conclusive endings or soaring climaxes or clear and direct opening expositions, since they are never found in life. Most deprecations of plot are based on the

[51] *The Poetry of Experience*, p. 135.

[52] Sources for these disputes about subject matter are so numerous that any form of brief citation would be misleading. For the reader who does not know the *loci classici*, a good place to start is Miriam Allott's *Novelists on the Novel* (New York, 1959), pp. 275–307.

claim that life does not provide plots, and literature should be like life.[53]

There is probably no inherent reason why a realistic structure should require any particular form of realistic *narrative technique*— to come to the third kind of realism. A fully "open-ended" work could very well end with a resounding claim by an omniscient author that the book is left inconclusive because life is like that. But in practice most programs demanding realistic structure have led to narrative rules. For some it has seemed that a story should be told as it might be told in real life, and they have thus been troubled to discover, for example, that Conrad's Marlow, in *Lord Jim*, could not possibly have told all that he does tell in the allotted time. For others, as we have seen, realistic narration must disguise the fact that it is narration at all, creating the illusion that the events are taking place unmediated by the author.

Attitudes toward these three variables, subject matter, structure, and technique, depend finally on notions of purpose or function or effect. There is a radical difference between those who seek some form of realism as an end in itself—including most of the realisms discussed in this chapter—and those for whom realism is a means to other ends. Writers whose realistic effects are sought only for what they consider more important ends are themselves of two basically different kinds. On the one hand, there are explicitly didactic authors, ranging from allegorists like Bunyan to philosophical propagandists like Sartre.[54] Satirists like Swift and Voltaire, though they may indulge in some realism for its own sake, will clearly sacrifice realism whenever their satirical ends require the sacrifice. On the other hand, many purely "mimetic" or objective writers, writers for whom the allegation of didacticism would be distressing, also treat realism as subordinate and functional to their special purposes. Much as Fielding and Dickens, Trollope and Thackeray may talk about their passion for truth to nature or the real, they are often willing, as some modern critics have complained, to sacrifice reality to tears or laughter.

---

[53] Allott, "Plot and Story," *ibid.*, pp. 241–51. See chap. v, pp. 120 ff.

[54] See Sartre, "What Is Writing?" and "Why Write?" in *What Is Literature?*

A more seriously confusing difference, however, is found among those who would agree that realism is in itself a sufficient end. On the one hand, there are writers like James, who seek an intense illusion of reality, as an effect to be realized in the reader through the use of whatever realistic subjects, techniques, and structures can be devised. As we have seen, James is quite clear that this effect is more important than any particular means that might serve it. In contrast, there are many who would make this or that subject, technique, or structure into an independent ideal, to be sought quite aside from consideration of readers or effects. The result is that two radically different kinds of literature, and two equally different kinds of criticism, often are thought to be identical.

Consider what has happened to James in the hands of Jamesians. Since James was seeking an intense illusion, in the reader, it did not matter to him if the visible structure of the work was "marred" with obvious signs that the work was written by a human being. So long as it was clear that this human being could not modify the facts of the story to suit his purposes, he could even comment quite freely on his story and his methods. "Mr. Longdon," we read in *The Awkward Age*, "looked the noble lady . . . straight in the face, and who can tell whether or no she acutely guessed from his expression that. . . ." And again, "As Mr. Van himself couldn't have expressed at any subsequent time to any interested friend the particular effect upon him of the tone of these words, his chronicler takes advantage of the fact not to pretend to a greater intelligence— to limit himself on the contrary to the simple statement that they produced in Mr. Van's cheek a flush just discernible." Whatever may be said for these repudiations of the "muffled majesty of irresponsible authorship," they are obviously not designed to free the book of all signs of its authorship. "If we were at this moment to take," the narrator of *The Bostonians* (1886) tells us, "an inside view of Mrs. Burrage (a liberty we have not yet ventured on), I suspect we should find. . . ." And in another moment he says, "Mrs. Burrage—since we have begun to look into her mind we may continue the process—had not meant. . . ." Of course this astonishing reminder of rigorous conventions comes from fairly "early James." But the later work is full of the sort of thing we have seen in *The*

Awkward Age. "If we should go into all that occupied our friend," the "chronicler" of *The Ambassadors* tells us, "we should have to mend our pen." And even in his last, unfinished novel, *The Sense of the Past*, reminders of artificial limitations lie thick upon James's page.[55]

To the critic who assumes that James sought a surface cleansed of all traces of the author, regarding an air of impersonal narration as an end in itself, such intrusions are self-evidently weaknesses, and it is easy for such a critic to quote James's own precepts, codified and elevated a notch or two, against the master. One recent critic contrasts James's practice in *The Ambassadors* with Lubbock's description of that practice, and he naturally finds a great many "lapses and shifts." Even those "intrusions" which James himself talks about in his Preface can then be quoted against him as evidence of "inconsistency" in pursuing "his struggle, in what he believed to be his finest work, to master the art of his craft." Where James had cited his shifting of point of view as evidence that intensity of effect was more important than any rule about being dramatic, the Jamesian can only conclude that James "presumably does not recognize his frequent lapses not only from Strether's point of view but from objective narration as well," and suggest that we can excuse "James the Old Intruder" because he "was still so close to the conventions of nineteenth-century fiction that he could never quite eschew their besetting manners and methods."[56]

It is thus in the failure to think clearly about ends and means that the prophets of realism have most often tarnished their remarkable achievements. To have made naturalness of technique an end in itself was, perhaps, an impossible goal in the first place. Whatever verisimilitude a work may have always operates within a larger artifice; each work that succeeds is natural—and artificial—in its own way. It is easy for us now to see what was not so clear at

---

[55] See, for example, p. 272 of the London edition of 1917.

[56] John E. Tilford, Jr., "James the Old Intruder," *Modern Fiction Studies*, IV (Summer, 1958), 157–64. Further evidence of the hardening process can be seen in a comparison of Joseph Warren Beach's early work on James with his new Preface to that work written thirty-six years later (*The Method of Henry James*, pp. lxxvi–lxxxi, 60–61). Flaubert has been subjected to the same treatment; it is easy to show that he violates standards of impersonality which he never sought to follow.

the beginning of the century: whether an impersonal novelist hides behind a single narrator or observer, the multiple points of view of *Ulysses* or *As I Lay Dying*, or the objective surfaces of *The Awkward Age* or Compton-Burnett's *Parents and Children*, the author's voice is never really silenced. It is, in fact, one of the things we read fiction for (chap. vii), and we are never troubled by it unless the author makes a great to-do about his own superior naturalness.

THE ORDERING OF INTENSITIES

Another result of the muddling of ends and means is the failure to recognize that no quality, however desirable, is likely to be suitable in the same degree in all parts of a work. Even the most elevated plateau is less interesting than a mountain, and it is misleading for criticism to talk as if the novelist succeeds best whose every line is as vivid and intense as every other.

If a novelist could achieve such a uniform intensity of whatever quality he cares about most, would he expect the reader to climb by himself to the height necessary for appreciation of that first elevated line? To the novelist who sees his task as in part that of *ordering* intensities, each valley and each peak in its proper place, there is no theoretical problem here; his only problem is to learn his craft. Willing to work with many different forms of intensity, and preparations for intensity, he can, like Henry James, manipulate his climaxes in recognition that every moment cannot be a climax. Physical immediacy, for example, sought by some modern novelists as if it were always a virtue, is a weapon that can easily destroy a work if used indiscriminately. In *The Brothers Karamazov* we feel many moments of vivid physical pain and pleasure, but Dostoevski knew when to hold back. We must feel Lisa's crushed finger as intensely as possible, and we feel it. "Lisa unbolted the door, opened it a little, put her finger in the crack and slammed the door with all her might, pinching her finger. Ten seconds after, releasing her finger, she walked softly, slowly to her chair, sat up straight in it and looked intently at her blackened finger and at the blood that oozed from under the nail. Her lips were quivering and she kept whispering rapidly to herself: 'I am a wretch, wretch, wretch, wretch.'" But when it comes to old Karamazov's and

Smerdyakov's death pangs we feel nothing. What would we say to Dostoevski if he had given with full vividness the pain in Grigory's skull when Dmitri strikes him with the pestle? Fortunately, he gives us almost nothing but Dmitri's sensations and reactions, so that Dmitri's crime is kept in what is, for this story, the proper perspective.

Precisely the same control is needed in the use of vivid psychic intimacy. Does anything seem more flaccid now than the "intensities" of some of those early experiments in stream-of-consciousness? "I'm flying . . . I'm dreaming . . . I'm asleep . . . I'm drea . . . drea —I'm . . . fly . . . The End." So passes away Schnitzler's poor Fräulein Else, back in 1923. But she is not really dead, not dead as Falstaff is dead after Mistress Quickly's description or as Don Quixote is dead:

> Death came at last for Don Quixote, after he had received all the sacraments and once more, with many forceful arguments, had expressed his abomination of books of chivalry. The notary who was present remarked that in none of those books had he read of any knight-errant dying in his own bed so peacefully and in so Christian a manner. And thus, amid the tears and lamentations of those present, he gave up the ghost; that is to say, he died. Perceiving that their friend was no more, the curate asked the notary to be a witness to the fact that Alonso Quijano the Good, commonly known as Don Quixote, was truly dead, this being necessary in order that some author other than Cid Hamete Benengeli might not have the opportunity of falsely resurrecting him and writing endless histories of his exploits.[57]

Even this last playful note, the most blatant kind of reminder that we are reading only a book, does not impugn the reality of the death as much as trying to get the very feel of it, by entering the Don's consciousness, might have done. The mistake of Schnitzler in *Fräulein Else* is not, of course, in entering a character's mind but in entering it at the wrong time for the wrong purpose.[58]

[57] Putnam translation.

[58] Needless to say, I am not suggesting that death is always an improper moment for intimate psychic rendering. Katherine Anne Porter's "The Jilting of Granny Weatherall" is a masterful "inside" presentation of the last moments of the heroine. By resisting the temptation to be literal and realistic in the heroine's language, and by drawing together in the final thoughts all the threads of the "jilting" theme, she

We should be careful, of course, not to underrate the technical achievement of modern authors as they have created degrees of psychic and physical vividness that would have been the envy of many earlier writers. Whenever such vividness is appropriate to the intended effect of the whole work, the new devices can prove useful (chap. x, below). They can even be sustained throughout a whole work, unmediated by any interpreting mind, if the work is short and if the emotions and ideas dealt with are simple. The author who, like Alain Robbe-Grillet, wants us to receive the very touch and feel of murderous jealousy, can now do so with an intensity that is almost unbearable. Simply by confining us to the sensations and thoughts of the disintegrating husband in *Jealousy*, Robbe-Grillet can make us experience a concentration of sensation impossible in any other mode.[59] He has, in fact, added a new fillip to this effect; by never describing the person, actions, or thoughts of the husband, but simply leaving us to infer his reality through what is left out, he locks us inside the camera box, as it were, more completely than in any previous fiction.

> All that remains is a large black spot contrasting with the dusty surface of the courtyard. This is a little oil which has dripped out of the motor, always in the same place.
>
> It is easy to make this spot disappear, thanks to the flaws in the rough glass of the window [through which the husband is, we have inferred, peering]: the blackened surface has merely to be brought into proximity with one of the flaws of the window-pane, by successive experiments.
>
> The spot begins by growing larger, one of its sides bulging to form a rounded protuberance, itself larger than the initial object. But a few fractions of an inch farther, this bulge is transformed into a series of tiny concentric crescents which diminish until they are only lines, while the other side of the spot shrinks, leaving behind it a stalk-shaped appendage which bulges in its turn for a second; then suddenly everything disappears.
>
> Behind the glass, now, in the angle determined by the central vertical frame and the horizontal cross-piece, there is only the gray-

---

achieves a very moving death: "For the second time there was no sign. Again no bridegroom and the priest in the house. She could not remember any other sorrow because this grief wiped them all away. Oh, no, there's nothing more cruel than this—I'll never forgive it. She stretched herself with a deep breath and blew out the light."

59 *La Jalousie* (Paris, 1957), trans. by Richard Howard as *Jealousy* (New York, 1959).

ish-beige color of the dusty gravel that constitutes the surface of the courtyard.

On the opposite wall, the centipede is there, in its tell-tale spot, right in the middle of the panel.

In *Jealousy* such repetitive and seemingly inconsequential detail is made to carry a great weight of emotion, because we become more and more deeply immersed in the tortured consciousness that produces the unimpassioned observations. But *Jealousy* is less than 35,000 words long—hardly a third longer than Molly Bloom's final interior monologue. We can endure unmediated, mindless sensation or emotion for as long as a hundred-and-fifty short pages. But it is no accident that *Jealousy* is very short. The effect of such a novel is of an extended dramatic monologue, an intense expression of one quality of mind and soul, deliberately not judged, deliberately left unplaced, isolated from the rest of human experience. It is, thus, less closely related to the traditional forms of fiction than to lyric poetry.[60]

It would be mere foolishness to claim that the passion for realism that has produced such experiments has been wrong. No theory that has helped to stimulate valuable fiction should be dismissed lightly, however one-sided it may appear. Further, the interest in realism is not a "theory" or even a combination of theories that can be proved right or wrong; it is an expression of what men of a given time have cared for most, and as such it cannot be attacked or defended with rational argument. One can show, I think, that it has sometimes had harmful consequences in the hands of dogmatists, but we can be quite sure that any exclusivist doctrine we tried to substitute for it would be fully as dangerous.

Fortunately, the alternative to dogmatic realism is not dogmatic antirealism. There are many other routes we can follow; whichever one we choose, our success will depend on our remembering the warning that Robert Louis Stevenson once gave James: what is the "making of one book, will in the next be impertinent or dull."[61]

---

[60] See Vivian Mercier, "Arrival of the Anti-Novel," *Commonweal*, LXX (May 8, 1959), 149–51.

[61] "A Humble Remonstrance," *Memories and Portraits* (London, 1887), p. 286. The essay has been reprinted several times, but it is not nearly so well known as James's "The Art of Fiction," which it purported to extend and correct.

Once we take this antidogmatism seriously, we find a flood of questions replacing "the one thing needful." Not just "How can an author achieve dramatic intensity?" Rather, "How can an author make sure that his most important dramatic moments will be heightened rather than obscured by their surroundings?"[62] "How can the author insure the greatest dramatic irony, not always, in all works, but whenever dramatic irony is desirable?" "How can an author maintain suspense—that much abused old-fashioned beauty, —when, like most authors, he really wants his readers to read through to the end?"[63] "How can he prevent a sentimental reading of this character or a hostile reading of that one?" "How can he insure that when this character lies, the reader will not be taken in—or, when desired, that he *will* be?" Answers to these and numerous similar questions will not necessarily lead to the restoration of commentary, much less to the restoration of any one kind of commentary. But they can provide a beginning in the effort to understand the rhetoric of fiction.

At this point in the mid-twentieth century we can see, after all, how easy it is to write a story that tells itself, freed of all authorial intrusion, shown with a consistent treatment of point of view. Even untalented writers can be taught to observe this fourth "unity." But we also know by now that in the process they have not necessarily learned to write good fiction. If they know only this, they know how to write fiction that will look modern—perhaps more "early modern" than late, but still modern. What they have yet to learn, if they know only this, is the art of choosing what to dramatize fully and what to curtail, what to summarize and what to heighten. And like any art, this one cannot be learned from abstract rules.

---

[62] ". . . when to dramatize and when to narrate, is the novelist's lesson" (George Meredith in *Westminster Review*, LXVII [April, 1857], 616, as quoted in Stang, *Theory of the Novel*, p. 105).

[63] I would not want to be asked for proof, but I suspect that many besides Yeats have praised *Ulysses* as a work of genius without being sufficiently interested even to finish it (see Richard Ellmann, *James Joyce*, p. 545).

"A novelist's characters must be with him as he lies down to sleep, and as he wakes from his dreams. He must learn to hate them and to love them."—TROLLOPE

"The less one feels a thing, the more likely one is to express it as it really is."—FLAUBERT

"An ecstatically happy prose writer . . . can't be moderate or temperate or brief. . . . He can't be detached. . . . In the wake of anything as large and consuming as happiness, he necessarily forfeits the much smaller but, for a writer, always rather exquisite pleasure of appearing on the page serenely sitting on a fence."—The narrator of J. D. Salinger's "Seymour: An Introduction"

"M. de Maupassant is remarkably objective and impersonal, but he would go too far if he were to entertain the belief that he has kept himself out of his books. They speak of him eloquently, even if it only be to tell us how easy . . . he has found this impersonality."—HENRY JAMES

"Now you are, through Maury, expressing your views, of course; but you would do so differently if you were deliberately stating them as your views."—MAXWELL PERKINS, in a letter to F. Scott Fitzgerald

General Rules, II:
"All Authors Should Be Objective"

A second type of general criterion common to many of the found-
ers of modern fiction deals with the author's state of mind or soul.
A surprising number of writers, even those who have thought of
their writing as "self-expression," have sought a freedom from the
tyranny of subjectivity, echoing Goethe's claim that "Every healthy
effort . . . is directed from the inward to the outward world."[1] From
time to time others have risen to defend commitment, engagement, involvement. But, at least until recently, the predominant
demand in this century has been for some sort of objectivity.

Like all such terms, however, objectivity is many things. Underlying it and its many synonyms—impersonality, detachment, dis-
interestedness, neutrality, etc.—we can distinguish at least three
separate qualities: neutrality, impartiality, and *impassibilité*.

NEUTRALITY AND THE AUTHOR'S "SECOND SELF"

Objectivity in the author can mean, first, an attitude of neutrality
toward all values, an attempt at disinterested reporting of all things

---

[1] "Conversations with Eckerman," January 29, 1826, trans. John Oxenford, as reprinted in *Criticism: The Major Texts*, ed. Walter Jackson Bate (New York, 1952),
p. 403.

good and evil. Like many literary enthusiasms, the passion for neutrality was imported into fiction from the other arts relatively late. Keats was saying in 1818 the kind of thing that novelists began to say only with Flaubert. "The poetical character . . . has no character. . . . It lives in gusto, be it foul or fair, high or low, rich or poor, mean or elevated. It has as much delight in conceiving an Iago as an Imogen. What shocks the virtuous philosopher, delights the camelion Poet. It does not harm from its relish of the dark side of things any more than from its taste for the bright one; because they both end in speculation."[2] Three decades later Flaubert recommended a similar neutrality to the novelist who would be a poet. For him the model is the attitude of the scientist. Once we have spent enough time, he says, in "treating the human soul with the impartiality which physical scientists show in studying matter, we will have taken an immense step forward."[3] Art must achieve "by a pitiless method, the precision of the physical sciences."[4]

It should be unnecessary here to show that no author can ever attain to this kind of objectivity. Most of us today would, like Sartre, renounce the analogy with science even if we could admit that science is objective in this sense. What is more, we all know by now that a careful reading of any statement in defense of the artist's neutrality will reveal commitment; there is always some deeper value in relation to which neutrality is taken to be good. Chekhov, for example, begins bravely enough in defense of neutrality, but he cannot write three sentences without committing himself. "I am afraid of those who look for a tendency between the lines, and who are determined to regard me either as a liberal or as a conservative. I am not a liberal, not a conservative, not a believer in gradual progress, not a monk, not an indifferentist. I should like to be a free artist and nothing more. . . . I have no preference either

---

[2] Letter to Richard Woodhouse, October 27, 1818, *The Poetical Works and Other Writings of John Keats*, ed. H. Buxton Forman (New York, 1939), VII, 129.

[3] *Correspondence* (October 12, 1853) (Paris, 1926–33), III, 367–68. For some of the citations from Flaubert in what follows I am indebted to the excellent monograph by Marianne Bonwit, *Gustave Flaubert et le principe d'impassibilité* (Berkeley, Calif., 1950). My distinction among the three forms of objectivity in the author is derived in part from her discussion.

[4] *Ibid.* (December 12, 1857), IV, 243.

for gendarmes, or for butchers, or for scientists, or for writers, or
for the younger generation. I regard trade-marks and labels as a superstition."[5] Freedom and art are good, then, and superstition bad?
Soon he is carried away to a direct repudiation of the plea for "indifference" with which he began. "My holy of holies is the human
body, health, intelligence, talent, inspiration, love, and the most
absolute freedom—freedom from violence and lying, whatever
forms they may take" (p. 63). Again and again he betrays in this
way the most passionate kind of commitment to what he often calls
objectivity.

> The artist should be, not the judge of his characters and their
> conversations, but only an unbiassed witness. I once overheard a
> desultory conversation about pessimism between two Russians;
> nothing was solved,—and my business is to report the conversation
> exactly as I heard it, and let the jury,—that is, the readers, estimate
> its value. My business is merely to be talented, i.e., to be able . . . to
> illuminate the characters and speak their language [pp. 58–59].

But "illuminate" according to what lights? "A writer must be as
objective as a chemist; he must abandon the subjective line; he
must know that dung-heaps play a very respectable part in a
landscape, and that evil passions are as inherent in life as good
ones" (pp. 275–76). We have learned by now to ask of such statements: Is it *good* to be faithful to what is "inherent"? Is it good to
include every part of the "landscape"? If so, why? According to
what scale of values? To repudiate one scale is necessarily to imply
another.

It would be a serious mistake, however, to dismiss talk about the
author's neutrality simply because of this elementary and under-
standable confusion between neutrality toward *some* values and
neutrality toward *all*. Cleansed of the polemical excesses, the attack
on subjectivity can be seen to rest on several important insights.

To succeed in writing some kinds of works, some novelists find it
necessary to repudiate all intellectual or political causes. Chekhov
does not want himself, *as artist*, to be either liberal or conservative.
Flaubert, writing in 1853, claims that even the artist who recognizes

---

[5] *Letters on the Short Story, the Drama and other Literary Topics*, selected and edited
by Louis S. Friedland (New York, 1924), p. 63.

the demand to be a "triple-thinker," even the artist who recognizes the need for ideas in abundance, "must have neither religion, nor country, nor social conviction."[6]

Unlike the claim to complete neutrality, this claim will never be refuted, and it will not suffer from shifts in literary theory or philosophical fashion. Like its opposite, the existentialist claim of Sartre and others that the artist should be totally *engagé*, its validity depends on the kind of novel the author is writing. Some great artists have been committed to the causes of their times, and some have not. Some works seem to be harmed by their burden of commitment (many of Sartre's own works, for example, in spite of their freedom from authorial comment) and some seem to be able to absorb a great deal of commitment (*The Divine Comedy, Four Quartets, Gulliver's Travels, Darkness at Noon, Bread and Wine*). One can always find examples to prove either side of the case; the test is whether the particular ends of the artist enable him to do something with his commitment, not whether he has it or not.

Everyone is against everyone else's prejudices and in favor of his own commitment to the truth. All of us would like the novelist somehow to operate on the level of our own passion for truth and right, a passion which by definition is not in the least prejudiced. The argument in favor of neutrality is thus useful in so far as it warns the novelist that he can seldom afford to pour his untransformed biases into his work. The deeper he sees into permanency, the more likely he is to earn the discerning reader's concurrence. The author as he writes should be like the ideal reader described by Hume in "The Standard of Taste," who, in order to reduce the distortions produced by prejudice, considers himself as "man in general" and forgets, if possible, his "individual being" and his "peculiar circumstances."

To put it in this way, however, is to understate the importance of the author's individuality. As he writes, he creates not simply an ideal, impersonal "man in general" but an implied version of "himself" that is different from the implied authors we meet in other

---

[6] *Corr.* (April 26–27, 1853), III, 183: ". . . ne doit avoir ni religion, ni patrie, ni même aucune conviction sociale. . . ."

men's works. To some novelists it has seemed, indeed, that they were discovering or creating themselves as they wrote. As Jessamyn West says, it is sometimes "only by writing the story that the novelist can discover—not his story—but its writer, the official scribe, so to speak, for that narrative."[7] Whether we call this implied author an "official scribe," or adopt the term recently revived by Kathleen Tillotson—the author's "second self"[8]—it is clear that the picture the reader gets of this presence is one of the author's most important effects. However impersonal he may try to be, his reader will inevitably construct a picture of the official scribe who writes in this manner—and of course that official scribe will never be neutral toward all values. Our reactions to his various commitments, secret or overt, will help to determine our response to the work. The reader's role in this relationship I must save for chapter v. Our present problem is the intricate relationship of the so-called real author with his various official versions of himself.

We must say various versions, for regardless of how sincere an author may try to be, his different works will imply different versions, different ideal combinations of norms. Just as one's personal letters imply different versions of oneself, depending on the differing relationships with each correspondent and the purpose of each letter, so the writer sets himself out with a different air depending on the needs of particular works.

These differences are most evident when the second self is given an overt, speaking role in the story. When Fielding comments, he gives us explicit evidence of a modifying process from work to

---

[7] "The Slave Cast Out," in *The Living Novel*, ed. Granville Hicks (New York, 1957), p. 202. Miss West continues: "Writing is a way of playing parts, of trying on masks, of assuming roles, not for fun but out of desperate need, not for the self's sake but for the writing's sake. 'To make any work of art,' says Elizabeth Sewell, 'is to make, or rather to unmake and remake one's self.' "

[8] In her inaugural lecture at the University of London, published as *The Tale and the Teller* (London, 1959). "Writing on George Eliot in 1877, Dowden said that the form that most persists in the mind after reading her novels is not any of the characters, but 'one who, if not the real George Eliot, is that second self who writes her books, and lives and speaks through them.' The 'second self,' he goes on, is 'more substantial than any mere human personality' and has 'fewer reserves'; while 'behind it, lurks well pleased the veritable historical self secure from impertinent observation and criticism' " (p. 22).

work; no single version of Fielding emerges from reading the satirical *Jonathan Wild*, the two great "comic epics in prose," *Joseph Andrews* and *Tom Jones*, and that troublesome hybrid, *Amelia*. There are many similarities among them, of course; all of the implied authors value benevolence and generosity; all of them deplore self-seeking brutality. In these and many other respects they are indistinguishable from most implied authors of most significant works until our own century. But when we descend from this level of generality to look at the particular ordering of values in each novel, we find great variety. The author of *Jonathan Wild* is by implication very much concerned with public affairs and with the effects of unchecked ambition on the "great men" who attain to power in the world. If we had only this novel by Fielding, we would infer from it that in his real life he was much more single-mindedly engrossed in his role as magistrate and reformer of public manners than is suggested by the implied author of *Joseph Andrews* and *Tom Jones*—to say nothing of *Shamela* (what would we infer about Fielding if he had never written anything but *Shamela!*). On the other hand, the author who greets us on page one of *Amelia* has none of that air of facetiousness combined with grand insouciance that we meet from the beginning in *Joseph Andrews* and *Tom Jones*. Suppose that Fielding had never written anything but *Amelia*, filled as it is with the kind of commentary we find at the beginning:

> The various accidents which befel a very worthy couple after their uniting in the state of matrimony will be the subject of the following history. The distresses which they waded through were some of them so exquisite, and the incidents which produced these so extraordinary, that they seemed to require not only the utmost malice, but the utmost invention, which superstition hath ever attributed to Fortune: though whether any such being interfered in the case, or, indeed, whether there be any such being in the universe, is a matter which I by no means presume to determine in the affirmative.

Could we ever infer from this the Fielding of the earlier works? Though the author of *Amelia* can still indulge in occasional jests and ironies, his general air of sententious solemnity is strictly in keeping with the very special effects proper to the work as a whole. Our picture of him is built, of course, only partly by the narrator's explicit commentary; it is even more derived from the kind of tale he chooses to tell. But the commentary makes explicit for us a relationship which is present in all fiction, even though it may be overlooked in fiction without commentary.

It is a curious fact that we have no terms either for this created "second self" or for our relationship with him. None of our terms for various aspects of the narrator is quite accurate. "Persona," "mask," and "narrator" are sometimes used, but they more commonly refer to the speaker in the work who is after all only one of the elements created by the implied author and who may be separated from him by large ironies. "Narrator" is usually taken to mean the "I" of a work, but the "I" is seldom if ever identical with the implied image of the artist.

"Theme," "meaning," "symbolic significance," "theology," or even "ontology"—all these have been used to describe the norms which the reader must apprehend in each work if he is to grasp it adequately. Such terms are useful for some purposes, but they can be misleading because they almost inevitably come to seem like purposes for which the works exist. Though the old-style effort to find the theme or moral has been generally repudiated, the new-style search for the "meaning" which the work "communicates" or "symbolizes" can yield the same kinds of misreading. It is true that both types of search, however clumsily pursued, express a basic need: the reader's need to know where, in the world of values, he stands—that is, to know where the author *wants* him to stand. But most works worth reading have so many possible "themes," so many possible mythological or metaphorical or symbolic analogues, that to find any one of them, and to announce it as what the work is *for*, is to do at best a very small part of the critical task. Our sense of the implied author includes not only the extractable meanings but also the moral and emotional content of each bit of action and suffering of all of the characters. It includes, in short, the intuitive apprehension of a completed artistic whole; the chief value to which *this* implied author is committed, regardless of what party his creator belongs to in real life, is that which is expressed by the total form.

Three other terms are sometimes used to name the core of norms and choices which I am calling the implied author. "Style" is sometimes broadly used to cover whatever it is that gives us a sense, from word to word and line to line, that the author sees more deeply and judges more profoundly than his presented characters. But, though style is one of our main sources of insight into the author's norms, in carrying such strong overtones of the merely verbal the word *style* excludes our sense of the author's skill in his choice of character and episode and scene and idea. "Tone" is similarly used to refer to the implicit evaluation which the author manages to convey behind his explicit presentation,[9] but it almost inevitably suggests again something limited to the merely verbal; some aspects of the implied author may be inferred through tonal variations, but his major qualities will depend also on the hard facts of action and character in the tale that is told.

Similarly, "technique" has at times been expanded to cover all discernible signs of the author's artistry. If everyone used "technique" as Mark Schorer does,[10] covering with it almost the entire range of choices made by the author, then it might very well serve our purposes. But it is usually taken for a much narrower matter, and consequently it will not do. We can be satisfied only with a term that is as broad as the work itself but still capable of calling attention to that work as the product of a choosing, evaluating person rather than as a self-existing thing. The "implied author" chooses, consciously or unconsciously, what we read; we infer him

---

[9] E.g., Fred B. Millett, *Reading Fiction* (New York, 1950): "This tone, the general feeling which suffuses and surrounds the work, arises ultimately out of the writer's attitude toward his subject. . . . *The subject derives its meaning from the view of life which the author has taken*" (p. 11).

[10] "When we speak of technique, then, we speak of nearly everything. For technique is the means by which the writer's experience, which is his subject matter, compels him to attend to it; technique is the only means he has of discovering, exploring, developing his subject, of conveying its meaning, and finally of evaluating it. . . . Technique in fiction is, of course, all those obvious forms of it which are usually taken to be the whole of it, and many others" ("Technique as Discovery," *Hudson Review*, I [Spring, 1948], 67–87, as reprinted in *Forms of Modern Fiction*, ed. Wm. Van O'Connor [Minneapolis, Minn., 1948], pp. 9–29; see esp. pp. 9–11).

as an ideal, literary, created version of the real man; he is the sum of his own choices.

It is only by distinguishing between the author and his implied image that we can avoid pointless and unverifiable talk about such qualities as "sincerity" or "seriousness" in the author. Because Ford Madox Ford thinks of Fielding and Defoe and Thackeray as the unmediated authors of their novels, he must end by condemning them as insincere, since there is every reason to believe that they write "passages of virtuous aspirations that were in no way any aspirations of theirs."[11] Presumably he is relying on external evidences of Fielding's lack of virtuous aspirations. But we have only the work as evidence for the only kind of sincerity that concerns us: Is the implied author in harmony with himself—that is, are his other choices in harmony with his explicit narrative character? If a narrator who by every trustworthy sign is presented to us as a reliable spokesman for the author professes to believe in values which are never realized in the structure as a whole, we can then talk of an insincere work. A great work establishes the "sincerity" of its implied author, regardless of how grossly the man who created that author may belie in his *other* forms of conduct the values embodied in his work. For all we know, the only sincere moments of his life may have been lived as he wrote his novel.

What is more, in this distinction between author and implied author we find a middle position between the technical irrelevance of talk about the artist's objectivity and the harmful error of pretending that an author can allow direct intrusions of his own immediate problems and desires. The great defenders of objectivity were working on an important matter and they knew it. Flaubert is right in saying that Shakespeare does not barge clumsily into his works. We are never plagued with his undigested personal problems. Flaubert is also right in rebuking Louise Colet for writing "La Servante" as a personal attack on Musset, with the personal passion destroying the aesthetic value of the poem (January 9–10,

---

11 *The English Novel* (London, 1930), p. 58. See Geoffrey Tillotson, *Thackeray the Novelist* (Cambridge, 1954), esp. chap. iv, "The Content of the Authorial 'I' " (pp. 55–70), for a convincing argument that the "I" of Thackeray's works should be carefully distinguished from Thackeray himself.

1854). And he is surely right when he forces the hero of the youthful version of *The Sentimental Education* (1845) to choose between the merely confessional statement and the truly rendered work of art.

But is he right when he claims that we do not know what Shakespeare loved or hated?[12] Perhaps—if he means only that we cannot easily tell from the plays whether the man Shakespeare preferred blondes to brunettes or whether he disliked bastards, Jews, or Moors. But the statement is most definitely mistaken if it means that the implied author of Shakespeare's plays is neutral toward all values. We do know what *this* Shakespeare loved and hated; it is hard to see how he could have written his plays at all if he had refused to take a strong line on at least one or two of the seven deadly sins. I return in chapter v to the question of beliefs in literature, and I try there to list a few of the values to which Shakespeare is definitely and obviously committed. They are for the most part not personal, idiosyncratic; Shakespeare is thus not recognizably subjective. But they are unmistakable violations of true neutrality; the implied Shakespeare is thoroughly engaged with life, and he does not conceal his judgment on the selfish, the foolish, and the cruel.

Even if all this were denied, it is difficult to see why there should be any necessary connection between neutrality and an absence of commentary. An author might very well use comments to warn the reader against judging. But if I am right in claiming that neutrality is impossible, even the most nearly neutral comment will reveal some sort of commitment.

> Once upon a time there lived in Berlin, Germany, a man called Albinus. He was rich, respectable, happy; one day he abandoned his wife for the sake of a youthful mistress; he loved; was not loved; and his life ended in disaster.
> This is the whole of the story and we might have left it at that had there not been profit and pleasure in the telling; and although there is plenty of space on a gravestone to contain, bound in moss, the abridged version of a man's life, detail is always welcome.[13]

---

[12] Qu'est qui me dira, en effet ce que Shakespeare a aimé, ce qu'il a haï, ce qu'il a senti?" (*Corr.*, I, 386).

[13] Vladimir Nabokov, *Laughter in the Dark* (New York, 1938), p. 1.

Nabokov may here have purged his narrator's voice of all commitments save one, but that one is all-powerful: he believes in the ironic interest—and as it later turns out, the poignancy—of a man's fated self-destruction. Maintaining the same detached tone, this author can intrude whenever he pleases without violating our conviction that he is as objective as it is humanly possible to be. Describing the villain, he can call him both a "dangerous man" and "a very fine artist indeed" without reducing our confidence in his open-mindedness. But he is not neutral toward all values, and he does not pretend to be.

IMPARTIALITY AND "UNFAIR" EMPHASIS

The author's objectivity has also sometimes meant an attitude of impartiality toward his characters. Much of what Flaubert and Chekhov wrote about objectivity is really a plea to the artist not to load the dice, not to take sides unjustly against or for particular characters. Chekhov wires to a friend, "I do not venture to ask you to love the gynecologist and the professor, but I venture to remind you of the justice which for an objective writer is more precious than the air he breathes" (*Letters on the Short Story*, p. 78). Sometimes this impartiality is made to sound like universal love or pity or toleration: "There is no one to blame, and should the guilt be traceable, that is the affair of the health officers and not of the artist. . . . She [your character] may act in any way she pleases, but the author should be kindly to the fingertips" (pp. 81, 82). Indeed, a very great deal of modern fiction has been written on the assumption, itself a basic commitment to a value, that to understand all is to forgive all. But this assumption is very different from the neutrality described in the first section. Writers who are successful in getting their readers to reserve judgment are not impartial about whether judgment should be reserved. As H. W. Leggett said, almost three decades ago, in a forgotten little classic on the role of what he calls the author's and reader's "code," modern fiction often presents occasions to the reader to "observe and refrain from judging . . . and a part at least of the reader's satisfaction is due to his consciousness of his own broadmindedness."[14]

---

[14] H. W. Leggett, *The Idea in Fiction* (London, 1934), p. 16.

In practice, no author ever manages to create a work which shows complete impartiality, whether impartial scorn, like Flaubert in *Bouvard et Pécuchet* attempting to "attack everything," or impartial forgiveness. Flaubert could sometimes write as if he thought Shakespeare and the Greeks were impartial in a sense they would have been astonished by. "The magnificent William sides with no one," and he refused to "declaim against usury" in *The Merchant of Venice*.[15] But Shakespeare never pretends that Goneril and Regan stand equal with Cordelia before the bar of justice, even though they are judged by the same standard. And in *The Merchant of Venice* he is so far from impartiality that he can really be accused of employing a double standard at Shylock's expense, at least in the latter part of the play. Certainly he does not work according to any abstract notion of impartial treatment for all characters. Similarly, the Greek dramatists never pretended that there was no basic distinction between men like Oedipus and Orestes on the one hand, and the fools and knaves on the other. Though they did not deal in "blacks and whites," as the popular attack on melodrama goes, they did not reduce all human worth to a gray blur.

Even among characters of equal moral, intellectual, or aesthetic worth, all authors inevitably take sides. A given work will be "about" a character or set of characters. It cannot possibly give equal emphasis to all, regardless of what its author believes about the desirability of fairness. *Hamlet* is not fair to Claudius. No matter how hard G. Wilson Knight labors to convince us that we have misjudged Claudius,[16] and no matter how willing we are to admit that Claudius' story is potentially as interesting as Hamlet's, *this* is Hamlet's story, and it cannot do justice to the king. *Othello* is not fair to Cassio; *King Lear* is not just to the Duke of Cornwall; *Madame Bovary* is unfair to almost everyone but Emma; and *A Portrait of the Artist as a Young Man* positively maligns everyone but Stephen.

But who cares? The novelist who chooses to tell *this* story cannot at the same time tell *that* story; in centering our interest, sympathy,

---

15 *Corr.* (November 2, 1852), III, 47; (December 9, 1852), 60–62.

16 *The Wheel of Fire* (rev. ed.; London, 1949), pp. 32–38.

or affection on one character, he inevitably excludes from our interest, sympathy, or affection some other character. Art imitates life in this respect as in so many others; just as in real life I am inevitably unfair to everyone but myself or, at best, my immediate loved ones, so in literature complete impartiality is impossible. Is *Ulysses* fair to the bourgeois Irish characters that throng about Bloom and Stephen and Molly? We can thank our stars that it is not.

It is true, nevertheless, that some works are marred by an impression that the author has weighed his characters on dishonest scales. But this impression depends not on whether the author explicitly passes judgment but on whether the judgment he passes seems defensible in the light of the dramatized facts. A clear illustration can be seen in *Lady Chatterley's Lover*. Lawrence can talk as passionately as the next man about the dangers of partiality: "Morality in the novel is the trembling instability of the balance. When the novelist puts his thumb in the scale, to pull down the balance to his own predilection, that is immorality.

"The modern novel tends to become more and more immoral, as the novelist tends to press his thumb heavier and heavier in the pan: either on the side of love, pure love: or on the side of licentious 'freedom.' "[17] What he hates, he tells us again and again, is the novel that is merely a "treatise." Though he is more aware than many have been that every novel implies "some theory of being, some metaphysic," he demands that "the metaphysic must always subserve the artistic purpose beyond the artist's conscious aim."[18]

Though critics of *Lady Chatterley's Lover* are agreed on little else, they seem to agree that the novelist has in this work pressed his thumb very heavily indeed in the pan containing his prophetic vision of a love that is neither "love, pure love" nor "licentious freedom," a love that can save us from the destructive forces of civilization. Critics who approve of the position praise the book—but in terms that make clear its courageous exposition of the truth.

---

[17] "Morality and the Novel" (1925), reprinted in *Phoenix* (London, 1936), pp. 528–29.

[18] "Study of Thomas Hardy," in *Phoenix* (London, 1936), as quoted by Allott, *Novelists on the Novel* (New York, 1959), p. 104.

Critics who think the thesis exaggerated or false may admit to Lawrence's gift but deplore the injustices he commits in defense of his lovers. But everyone seems to deal with the book in terms of its thesis.[19] Even the critics who feel, with Mark Schorer, that Lawrence managed to make "the preacher" and "the poet" coincide "formally" cannot discuss the book without spending most of their energies on the preachments.[20]

Significantly enough the question of Lawrence's impartiality seems completely unrelated to his choice of technical devices. Whether we accept or reject Lawrence's vision of a new salvation, our decision is not based on whether he uses this or that form of authorial preachment; objections against Lawrence's bias have more often dealt with his portrayal of Mellors, the gamekeeper, than with the fact that he allows authorial commentary of various kinds. When Mellors presents at great length his belief that "if men could fuck with warm hearts, and the women take it warm-heartedly everything would come all right" (chap. xiv), the panacea may strike us as inadequate to the point of comedy or as an inspiring portrait of a brave new world acomin', but we will receive little help in our choice by asking whether the beliefs are given in dramatic form. Those of us who reject this side of the book do so finally on the grounds that what Mellors says implies for us a version of D. H. Lawrence that we cannot admire; there is an unbridgeable disparity between the implied author's proffered salvation and our own views.[21]

---

[19] Stanley Kauffmann, "'Lady Chatterley' at Last," *The New Republic*, May 25, 1959, p. 16; Paul Lauter, "Lady C. with Love and Money," *The New Leader*, September 21, 1959: "Lawrence refines the gamekeeper with each revision of the novel, perhaps to make him more acceptable to Connie (and to the reader) as a lover. His finish in the final version, however, is partly a concession to the very society to which he stands opposed. . . . What does make Mellors eligible for salvation? Why cannot Michaelis or Tommy Dukes then enter?" (p. 24).

[20] See Schorer's Introduction to the Grove Press reprint (New York, 1959), esp. pp. 21 ff.

[21] See, for example, Colin Welch's attack on the book in "Black Magic, White Lies," *Encounter*, XVI (February, 1961), 75–79: "What it preaches is this: that mankind can only be regenerated by freeing itself from the tyranny of the intellect and the soul, from the tyranny of Jesus Christ, and by prostrating itself before its own phallus . . ." (p. 79). Whether one accepts Welch's charges or the defense of Lawrence by Rebecca West and Richard Hoggart in the following issue of *Encounter*, it is clear

What we object to, then, is the Lawrence implied by some of the drama, not necessarily the Lawrence given in the commentary. The little disquisition in chapter nine on the powers and limitations of fiction, which a critic has deplored as evidence of "unsteadiness of control in points of view,"[22] really shows Lawrence in very attractive form. Since we recognize the validity of the author's attack on the conventional fiction that appeals only to the vices of the public, the fiction that is humiliating because it glorifies the most corrupt feelings under the guise of "purity," we grant to the author the superiority of his effort to use the novel to "reveal the most secret places of life." Lawrence's essential integrity seems to us beyond question after such a passage—at least until we encounter another long-winded outburst by Mellors.

In short, whatever unfairness there is in this book lies at the core of the novel; so long as Lawrence is determined to damn everyone who does not follow Mellors' way, to labor for surface impartiality would be pointless. If we finish the book with a sense of embarrassment at its special pleading, if we read Mellors' final pseudobiblical talk of "the peace that comes of fucking" and of his "Pentecost, the forked flame between me and you," with regrets rather than conviction, it is ultimately because no literary technique can conceal from us the confused and pretentious little author who is implied in too many parts of the book. Even our memory of the very different author implied by the better novels—*Women in Love*, say— is not enough to redeem the bad portions of this one.

"Impassibilité"

The author's objectivity can mean, finally, what Flaubert called *impassibilité*, an unmoved or unimpassioned feeling toward the characters and events of one's story. Although Flaubert did not maintain the distinction clearly, this quality is distinct from neutrality of judgment about values; an author could be committed to one or another value and still not feel with or against any of his

---

that what is in dispute is Lawrence's success in winning us to accept his basic vision; no tinkering with the proportions of telling and showing will make much difference here.

[22] Kauffmann, *op. cit.*, p. 16.

characters. At the same time, it is clearly distinct from impartiality, since the artist could feel a lively hate or love or pity for all of his characters impartially. There seems to be a genuine temperamental difference among authors in the amount of detachment of this kind they find congenial[23]—somewhat like the difference between actors who "feel" their roles and actors like the heroine of Somerset Maugham's *Theatre*, who finds that as soon as she feels a role her power to perform effectively is destroyed. Trollope in his *Autobiography* describes himself as wandering alone in the woods, crying at the grief of his characters and "laughing at their absurdities, and thoroughly enjoying their joy." It was perhaps natural that authors like Flaubert should have reacted to a similarly impassioned approach in some of the French romantics by pretending to an equally impassioned rejection of passion.

But this hardly suggests that there is any natural connection between the author's *impassibilité* and any one kind of rhetoric or any particular level of achievement. Authors at either extreme of the scale of emotional involvement might write works which were full of highly personal commentary, stories that were altogether "told," or works that were strictly dramatic, strictly "shown."

One sign that there is no connection between the author's feelings and any necessary technique or achieved quality of his work is the fact that we can never securely infer, without external evidence, whether an author has *felt* his work or written with cold detachment. Did Fielding hate Jonathan Wild or weep for Amelia? Was he personally amused when Parson Adams, on his way to London to sell sermons which Fielding and the reader know to be unmarketable, discovers that he has left them at home?

Saintsbury praised Fielding for his "detachment" in *Jonathan Wild*, presumably because the narrator is maintained throughout as a character who differs obviously and markedly from any real Fielding we could possibly imagine. But is there any reason to suppose that Fielding was less detached from his materials when dealing with the lovable fool Adams than when portraying Wild? We too easily fall into the habit of talking as if the narrator who

---

23 See Chekhov, *Letters*, pp. 97–98.

says, "O my good readers!" were Fielding, forgetting that for all we know he may have worked as deliberately and with as much detachment in creating the wise, urbane narrator of *Joseph Andrews* and *Tom Jones* as he did in creating the cynical narrator of *Jonathan Wild*. What was said above about the relation between the author's own values and the values supported by his second self applies here in precisely the same sense. A great artist can create an implied author who is either detached or involved, depending on the needs of the work in hand.

We see, then, that none of the three major claims to objectivity in the author has any necessary bearing on technical decisions. Though it may be important at a given moment in the history of an art or in the development of a writer to stress the dangers of a misguided commitment, partiality, or emotional involvement, the tendency to connect the author's objectivity with a required impersonality of technique is quite indefensible.

Subjectivism Encouraged by Impersonal Techniques

Impersonal narration may, in fact, encourage the very subjectivism that it is supposed to cure. The effort to avoid signs of explicit evaluation can be peculiarly dangerous for the author who is fighting to keep himself out of his works. Although it is true that commentary can be a medium for meretricious subjective outpourings, the effort to construct such commentary can, in some authors, create precisely the right kind of wall between the author's weaker self and the self he must create if his book is to succeed. The art of constructing reliable narrators is largely that of mastering all of oneself in order to project the *persona*, the second self, that really belongs in the book. And, in laying his cards on the table, an author can discover in himself, and at least then find some chance of combating, the two extremes of subjectivism that have marred some impersonal fiction.

Indiscriminate sympathy or compassion.—By giving the impression that judgment is withheld, an author can hide from himself that he is sentimentally involved with his characters, and that he is asking for his reader's sympathies without providing adequate reasons. The older technique of reliable narration, as Q. D. Leavis says, forced the author and reader to remain somewhat distant from even the most sympathetic character. But she finds that often in the modern best seller "the author has poured his own day-dreams, hot and hot, into dramatic form, without bringing them to any such touchstone as the 'good sense, but not common-sense' of a cultivated society: the author is himself—or more usually herself— identified with the leading character, and the reader is invited to share the debauch."[24]

Such sentimentality was of course possible in older forms of fiction. "Our hero" could often get away with murder, while his enemies were condemned for minor infractions of the moral code. But the modern author can reject the charge of sentimentality by saying, in effect, "Who, me? Not at all. It is the reader's fault if he feels any excessive or unjustified compassion. *I* didn't say a word. I'm as tight-lipped and unemotional as the next man." Such effects are most evident, perhaps, in the worst of the tough-guy school of detective fiction. Mickey Spillane's Mike Hammer can, in effect, do no wrong—for those who can stomach him at all. But many of Spillane's readers would drop him immediately if he intruded to make explicit the vicious morality on which enjoyment of the books is based: "You may notice, reader, that when Mike Hammer beats up an Anglo-Saxon American he is less brutal than when he beats up a Jew, and that when he beats up a Negro he is most brutal of all. In this way our hero discriminates his punishment according to the racial worth of his victims." It is wise of Spillane to avoid making such things explicit.

If, as Chekhov said, "Subjectivity is an awful thing—even for the reason that it betrays the poor writer hand over fist," we can now see that the kind of subjectivity he deplored is not by any means

---

[24] *Fiction and the Reading Public* (London, 1932), p. 236. See also Roger Vailland, "La Loi du Romancier," *L'Express* (Paris), July 12, 1957, pp. 13, 15. Vailland found that he was ready to write "de vrais romans" only when he had ceased to be the hero of his own daydreams. "J'en étais complètement absent; je m'en suis brusquement aperçu; preuve était donc faite que mon rêve ne constituait pas un moyen détourné de me rapprocher de la bergère [the heroine of the daydream]" (p. 14).

prevented by the standard devices of so-called objectivity. In what is perhaps a different sense of the word, we can see that even the most rigorously impersonal techniques can *betray* the poor writer hand over fist. Betrayal for betrayal, there is probably less danger for author and reader in a literature that lays its cards on the table, in a literature that betrays to the poor writer just how poor a thing he has created.

Indiscriminate irony.—We have no word like sentimentality to cover the opposite fault of the author who allows an all-pervasive, "un-earned" irony to substitute for an honest discrimination among his materials. The fault is always hard to prove, but most of us have, I suspect, encountered novelists who people their novels with very short heroes because they themselves want to appear tall. The author who maintains his invulnerability by suggesting irony at all points but never holding himself responsible for definition of its limits can be as irresponsible as the writer of best sellers based on naïve identification.[25]

Henry James talks of Flaubert's "two refuges" from the need to look at humanity squarely. One was the exotic, as in *Salammbo* and *The Temptation of Saint Anthony*, the "getting away from the human" altogether. The other was irony, which enabled him to deal with the human without having to commit himself about it directly. But, James asks, "when all was said and done was he absolutely and exclusively condemned to irony?" Might he "not after all have fought out his case a little more on the spot?" Coming from James, this is a powerful question. One cannot help feeling, as one reads many of the "objective" yet corrosive portraits that have been given us since James, that the author is using irony to protect himself rather than to reveal his subject. If the author's characters reveal themselves as fools and knaves when we cast a cold eye upon them, how about the author himself? How would he look if his true opinions were served up cold? Or does he have no opinions?

Like the female novelist satirized by Randall Jarrell, these novelists can show us "the price of every sin and the value of none."

---

[25] See May Sarton, "The Shield of Irony," *The Nation*, April 14, 1956, pp. 314–16.

Her books were a systematic, detailed, and conclusive condemnation of mankind for being stupid and bad; yet if mankind had been clever and good, what would have become of Gertrude? . . . When she met someone who was either good or clever, she looked at him in uneasy antagonism. Yet she need not have been afraid. Clever people always came to seem to her, after a time, bad; good people always came to seem to her, after a time, stupid. She was always able to fail the clever for being bad, the good for being stupid; and if somebody was both clever and good, Gertrude stopped grading. If a voice had said to her, "Hast thou considered my servant Gottfried Rosenbaum, that there is none like him in Benton, a kind and clever man," she would have answered: "I can't *stand* that Gottfried Rosenbaum."[26]

Subjectivism of these two kinds can ruin a novel; the weaker the novel, on the whole, the more likely we are to be able to make simple and accurate inferences about the real author's problems based on our experience of the implied author. There is this much truth to the demand for objectivity in the author: signs of the real author's untransformed loves and hates are almost always fatal. But clear recognition of this truth cannot lead us to doctrines about technique, and it should not lead us to demand of the author that he eliminate love and hate, and the judgments on which they are based, from his novels. The emotions and judgments of the implied author are, as I hope to show, the very stuff out of which great fiction is made.[27]

---

[26] *Pictures from an Institution* (New York, 1954), p. 134.

[27] Mauriac discusses this complex problem brilliantly in *Le romancier et ses personnages* (Paris, 1933), esp. pp. 142–43: "Derrière le roman le plus objectif, s'il s'agit d'une belle œuvre, d'une grande œuvre, se dissimule toujours ce drame vécu du romancier, cette lutte individuelle avec ses démons et avec ses sphinx. Mais peut-être est-ce précisément la réussite du génie que rien de ce drame personnel ne se trahisse au dehors. Le mot fameux de Flaubert: 'Mme Bovary, c'est moi-meme,' est très compréhensible,—il faut seulement prendre le temps d'y réfléchir, tant à première vue l'auteur d'un pareil livre y paraît être peu mêlé. C'est que *Madame Bovary* est un chef-d'œuvre,—c'est-à-dire une œuvre qui forme bloc et qui s'impose comme un tout, comme un monde séparé de celui qui l'a créé. C'est dans la mesure où notre œuvre est imparfaite qu'à travers les fissures se trahit l'âme tourmentée de son misérable auteur."

"It has been through Flaubert that the novel has at last caught up with poetry."—Allen Tate

"Maybe every novelist wants to write poetry first."—William Faulkner

"You must have your eyes forever on your Reader. That alone constitutes Technique!"—Ford Madox Ford

"The writer expresses. He does not communicate." "The plain reader be damned."—Planks 11 and 12 of the Jolas "Manifesto," 1926

"I don't care about John Doe's opinion on mine or anyone else's work. Mine is the standard which has to be met. . . ." —William Faulkner

"An author who assures you that he writes for himself alone and that he does not care whether he is heard or not is a boaster and is deceiving either himself or you."—François Mauriac

"I remember Yeats: 'I have spent the whole of my life trying to get rid of rhetoric . . . I have got rid of one kind of rhetoric and have merely set up another.' "—Ezra Pound in *Make It New*

General Rules, III:
"True Art Ignores the Audience"

"True Artists Write Only for Themselves"

Rules about realistic works and about objective authors lead naturally to the third kind, prescriptions about readers. It is not, after all, only an image of himself that the author creates. Every stroke implying his second self will help to mold the reader into the kind of person suited to appreciate such a character and the book he is writing. But this act of communication, fundamental to the very existence of literature, has in modern criticism often been ignored, lamented, or denied. True artists, we have been told again and again, take no thought of their readers. They write for themselves. The true poet writes to express himself, or to find himself, or "to get rid of the book"[1]—and let the reader be damned. "Is the writer under any obligation to the reader?" an interviewer asked Faulkner, and he received a reply that might not have shocked Keats but would surely have troubled Dickens or Trollope. "I don't care about John Doe's opinion on mine or anyone else's work. Mine is the standard which has to be met, which is when the work makes me feel the

---

[1] Vladimir Nabokov, "On a Book Entitled Lolita," *Lolita* (New York, 1958), p. 313.

way I do when I read *La Tentation de Saint Antoine*, or the Old
Testament. They make me feel good. So does watching a bird make
me feel good."[2]

In the last few decades it is really only in handbooks about how
to write best sellers that we find very much open advice to the
author to think of his reader and write accordingly. The predominant fashion among serious writers has been to consider any recognizable concern for the reader as a commercial blemish on the
otherwise spotless face of art.[3] If someone is rude enough to ask
who the serious writers are, the answer is easy: they are those
whom one could never suspect of writing with the reader in mind!

Though we may be amused by the cultic solemnities of those
who suspect rhetorical concerns, there are good reasons for their
suspicion. Do we not see, in every bit of hack work on the best-
seller lists, evidence of what happens to art when the audience's
demands are allowed to control what the artist does? Rather than
enter into the morass of conflicting and degrading rhetorical demands, is it not safer to assume that any compliance with the reader's needs is both inartistic and dangerous? "I write. Let the reader
learn to read"—such a motto, adopted openly by Mark Harris recently, might serve as the credo for many modern novelists. "There
is easy reading. And there is literature," he says. "There are easy
writers, and there are writers. . . . The novelist depends upon that
relatively small audience which brings to reading a frame of reference, a sophistication, a level of understanding not lower than
the novelist's own. . . . I resist, as true novelists do, the injunction
(usually a worried editor's) to be clearer, to be easier, to explain,
if I feel that the request is for the convenience of the reader at the
expense of craft."[4]

"I write. Let the reader learn to read." An author who makes
this his motto, in the name of artistic integrity, can hardly be ex-

---

[2] Jean Stein, "Interview with William Faulkner," *The Paris Review*, IV (Spring,
1956), 28–52. Quotation is from p. 38.

[3] This is not to say that what I am calling rhetoric has been entirely ignored. See
Bibliography, Sec. IV.

[4] "Easy Does It Not," in *The Living Novel*, ed. Granville Hicks (New York, 1957),
pp. 113–16.

pected to tolerate the attitudes of earlier novelists like Trollope, who claimed that the novelist's first duty is to "make himself pleasant," and that to do so he must render his meaning "without an effort to the reader."[5] Why should the author be bound to the tyrannical reader? In a time when to talk of the "reader" can no longer mean what it could still mean for Trollope, when to render your meaning without an effort to most readers might very well mean to stop writing entirely, the serious author must surely brace himself against the demand that he take the reader into account. How can he avoid the attitude of Virginia Woolf, who saw the ordinary reader as a tyrant who has the novelist "in thrall to provide a plot, to provide comedy, tragedy, love interest"?[6]

THEORIES OF PURE ART

The question cannot be answered by looking at the reader alone. Suspicion of the reader has usually been based on theories of pure art or pure poetry which demand that this, that, or the other element be purged in order that what remains might consist of nothing but pure elements fused in an intrinsic, internal relationship. Though such theories have varied widely in what they would ban, most of them have excluded all obvious rhetoric, since it is clearly not a part of the "pure poetic object."[7]

---

[5] *An Autobiography*, ed. Frederick Page (London, 1950), pp. 234–35.

[6] "Modern Fiction," *The Common Reader* (London, 1925; New York, 1953), pp. 153–54. The essay was written in 1919. The battle between the more and more demanding author and the less and less capable reader has so many facets that I cannot even define the issues here, let alone assign praise and blame. For accounts of the deterioration of the reading public, see Q. D. Leavis, *Fiction and the Reading Public* (London, 1932), and Richard D. Altick, *The English Common Reader: A Social History of the Mass Reading Public, 1800–1900* (Chicago, 1957).

  Attacks on the reading public are still frequent. "It is apparent," Granville Hicks concludes his edition of statements by ten younger novelists (*The Living Novel*), "that all is not well with the novel today, but the problem is essentially a problem of readers, not a problem of writers" (p. 216). Yet at least two of the novelists in his volume, Ralph Ellison and Harvey Swados, have a good deal to say about the novelist's problem in dealing with values as they relate to the reader. The problem of whether the anti-rhetorical pose of the early "modern" novelists is dying out must be left, however, for someone who can follow the contemporary picture more closely than I.

[7] Robert Penn Warren lists ten elements that he has found one critic or another purging in order to leave only pure poetry: "1. Ideas, truths, generalizations, 'meaning.' 2. Precise, complicated, 'intellectual' images. 3. Unbeautiful, disagreeable, or

There was nothing new in the contrast of poetry with rhetoric or with mere prose. Indeed, the notion that recognizably rhetorical elements in poetry are at best necessary evils can be found in poetic theory from Aristotle on. "The poet should speak as little as possible in his own person," Aristotle says, "for it is not this that makes him an imitator" (Butcher trans. xxiv. 7). To use more modern terminology, it is not his intrusive commentary that makes him a true poet or creative artist. Similarly, the chorus should "be regarded as one of the actors; it should be an integral part of the whole, and share in the action, in the manner not of Euripides but of Sophocles. As for the later poets, their choral songs pertain as little to the subject of the piece as to that of any other tragedy" (xviii. 7). Finally, he repudiates the last of the three most obviously rhetorical temptations of drama, the use of spectacular staging. The plot, he says, should take care of the emotional effect, and to produce this effect by "spectacular means"—that is, by the producer's rhetoric—is a "less artistic method, and dependent on extraneous aids" (xiv. 2).

Unlike many modern aestheticians, Aristotle never completely repudiates the rhetorical dimension of poetry. He clearly recognizes that one thing the poet does is to produce effects on audiences. In exciting feelings "such as pity, fear, anger, and the like," and in suggesting "importance or its opposite," poetry is, in fact, closely related to rhetoric. Indeed, when he comes to discuss "Thought," Aristotle relegates it to "the *Rhetoric*, to which inquiry the subject more strictly belongs" (xix. 1). But despite this close relation to the study of rhetoric, poetics is not the study of effects designed to suit the characteristics of particular audiences. The audience to be worked upon is kept constant; only in studying

---

neutral materials. 4. Situation, narrative, logical transition. 5. Realistic details, exact descriptions, realism in general. 6 Shifts in tone or mood. 7. Irony. 8 Metrical variation, dramatic adaptations of rhythm, cacophony, etc. 9. Meter itself. 10. Subjective and personal elements" ("Pure and Impure Poetry," *Kenyon Review*, Spring, 1943, as reprinted in *Critiques and Essays in Criticism: 1920–48*, ed. Robert W. Stallman [New York, 1949], p. 99). For a persuasive argument against using purity as a universal standard, see Frederick Pottle, *The Idiom of Poetry* (Ithaca, N.Y., 1941).

rhetoric proper must we trouble about the peculiarities of audiences and the adaptation of our case to fit those peculiarities.[8]

But though he sees that poetry always works upon an audience, and thus always has a close relationship to rhetoric, Aristotle deplores all obvious, separable rhetoric, as we have just seen, because it is "extraneous." On the one hand we have what is integral and hence poetic: the imitated action. On the other we have the author's and chorus' comments which, like spectacular staging, always threaten to become extraneous and hence, by definition, less poetic.

The distinction between intrinsic and extrinsic has often proved to be helpful, and it is not surprising that it has been used again and again throughout the history of criticism. But it is much too general to take us very far in our critical task. What do we mean, after all, by "extraneous"? Most of us can accept the essential poetic truth first formulated by Aristotle—that each successful imaginative work has its own life, its own soul, its own principles of being, quite independently of the prejudices or practical needs of this or that audience, and that our poetic devices should be an "integral part of the whole." The poet, we will say, "should speak as little as possible in his own person." But why, then, speak at all? If Homer is better than the others for appearing rarely—though as we have seen already he appears far more often than Aristotle's comment would suggest—can we not out-Homer Homer by not appearing at all, by *showing* everything and *telling* nothing? If Sophocles is better than Euripides for involving his chorus in the action to at least some extent, would he have been better still if he had been able to involve them completely, eliminating all of their mere commentary?

Aristotle never carries the case that far, and there are good reasons, in addition to the hints of his chapter xix, to believe that he

---

8 Aristotle's attempt to distinguish rhetoric from poetics soon was abandoned, however, in the works of the various rhetoricians. See Bernard Weinberg, "Robertello on the *Poetics*," in *Critics and Criticism*, ed. R. S. Crane (Chicago, 1952), pp. 319–48; Richard McKeon, "The Concept of Imitation in Antiquity," *ibid.*, esp. pp. 168–74. On some current varieties of "rhetorical" criticism, see R. S. Crane, *The Languages of Criticism and the Structure of Poetry* (Toronto, 1953), esp. pp. 115–28, 197.

would have objected strenuously to doing so. He wanted the great-est possible effect appropriate to the tragic imitation, not the most rigorous adherence to abstract rules of purity. Unlike many modern critics, he says that the poet should speak "as little *as possible*" in his own person—that is, short of harming his poetic effect by his reticence. Too much and too little are, as always in Aristotle, de-termined by particular ends, and he never forgets that what might be too much in one work might equally well be too little in another.

No such restraint has marked the pronouncements of some mod-ern champions of poetic integrity. Paul Valéry, for example, whose essay on "Pure Poetry" has been echoed again and again by English and American poets and novelists, begins by distinguishing a pure poetic quality common to all true poetry. Poetry comes into ex-istence only when "words show a *certain deviation* from the most di-rect, that is, the most *insensible*, expression of thought," only when "these deviations foreshadow, as it were, a world of relationships distinct from the purely practical world." The poet grasps "frag-ments" of this "noble and living," impractical world, and develops and cultivates them into poetry "in so far as it is an effect of art."

The man who would write *pure* poetry must, obviously enough in such a program, try to make entire works out of these poetic moments. "The problem of pure poetry is this: . . . whether by means of a work, in verse or not, one can give the impression of a complete system of *reciprocal* relations between our ideas and images on the one hand and our means of expression on the other." Valéry maintains that it is impossible to construct such a work, freed of all non-poetic elements, with every detail integrally fused with every other detail, but "poetry is always a striving after this purely ideal state. In fact, what we call a *poem* is in practice com-posed of fragments of pure poetry embedded in the substance of a discourse."[9] It is not surprising that for Valéry the ideal art should be music. "I shall compare *what is given to the poet* and *what is given to the musician*. Happy musician!" (p. 189).

This envious analogy with the ideal purity of music would have

[9] "Pure Poetry," *The Art of Poetry*, trans. Denise Folliot (New York, 1958), pp. 184–85.

puzzled Aristotle, but it has for a century dominated discussions of artistic purity. If all art is trying for the same effect—a kind of pure realization of another world or a disinterested contemplation of pure form—then obviously music (or sometimes painting, the more abstract the better) should be our model. "All art constantly aspires towards the condition of music," Walter Pater said nearly eighty years ago, because it is in music that the "artistic ideal" of a "perfect identification of matter and form," of ends and means, of subject and expression, is achieved.[10] He never applied his musical model to fiction, so far as I know, but it has been adopted and extended by critics of fiction up to the present.[11]

We see in this drive for purity a curious contrast with the general demand for realism. Though some realisms can be harmonized with some notions of poetic purity, the typical demand for realistic effect is likely to clash with the typical demand for a pure rendering of the ideal aesthetic realm. James would have been distressed by any suggestion that his fiction be purged of its moral problems and human emotions. Sartre is emphatic in his attack on the "impossible dream of giving an impartial picture of Society and the human condition." For him, men reveal themselves, "in their truth," only when they are shown "in love, in hate, in anger, in fear, in joy, in indignation, in admiration, in hope, in despair."[12] But the typical

---

[10] "The School of Giorgione," The Renaissance (London, 1888; Modern Library ed., n.d.), pp. 111–14.

[11] See David Daiches, Virginia Woolf (Norfolk, Conn., 1942), p. 129, for one of many suggestions in modern criticism that what the novelist is trying to do—in this case "distil life into an essence"—can, perhaps, be done better by the musician. Anyone acquainted with modern criticism will be able to think of many efforts to compare the work of novelists like Gide, Proust, Mann, Joyce, and Faulkner to music. It is no accident that Dujardin, who prided himself on originating stream-of-consciousness (monologue intérieur) in fiction, should have undertaken his work with the "mad ambition to transport into literature the methods of Wagner" (Le monologue intérieur. Son apparition. Ses origines. Sa place dans l'œuvre de James Joyce [Paris, 1931], p. 97). See Abrams, The Mirror and the Lamp (New York, 1953), chap. iii, sec. i, for the use of the analogy with music throughout the nineteenth century.

[12] What Is Literature? trans. Bernard Frechtman (London, 1950), p. 13. For a theoretical discussion of the inherent "impurity" of literature, the inevitable reference to a reality that is "outside," see Murray Krieger, The New Apologists for Poetry (Minneapolis, Minn., 1956), pp. 129 ff.

purist is likely to see moral problems and human emotions as the prime source of literary impurity.

Curiously enough, both the quest for realism and the quest for purity, even in their most extreme forms, have yielded the same attack on rhetorical impurities in fiction. As we saw in chapter ii, if fiction is to seem *real*, it must not be laden with signs of artifice. And we find here that if fiction is to be *pure*, if it is to "catch up with poetry," if it is to have anything like equal status with the more obviously pure arts, the author must somehow find a way to create a cleansed object which can speak for itself. Just as many poets in the modern period, whether symbolists, imagists, or whatever, felt that the "natural object is always the adequate symbol,"[13] so the novelists and critics of widely different schools have echoed again and again the belief of Flaubert that the fully expressed "natural" event will convey its own meanings far better than any explicit evaluative commentary might do.[14] "When I read in a novel, 'John was peevish,'" says Ortega, "it is as though the writer invited me to visualize, on the strength of his definition, John's peevishness in my own imagination. That is to say, he expects me to be the novelist. What is required, I should think, is exactly the opposite: that he furnish the visible facts so that I obligingly discover and define John to be peevish" (p. 59). Some decades before this formulation

---

[13] Ezra Pound, "A Stray Document," (1913), reprinted in *Make It New* (New Haven, Conn., 1935) and in M. D. Zabel, *Literary Opinion in America* (rev. ed.; New York, 1951), p. 170. See also Pound's letter to W. Carlos Williams, October 21, 1908, *Letters 1907-1941*, ed. D. D. Paige (New York, 1950), pp. 3-4; and Hugh Kenner, *The Art of Poetry* (New York, 1959): "A thing is what it is. A large part of the poet's job is knowing what it is, and then recognizing that its nature is of more enduring interest than the workings of his mind in its presence. If its nature implies certain moral truths, the successful poet will persuade us that he is elucidating these because they are contained in his subject, rather than inventing them because he feels that way" (p. 174).

[14] See Auerbach, *Mimesis: The Representation of Reality in Western Literature*, trans. Willard Trask (Anchor Book ed., 1957), p. 486. See also R. G. Collingwood, *The Principles of Art* (first pub. 1938; New York, 1958): "... the use of epithets in poetry, or even in prose where expressiveness is aimed at, is a danger. If you want to express the terror which something causes, you must not give it an epithet like 'dreadful.' For that describes the emotion instead of expressing it, and your language becomes frigid, that is inexpressive, at once. A genuine poet, in his moments of genuine poetry, never mentions by name the emotions he is expressing" (p. 112).

of the need for purity, the unknown James Joyce, revising the sprawling fat manuscript which finally became the lean, pure *Portrait of the Artist as a Young Man*, carefully expunged most of the adverbs and adjectives and finally all but a scarcely recognizable remnant of the authorial commentary. We see clear evidences of the process in the intermediate manuscript, *Stephen Hero*. Having once written, "Stephen stuck his spoon angrily through the bottom of the [egg] shell," he reconsidered and crayoned out "angrily." Why? Because it was clearly the author refusing to let the natural, the pure object—in this case a physical action—speak for itself.

We can see then that T. S. Eliot was not creating a new concept when he talked of the "objective correlative." "The only way," he begins his much quoted definition, "of expressing emotion in the form of art is by finding an 'objective correlative'; in other words, a set of objects, a situation, a chain of events which shall be the formula of that *particular* emotion; such that when the external facts, which must terminate in sensory experience, are given, the emotion is immediately evoked."[15] This "objective correlative" has become so much a part of our critical language that we often forget to ask whether there is any such thing as a natural poetic object which will serve, in itself, as a formula for particular emotions. The truth is that dozens of different concepts of what is "natural" have been covered by this convenient notion of the object which correlates with the natural, inevitable response. Before we allow ourselves to purge our literature of any one form of artificiality, we should be quite clear what we mean when we say that "the natural object is always the adequate symbol."

We can admit, of course, that the choice of evocative "situations and chains of events" is the writer's most important gift—or, as Aristotle put a similar point, the "most important of all is the structure of the incidents." The gift of choosing the right "object" is indispensable, whether that object is a thought, a gesture, a descriptive detail, or a great character involved in a significant action. When Gogol created Akaky Akakievitch Bashmatchkin, the poor

---

[15] "Hamlet and His Problems," *Athenaeum*, September 26, 1919, as reprinted in *Critiques and Essays*, ed. Stallman, p. 387.

clerk of "The Overcoat," almost anonymous behind his "unusual, artificial" name, a victim of bureaucracy, fate, and his own weakness, representative of all foolish, helpless clerks, he had already performed the major part of his rhetorical task. When he further hit upon the notion of using an overcoat as a sign of his hero's aspirations, deception, and final destruction, he had again chosen the "natural object" most amenable to his purposes. As we watch the impoverished Bashmatchkin, desperately cold and shabby, desperately saving his pennies for an overcoat which stands in his mind more and more as a symbol of security, social standing, and happiness, we are led with great effectiveness toward the theft of the coat and the hero's death. No amount of direct appeal to sympathy or direct attack on the brutality of "the system" could possibly serve as well. One need only think of the obvious inferiority of any other article of clothing to see how appropriate the choice of this one "natural object" was.

If this is true, how can we question the claim that the "natural object" is adequate? Must not the very presence of Gogol's many other, more easily recognizable, appeals to the reader be a sign of inadequate faith in his choice of the right natural objects?

The "Impurity" of Great Literature

The question may not be answerable short of a fundamental philosophical confrontation. Most of the programs of purity have conceded that complete purity is impossible. Based on a Platonic notion of a perfect condition toward which all the arts aspire, such programs can admit the radical imperfection of every particular art work without impugning the validity of the quest for perfection. To show that all great literature has in fact made use of rhetoric will seem quite pedestrian and irrelevant to the critic who has already conceded that though "poetry wants to be pure," most poems "do not want to be too pure."[16] But I must perform this literal-minded task nevertheless. If the most admired literature is in fact radically contaminated with rhetoric, we must surely be led to ask whether the rhetoric itself may not have had something to

16 Warren, "Pure and Impure Poetry," in *Critiques and Essays*, ed. Stallman, p. 86.

do with our admiration. If we find that it has, some readers may still at that point want to rejoin the Platonists and argue, as 'Plato sometimes argued, that literature as a whole is bad precisely because it must depend on base human appeals. But at least they should find themselves less confident in applying general standards of purity as criteria in judging the worth of individual works. If even the greatest literature depends on "impurities" for its greatness, and if, as we all know, some of the purest literature is very bad indeed, degrees of purity are useless as general criteria.

The truth is that, if recognizable appeals to the reader are a sign of imperfection, perfect literature is impossible to find; in the great works, not just of fiction but of all kinds, we find such appeals wherever we look. The most obvious are of course rhetorical intrusions in fiction, but to the careful eye most plays and most lyric poems reveal similar "commentary." In any Greek play, for example, we find much that would have to be expunged if we objected to everything directed at the audience's emotional reactions. Coleridge says that the choruses often seem to be purely rhetorical, created "as ideal representatives of the real audience, and of the poet himself in his own character, assuming the supposed impressions made by the drama, in order to direct and rule them."[17] Nearly one-fourth of *Agamemnon* is given over to commentary by the chorus when no other characters are present and when no internal decisions or actions are at stake. However plausible such commentary can be made to seem—and by some modern standards of realism it is implausible indeed—it is clearly directed outward, reminding us that we are watching a play, and demonstrating the poet's willingness to leave "the natural object" for a while in order to comment on its meaning or control our emotional response.

> What is this insistent fear
> Which in my prophetic heart
> Set and steady beats with evil omen,
> Chanting unbidden a brooding, oracular music?[18]

---

[17] "Greek Drama," *Essays and Lectures on Shakspeare* (Everyman ed., [1907]), p. 17.

[18] *Agamemnon*, trans. George Thompson, in *Six Greek Plays in Modern Translation*, ed. Dudley Fitts (New York, 1955), pp. 34–35.

What is this insistent fear indeed but a way of preparing the audience emotionally for what is to follow?

Similarly in Shakespeare, whom Flaubert praised for his divine objectivity, we find much choral commentary obviously directed toward the spectator, often enough with no evident internal function. If we tried to purge Shakespeare of rhetorical impurities, would we not find ourselves objecting, for example, to all of the chanting and dancing performed by the witches in *Macbeth*, when no one else but the spectator is present? And what of the many soliloquies and asides? Many of these direct addresses to the spectator are radically "out of character." Iago's private statements, as many critics have recognized, are seriously misleading if taken as the realistic meditation of a consistent, thought-ridden melancholic. They make dramatic sense only as unapologetic explanations to the audience of motives, threats, and probabilities that could not easily be made clear in convincing dialogue.

Perhaps in our search for purity we should choose something more modern and more clearly purified. But in modern lyric poetry of the purest kind, do we find nothing but "objective correlatives," nothing but pure lyricism or pure drama, with all of the rhetoric removed? Not usually. What we find is, very often, a disguised rhetoric. The obliquity of a Greek epigraph to a poem by Eliot may easily lead us to overlook what Eliot has in reality done to us. When he quotes Heraclitus in Greek to the effect that "it is a duty to follow the common law," and that "the way up and the way down is one and the same," he may be accused of difficulty and even of obscurantism, but not of committing impurities in public. Yet what is the effect on the reader who knows Greek well enough to translate the epigraphs to "Burnt Norton" or who ferrets out someone else's translation? It is to tell him, "In reading the following poem, remember the saying of Heraclitus: the way up and the way down is one and the same."

Who says that "Mistah Kurtz, he dead" is relevant to what follows? Certainly not the hollow men who speak dramatically in the poem. It is really the poet, announcing his subject and putting us into a frame of mind suitable to that subject. Finally, we must not forget the rhetoric of titles. "The Waste Land"? "The Hollow Men"? Who says so?

But recognizable rhetoric is by no means confined to what is spoken directly and exclusively to the audience or reader. In many completely dramatic works with no choral commentary whatever, there are scenes which are obviously rhetorical in intent. In *Ghosts*, for example, what really is the function of the long discussion between Mrs. Alving and Manders concerning whether the new orphanage should be insured?. Obviously, it is to inform the spectator of the foolish, weak conventionality of Manders. Sometimes Ibsen uses such scenes simply to make the play more easily intelligible, but sometimes they are used to argue for ideas that the spectator must understand, and at least tentatively entertain, if he is to grasp the play. "Do you know when and where I *have* met with immorality in artists' circles?" the young Oswald, whom one might expect to be preoccupied with the more pressing problem of his approaching insanity, takes time to ask. And he then delivers a tirade against "your model husbands and fathers." Like Mrs. Alving's later indictment of the "second-rate town" which could offer Alving none of the "joy of life," it is more necessary for the reader's comprehension than for any effect on anyone within the play. Does Mrs. Alving really need to convince Oswald of the stifling effect of the small town? No, but she does have the problem of convincing the spectators.[19]

We find the same sort of thing in fiction. Even the finest novelists often create scenes which on analysis seem unnecessary except as they aid the reader. They are appropriate to their contexts, but the critic who tries to defend their author's economy must refer to the audience's needs rather than to any completion of necessary details in the "natural object."

The best discussion of how a novelist works to integrate such scenes into the more nearly indispensable materials is in the pref-

---

[19] More obvious examples can be found in earlier drama. The scene between Cassandra and the chorus in *Agamemnon*, the longest scene in the play, coming at a time when all of the important action is going on unobserved backstage, is a splendid example. It takes up nearly one-fifth of the play, a length that can be justified only as psychological preparation of the audience for Agamemnon's cry.

aces and notebooks of Henry James. Again and again James admits
to inventing what he calls *ficelles*, characters whose main reason
for existence is to give the reader in dramatic form the kind of help
he needs if he is to grasp the story. Speaking of his reasons for inventing Waymarsh and Maria Gostrey in *The Ambassadors*, James
admits that his effort to make everything dramatic requires the invention of carefully dissimulated rhetoric. Maria Gostrey is "keenly
clutched at," as such a *ficelle*, "without even the pretext, either, of
her being, in essence, Strether's friend. She is the reader's friend
much rather—in consequence of dispositions that make him so
eminently require one; and she acts in that capacity, and *really* in
that capacity alone, with exemplary devotion, from beginning to
end of the book. She is an enrolled, a direct, aid to lucidity; she is
in fine, to tear off her mask, the most unmitigated and abandoned
of *ficelles*."[20] And without apology, James then generalizes about
the whole relation of what is "of the essence" to what is rhetorical:
"To project imaginatively, for my hero, a relation that has nothing
to do with the matter (the matter of my subject) but has everything to do with the manner (the manner of my presentation of
the same) and yet to treat it, at close quarters and for fully economic expression's possible sake, as if it were important and essential—
to do that sort of thing and yet muddle nothing may easily become, as one goes, a signally attaching proposition . . ." (p. 324).

It can be a signally attaching proposition for the reader as well,
if he attempts to discover where, in the process of growth of James's
subjects, the essential "matter" leaves off and the rhetorical "manner" begins. James usually starts with "some conceived or encountered individual," some character to be realized. Gradually he develops other characters, necessary either for the reader's comprehension or for the propulsion of the developing action; he often
makes no distinction between the two at this stage. And he will go
on, inventing more and more until he comes to something that he
will label a *ficelle*.

Sometimes he talks of the completed process as if it were all

---

20 Preface to New York Edition, as reprinted in *The Art of the Novel*, ed. R. P. Blackmur (New York, 1934; 1947), p. 322.

rhetorical, except for the initial vision of the major character. In *The Portrait of a Lady*, Isabel Archer is described in the "Preface," written long after the novel, as the essential subject; the rest is done to help the reader see her as James wants her to be seen. Yet when he comes to the invention of Henrietta Stackpole, he describes her as much further from what is essential than his other inventions surrounding Isabel. He calls her but a wheel to the coach not belonging "to the body of that vehicle." "There the subject alone is ensconced, in the form of its 'hero and heroine,' and of the privileged high officials, say, who ride with the king and queen." The poor *ficelle* runs beside the coach for all she is worth, out of breath, never so much as getting "her foot on the step" (pp. 52–55).

Thus we have the other main characters invented to reveal Isabel, and the *ficelle* invented to help reveal all of them. When we add such "friends of the reader" to the explicit commentary—in the opening paragraph, for example, with its ornate and personal description of "afternoon tea"—we find a large share of the book falling on the side of rhetoric consciously directed to the reader; almost nothing except Isabel's character is left on the side of "subject."

Why is it that we do not, cannot, honestly object to all of this concern for the reader? And what is it that distinguishes this acceptable rhetoric from the tricks and contrivances to which we do object? In chapter vii I try to grapple with these questions. At this point I can only touch on two important directions in which the answer might be found.

In the first place, there is an "intrinsic" aspect about acceptable rhetoric, even when it is easily recognizable and even when it can be separated from the work with no serious curtailment of effect. The extrinsic-intrinsic distinction breaks down whenever we try to use it as a standard for giving marks to the various parts of a good book—whenever we try to decide whether this or that part is "in" or "out." Is the Gloucester subplot in *King Lear* less intrinsic than Lear's own experiences? Certainly, if we mean that to be judged intrinsic an element must be indispensable. Horrified as we may be by the suggestion, we can be quite sure that if Shakespeare had not thought of the Gloucester plot, Lear would still be an acceptable, intelligible, moving play; no one would complain that there is something missing. The subplot seems to have been invented as a way of heightening Lear's tragedy, and hence it is, from our present viewpoint, rhetorical. But is it less artistic, less desirable, less "intrinsic" for that? There are other elements in the play even more readily expendable than Gloucester's family tragedy. Do we want to find ourselves accusing Shakespeare of deficient artistry because he did not let the pure, poetic moments—say Lear's impassioned speeches on the heath or the death scene—speak for themselves?

James himself was deeply impressed by the process whereby substance and form, subject and treatment, matter and manner become fused. "The sacrament of execution indissolubly marries them, and the marriage, like any other marriage, has only to be a 'true' one for the scandal of a breach not to show." And he challenges the reader, "Prove this value, this effect, . . . to be of my treatment, prove that I haven't so shaken them together as the conjurer I profess to be must consummately shake, and I consent but to parade as before a booth at the fair" (p. 116).

This is no idle boast, but we should be very clear about what it means. It most certainly cannot mean that there are no recognizably rhetorical elements in *The Portrait of a Lady*. What it must mean, for James as for us, is that there are no elements that are *only* rhetorical; when the book is completed, everything, including the rhetoric, "belongs," everything has become intrinsic—though even to use the word we must understand it in our broadened sense. The original twofold distinction has once again broken down, and we must admit to various degrees of "intrinsicness" (see chap. vii, pp. 205–9, below).

Perhaps a more profitable, or at least less cumbersome, explanation for our willingness to accept the rhetoric of *ficelles*, and even of James's commentary, can be found in looking closely at what is meant by the "core," the "essence," the "true subject" itself. Regardless of how we conceive the core of any literary work, will it be entirely freed of a rhetorical dimension? On the contrary, at the very moment of initial conception, at the instant when James exclaims to himself, "Here is my subject!" a rhetorical aspect is contained within the conception: the subject is thought of as *something that can be made public*, something that can be made into a communicated work. In so far as it turns out to be a true subject, its means of communication will spring from the essence and seem, when perfected, in harmony with it.

This is not to say that the novelist must think consciously of his audience, or that novelists who worry about their readers will necessarily write better than those who do not. No doubt some authors work better when they think of their writing as self-expression and of their technique as self-discovery. But, regardless of how we define art or artistry, the very concept of writing a story seems to have implicit within it the notion of finding techniques of expression that will make the work accessible in the highest possible degree. To think of Isabel as a potential subject is to think of her as something to be transformed into "public property," not as something to be hoarded in the precious inner life of the author.

When we read without critical preconceptions, we ordinarily take this dimension of literature for granted; we are not in the least shocked when we discover that the author has, in fact, worked to make his subject available to us. We think of the writer as someone who addresses us, who wants to be read, and who does what he can to make himself readable. This common-sense attitude has been complicated by modern experience, particularly by the multiplying and fragmenting of "publics" and by the many private stratagems that authors have felt forced to adopt in response. But even the most uncompromising avant-garde writers can never maintain for long the pose of not wanting to be read.[21]

If I am right in saying that the rhetorical dimension in literature is inescapable, evidence can be found in any successful scene, how-

---

[21] See, for example, Ellmann's account of Joyce's almost pathetic eagerness to get reports on the criticism of each work before, and as, it appeared. Part of Joyce's interest in sales may have been merely commercial, but it is clear that he wanted desperately to be read (*James Joyce, passim*).

ever pure, regardless of whether the author was thinking of his reader as he wrote. But my main point here does not depend on this deliberate expansion of the term "rhetoric," an expansion that may to some seem merely verbal. The more important point is the prevalence in the works we admire of rhetoric in the narrower sense —elements that are recognizable, separable, "friends of the reader." Such elements may not, in fact, be found in every successful literary work. If someone can find a great novel, play, or poem, acknowledged to be such by a fair number of competent readers, and yet entirely free of recognizable rhetoric, I shall be surprised but not disturbed. This first defense of rhetoric does not depend on proving that it is indispensable but rather in showing that in fact it has generally been not only tolerated but embraced by competent writers. To those who would still reply that the authors should have known better, the theoretical considerations of the next section are directed. For now, it will be most useful to conclude with a dramatized scene that might seem, on first reading, to be entirely pure.

Early in Forster's *A Passage to India* Dr. Aziz, retreating in anger from the world of the hated Britishers where he has just been rebuffed, retires into a favorite mosque to rest. In the midst of his meditations, he notices an Englishwoman in the moonlight.

> Suddenly he was furiously angry and shouted: "Madam! Madam! Madam!"
> "Oh! Oh!" the woman gasped.
> "Madam, this is a mosque, you have no right here at all; you should have taken off your shoes; this is a holy place for Moslems."
> "I have taken them off."
> "You have?"
> "I left them at the entrance."
> "Then I ask your pardon."
> Still startled, the woman moved out, keeping the ablution-tank between them. He called after her, "I am truly sorry for speaking."
> "Yes, I was right, was I not? If I remove my shoes, I am allowed?"
> "Of course, but so few ladies take the trouble, especially if thinking no one is there to see."
> "That makes no difference. God is here."

He is almost overwhelmed by this unexpected sensitivity. Immediately a friendship begins, a friendship that survives even the shock of his discovery that she is elderly. They find themselves discussing the wife of his superior officer.

> His voice altered. "Ah! A very charming lady."
> "Possibly, when one knows her better."
> "What? What? You didn't like her?"
> "She was certainly intending to be kind, but I did not find her exactly charming."
> He burst out with: "She has just taken my tonga without my permission—do you call that being charming?—"

And soon he is exclaiming, "You understand me, you know what others feel. Oh, if others resembled you!"

How would we answer if someone asked us whether this scene might not be expunged from the novel? One kind of answer would refer to the internal relationships of character and event. If the major events of A Passage to India are to take place, an initial friendship between Aziz and Mrs. Moore is indispensable. The scene quoted is, in this respect, a necessary step in the chain of events. If Forster is to have his novel at all, this scene must occur.

An alternative but not conflicting answer would deal with the reader's needs. Certain meanings, for example, will be overlooked if the scene is curtailed or expunged; the first section is entitled "Mosque," and, when matched thematically with the other two sections, "Caves" and "Temple," it yields level after level of meaning about the lives of the two races that encounter each other in this meeting.[22] The meanings might be there—not just in Forster's mind but realized in the later sections—and still be missed without the clues provided here.

Equally important, the scene is required for what it does to the reader's emotional involvement with these two people. As they become friends, they win our friendship. As they impress each other with their warmth and generosity, they impress us as well. By the end of the scene we have been prepared, without necessarily becoming aware of it, for a proper response to the less sympathetic Englishmen who follow. Indeed, one's sympathies have become so deeply involved that one feels strong resentment later when Mrs.

---

[22] See E. K. Brown, Rhythm in the Novel (Toronto, 1950), esp. p. 114.

Moore's son interrogates her in a "scratchy, dictatorial" manner about her encounter. "He called to you in the mosque, did he? How? Impudently? What was he doing there himself? . . . So he called to you over your shoes. Then it was impudence. It's an old trick. I wish you had had them on." And so the impact of this first scene rolls on; our likes and dislikes, our sense of the meaning of things, our interest in what is to happen to those we like and those we mistrust all spring out of this initial encounter.

Dramatic necessity and rhetorical function seem, then, to be thoroughly united here. Whatever we take to be the heart of the work, whether action, symbolic structure, or significant form (our vocabulary preferences are unimportant at this point), seems to justify this scene, or something like it. And each stroke works outward upon us as it works internally.

Yet it is obvious that even here rhetorical decisions in the narrower sense have played a part. Why is the scene so long and so vivid? It is difficult to answer without talking of the novel's "need" to communicate itself. Its need to *be* itself could have been satisfied with much less. "The friendship between Aziz and Mrs. Moore had begun when they met by chance in a mosque. Aziz had been overwhelmed by the discovery that. . . ." Or we might even have been told directly and simply that "Aziz and Mrs. Moore had become friends, recognizing in each other. . . ." Forster could then have shown us the scene at Fielding's house, during which Aziz invites Mrs. Moore and Miss Quested to visit the caves, and we would never know what we had missed.

It is easy to think of arguments against this revision, but surely the most powerful refer in one way or another to the reader's needs. If we are to feel such-and-such, if we are to recognize so-and-so, if we are to wish for this outcome and fear that outcome, we must have experienced the friendship vividly. It is popular these days to say that the scene must be "realized." But made real for whom? Even in the most summary account it is in some sense "real." And for the author himself the facts and emotions it reveals are presumably real without providing the scene at all. But nothing is real for the reader until the author makes it so, and it is for the reader that the author chooses to make this scene as powerful as possible.

It might be answered that any sincere author will expand such a scene only "for himself." Though this doesn't happen to agree with what Forster has said about the novelist's relations to his readers, it does agree, as we have seen, with what many others have felt about themselves. It can be a dangerous position, but we need not reject it completely if we keep in mind the distinction between the real author and his second self. The real Forster does not need this scene; he knows all this and more about his characters. Only if he imagines himself temporarily as his own reader, approaching his work without special knowledge, can we think of him as troubling to write this scene for "himself." Yet if he postulates himself as reader in this sense, what is he doing that is different from writing with "the reader" in mind? To express this *public* self and to affect a public made up of similar selves become identical processes, and the distinction between expressive and rhetorical theories of literature disappears.

Whether or not this is a fruitful way of harmonizing self-expression and rhetoric, we must conclude that in Forster's novel, as in our other examples, recognizable rhetorical elements are used by the author and accepted by us as part of the realization of his subject. He may dramatize or he may comment directly (p. 188, below) but one eye is always on the reader, even as he works to bring the "novel itself" to perfection.

Is a Pure Fiction Theoretically Desirable?

If what I have said about rhetoric in the larger sense is true, then a pure fiction is impossible, and it would be meaningless to ask whether or not it is desirable. But fiction can be partially purified of rhetoric in the narrower sense. Can we say that the purer a novel is, the better? Is the author who relies most on the inherent force of the "natural object" more artistic than the author who consciously labors to heighten some elements in that object and to throw others into shadow?

We may finally be forced to conclude, with Aristotle and with most important modern critics, that the author should use as little recognizable rhetoric "as possible." But before we do so we should be quite clear about the limits of possibility in literary communication.

1. Even if a presented object seems to the author to call for a natural response based on universals, he can never count on those universals being responded to with any intensity unless he gives good reasons. He must recognize that all readers are daily bombarded with real events which should call for the most intense, universal reactions; murder, rape, pillage, famine, innocent suffering, villainous machinations, and maniacal cruelty can all be found in the evening paper, sometimes with, sometimes without, rhetorical heightening. The art work is not satisfied, however, with the mild, undifferentiated reactions such accounts produce. "You would have me," Chekhov writes a friend, "when I describe horse-thieves, say: 'Stealing horses is an evil.' But that has been known for ages without my saying so. . . . When I write, I reckon entirely upon the reader to add for himself the subjective elements that are lacking in the story."[23] But Shakespeare did not simply present Gloucester's suffering as a journalistic account, leaving the subjective elements to the spectator. Though the evil of putting out old men's eyes had "been known for ages" without his "saying so," he works at heightening the revulsion of his audience in many ways. Gloucester's own outburst, the longest speech in the scene, is itself calculated to rouse us against the tormentors: "Because I would not see thy cruel nails / Pluck out his [Lear's] poor old eyes; nor thy fierce sister / In his anointed flesh stick boarish fangs." The prolongation of the gouging, one eye at a time, the horrified intervention of the servant, driven to the crime of insubordination by what he sees, and finally the cries of the tormentors themselves—Regan shrieking for the completion of the deed, Cornwall with his, "Out, vile jelly! Where is thy lustre now?"—all this shows us Shakespeare's conviction that no amount of reaction to this scene could be too much. He knew that, though we would be horrified by the mere spectacle, he could not count on the degree of horror he desired without heightening our reaction beyond whatever might be considered a natural response.

---

[23] *Letters on the Short Story, the Drama and Other Literary Topics,* ed. Louis S. Friedland (New York, 1920), p. 64.

2. Most dramatic events are much more ambiguous than this scene, much more evidently based on merely conventional responses, requiring a rhetoric to place them for the reader. And even the most permanent values receive altered conventional expression from man to man, region to region, and time to time. The greatest artists do, indeed, plumb to permanent values; I am convinced that my pity for King Lear, my affection for Elizabeth Bennet and Alyosha, and my fear of Iago and the Master of Ballantrae are based on beliefs that are not merely conventional in origin. I am convinced that Faulkner is right when he calls the motives of *As I Lay Dying* universal and natural. "I simply imagined," he says, "a group of people and subjected them to the simple universal natural catastrophes which are flood and fire with a simple natural motive [burial] to give direction to their progress."[24] Men in general will never cease to care about the two values of filial piety and respect for the dead, pitted against "flood and fire"—so long as there are readers who care for literature at all. But any artist would be foolish indeed if he simply pointed, in effect, to the spectacle of innocent suffering or inexplicable evil or dogged loyalties and expected me to react as I do to these complex characters and events. The fact is that Faulkner has taken elaborate technical measures— short of explicit commentary—to help me to chart my path through this comic-heroic jungle. Even so, he leaves me at many points thoroughly baffled—and I am not alone.[25] More often than not we may not even recognize, if left unassisted, what it is that we have been shown. It might be said that we *ought* to. But *why* ought we? Could I reasonably expect Faulkner, say, or Joyce, to recognize my natural objects for what they *really* are, if I simply presented a fictional world to them with no clues as to how I viewed that world?

---

24 Jean Stein, "Interview with William Faulkner," p. 39.

25 See Edward Wasiolek's "*As I Lay Dying:* Distortion in the Slow Eddy of Current Opinion," *Critique,* III (Spring–Fall, 1959), 15–23. "Is our attitude to be identified with that of the Bundrens, or is it to be kept at an ironic distance? . . . Faulkner is able to control, by the selection of detail and situation, the way in which he wishes us to look upon the Bundrens' struggle" (p. 17). Perhaps "able" is not quite the word, since Wasiolek finds that views opposite to his own have been "fixed in the slow eddy of current critical opinion." I find his argument very persuasive, but I would never trust myself to arrive at it on my own, even after much work on the book and with all of Faulkner's control by "selection of detail and situation."

Of course, we all admire the virtues tremendously, whatever names we use for them ("beat" or "wise," showing "courage" or "guts," etc.). And we are all passionately fond of the truth. But I can never rely on myself to recognize decency or courage when I see them, and more often than not the truth annoys me on first encounter or is dismissed as falsehood.

The notion of firmly constituted natural objects inducing natural responses came into literature originally in emulation of the nine-teenth-century scientist, dealing dispassionately, objectively, with concrete reality. It was never as fruitful an idea in literature as it was in science. Now that the scientists have given up the claim that they are seeking one single formulation of a firmly constituted reality, unaffected by the limitations and interests of the observer, perhaps we should once again pack up our bags and follow after. Undifferentiated reality is never given to men in a "natural," un-adorned form. Without surrendering to relativism, one can rec-ognize that our different interests and predispositions lead us to take different aspects of reality for different purposes. The same fact can be many different facts, depending on differences in our general orientation. Thus, every literary "fact"—even the most un-adorned picture of some universal aspect of human experience—is highly charged by the meanings of the author, whatever his preten-sions to objectivity.

What this means is that any story will be unintelligible unless it includes, however subtly, the amount of telling necessary not only to make us aware of the value system which gives it its meaning but, more important, to make us willing to accept that value sys-tem, at least temporarily. It is true that the reader must suspend to some extent his own disbeliefs; he must be receptive, open, ready to receive the clues. But the work itself—any work not written by myself or by those who share my beliefs—must fill with its rhetoric the gap made by the suspension of my own beliefs.

Even something as universally deplored as cruelty to children can be molded to radically different effects. When Huck's pap pursues him with the knife, or when the comic-strip father beats his child because he's had a bad day at the office; when Jim in "Haircut" and Jason in *The Sound and the Fury* disappoint the children about a

circus; when Elizabeth Bowen's heroine experiences the death of
the heart; when Saki's little pagan is punished by his aunt; when
Medea kills her children; when Macbeth kills Lady Macduff's children; when Swift's Modest Proposer arranges to have the infants
boiled and eaten; when Pip is trapped by Miss Havisham; when
Farrington in Joyce's "Counterparts" beats his son; and, finally,
when the child is beaten to death in *The Brothers Karamazov*, our
feelings toward the perpetrators range from unconcerned amusement to absolute horror, from pitying forgiveness to hatred, depending not primarily upon any natural relation between the bare
events and our reaction but upon a judgment rendered by the
author.[26]

3. Even if there are permanent, universal responses embodied in
the work, then, they are unlikely to move us strongly and they may
be unclear—without the author's rhetoric. What is more troublesome is that fiction, in its very drive for reality, is inclined to deal
with a great number of mere conventions, meaningless except in a
context. Any good hack writer knows that a woman lighting a
cigarette, say, does not mean the same thing in a novel written in
1960 as she would have meant in a novel written in 1860. Modes
of dress and hair style, types of gentlemanly behavior, sexual conduct—all areas of life where convention operates—can be used to
establish character, but only within limits of time and place carefully defined and controlled by the author.[27] Promiscuity in a

---

[26] For an especially poignant use of cruelty to children, see Dostoevski's "The Dream
of a Ridiculous Man," *A Gentle Creature and Other Stories*, trans. David Magarshack
(London, 1950).

The same point can be made about any general action—marriage, childbirth, suicide,
love. Consider the following murders: Macbeth murders Duncan, and we pity Macbeth
rather than Duncan; Markheim murders the pawnbroker, and we hope for Markheim's salvation; Monsieur Verdoux murders a series of wealthy women, and we side
with him against a rotten civilization; the would-be heir in *Kind Hearts and Coronets*
murders a half-dozen or so of his relatives and we simply laugh; Zuleika Dobson "murders" the whole of the undergraduate body at Oxford and we laugh, quite complicatedly;
Ch'en, in *Man's Fate*, murders a stranger in cold blood and we are terrified—for
Ch'en. There is no need to list the many murders in which the more "natural" responses of hatred toward the murderer and pity for the victim are made to predominate.

[27] "A hundred and fifty years ago people knew their places and the conduct expected
of them, so that, when they varied from an accepted norm, their variations would
really tell you something about their state of mind. When Anne Elliot, for instance,
found that Sunday travelling had been a common thing with her cousin, she deduced,

heroine is not nearly so damning a fault in the 1960's as was even the involuntary fornication of Tess seventy years ago. Mauriac tells of a modern woman who could not understand what all the fuss is about in *Phèdre:* what could be more natural than falling in love with one's stepson!

The result of such shifts is that an author may purify his work to meaninglessness, if he relies on correlatives that are in fact in no way objective. The reader is always faced with the question of what a particular gesture, a particular detail *means?* It is not enough to say that it need not mean anything because it simply *is.* The meaningless accumulation of accurately observed detail cannot satisfy us for long; only if the details are made to *tell,* only if they are weighted with a significance for the lives shown, will they be tolerable. If James T. Farrell shows McGinty, in the opening sentence of *Gas-House McGinty* (1933), missing a spittoon, what does it mean? The fact that he was spitting at all may suggest something about him, though surely not much. The fact that it is a *spittoon* says a little about his milieu. But what about the act of *missing* the spittoon? Does it mean anything more than would hitting the bullseye? Perhaps, perhaps not. "Munching his fourth olive, McGinty thought that Boyle [the proprietor] ought to have stuffed olives." Is this intended to count for something? Perhaps it is simply indicative of McGinty's being fat, which we already know sufficiently well. Perhaps it means something more. If the reader fails to catch the full significance of each loaded fact, he is of course seriously misreading. But, on the other hand, if he assumes that his author is choosing details consciously and packing them with significance, he may find himself overinterpreting.

The young Stephen Dedalus, when he stuck his spoon angrily through the eggshell, was one kind of objective fact, but he might

---

and had a perfect right to deduce, that he had been 'at least careless on all serious matters.' Even when I was a child I still used to be told all sorts of improbable signs by which you could recognize who was a lady and who was not. To-day most of that sign-language is obsolete, with the result that an external description bears less and less relation to the facts of consciousness, and it becomes increasingly necessary for the novelist to use his own imagination in tracing the connection" (Mary Scrutton, "Addition to Fiction," *The Twentieth Century* [April, 1956], pp. 367–68). If this is true of externals like traveling on Sunday, it is just as true of thoughts and attitudes.

easily become another after Joyce has expunged the "angrily." An eggshell, we might pedantically remind the pedant Joyce, can be destroyed in many moods besides anger. Meditatively? Nervously? Absent-mindedly? Carelessly? With exhilaration? Of course "the context would show"—sometimes. But is the context then part of the "object"? If so, why may not the author provide, as part of the object, scenes designed to make the context clear to the reader but not really necessary to the "object"? And if the object itself can be expanded in this way, as James is seen doing with Henrietta Stackpole, where do we stop? May we not then add an adverb or two, and even a comment or so? Where does the context stop? If the context is needed for the objective correlative really to correlate, and if the context becomes the whole work, then we are in the curious position of saying, if we adopt Eliot's formula for the objective correlative, that the "only way to evoke emotion in art is to create complete art works that will stand as a formula for that emotion"—true enough, because tautological, but not particularly helpful in clearing out the rhetoric.

4. Finally, some of the most powerful literature is based on a successful reversal of what many readers would "naturally" think of as a proper response. Such reversals can only be achieved if the author is able to call to our attention relationships and meanings that the surface of the object obscures. If Macbeth's merciless rise to power and his brutal tyranny is naturally suited to any universal emotional response, it would be a combination of fear and hatred and the pleasures of revenge. The less rhetorical manipulation such a story is subjected to, the less sympathy it is likely to induce. If Shakespeare's intent had been a revenge tragedy, he might conceivably have foregone any special rhetoric and let the murder and tyranny, seen from the outside, speak for themselves. It is hard to imagine that the result would have been very distinguished even coming from Shakespeare, but at least it would have been freer of obvious manipulations of our sympathy than is the actual version. As it is, Shakespeare employs an elaborate rhetoric to control our sympathies: Macbeth's suffering conscience, dramatized at length, speaks a stronger message than is carried by his undramatized crimes.[27]

---

[27] Julian Markels develops this point in "The Spectacle of Deterioration: *Macbeth* and the 'Manner' of Tragic Imitation," *Shakespeare Quarterly*, XII (Summer, 1961), 293–303.

Aristotle claimed that the tragic poet should be able to narrate his plot in simple form and produce, in reduced degree, the tragic emotions. True enough, perhaps, if his plot is that of Oedipus or Lear or Othello. But suppose he wants his audience to pity what looks to any external view to be a wicked man, or to love, as in *Emma*, what looks to any external view to be a vain and meddling woman—what then? Why then all the rhetorical resources at his command—every resource of style, of transformed sequence, of manipulated "inside views," and of commentary if need be—will be called in aid.

In short, all of the clichés about the natural object being self-sufficient are at best half-truths. Though some characters and events may speak by themselves their artistic message to the reader, and thus carry in a weak form their own rhetoric, none will do so with proper clarity and force until the author brings all his powers to bear on the problem of making the reader see what they really are. The author cannot choose whether to use rhetorical heightening. His only choice is of the kind of rhetoric he will use.

"Only when the moral beliefs of the reader tally exactly with those on which a story is based will the reader have the whole of the emotion which it is potentially able to produce in him."—MONTGOMERY BELGION

"How does one in the novel (the novel which is a work of art and not a disguised piece of sociology) persuade the American reader to identify that which is basic in man beyond all differences of class, race, wealth, or formal education?"—RALPH ELLISON

"The intention of the writer, therefore, is to hold the reader to a sense of the weight of each action. The writer cannot be sure that his million [readers] will view the matter as he does. He therefore tries to define an audience. By assuming what it is that all men ought to be able to understand and agree upon, he creates a kind of humanity, a version of it composed of hopes and realities in proportions that vary as his degree of optimism. . . . The writer must find enduring intuitions of what things are real and what things are important. His business is with these enduring intuitions which have the power to recognize occasions of suffering or occasions of happiness, in spite of all distortion and blearing."—SAUL BELLOW

CHAPTER FIVE

General Rules, IV:
Emotions, Beliefs, and the
Reader's Objectivity

"TEARS AND LAUGHTER ARE, AESTHETICALLY, FRAUDS"

"It is not simply that fiction is artificial and rhetorical; it is tainted."
So some critics might reply, believing that the very arguments I
have advanced are proof of the inferiority of fiction to other, more
nearly pure, forms of literature. One man's purity is another man's
taint, and the very emotional effect for the sake of which an author
like James will purge his work of the author's voice will for another, purer author require purging. "Not only," Ortega says, "is
grieving and rejoicing at such human destinies as a work of art
presents or narrates a very different thing from true artistic pleasure, but preoccupation with the human content of the work is in
principle incompatible with aesthetic enjoyment proper."[1] For
him not only must true art exclude rhetoric,[2] it must exclude reality

---

[1] *The Dehumanization of Art, and Other Writings on Art and Culture* (Madrid, 1925),
trans. Willard R. Trask (Garden City, N.Y., 1956), p. 9.

[2] "Notes on the Novel," *ibid.*, pp. 58–60 and *passim*.

itself in so far as reality is made up of human content. "But an object of art is artistic only in so far as it is not real" (p. 10). "Even though pure art may be impossible there doubtless can prevail a tendency toward a purification of art. Such a tendency would effect a progressive elimination of the human, all too human, elements predominant in romantic and naturalistic production" (p. 11). "Tears and laughter are, aesthetically,. frauds" (p. 25).

Speaking for "the most alert young people of two successive generations—in Berlin, Paris, London, New York, Rome, Madrid" who have found that they detest traditional art (p. 12), he describes their achievement as the "dehumanization" of art in the name of form, form contemplated rather than form experienced, form purged of everything that is not purely aesthetic. Thus, those whom Ortega describes would not only eliminate all mere narration in fiction, they would bypass all of James's elaborate effort to disguise telling; they would eliminate all "reference, allusion, narration" and simply present "the things themselves," the "visible facts" (pp. 58, 59). Although a certain amount of plot based on emotional response may be indispensable, it should be recognized as a necessary evil, with "no aesthetic value or only a reflected and secondary one" (p. 76).

Naturally, the reader of such works must be himself purged of emotional involvement. Again and again one reads attacks on readers who want to be excited with "action" or "plot" or sentimental romance. The proper reader, it is understood, will not demand intensity of hopes and fears based on such low "melodramatic" qualities as moral goodness or innocent suffering; rather he will be willing to take his pleasure from "aesthetic" and "intellectual" qualities, or from a contemplation of the artist's skill. The highest goal in art, Flaubert said, is "not to raise laughter nor tears"—how many times this formula was to be repeated in the next hundred years!—but to "work as nature works, that is to say, to make the reader dream."[3] Even James, who could never have approved the extreme form of dehumanization described by Ortega, pleads for a reader who is capable of rising above involvement in the mere

---

[3] *Correspondence* (August 26, 1853) (Paris, 1926–33), III, 322.

"story" to an analytical appreciation of "the story of one's story itself."[4] What he requires is intelligence, discrimination, and analytical interest, and although, as we have seen, he is willing to accept responsibility in raising the reader to this level, he still presupposes a reader ready for the proper analytical response.

Many later critics have extended the contrast between true appreciation and a base, popular, commercial interest in plot and emotions. Probably few now would go so far as the early moderns described by Ortega, for whom true art is "anti-popular," dividing "the public into two groups," deliberately compelling "the average citizen to realize that he is just this—the average citizen, a creature incapable of receiving the sacrament of art, blind and deaf to pure beauty." But in the many modern denigrations of story or plot, one senses again and again the trend which Ortega dares to express in its extreme form: true art is based on impulses that are "not of a generically human kind." It is not "for men in general but for a special class of men who may not be better but who evidently are different."[5]

Many of the attacks on allegedly non-aesthetic matters like plot and emotional involvement have been based on the modern rediscovery of "aesthetic distance." After an unrestrained binge of romantic emotionalism and literal naturalism, authors began to discover, as the nineteenth century moved to an end, that in removing the various artificialities of earlier literature they had raised more problems than they had solved; it became more and more clear that if the gap between art and reality were ever fully closed, art would

---

[4] Preface to *The Ambassadors*, in *The Art of the Novel*, ed. R. P. Blackmur (New York, 1934; 1937), p. 313.

[5] *Ibid.*, pp. 5–8. Cf. E. M. Forster, *Aspects of the Novel* (New York, 1927), p. 45: "Yes—oh, dear, yes—the novel tells a story. . . . That is the highest factor common to all novels, and I wish it was not so, that it could be something different—melody, or perception of the truth, not this low atavistic form." In *The Mirror and the Lamp* (New York, 1953), Abrams shows that already early in the nineteenth century, the criterion of purity had led many to elevate lyric poetry and to demote longer narrative forms. He shows John Stuart Mill, for example, in interesting anticipation of the moderns: "An epic poem 'in so far as it is epic (i.e. narrative) . . . is not poetry at all,' but only a suitable frame for the greatest diversity of genuinely poetic passages; while the interest in plot and story 'merely as a story' characterizes rude stages of society, children, and the 'shallowest and emptiest' of civilized adults" (p. 23).

be destroyed. But it was not until this century that men began to take seriously the possibility that the power of artifice to keep us at a certain distance from reality could be a virtue rather than simply an inevitable obstacle to full realism. In 1912 Edward Bullough formulated the problem of what he called "psychic distance" as that of making sure that a work is neither "over-distanced" nor "under-distanced." If it is over-distanced, it will seem, he said, improbable, artificial, empty, or absurd, and we will not respond to it. Yet if it is "under-distanced," the work becomes too personal and cannot be enjoyed as art. For example, if a man who believes that he has reason to be jealous of his wife attends *Othello*, he will be moved too deeply and in a manner not properly aesthetic.[6] It is this second danger that was really an expression of something new in the air; when Bullough suggested that the artist should take steps to prevent under-distancing, he was in the vanguard of a great parade of authors and critics who have become enthusiastic for this or that "alienation effect," or who have deplored the common reader's demand that he should be deeply and emotionally involved in what he reads. Bertolt Brecht's effort to produce plays "of a non-Aristotelian kind," "plays which are not based on empathy," is only an extreme form of what many artists have sought, in their effort to break the bond with tyrannical reality.[7]

The emphasis on the need for control of distance is obviously

---

6 " 'Psychical Distance' as a Factor in Art and an Aesthetic Principle," *British Journal of Psychology*, V (1912), 87–98, as reprinted in *The Problems of Aesthetics*, ed. Eliseo Vivas and Murray Krieger (New York, 1953), pp. 396–405.

7 See, for example, Brecht's "Chinese Acting," trans. Eric Bentley, in *Furioso* (Fall, 1949). A history should be written of the concept of aesthetic distance. One element in such a history would be the growing knowledge, early in the century, of oriental literature, with its extremely unrealistic setting, costumes, and acting manners. Donald Keene shows some similarities between anti-realist theories of the eighteenth-century puppet dramatist, Chikamatsu, and certain western theories, beginning with the Imagists (*Japanese Literature* [London, 1953], esp. chap. iii). Brecht's so called epic theatre, with its emphasis on unrealistic "alienation effects," is explicitly patterned upon certain effects in the Chinese theatre. "In the Chinese theatre," Brecht says, "the alienation effect is achieved in the following way. The Chinese performer does not act as if, in addition to the three walls around him, there were also a fourth wall. *He makes it clear that he knows he is being looked at. . . . The actor looks at himself*" (op. cit., p. 69). But such external influences by no means account for the readiness with which serious artists pursued the very sense of distance which the preceding generations had struggled to overcome.

sound. But the novelist will find himself in difficulties if he tries to discover some ideal distance that all works ought to seek. "Aesthetic distance" is in fact many different effects, some of them quite inappropriate to some kinds of works. More important, distance is never an end in itself; distance along one axis is sought for the sake of increasing the reader's involvement on some other axis. When Chikamatsu, for example, urges that poets avoid all emotional epithets, he does so in order to increase the emotional effect in the reader. "I take pathos to be entirely a matter of restraint. . . . It is essential that one not say of a thing that 'it is sad,' but that it be sad of itself."[8] When Brecht, on the other hand, asks for a "pervading coolness" (p. 71), he may seem at first to desire an increase in distance of all kinds. But what he really wants is to increase the emotional distance in order to involve the reader's social judgment more deeply.

The closer we look at the concept of distance the more complicated it appears. Of course, if we were content to see all literature as aspiring to one kind of involvement and one kind only—a sense of realism, an ecstatic contemplation of pure form, or whatever—we could feel comfortable about seeking one kind of distance as well. Each critic could then offer his formula and try to convert readers to it: As much realism as possible, but enough distance from reality to preserve a sense of form; As close to pure form as possible, with only so much of impurities like plot as cannot be done without; and so on. But is our experience with actual works ever as simple as this approach suggests? Every literary work of any power—whether or not its author composed it with his audience in mind—is in fact an elaborate system of controls over the reader's involvement and detachment along *various* lines of interest. The author is limited only by the range of human interests.

Resisting, then, the natural temptation to substitute my own universal rules about which interests should be heightened and which suppressed to make the greatest literature, I must develop here an elementary—and perhaps to some readers rather obvious—catalogue of the interests that novelists have, in fact rather than in

---

[8] Keene, *op. cit.*, p. 8.

theory, played upon in constructing their works. Once the catalogue is completed, we may still be convinced that one type of interest is far superior to all others, but even so our legislations in its favor should be based on a fairly comprehensive look at the range of interests or appetites[9] which our rules would forbid. The various kinds of purge—whether of unrealistic author's voice, of impure human emotions, or of the moral judgments which help to produce them—can be understood only in the context of what cannot be purged: some kind of interest that will grasp and sustain the reader throughout the work.

In setting up interest as a general criterion, I am aware of indulging in what may look like the apriorism that I have criticized. Why must all works be interesting? And interesting to whom? Cannot a work be simply "true" or "expressive" or "finely composed"—with the reader left to make of it what he can? To answer these questions properly would lead me far afield. Perhaps it will be sufficient to say here that *interest* is dictated to me by the nature of my topic: if I am to deal with literature as it affects readers, some kind of interest will always be central. Different general values would be dictated if I were trying to deal with works as reflections of reality, in which case truth would probably be my over-all term; or as expressions of the author's mind or soul, in which case some general term like sincerity or expressiveness might be central; or, finally, as realizations of formal excellence, in which case general terms like coherence, complexity, unity, or harmony would prove central. Literary works are, in fact, all of these things; one's choice of which aspect to emphasize is largely determined by the kind of question one wants to answer. What is more, there are unavoidable limitations in any one choice, as Abrams has shown so persuasively in *The Mirror and the Lamp*. There are also dangers and temptations that are avoidable—but only by the critic who can resist imposing his general commitment arbitrarily upon the rich variety of

---

[9] See Kenneth Burke, "Psychology and Form," *Counter-Statement* (Los Altos, Calif., 1953), p. 31. Readers who know Burke's *Lexicon Rhetoricae* will notice in my threefold classification as I develop it below some similarities to his "five aspects of form": syllogistic progression, qualitative progression, repetitive form, conventional form, and minor or incidental forms. But I am classifying interests, not forms; forms are almost always built upon several interests.

actual authors, works, and audiences. Whether I have done so in what follows is not, unfortunately, a question I can settle simply by laying my hand on my heart and swearing that I have tried.

Types of Literary Interest (and Distance)

The values which interest us, and which are thus available for technical manipulation in fiction, may be roughly divided into three kinds. (1) Intellectual or cognitive: We have, or can be made to have, strong intellectual curiosity about "the facts," the true interpretation, the true reasons, the true origins, the true motives, or the truth about life itself. (2) Qualitative: We have, or can be made to have, a strong desire to see any pattern or form completed, or to experience a further development of qualities of any kind. We might call this kind "aesthetic," if to do so did not suggest that a literary form using this interest was necessarily of more artistic value than one based on other interests. (3) Practical: We have, or can be made to have, a strong desire for the success or failure of those we love or hate, admire or detest; or we can be made to hope for or fear a change in the quality of a character. We might call this kind "human," if to do so did not imply that 1 and 2 were somehow less than human. This hope or fear may be for an intellectual change in a character or for a change in his fortune; one finds this practical aspect even in the most uncompromising novel of ideas that might seem to fall entirely under 1. Our desire may, second, be for a change of quality in a character; one finds this practical aspect even in the purely "aesthetic" novel of sensibility that might seem to fall entirely under 2. Finally, our desire may be for a moral change in a character, or for a change in his fortune —that is, we can be made to hope for or to fear particular moral choices and their results.

Intellectual interests.—We always want to find out the facts of the case, whether the simple material circumstances, as in most mystery stories, or psychological or philosophical truths which explain the external circumstances. Even in so-called plotless works we are pulled forward by a desire to discover the truth about the world of the book. In works relying heavily on this interest, we know that the book is completed when we once see the complete picture. In Hermann Hesse's *Siddhartha*, for example, our major interest is in Siddhartha's quest for the truth about how a man should live. If we do not think that the question of how a man should live is important, or that this author's insights on the question are likely to prove valuable, we can never care very much for this novel, even though we may enjoy some of the lesser pleasures offered by it. In many serious modern novels we look for an answer to the question, "What do these lives mean?" In others we look for completed patterns of theme, image, or symbol.

Very few imaginative works, however, rely entirely on a desire for intellectual completion. The pure literary forms that belong properly to this kind of suspense are the philosophical treatise which arouses our curiosity about an important question and the purely ratiocinative detective novel.

Completion of qualities.—Most imaginative works, even those of a kind that might seem to be cognitive or didactic in the sense of being built only on speculative or intellectual interests, rely in part on interests very different from intellectual curiosity; they make us desire a quality. Though some of the qualities which some works provide are often discussed under cognitive terms like "truth" and "knowledge," clearly the satisfaction we receive from the following qualities is to some degree distinct from the pleasure of learning.

a) *Cause-effect.*—When we see a causal chain started, we demand—and demand in a way that is only indirectly related to mere curiosity—to see the result. Emma meddles, Tess is seduced, Huck runs away—and we demand certain consequences. This kind of sequence, so strongly stressed by Aristotle in his discussion of plot, is, as we have seen, often played down or even deplored by modern critics and novelists. Yet our desire for causal completion is one of the strongest of interests available to the author. Not only do we believe that certain causes do in life produce certain effects; in literature we believe that they should. Consequently, we ordinary readers will go to great lengths, once we have been caught up by an author who knows how to make use of this interest, to find out whether our demands will be met.

The suspension from cause to effect is of course closely related, on the one hand, to curiosity—that is, to a cognitive interest; we know that whatever fulfilment of our expectations we are given will be given with a difference, and we are inevitably curious about what the difference will be. All good works surprise us, and they surprise us largely by bringing to our attention convincing cause-and-effect patterns which were earlier played down. We can predict that disaster will result from Achilles' anger; we could never predict the generosity to Priam as a crucial part of the "disaster," even though when it comes it can be seen to follow properly as a result from other causes in Achilles' nature and situation.

On the other hand, this interest is easily confused with practical interests, which are described below. It is qualitative, nonetheless, because it operates quite independently of our interests in the welfare of human beings. In fact it can conflict with those interests. The hero commits a crime—and we are torn between our appetite for the proper effect, discovery and punishment, and our practical desire for his happiness.

b) *Conventional expectations.*—For experienced readers a sonnet begun calls for a sonnet concluded; an elegy begun in blank verse calls for an elegy completed in blank verse. Even so amorphous a genre as the novel, with hardly any established conventions, makes use of this kind of interest: when I begin what I think is a novel, I expect to read a novel throughout, unless the author can, like Sterne, transform my idea of what a novel can be.

We seem to be able to accept almost anything as a literary convention, no matter how inherently improbable. Even the most outlandish of mannerisms, like Euphuism or Finneganswakism, can perform the essential task of maintaining our sense of the artistic integrity of *this work* as distinct from all others and as distinct from life. Again, authors may surprise us by violating conventions, but only so long as conventional expectations are available in a given public to be played upon. When everyone prides himself on violating conventions, there is nothing left to violate; the fewer the conventions the fewer the surprises.

c) *Abstract forms.*—There seems to lie behind each convention some more general pattern of desires and gratifications that it serves. Balance, symmetry, climax, repetition, contrast, comparison —some pattern derived from our experience is probably imitated by every successful convention. The conventions which continue to give pleasure when they are no longer fashionable are based on patterns of reaction that lie very deep. Fashions in verse form come and go, for example, but meter and rhyme and the other musical devices of poetry do not lose their importance.

With the surrender of verse, and with no conventional agreement whatever about what is good narrative prose style, writers of longer narratives have been forced to engage in a constant search for new ways of giving body to abstract forms.

d) "Promised" qualities.—In addition to these qualities, common to many works, each work promises in its early pages a further provision of distinctive qualities exhibited in those pages. Whether the quality is a peculiar stylistic or symbolic brilliance, an original kind of wit, a unique sublimity, irony, ambiguity, illusion of reality, profundity, or convincing character portrayal, there is an implied promise of more to come.

Our interest in these qualities may be static; we do not hope for or find a change in the quality but simply move forward looking for more of the same. Some good works rely heavily on this kind of interest (Montaigne's *Essays*, Burton's *Anatomy of Melancholy*, collections of table talk and facetiae, modern novels of stylistic experimentation like Gertrude Stein's *Melanctha*). Many of the realistic and naturalistic novels which were once popular and which now seem tedious relied somewhat too heavily on the sustained appeal of what was often called truth. Reading for the first time a novel dealing in the new vivid way with any new subject matter—whether the social reality about prostitution, slums, or the wheat market or the psychological reality about Irish Jews or American psychopaths —many readers were so fascinated by the new sense of reality, quite aside from the appeal of the facts as information, that little else was needed to carry them through to the end. But once this quality had become common, its appeal faded. Now that most commercial writers know how to portray violent physical reality, for example, with a vividness that would at one time have established an international reputation, only those novels which provide something more than physical reality survive.

The same danger threatens interest in any technique, even when the inherently more interesting procedure is adopted of providing some progressive change in the quality. Following James's masterful explorations of what "composition" could do for the novel, it was easy to believe that the reader's interest in technique was an adequate substitute for other interests, rather than at best a useful adjunct and at worst a harmful distraction. And some novels were written which encouraged this interest. When James and his eleven colleagues wrote *The Whole Family: A Novel by Twelve Authors* (1908), each author writing one chapter, each chapter using a different central intelligence to throw a different light on the events, no reader could help being mainly interested in the point of view rather than in what the point of view revealed: "I wonder what James will make of *his* chapter?"[10] But even with this much "suspense" introduced, interest in technique alone is likely to prove trivial.

Practical interests.—If we look closely at our reactions to most great novels, we discover that we feel a strong concern for the characters as people; we care about their good and bad fortune. In most works of any significance, we are made to admire or detest, to love or hate, or simply to approve or disapprove of at least one central character, and our interest in reading from page to page, like our judgment upon the book after reconsideration, is inseparable from

---

[10] See also *The Affair at the Inn* (London, 1904) by Kate Douglas Wiggin, Mary Findlater, Jane Findlater, Allan McAuley. Each author "did" one character. Protests against this tendency to let interest in the quality of the telling replace interest in what is told can be found throughout modern criticism. Beach claimed that the net effect of *The Awkward Age* depended too much on "the recognition of the author's cleverness" (*The Method of Henry James* [New Haven, Conn., 1918; Philadelphia, 1954], p. 249). David Daiches finds that the pleasure in Virginia Woolf's *The Years* "derives more from a recognition of virtuosity, let us say, than from our complete domination by the novel as an integrated work of art"; though he tries to allow for the former recognition as a legitimate literary pleasure, it is clear that for him it is inferior to what is really "an integrated work of art" (*Virginia Woolf* [Norfolk, Conn., 1942], p. 120).

Compare Faulkner's complaint about Sherwood Anderson: "His was that fumbling for exactitude, the exact word and phrase within the limited scope of a vocabulary controlled and even repressed by what was in him almost a fetish of simplicity, to milk them both dry, to seek always to penetrate to thought's uttermost end. He worked so hard at this that it finally became just style: an end instead of a means: so that he presently came to believe that, provided he kept the style pure and intact and unchanged and inviolate, what the style contained would have to be first rate: it couldn't help but be first rate, and therefore himself too" (*Atlantic Monthly* [June, 1953], p. 28).

this emotional involvement. We care, and care deeply, about Raskolnikov and Emma, about Father Goriot and Dorothea Brooke. Whatever happens to them, we wish them well. It is of course true that our desires concerning the fate of such imagined people differ markedly from our desires in real life. We will accept destruction of the man we love, in a literary work, if destruction is required to satisfy our other interests; we will take pleasure in combinations of hope and fear which in real life would be intolerable. But hope and fear are there, and the destruction or salvation is felt in a manner closely analogous to the feelings produced by such events in real life.

Any characteristic, mental, physical, or moral, which in real life will make me love or hate other men will work the same effect in fiction. But there is a large difference. Since we are not in a position to profit from or be harmed by a fictional character, our judgment is disinterested, even in a sense irresponsible. We can easily find our interests magnetized by characters who would be unbearable as acquaintances. But the fact remains that what I am calling practical interests, and particularly moral qualities as inferred from characteristic choices or as stated directly by the author, have always been an important basis for literary form. Our interest in the fate of Oedipus and Lear, of David Copperfield and Richard Feverel, of Stephen Dedalus and Quentin Compson, springs in part from our conviction that they are people who matter, people whose fate concerns us not simply because of its meaning or quality, but because we care about them as human beings.

Such concerns are not simply a necessary but impure base, as Ortega would have it, to "make contemplation possible" but "with no aesthetic value or only a reflected or secondary one" (pp. 80, 76). In many first-rate works they are the very core of our experience. We may refuse assent when an author tries to manipulate us too obviously or cheaply with a casual bestowal of goodness or intellectual brilliance or beauty or charm. We all have use for epithets like "melodramatic" to apply against abuses of this kind. But this does not mean that human interest in itself is cheap. It is true that our involvement in the fate of Raskolnikov is not different in kind from the involvement sought by the most sentimental of novels. But in the great work we surrender our emotions for reasons that leave us with no regrets, no inclination to retract, after the immediate spell is past. They are, in fact, reasons which we should be ashamed *not* to respond to.

The best of these has always been the spectacle of a good man facing moral choices that are important. Our current neglect of moral terms like "good man" and "bad man" is really unfortunate if it leads us to overlook the role that moral judgment plays in most of our worthwhile reading. There is a story of the psychoanalyst who listened patiently and without judgment to the criminal self-revelations of his patient—until suddenly, as the patient was leaving, the analyst was filled with surprised revulsion. Try as we will to avoid terms like "moral" and "good"—and despite the mounting chorus against relativism, many still do try—we cannot avoid judging the characters we know as morally admirable or contemptible, any more than we can avoid judgments on their intellectual ability. We may tell ourselves that we do not condemn stupidity and viciousness, but we believe that men ought not to be stupid and vicious nonetheless. We may explain the villain's behavior by relating him to his environment, but even to explain away is to admit that something requires excuse.

Actually, there has been less of a retreat from moral judgment than appears on the surface, because of the shift, in modern fiction, to new terms for goodness and wickedness. Modern literature is in fact full of conventionally "virtuous" villains, fatally flawed by their blind adherence to outmoded norms, or by their intolerance of true but unconventional goodness (the missionaries in Maugham's "Rain," the "quiet American" in Greene's novel). Perhaps the prototype is Huck Finn's Miss Watson, who is determined to "live so as to go to the good place." It is easy for the author to make us agree with Huck, who "couldn't see no advantage in going where she was going, so I made up my mind I wouldn't try for it." But few have ever made the mistake of thinking that Huck has repudiated virtue in repudiating Miss Watson's idea of virtue.

Much of what looks like purely aesthetic or intellectual quality in a character may in fact have a moral dimension that is highly effective, though never openly acknowledged between author and reader. When compared with Dickens, for example, James Joyce may seem explicitly amoral. Joyce's overt interests are entirely in matters of truth and beauty. Conventional moral judgments never occur in his books except in mockery. And yet the full force of *A Portrait of the Artist* depends on the essentially moral quality of Stephen's discovery of his artistic vocation and of his integrity in following where it leads. His repudiations of conventional morality —his refusal to enter the priesthood, his rejection of communion, his decision to become an exile—are in fact read as signs of aesthetic integrity—that is, of superior morality. Joyce would probably never call him a "good" boy, though later an older and mellower Joyce was willing to describe Bloom as "a good man," a "complete man."[11] For us Stephen is, in part, a good boy. His pursuit of his own vision is uncompromising; he is headed for Joyce's heaven.[12] We may pretend that we read Joyce objectively and disinterestedly, without the sentimental involvements required of us in Victorian fiction. But most of us would never get beyond page one if the novel were only a portrait of an aesthetic sensibility receiving its Joycean epiphanies.[13]

Whatever Joyce's intentions, for example, with such episodes as the cruel pandybatting of the innocent Stephen, Joyce clearly profits from our irresistible sympathy for the innocent victim. Once such sympathy is established, each succeeding episode is felt deeply, not simply contemplated. The Victorian hero often enough won our sympathies because his heart was in the right place. Many modern heroes win our allegiance because their aesthetic sensibilities will not be denied, or because they live life to the hilt, or simply because they are victims of their surroundings. This is indeed a shift

---

11 Quoted from Frank Budgen in R. Ellmann, *James Joyce* (New York, 1959), p. 449.

12 For a contrary view, see Caroline Gordon, *How To Read a Novel* (New York, 1957), p. 213. For a convincing argument that Joyce is interested in moral satire, not simply in aesthetic values, see Lawrance Thompson, *A Comic Principle in Sterne—Meredith —Joyce* (Oslo, 1954). "There's moral indignation, even though both Stuart Gilbert and David Daiches insist that Joyce's concern is not moral, only aesthetic" (p. 26). See also Joyce's letter to Grant Richards about *Dubliners*, "My intent was to write a chapter of the moral history of my country, and I chose Dublin for the scene, because that city seemed to be the center of paralysis . . ." (quoted in Thompson, p. 25).

13 To see how essential judgment was to Joyce's conception of his work, see Ellmann, *op. cit.*, pp. 380 ff.

of emphasis, but we should not let popular talk about the "affective fallacy" deceive us: the very structure of fiction and, hence, of our aesthetic apprehension of it is often built of such practical, and in themselves seemingly "non-aesthetic," materials.

COMBINATIONS AND CONFLICTS OF INTERESTS

Since men do have strong intellectual, qualitative, and practical interests, there is no reason why great novels cannot be written relying primarily on any one kind. But it is clear that no great work is based on only one interest. Whenever a work tends toward an exclusive reliance on intellectual interests, on the contemplation of qualities, or on practical desires we all look for adjectives to whip the offender with; a mere "novel of ideas," a mere "desiccated form," a mere "tear-jerker" will offend all but the small handful of critics and authors who are momentarily absorbed in pushing one interest to the limit.[14] But it is a rare critic who can distinguish the novels that are really marred by narrowness from those "narrow" novels which, like Jane Austen's, develop a wide range of interests within a narrow social setting.

In any case, for good or ill, we all seem convinced that a novel or play which does justice to our interest in truth, in beauty, and in goodness is superior to even the most successful "novel of ideas," "well-made play," or "sentimental novel"—to name only a selection from the partialities that conventional labels describe. Our emotional concern in Shakespeare is firmly based on intellectual, qualitative, and moral interests. It is a serious mistake to talk as if this richness were simply a matter of stuffing in something for the pit and something else for the gallery. To separate the plot, the manifold qualitative pleasures (including the patterns of imagery and the rich bawdry), or the profound intellectual import and to erect one of the fragments as superior to the others is precisely what a

---

14 Cf. David Daiches' distinction between the "intellectual fallacy, where the most 'real' facts about men and women are considered to be their states of mind rather than of heart," and the "sentimental fallacy" of constructing novels or plays "out of purely emotional patterns" (*Virginia Woolf*, pp. 27–28). Though Daiches explicitly denies that works committing either "fallacy" are necessarily inferior, it seems clear that he would rate a work which somehow avoided both of these "exaggerations" above even the best work committing one or the other fallacy.

direct experience of the plays teaches us not to do. We experience a miraculous unity of what might have remained dissociated but for Shakespeare's ability to involve our minds, hearts, and sensibilities simultaneously.

Another master of the same kind of richness is Dostoevski. In *Crime and Punishment* we experience a wide variety of intellectual appeals. We are curious about the philosophical and religious and political battle between nihilism and relativism on the one hand and salvation on the other. We are also simply curious about whether Porphyry will catch his mouse. We are curious about a thousand and one details that are resolved in the course of the work. Second, we are constantly titillated with qualitative hungers: we have seen the crime and we demand the punishment; we would like more of this remarkably profound use of dreams, and we are given more; we would like more of this skill in transforming disagreeable characters into sympathetic portraits, and Dostoevski does not disappoint us. Finally, our *practical* judgments and the resulting emotions are powerfully involved. We sympathize with Raskolnikov in a peculiarly intense fashion from beginning to end; we wish passionately, though without much hope, for his happiness, and we fear the very punishment which our interest in cause-and-effect patterns demands. We sympathize also with many others, particularly with Sonia. Those aesthetic frauds, tears and laughter, are prominent throughout, but we do not experience them as isolated, sentimental moments, divorced from our intellectual and aesthetic hungers and rewards.

So far, so good. It would be a mistake, however, to make a simple plea for authors to enrich their palettes, as if all appeals had to be in all works, the more the better. The danger is not so much that enough interests won't be packed in, but that pursuit of secondary interests may diminish interests that the author most desires. Even though most great works embody to some degree all three types of interest, some of the particular interests under each type are incompatible with each other and with some types of rhetoric. It was, in fact, a recognition of this incompatibility of interests that led to the notion that overt rhetoric, useful as it was in heightening some practical interests, hampered some qualitative interests, particularly the qualities of realism or purity. But there are other incompatibilities that have not been so fully described.

An author may want, for instance, to cultivate the reader's interest in the quality of ambiguity. He cannot do so, however, and at the same time convey the full intellectual pleasure of gratified curiosity or use fully the reader's moral and emotional interests. There is a pleasure in seeing someone whom we like triumph over difficulties and there is a pleasure in recognizing that life is so complex that no one ever triumphs unambiguously. Both pleasures cannot be realized to the full in the same work. If I am to rejoice, for example, in Stephen's flight into exile as the final sign of his growth into the true artist, I cannot at the same time delight fully in his creator's cleverness in leaving the meaning of that flight ambiguous; the more ambiguity the less triumph.

If he is clear about where his focus lies, a great artist can of course do some justice to the complexities of the world and still achieve a high degree of emotional involvement. Dostoevski, like Shakespeare, derives some of his pre-eminence from his ability to show what a murky business the moral world really is while still keeping the lines of our moral sympathies clear. His criminals remain deeply sympathetic because he knows, and makes us know, why they are criminals and why they are still sympathetic. Not genuine ambiguity, but rather complexity with clarity, seems to be his secret. If he were to leave the basic worth of Raskolnikov or Dmitri ambiguous, or if he were to leave us in doubt concerning Ivan's sincerity in his dialectic with Alyosha, we could never be moved as deeply as we are by their fate.

The real world is of course ambiguous. When my king goes to his doom, I am never sure whether to weep or cheer; or if I am sure, I find out soon that I may very well have been wrong. My true love turns out to have, not a heart of stone—as might very well have happened in the older fiction and drama—but a heart that leaves me baffled. Like myself, she is neither good nor bad, but a puzzling mixture. If literature is to deal realistically with life, then, must it not dwell on the neutral tones rather than the scarlets and deep sky blues? Yes—if verisimilitude and naturalness are more important than anything else. But high dramatic effects depend on heighten-

ing. Demigods, heroes, villains, poetic Othellos and Iagos—these
are not realistic in the sense of being like our everyday reality. And,
on the other hand, Maggie, the girl of the streets, will not appear
as a queen, even potentially, if she is treated with strict realism;
only if the narrator feels free to manipulate his materials in order to
show what she might have been or how her fate is representative of
a society—in short, why it is more significant than the disasters one
reads about in today's paper—will we care about her with anything
like the concern we grant willingly to the unrealistic Desdemona.
A Joyce may provide enough other interests to be able to risk our
question, "Who cares about the fate of Molly Bloom?" but what is
Farrell to reply when I ask, "Who cares about the unheroic hero of
Gas-House McGinty?"[15]

Similarly, if an author wishes to take me on a long quest for the
truth and finally present it to me, I will feel the quest as a boring
triviality unless he gives me unambiguous signs of what quest I am
on and of the fact that I have found my goal when I get there; his
private conviction that the question, the goal, and their importance
are clear, or that clarity is unimportant, will not be sufficient. For
his purposes a direct authorial comment, destroying the illusion
that the story is telling itself, may be what will serve his desired
effect rather than kill it.

There is a pleasure from learning the simple truth, and there is a
pleasure from learning that the truth is not simple. Both are legitimate sources of literary effect, but they cannot both be realized to
the full simultaneously. In this respect, as in all others, the artist
must choose, consciously or unconsciously. To write one kind of
book is always to some extent a repudiation of other kinds. And regardless of an author's professed indifference to the reader, every
book carves out from mankind those readers for which its peculiar
effects were designed.

---

15 What I am saying here is related to the case made by E. E. Stoll about the artificial,
and hence unrealistic, heightening of sympathy in Shakespeare's characters. "To sympathize you must know the facts; when you don't know them, your interest is of another sort; and while the incentive of suspense in Shakespeare and the ancients is an
anxious sympathy, in Ibsen and the moderns it is an excited curiosity" (*Shakespeare
and Other Masters* [Cambridge, Mass., 1940], p. 14; see also pp. 27, 28, 240).

THE ROLE OF BELIEF

With this broadened spectrum of interests in mind, we should now be in a somewhat more favorable position to consider the question of the author's and reader's beliefs. "Most contemporary students of literature would agree that a writer's ideas have as little to do with his artistic talent as his personal morals. . . . Not many people would agree with the views of man held by Homer, Dante, Baron Corvo, or Ezra Pound; but whether or not we agree with them should have little to do with whether or not we accept or reject their art." So writes Maurice Beebe, editor of *Modern Fiction Studies*,[16] expressing once more a position that has been repeated again and again since the famous claim by I. A. Richards that "we need no beliefs, and indeed we must have none, if we are to read *King Lear*."[17] On the other hand, the editor of a recent symposium on belief in literature finds common ground among all the participants in the conviction that literature "involves assumptions and beliefs and sympathies with which a large measure of concurrence is indispensable for the reading of literature as literature and not another thing."[18]

The seeming disagreement here is striking. But it is partly dissolved when we remember the distinction we have made between the real author and the implied author, the second self created in the work. The "views of man" of Faulkner and E. M. Forster, as they go about making their Stockholm addresses or writing their essays, are indeed of only peripheral value to me as I read their novels. But the implied author of each novel is someone with whose beliefs on all subjects I must largely agree if I am to enjoy his work. Of course, the same distinction must be made between myself as

[16] Summer, 1958, p. 182.

[17] "Poetry and Beliefs," *Science and Poetry* (1926), as reprinted in R. W. Stallman (ed.), *Critiques and Essays* (New York, 1949), pp. 329–33. A short bibliography of criticism of Richards' position is given in Stallman, p. 333. It should be noted that in the context of his distinction between "statement" and "pseudo-statement" the word *belief* does not mean what Richards' critics have generally taken it to mean; rather it means something like "convictions about ultimate reality based on solid evidence."

[18] *Literature and Belief: English Institute Essays, 1957*, ed. M. H. Abrams (New York, 1958), p. x.

reader and the often very different self who goes about paying bills, repairing leaky faucets, and failing in generosity and wisdom. It is only as I read that I become the self whose beliefs must coincide with the author's. Regardless of my real beliefs and practices, I must subordinate my mind and heart to the book if I am to enjoy it to the full. The author creates, in short, an image of himself and another image of his reader; he makes his reader, as he makes his second self, and the most successful reading is one in which the created selves, author and reader, can find complete agreement.

This distinction, however, only partly dissolves the contradiction about the role of beliefs, because the divorce between my ordinary self and the selves I am willing to become as I read is not complete. Walker Gibson, in an excellent essay on "Authors, Speakers, Readers, and Mock Readers,"[19] says that the book we reject as bad is often simply a book in whose "mock reader we discover a person we refuse to become, a mask we refuse to put on, a role we will not play." We may exhort ourselves to read tolerantly, we may quote Coleridge on the willing suspension of disbelief until we think ourselves totally suspended in a relativistic universe, and still we will find many books which postulate readers we refuse to become, books that depend on "beliefs" or "attitudes"—the term we choose is unimportant here[20]—which we cannot adopt even hypothetically as our own.

We can see that from this standpoint the trouble I had with Lawrence's implied second self (pp. 79–81, above) can equally well be described as my inability or refusal to take on the characteristics he requires of his "mock reader." Whatever may be said by Laurentians of the weaknesses in my own real character that might account for my refusal, I simply cannot read his polemic without smiling when I should be panting, scoffing when I should be feeling awe. Whether I should blame myself or Lawrence for this, I can never be quite sure. Perhaps we are both partly at fault. Even if I cannot resist blaming him, at least a little, it is difficult to know whether his failure to carry me along is a failure of craftsmanship

---

[19] *College English*, XI (February, 1950), 265–69.

[20] Many writers have rejected "beliefs" only to bring them back under another term like "attitudes." See "Poetry and Belief," *T.L.S.* (August 17, 1956), pp. xvi–xvii.

or a fundamental incompatibility that no amount of craftsmanship could overcome. But it is impossible for me to conclude that incompatibility of beliefs is irrelevant to my judgment of Lawrence.

We cannot fully enjoy James's *Ambassadors*, for another example, if we insist as we read that spontaneity of consciousness must always be subordinated to the puritan conscience—if we refuse, that is, to entertain the implied author's values at something like his own estimate. Strether's discovery in Paris of what it means to *live* will be for us a fall rather than a triumph, and the book will be for us less effective. His discovery must seem a good thing, not just in his or James's views, in which we can take an interest, but in our own. And afterwards, if the book is to maintain our respect, if it is to be remembered as something more than a pleasant experience based on ephemeral trickery, we must be able to entertain the beliefs on which Strether's discovery is based as among the intellectually and morally defensible views of life. One of our most common reading experiences is, in fact, the discovery on reflection that we have allowed ourselves to become a "mock reader" whom we *cannot* respect, that the beliefs which we were temporarily manipulated into accepting cannot be defended in the light of day.

It is true, as Beebe reminds us, that we can read with pleasure the works of a great many authors, some of whose beliefs we reject: Dante, Milton, Hopkins, Yeats, Eliot, Pound—the list varies, of course, with the position of the critic. But is it really true that the serious Catholic or atheist, however sensitive, tolerant, diligent, and well-informed about Milton's beliefs he may be, enjoys *Paradise Lost* to the degree possible to one of Milton's contemporaries and co-believers, of equal intelligence and sensitivity? Can a devout Protestant or Jew who abhors clerical celibacy enjoy Hopkins' "The Habit of Perfection" as a devout Catholic of equal literary sensibility and experience enjoys it? We must be very clear that we are talking now about literary experience, not about the pleasures of finding one's prejudices echoed. The question is whether the enjoyment of literature as literature, and not as propaganda, inevitably involves our beliefs, and I think that the answer is inescapable. Anyone who has ever read the same novel "before and after," noticing that strange loss of power a novel betrays when one has re-

pudiated its norms, whether of Church or Party, of faith in progress, nihilism, existentialism, or whatever, knows that our convictions even about the most purely intellectual matters cannot help
fundamentally affecting our literary responses.

Purists may reply that, even though all readers do in fact allow
their beliefs to get in the way of an objective view of the work, they
should not do so. Which puts us right back where we started: if we
want to deal with an ideal literature that has never existed on land
or sea, and postulate an ideal reader who could never possibly exist,
and then judge all books and all readers as they more or less approximate to this pure state, that is our privilege. But as the facts are,
even the greatest of literature is radically dependent on the concurrence of beliefs of authors and readers. In an excellent discussion
of this problem, M. H. Abrams says what would not need to be
said at all if a generation of exhortation to "objectivity" had not
led us astray:

> Is an appreciation of the Ode [on a Grecian Urn], then, entirely
> independent of the reader's beliefs? Surely not. As it evolves, the
> poem makes constant call on a complex of beliefs which are the
> product of ordinary human experiences with life, people, love, muta-
> bility, age, and art. These subsist less in propositional form than in
> the form of unverbalized attitudes . . . ; but they stand ready to pre-
> cipitate into assertions the moment they are radically challenged. . . .
> If the poem works, our appreciation of the matters it presents is not
> aloofly contemplative, but actively engaged. . . . We are interested
> in a fashion that brings into play our entire moral economy and
> expresses itself continuously in attitudes of approval or disapproval,
> sympathy or antipathy.[21]

This does not mean, of course, that Catholics cannot enjoy *Paradise Lost* more than they might a second-rate Catholic epic, or that
Protestants cannot enjoy "The Habit of Perfection" more than
they might a second-rate Protestant hymn. It means simply that
differences of belief, even in the sense of abstract, speculative systems, are always to some extent relevant, often seriously hampering,
and sometimes fatal. Imagine a beautifully written tragedy with a
convinced Nazi SS man as hero, his tragic error consisting of a

---

[21] *Literature and Belief*, pp. 16–17.

temporary, and fatal, toying with bourgeois democratic ideals. Is there any one of us, regardless of our commitment to objectivity, who could seriously claim that agreement or disagreement with the author's ideas in such a work would have nothing to do with our accepting or rejecting his art?

It is true that some great works seem to rise above differences of speculative system and to win readers of all camps. Shakespeare is the pre-eminent example. The norms in his plays are indeed compatible with more philosophies than are comprehended in most of our dogmas; it is precisely this centrality, this lack of bias, this capacity to cut to the heart of problems which all philosophies attempt to deal with in conceptual terms, that makes his plays what we call universal. Great art can bring men of different convictions together by translating, as it were, their different vocabularies into a tangible experience that incorporates what they mean. It thus mediates among philosophies: Platonist and Aristotelian, Catholic and Protestant, liberal and conservative, can agree that these lives are comic and those tragic, that this behavior is vicious and that admirable, that somehow, in fact, these plays express existentially, as the current fashion puts it, what life means.

But this is far from saying that great literature is compatible with *all* beliefs. Though Shakespeare seems, when looked at superficially, to "have no beliefs," though it is indeed impossible to extract from the plays any one coherent philosophical or religious or political formulation that will satisfy all readers, it is not difficult to list innumerable norms which we must accept if we are to comprehend particular plays, and some of these do run throughout his works. It is true that these beliefs are for the most part self-evident, even commonplace—but that is precisely because they are acceptable to most of us. Shakespeare requires us to believe that it is right to honor our fathers, and that it is wrong to kill off old men like Lear or grind out the eyes of old men like Gloucester. He insists that it is always wrong to use other people as instruments to one's own ends, whether by murder or slander, that it is good to love, but wrong to love selfishly, that helpless old age is pitiable, and that blind egotism deserves punishment. He never lets us forget that the world is made up of good and evil in very strange and frightening

mixtures or that suffering is an essential part of the world's constitution, but he also remembers that it can produce a ripeness which
in a sense justifies all: in his plays, suffering, like everything else,
makes a kind of sense in an ordered universe. Such a list of persistent norms is surprisingly similar to the norms derived from other
really great authors, as well as those found in many very mediocre
ones. Certainly, to work in accordance with such universals is not
enough to make an author great. But to accept them in the works
where they are pertinent is a fundamental step before greatness can
be experienced.

We seldom talk in these terms about great literature only because we take them for granted or because they seem old-fashioned.[22] Only a maniac, presumably, would side with Goneril and
Regan against Lear. It is only when a work seems explicitly doc-
trinaire, or when reasonable men can be in serious disagreement
about its values, that the question of belief arises for discussion.
Even when it does arise, it is often misleading if we think of beliefs in terms of speculative theories. The great "Catholic" or
"Protestant" works are not, in their essentials, Catholic or Protestant at all. Even though a Catholic may be presumed to derive additional pleasures and insights not available to the non-Catholic in
reading Mauriac's *Knot of Vipers*, the picture it gives of a man
made miserable through his own spiritual confusion depends for its
effect on values common to most views of man's fate. Any reader
who believes that human misery is pitiable and that to feel constant
envy and fear and mistrust is to be miserable must pity this man.
Anyone who believes that it is good, or important, for a miserable,

---

22 After a similar, though more comprehensive, listing of Shakespeare's values, Alfred
Harbage seems to hear in the background, as I do, a chorus of very modern voices
protesting that he has got it all wrong. He turns, as it were, and faces them, and to me
he has it all right: "If anyone can ask how an artist of the intelligence postulated above
could have accepted the values described in this book—so cribbed and 'Victorian,' so
bourgeois and grubby—. . . . [I answer that] A great poet could accept the values because they were great values. They represented a synthesis of such products of Judaic
and Hellenistic philosophy as had shown the highest power of survival—literally, the
best that had been known and thought in the world. Nothing since Shakespeare's time
has impeached the evidence of an ordered universe, however diffidently it must
now be defined, or of the superiority of an ethic of love . . ." (*Shakespeare and the
Rival Traditions* [New York, 1952], p. 296).

loveless man to find some repentance and love, however slight, before he dies, cannot help responding to this conclusion. The non-
Catholic reader's lack of concern over whether the protagonist will
receive extreme unction—a problem that plays a minor role in the
book—will no doubt reduce his response to some degree. But the
knot of vipers gnaws as excruciatingly for an unbeliever as for the
most orthodox reader.

Although such universals inevitably operate to some extent in all
successful literature, it is true that most works whose authors have
asked the reader to be "objective" have in fact depended strongly
on the substitution of unconventional or private values—often in
modern criticism called "myths"—for more conventional or public
standards. Far from asking for objectivity, their authors have really
asked for commitment on an unusual axis. The strangeness of much
modern literature when it is first encountered comes in large part
from this substitution—often unacknowledged and unsupported by
any clarification or intensification—of a new and peculiar scale of
norms for the old.

Thus the "novel of sensibility," as written by Virginia Woolf
and others, deliberately rejected most of the values on which the effects of older fiction were based. In *To the Lighthouse* there is little
effort to engage our feelings strongly for or against one or more
characters on the basis of their moral or intellectual traits. Instead,
the value of "sensibility" has been placed at the core of things; those
characters who, like Mrs. Ramsay, have a highly developed sensibility are sympathetic; the "villains" are those who, like Mr. Ramsay, are insensitive. We read forward almost as much to discover
further instances of sensibility as to discover what happens to the
characters. The revelation of the whole, such as it is, is of the over-
all *feeling* rather than the meaning of events.[23] But this, of course,

---

23 "The new philosophy opened up sources of interest for the novel which allowed it
to dispense with whatever values such writers as George Eliot and Henry James had
depended on in a still remoter period. Like naturalism, it brought with it its own
version of an esthetic; it supplied a medium which involved no values other than the
primary one of self-expression" (William Troy, "Virginia Woolf: The Novel of Sensibility," *The Symposium*, III [January–March, 1932], 53–63; and [April–June, 1932],
153–66, as reprinted in Zabel, *Literary Opinion in America* [rev. ed.; New York, 1951],
p. 324).

does not mean that belief is irrelevant. The reader who does not value sensibility as highly as Virginia Woolf will fail to enjoy much of her work unless he is persuaded by it, as he reads, to shift his judgment.

Similarly, if I say to myself, as I read *Ulysses*, "Bloom is a bad man because he masturbates in public," or "Camus' *Stranger* is wicked because he commits murder," I am obviously barred from any complete experience of *Ulysses* or *The Stranger*. It is true, I think, that moral values of another kind are in operation in both works.[24] But it is also true that neither Joyce nor Camus cares very much whether his characters are good in any sense of the word except the author's own. On the other hand, in the later works of Tolstoy, the chief value is a narrowly moral one; a host of beliefs that one must accept to read Joyce or Camus, Faulkner or Hemingway are not only ignored but actively combated by the rhetoric of a story like "Where Love Is, God Is Also."

The problem for the reader is thus really that of discovering which values are in abeyance and which are genuinely, though in modern works often surreptitiously, at work. To pass judgment where the author intends neutrality is to misread. But to be neutral or objective where the author requires commitment is equally to misread, though the effect is likely to be less obvious and may even be overlooked except as a feeling of boredom. At the beginning of the modern period, no doubt the danger of dogmatic overjudgment was the greater one. But for at least two decades now, I am convinced, far more misreading has resulted from what I can only call dogmatic neutrality.

BELIEF ILLUSTRATED: "THE OLD WIVES' TALE"

The best proof of our dependence on beliefs as we read is a detailed look at our reactions to any passage. But the evidence is clearest when one deals with a passage the values of which one can neither fully accept nor fully reject.

In *The Old Wives' Tale* (1908), Arnold Bennett shows the

---

[24] For a convincing argument that morality is important in *Ulysses*, see Lawrance Thompson, *A Comic Principle in Sterne—Meredith—Joyce*. See also p. 132, above.

young heroine, Sophia, eloping with Gerald Scales. They meet in a hotel bedroom. In the manner which so annoyed Virginia Woolf, Bennett's narrator hovers over his characters, looking at the thoughts now of one, now of the other, and commenting as he pleases:

> She was his capture; he held her close. . . . Something in him had forced her to lay her modesty on the altar of his desire. And the sun brightly shone. So he kissed her yet more ardently, and with the slightest touch of a victor's condescension; and her burning response more than restored the self-confidence which he had been losing.
> "I've got no one but you now," she murmured in a melting voice.
> She fancied in her ignorance that the expression of this sentiment would please him. She was not aware that a man is usually rather chilled by it, because it proves to him that the other is thinking about his responsibilities and not about his privileges. Certainly it calmed Gerald, though without imparting to him her sense of his responsibilities. He smiled vaguely. To Sophia his smile was a miracle continually renewed; it mingled dashing gaiety with a hint of wistful appeal in a manner that never failed to bewitch her. A less innocent girl than Sophia might have divined from that adorable half-feminine smile that she could do anything with Gerald except rely on him. But Sophia had to learn [Book III, chap. i].

What strikes one most obviously here are the "practical interests." If we are to react to Sophia's great mistake as Bennett obviously intends, we must first of all feel contempt for Gerald. He has therefore been named "Scales," and in the quotation he is explicitly described as self-satisfied, condescending, irresponsible, unreliable. His actions—which in much modern fiction would be left to speak entirely for themselves—support this explicit commentary: he is contemptible throughout, and it is obvious that we cannot enjoy the dramatic irony of this scene if we do not feel mistrust and contempt for him.

"But Sophia had to learn." Not only must we pass judgment on the slimy seducer, we must agree with the narrator's judgment on Sophia. And this is a fairly complex judgment, more complex than most of us would arrive at with any precision on our own. We must take her side against Gerald, but we must at the same time judge her to be foolish and blind. She is partly to blame for the impending disaster, yet she is "innocent" and hence pitiable. To think her so we must be willing to agree that her type of innocent ignorance is more excusable and hence more pitiable than Gerald's selfish folly. To aid us in this judgment—which might easily be reversed by a skilful novelist—we have her honesty as against his scheming. But Bennett is not at all sure that this will be enough. He dwells upon her as an innocent victim, and on the next page he tries once again to make clear who is to be pitied. "She looked pitiably young, virgin, raw, unsophisticated; helpless in the midst of dreadful dangers."

Bennett asks us, in short, to accept Sophia as a good though foolish person, and Gerald as a bad and foolish one. If we approve of Gerald's behavior in spite of Bennett's efforts, if we detest self-pitying, ignorant young girls, or if, to move in the other direction, we refuse to pity any unmarried young woman who gives a "burning response" to "ardent" kissing in a hotel room, we can hardly react as Bennett intends. And we shall probably be unable to read on, unless we find compensating beliefs which we can share with the author. Thus, our ethical evaluation of the two characters is essential to the passage and to the book as a whole.

But we must not only agree with the author's judgment about seduction, ignorance, dishonesty, sexual passion in young girls, and marriage. We find fully as many appeals to our qualitative interests, though they may seem to be subordinated here. Whether we choose to call our concurrence about such interests "beliefs," it is clear that our reading does depend on our agreement with Bennett's implicit judgment that we are better off spending our time on this written spectacle than looking out of our windows, say, at the passing parade, or reading of a seduction in *True Story Magazine*. We must agree, for example, that it is artistically permissible to tell a story in this intrusive manner, with liberal commentary from the all-wise author. Once we refuse to accept not only this value in general, but the particular manifestation of it here, the story suffers in our eyes. If the quality of each intrusion is not self-justifying, if the style and manner of the revealed author are not in themselves compelling, then our disbelief in this aspect of the story will hamper our enjoyment of the whole.

The trouble is not in the least that the author is present, but that the author who is present gives himself away again and again as not caring sufficiently about what he does: "Something in him," "altar of desire," "burning response," "melting voice"—Bennett has made himself responsible for these banalities, and we find some difficulty in forgiving him. As we shall see later on, the author who attributes the style of his work to a narrator who is to some degree unreliable can get away with murder in this regard, providing himself with a pat excuse if we find weaknesses: "They are characteristic of my narrator, not of me" (see chap. xi).

Finally, our intellectual beliefs are deeply implicated. Since the author intrudes explicitly, our agreement or disagreement is called to mind more than it might be otherwise. Though the Bennett who is implied here is less convincing as the wise, ironic commentator than are the created authors of Fielding or Austen or Meredith, or even of Faulkner, to me the passage is strongest when the author comments directly: Bennett's ironic view of his creatures to some extent redeems them from the damnation conferred by his style. "She was not aware that a man is usually rather chilled by it," he says of her confession of dependence, "because it proves to him that the other is thinking about his responsibilities and not about his privileges. Certainly it calmed Gerald"—this may not be the equal of Fielding, but it is good enough to save the passage from seeming like an unintentional anticipation of the intentionally drab and meaningless seduction in Eliot's *The Waste Land*. Though I would agree that there is, throughout the novel, much too much of this narrator, to eliminate him would make the book unbearably dull.

Clearly such a judgment depends on my concurrence with Bennett's speculations. Whenever I find myself disagreeing with him, either in his explicit commentary about the meaning of life in the Five Towns or in the implicit judgment conveyed by all the less obvious forms of the author's voice, the book suffers in my eyes. To pretend that we read otherwise, to claim that we can make ourselves into objective, dispassionate, thoroughly tolerant readers is in the final analysis nonsense.

"But he [the narrator] little knows what surprises lie in wait for him, if someone were to set about analysing the mass of truths and falsehoods which he has collected here."—"Dr. S.," in *Confessions of Zeno*

"I give you notice betimes, because I design not to surprize you, as some malicious Authors are wont to do, who aim at nothing else."—Antoine Furetière, *Le roman bourgeois*, (1666)

"Perhaps I shall eliminate the preceding chapter. Among other reasons, there is, in the last few lines, something that might be construed as an error on my part. . . . Let us look into the future. Seventy years from now, a thin, sallow, grey-haired fellow, who loves nothing but books, is bent over the preceding page trying to find the error."—Machado de Assis, *Epitaph of a Small Winner*

CHAPTER SIX

Types of Narration

We have seen that the author cannot choose to avoid rhetoric; he can choose only the kind of rhetoric he will employ. He cannot choose whether or not to affect his readers' evaluations by his choice of narrative manner; he can only choose whether to do it well or poorly. As dramatists have always known, even the purest of dramas is not purely dramatic in the sense of being entirely presented, entirely shown as taking place in the moment. There are always what Dryden called "relations" to be taken care of, and try as the author may to ignore the troublesome fact, "some parts of the action are more fit to be represented, some to be related."[1] But related by whom? The dramatist must decide, and the novelist's case is different only in that the choices open to him are more numerous.

If we think through the many narrative devices in the fiction we know, we soon come to a sense of the embarrassing inadequacy of our traditional classification of "point of view" into three or four kinds, variables only of the "person" and the degree of omniscience. If we name over three or four of the great narrators—say Cervantes' Cid Hamete Benengeli, Tristram Shandy, the "I" of *Middlemarch*,

---

[1] *An Essay of Dramatic Poesy* (1668). Though this quotation comes from Lisideius, in his defense of French drama, and not from Neander, who seems to speak more nearly for Dryden, the position is taken for granted in Neander's reply; the only dispute is over which parts are more fit to be represented.

and Strether, through whose vision most of *The Ambassadors* comes to us, we realize that to describe any of them with terms like "first-person" and "omniscient" tells us nothing about how they differ from each other, or why they succeed while others described in the same terms fail.[2] It should be worth our while, then, to attempt a richer tabulation of the forms the author's voice can take, both as a summary of the preceding chapters and as a basis for Parts II and III.

PERSON

Perhaps the most overworked distinction is that of person. To say that a story is told in the first or the third person[3] will tell us nothing of importance unless we become more precise and describe how the particular qualities of the narrators relate to specific effects. It is true that choice of the first person is sometimes unduly limiting; if the "I" has inadequate access to necessary information, the author may be led into improbabilities. And there are other effects that may dictate a choice in some cases. But we can hardly expect to find useful criteria in a distinction that throws all fiction into two, or at most three, heaps. In this pile we see *Henry Esmond*, "A Cask of Amontillado," *Gulliver's Travels*, and *Tristram Shandy*. In that, we have *Vanity Fair*, *Tom Jones*, *The Ambassadors*, and *Brave New World*. But in *Vanity Fair* and *Tom Jones* the commentary is in the first person, often resembling more the intimate effect of *Tristram Shandy* than that of many third-person works. And again, the effect of *The Ambassadors* is much closer to that of

---

[2] There is no point in listing any of the conventional classifications here in order to reject them. They range from the simplest and least useful, in a clever popular essay by C. E. Montague (" 'Sez 'e' or 'Thinks 'e,' " *A Writer's Notes on His Trade* [London, 1930; Pelican ed., 1952], pp. 34–35) to the valuable study by Norman Friedman ("Point of View," *PMLA*, LXX [December, 1955], 1160–84).

[3] Efforts to use the second person have never been very successful, but it is astonishing how little real difference even this choice makes. When I am told, at the beginning of a book, "You have put your left foot. . . . You slide through the narrow opening. . . . Your eyes are only half open . . . ," the radical unnaturalness is, it is true, distracting for a time. But in reading Michel Butor's *La Modification* (Paris, 1957), from which this opening comes, it is surprising how quickly one is absorbed into the illusory "present" of the story, identifying one's vision with the "vous" almost as fully as with the "I" and "he" in other stories.

the great first-person novels, since Strether in large part "narrates" his own story, even though he is always referred to in the third person.

Further evidence that this distinction is less important than has often been claimed is seen in the fact that all of the following functional distinctions apply to both first- and third-person narration alike.

DRAMATIZED AND UNDRAMATIZED NARRATORS

Perhaps the most important differences in narrative effect depend on whether the narrator is dramatized in his own right and on whether his beliefs and characteristics are shared by the author.

The implied author (the author's "second self").—Even the novel in which no narrator is dramatized creates an implicit picture of an author who stands behind the scenes, whether as stage manager, as puppeteer, or as an indifferent God, silently paring his fingernails. This implied author is always distinct from the "real man"—whatever we may take him to be—who creates a superior version of himself, a "second self," as he creates his work (chap. iii).[4]

In so far as a novel does not refer directly to this author, there will be no distinction between him and the implied, undramatized narrator; in Hemingway's "The Killers," for example, there is no narrator other than the implicit second self that Hemingway creates as he writes.

Undramatized narrators.—Stories are usually not so rigorously impersonal as "The Killers"; most tales are presented as passing through the consciousness of a teller, whether an "I" or a "he." Even in drama much of what we are given is narrated by someone, and we are often as much interested in the effect on the narrator's own mind and heart as we are in learning what *else* the author has to tell us. When Horatio tells of his first encounter with the ghost in *Hamlet*, his own character, though never mentioned, is important to us as we listen. In fiction, as soon as we encounter an "I,"

---

[4] A fine account of the subtleties that underlie the seemingly simple relations between real authors and the selves they create as they write can be found in "Makers and Persons," by Patrick Cruttwell, *Hudson Review*, XII (Winter, 1959–60), 487–507.

we are conscious of an experiencing mind whose views of the experience will come between us and the event. When there is no such "I," as in "The Killers," the inexperienced reader may make the mistake of thinking that the story comes to him unmediated. But no such mistake can be made from the moment that the author explicitly places a narrator into the tale, even if he is given no personal characteristics whatever.

Dramatized narrators.—In a sense even the most reticent narrator has been dramatized as soon as he refers to himself as "I," or, like Flaubert, tells us that "we" were in the classroom when Charles Bovary entered. But many novels dramatize their narrators with great fulness, making them into characters who are as vivid as those they tell us about (*Tristram Shandy, Remembrance of Things Past, Heart of Darkness, Dr. Faustus*). In such works the narrator is often radically different from the implied author who creates him. The range of human types that have been dramatized as narrators is almost as great as the range of other fictional characters—one must say "almost" because there are some characters who are not fully qualified to narrate or "reflect" a story (Faulkner can use the idiot for *part* of his novel only because the other three parts exist to set off and clarify the idiot's jumble).

We should remind ourselves that many dramatized narrators are never explicitly labeled as narrators at all. In a sense, every speech, every gesture, narrates; most works contain disguised narrators who are used to tell the audience what it needs to know, while seeming merely to act out their roles.

Though disguised narrators of this kind are seldom labeled so explicitly as God in Job, they often speak with an authority as sure as God's. Messengers returning to tell what the oracle said, wives trying to convince their husbands that the business deal is unethical, old family retainers expostulating with wayward scions—these often have more effect on us than on their official auditors; the king goes ahead with his obstinate search, the husband carries out his deal, the hell-bound youth goes on toward hell as if nothing had been said, but we know what we know—and as surely as if the author himself or his official narrator had told us. "She's laughing at you to your face, brother," Cleante says to Orgon in *Tartuffe*, "and frankly, without meaning to anger you, I must say she's quite right. Has there ever been the like of such a whim? . . . You must be mad, brother, I swear."[5] And in tragedy there is usually a chorus, a friend, or even a forthright villain, to speak truth in contrast to the tragic mistakes of the hero.

The most important unacknowledged narrators in modern fiction are the third-person "centers of consciousness" through whom authors have filtered their narratives. Whether such "reflectors," as James sometimes called them, are highly polished mirrors reflecting complex mental experience, or the rather turbid, sense-bound "camera eyes" of much fiction since James, they fill precisely the function of avowed narrators—though they can add intensities of their own.

> Gabriel had not gone to the door with the others. He was in a dark part of the hall gazing up the staircase. A woman was standing near the top of the first flight, in the shadow also. He could not see her face but he could see the terracotta and salmon-pink panels of her skirt which the shadow made appear black and white. It was his wife. She was leaning on the banisters, listening to something. . . . He asked himself what is a woman standing on the stairs in the shadow, listening to distant music, a symbol of [Joyce's "The Dead"].

The very real advantages of this method, for some purposes, have provided a dominant theme in modern criticism. Indeed, so long as our attention is on such qualities as naturalness and vividness, the advantages seem overwhelming. Only as we break out of the fashionable assumption that all good fiction tries for the same kind of vivid illusion in the same way are we forced to recognize disadvantages. The third-person reflector is only one mode among many, suitable for some effects but cumbersome and even harmful when other effects are desired (chaps. xi–xiii, below).

Observers and Narrator-Agents

Among dramatized narrators there are mere observers (the "I" of *Tom Jones, The Egoist, Troilus and Criseyde*), and there are narrator-agents, who produce some measurable effect on the course of

---

[5] From an unpublished translation by Marcel Gutwirth.

events (ranging from the minor involvement of Nick in *The Great Gatsby*, through the extensive give-and-take of Marlow in *Heart of Darkness*,[6] to the central role of Tristram Shandy, Moll Flanders, Huckleberry Finn, and—in the third person—Paul Morel in *Sons and Lovers*). Clearly, any rules we might discover about observers may not apply to narrator-agents, yet the distinction is seldom made in talk about point of view (chap. xii).

SCENE AND SUMMARY

All narrators and observers, whether first or third person, can relay their tales to us primarily as scene ("The Killers," *The Awkward Age*, the works of Ivy Compton-Burnett and Henry Green), primarily as summary or what Lubbock called "picture" (Addison's almost completely non-scenic tales in *The Spectator*), or, most commonly, as a combination of the two.

Like Aristotle's distinction between dramatic and narrative manners, the somewhat different modern distinction between showing and telling does cover the ground. But the trouble is that it pays for broad coverage with gross imprecision. Narrators of all shapes and shades must either report dialogue alone or support it with "stage directions" and description of setting. But when we think of the radically different effect of a scene reported by Huck Finn and a scene reported by Poe's Montresor, we see that the quality of being "scenic" suggests very little about literary effect. And compare the delightful summary of twelve years given in two pages of *Tom Jones* (Book III, chap. i) with the tedious showing of even ten minutes of uncurtailed conversation in the hands of a Sartre when he allows his passion for "durational realism" to dictate a scene when summary is called for. As was shown in chapters i and ii, the contrast between scene and summary, between showing and

---

[6] For a careful interpretation of the development and functions of Marlow in Conrad's works, see W. Y. Tindall, "Apology for Marlow," in *From Jane Austen to Joseph Conrad*, ed. Robert C. Rathburn and Martin Steinmann, Jr. (Minneapolis, Minn., 1958), pp. 274–85. Though Marlow is often himself a victim of Conrad's ironies, he is generally a reliable reflector of the clarities and ambiguities of the implied author. A much fuller treatment, and a remarkable work for an undergraduate, is James L. Guetti, Jr., *The Rhetoric of Joseph Conrad* ("Amherst College Honors Thesis," No. 2 [Amherst, Mass., 1960]).

telling, is likely to be of little use until we specify the kind of narrator who is providing the scene or the summary.

COMMENTARY

Narrators who allow themselves to tell as well as show vary greatly depending on the amount and kind of commentary allowed in addition to a direct relating of events in scene and summary. Such commentary can, of course, range over any aspect of human experience, and it can be related to the main business in innumerable ways and degrees. To treat it as a single device is to ignore important differences between commentary that is merely ornamental, commentary that serves a rhetorical purpose but is not part of the dramatic structure, and commentary that is integral to the dramatic structure, as in *Tristram Shandy* (chaps. vii–viii, below).

SELF-CONSCIOUS NARRATORS

Cutting across the distinction between observers and narrator-agents of all these kinds is the distinction between *self-conscious narrators* (chap. viii), aware of themselves as writers (*Tom Jones, Tristram Shandy, Barchester Towers, The Catcher in the Rye, Remembrance of Things Past, Dr. Faustus*), and narrators or observers who rarely if ever discuss their writing chores (*Huckleberry Finn*) or who seem unaware that they are writing, thinking, speaking, or "reflecting" a literary work (Camus's *The Stranger*, Lardner's "Haircut," Bellow's *The Victim*).

VARIATIONS OF DISTANCE

Whether or not they are involved in the action as agents or as sufferers, narrators and third-person reflectors differ markedly according to the degree and kind of distance that separates them from the author, the reader, and the other characters of the story. In any reading experience there is an implied dialogue among author, narrator, the other characters, and the reader. Each of the four can range, in relation to each of the others, from identification to complete opposition, on any axis of value, moral, intellectual, aesthetic, and even physical. (Does the reader who stammers react to the stammering of H. C. Earwicker as I do? Surely not.) The elements usually discussed under "aesthetic distance" enter in of course; distance in time and space, differences of social class or conventions of speech or dress—these and many others serve to control our sense that we are dealing with an aesthetic object, just as the paper moons and other unrealistic stage effects of some modern drama have had an "alienation" effect. But we must not confuse these with the equally important effects of personal beliefs and qualities, in author, reader, narrator, and all others in the cast of characters.

1. The *narrator* may be more or less distant from the *implied author*. The distance may be moral (Jason vs. Faulkner, the barber vs. Lardner, the narrator vs. Fielding in *Jonathan Wild*). It may be intellectual (Twain and Huck Finn, Sterne and Tristram Shandy on the influence of noses, Richardson and Clarissa). It may be physical or temporal: most authors are distant from even the most knowing narrator in that they presumably know how "everything turns out in the end." And so on.

2. The *narrator* also may be more or less distant from the *characters* in the story he tells. He may differ morally, intellectually, and temporally (the mature narrator and his younger self in *Great Expectations* or *Redburn*); morally and intellectually (Fowler the narrator and Pyle the American in Greene's *The Quiet American*, both departing radically from the author's norms but in different directions); morally and emotionally (Maupassant's "The Necklace," and Huxley's "Nuns at Luncheon," in which the narrators affect less emotional involvement than Maupassant and Huxley clearly expect from the reader); and thus on through every possible trait.

3. The *narrator* may be more or less distant from the *reader's* own norms; for example, physically and emotionally (Kafka's *The Metamorphosis*); morally and emotionally (Pinkie in *Brighton Rock*, the miser in Mauriac's *Knot of Vipers*, and the many other moral degenerates that modern fiction has managed to make into convincing human beings).

With the repudiation of omniscient narration, and in the face of inherent limitations in dramatized reliable narrators, it is hardly surprising that modern authors have experimented with unreliable narrators whose characteristics change in the course of the works they narrate. Ever since Shakespeare taught the modern world what the Greeks had overlooked in neglecting character change (compare *Macbeth* and *Lear* with *Oedipus*), stories of character development or degeneration have become more and more popular. But it was not until authors had discovered the full uses of the third-person reflector that they could effectively show a narrator changing *as he narrates*. The mature Pip, in *Great Expectations*, is presented as a generous man whose heart is where the reader's is supposed to be; he watches his young self move away from the reader, as it were, and then back again. But the third-person reflector can be shown, technically in the past tense but in effect present before our eyes, moving toward or away from values that the reader holds dear. Authors in the twentieth century have proceeded almost as if determined to work out all of the possible plot forms based on such shifts: start far and end near; start near, move far, and end near; start far and move farther; and so on. Perhaps the most characteristic, however, have been the astonishing achievements in the first of these, taking extremely unsympathetic characters like Faulkner's Mink Snopes and transforming them, both through character change and technical manipulation, into characters of dignity and power. We badly need thoroughgoing studies of the various plot forms that have resulted from this kind of shifting distance.

4. The *implied author* may be more or less distant from the *reader*. The distance may be intellectual (the implied author of *Tristram Shandy*, not of course to be identified with Tristram, more interested in and knowing more about recondite classical lore than any of his readers), moral (the works of Sade), or aesthetic. From the author's viewpoint, a successful reading of his book must eliminate all distance between the essential norms of his implied author and the norms of the postulated reader. Often enough, there is very little fundamental distance to begin with; Jane Austen does not have to convince us that pride and prejudice are undesirable. A bad book, on the other hand, is often most clearly recognizable because the implied author asks that we judge according to norms that we cannot accept.

5. The *implied author* (carrying the reader with him) may be

more or less distant from *other characters*. Again, the distance can be on any axis of value. Some successful authors keep most of their characters very far "away" in every respect (Ivy Compton-Burnett), and they may work very deliberately, as William Empson says of T. F. Powys, to maintain an artificiality that will keep their characters "at a great distance from the author."[7] Others present a wider range from far to near, on a variety of axes. Jane Austen, for example, presents a broad range of moral judgment (from the almost complete approval of Jane Fairfax in *Emma* to the contempt for Wickham in *Pride and Prejudice*), of wisdom (from Knightley to Miss Bates or Mrs. Bennet), of taste, of tact, of sensibility.

It is obvious that on each of these scales my examples do not begin to cover the possibilities. What we call "involvement" or "sympathy" or "identification," is usually made up of many reactions to author, narrators, observers, and other characters. And narrators may differ from their authors or readers in various kinds of involvement or detachment, ranging from deep personal concern (Nick in *The Great Gatsby*, MacKellar in *The Master of Ballantrae*, Zeitblom in *Dr. Faustus*) to a bland or mildly amused or merely curious detachment (Waugh's *Decline and Fall*).

For practical criticism probably the most important of these kinds of distance is that between the fallible or unreliable narrator and the implied author who carries the reader with him in judging the narrator. If the reason for discussing point of view is to find how it relates to literary effects, then surely the moral and intellectual qualities of the narrator are more important to our judgment than whether he is referred to as "I" or "he," or whether he is privileged or limited. If he is discovered to be untrustworthy, then the total effect of the work he relays to us is transformed.

Our terminology for this kind of distance in narrators is almost hopelessly inadequate. For lack of better terms, I have called a narrator *reliable* when he speaks for or acts in accordance with the norms of the work (which is to say, the implied author's norms),

---

[7] *Some Versions of Pastoral* (London, 1935), p. 7. For an excellent discussion of Powys' deliberate artificiality, see Martin Steinmann's "The Symbolism of T. F. Powys," *Critique*, I (Summer, 1957), 49–63.

unreliable when he does not. It is true that most of the great reliable narrators indulge in large amounts of incidental irony, and they are thus "unreliable" in the sense of being potentially deceptive. But difficult irony is not sufficient to make a narrator unreliable. Nor is unreliability ordinarily a matter of lying, although deliberately deceptive narrators have been a major resource of some modern novelists (Camus' *The Fall*, Calder Willingham's *Natural Child*, etc.).[8] It is most often a matter of what James calls *inconscience*; the narrator is mistaken, or he believes himself to have qualities which the author denies him. Or, as in *Huckleberry Finn*, the narrator claims to be naturally wicked while the author silently praises his virtues behind his back.

Unreliable narrators thus differ markedly depending on how far and in what direction they depart from their author's norms; the older term "tone," like the currently fashionable terms "irony" and "distance," covers many effects that we should distinguish. Some narrators, like Barry Lyndon, are placed as far "away" from author and reader as possible, in respect to every virtue except a kind of interesting vitality. Some, like Fleda Vetch, the reflector in James's *The Spoils of Poynton*, come close to representing the author's ideal of taste, judgment, and moral sense. All of them make stronger demands on the reader's powers of inference than do reliable narrators.

VARIATIONS IN SUPPORT OR CORRECTION

Both reliable and unreliable narrators can be unsupported or uncorrected by other narrators (Gully Jimson in *The Horse's Mouth*,

---

8 Alexander E. Jones in a recent essay argued convincingly for a "straight" reading of *The Turn of the Screw*, offering as one reason that "the basic convention of first-person fiction is necessarily a confidence in the narrator. . . . Unless James has violated the basic rules of his craft, the governess cannot be a pathological liar" (*PMLA*, LXXIV [March, 1959], 122). Whatever may have been true in James's time, it is clear that in modern fiction there is no longer any such convention. The only convention that can be relied on, as I show in chapter eleven, is that if a narrator presents himself as speaking or writing to the reader, he really is doing so. The content of what he says may turn out to be dream (Schwartz's "In Dreams Begin Responsibilities"), or falsehood (Jean Cayrol's *Les corps étrangers*), or it may not "turn out" at all—that is, it may be left indeterminately between dream, falsehood, fantasy, and reality (Unamuno's *Mist*, Beckett's *Comment c'est*).

Henderson in Bellow's *Henderson the Rain King*) or supported or corrected (*The Master of Ballantrae, The Sound and the Fury*). Sometimes it is almost impossible to infer whether or to what degree a narrator is fallible; sometimes explicit corroborating or conflicting testimony makes the inference easy. Support or correction differs radically, it should be noted, depending on whether it is provided from within the action, so that the narrator-agent might benefit from it in sticking to the right line or in changing his own views (Faulkner's *Intruder in the Dust*), or is simply provided externally, to help the reader correct or reinforce his own views as against the narrator's (Graham Greene's *The Power and the Glory*). Obviously, the effects of isolation will be extremely different in the two cases.

PRIVILEGE

Observers and narrator-agents, whether self-conscious or not, reliable or not, commenting or silent, isolated or supported, can be either privileged to know what could not be learned by strictly natural means or limited to realistic vision and inference. Complete privilege is what we usually call omniscience. But there are many kinds of privilege, and very few "omniscient" narrators are allowed to know or show as much as their authors know.

We need a good study of the varieties of privilege and limitation and their function. Some limitations are only temporary, or even playful, like the ignorance Fielding sometimes imposes on his "I" (as when he doubts his own powers of narration and invokes the Muses for aid (*Tom Jones*, Book XIII, chap. i). Some are more nearly permanent but subject to momentary relaxation, like the generally limited, humanly realistic Ishmael in *Moby Dick*, who can yet break through his human limitations when the story requires (" 'He waxes brave, but nevertheless obeys; most careful bravery that!' murmured Ahab"—with no one present to report to the narrator). And some are confined to what their literal condition would allow them to know (first person, Huck Finn; third person, Miranda and Laura in Katherine Anne Porter's stories).

The most important single privilege is that of obtaining an inside view of another character, because of the rhetorical power that such a privilege conveys upon a narrator. There is a curious ambiguity in the term "omniscience." Many modern works that we usually classify as narrated dramatically, with everything relayed to us through the limited views of the characters, postulate fully as much omniscience in the silent author as Fielding claims for himself. Our roving visitation into the minds of sixteen characters in Faulkner's *As I Lay Dying*, seeing nothing but what those minds contain, may seem in one sense not to depend on an omniscient author. But this method is omniscience with teeth in it: the implied author demands our absolute faith in his powers of divination. We must never for a moment doubt that he knows everything about each of these sixteen minds or that he has chosen correctly how much to show of each. In short, impersonal narration is really no escape from omniscience—the true author is as "unnaturally" all-knowing as he ever was. If evident artificiality were a fault—which it is not— modern narration would be as faulty as Trollope's.

Another way of suggesting the same ambiguity is to look closely at the concept of "dramatic" storytelling. The author can present his characters in a dramatic situation without in the least presenting them in what we normally think of as a dramatic manner. When Joseph Andrews, who has been stripped and beaten by thieves, is overtaken by a stagecoach, Fielding presents the scene in what by some modern standards must seem an inconsistent and undramatic mode. "The poor wretch, who lay motionless a long time, just began to recover his senses as a stage-coach came by. The postilion, hearing a man's groans, stopped his horses, and told the coachman, he was certain there was a dead man lying in the ditch. . . . A lady, who heard what the postilion said, and likewise heard the groan, called eagerly to the coachman to stop and see what was the matter. Upon which he bid the postilion alight, and look into the ditch. He did so, and returned, 'That there was a man sitting upright, as naked as ever he was born.' " There follows a splendid description, hardly meriting the name of scene, in which are recorded the selfish reactions of each passenger. A young lawyer points out that they might be legally liable if they refuse to take Joseph up. "These words had a sensible effect on the coachman, who was well acquainted with the person who spoke them; and the old gentleman above mentioned, thinking the naked man would afford him frequent opportunities of showing his wit to the lady, offered to join with the company in giving a mug of beer for his fare; till, partly alarmed by the threats of the one, and partly by the promises of the other, and being perhaps a little moved with compassion at the poor creature's condition, who stood bleeding and shivering with the cold, he at length agreed." Once Joseph is in the coach, the same kind of indirect reporting of the "scene" continues, with frequent excursions, however superficial, into the minds and hearts of the assembly of fools and knaves, and occasional guesses when complete knowledge seems inadvisable. If to be dramatic is to show characters dramatically engaged with each other, motive clashing with motive, the outcome depending upon the resolution of motives, then this scene is dramatic. But if it is to give the impression that the story is taking place by itself, with the characters existing in a dramatic relationship vis-à-vis the spectator, unmediated by a narrator and decipherable only through inferential matching of word to word and word to deed, then this is a relatively undramatic scene.

On the other hand, an author can present a character in this latter kind of dramatic relationship with the reader without involving that character in any internal drama at all. Many lyric poems are dramatic in this sense and undramatic in any other. "That is no country for old men—" Who says? Yeats, or his "mask," says. To whom? To us. How do we know that it is Yeats and not some character as remote from him as Caliban is remote from Browning in "Caliban upon Setebos"? We infer it as the dramatized statement unfolds; the need for the inference is what makes the lyric dramatic in this sense. Caliban, in short, is dramatic in two senses; he is in a dramatic situation with other characters, and he is in a dramatic situation over against us. Yeats's poem is dramatic in only one sense.

The ambiguities of the word dramatic are even more complicated in fiction that attempts to dramatize states of consciousness directly. Is *A Portrait of the Artist as a Young Man* dramatic? In some respects, yes. We are not told about Stephen. He is placed on the stage before us, acting out his destiny with only disguised helps or comments from his author. But it is not his actions that are dramatized directly, not his speech that we hear unmediated. What is dramatized is his mental record of everything that happens. We see his consciousness at work on the world. Sometimes what it records is itself dramatic, as when Stephen observes himself in a scene with other characters. But the report itself, the internal record, is dramatic in the second sense only. The report we are given of what goes on in Stephen's mind is a monologue uninvolved in any modifying dramatic context. And it is an infallible report, even less subject to critical doubts than the typical Elizabethan soliloquy. We accept, by convention, the claim that what is reported as going on in Stephen's mind really goes on there, or in other words, that Joyce knows how Stephen's mind works. "The equation of the page of his scribbler began to spread out a widening tail, eyed and starred like a peacock's; and, when the eyes and stars of its indices had been eliminated, began slowly to fold itself together again. The indices appearing and disappearing were eyes opening and closing; the eyes opening and closing were stars. . . ." Who says so? Not Stephen, but the omniscient, infallible author. The report is direct, and it is clearly unmodified by any "dramatic" context—that is, unlike a speech in a dramatic scene, it does not lead us to suspect that the thoughts have been in any way aimed at an effect. We are thus in a dramatic relation with Stephen only in a limited sense—the sense in which a lyric poem is dramatic.[9]

INSIDE VIEWS

Finally, narrators who provide inside views differ in the depth and the axis of their plunge. Boccaccio can give inside views, but they are extremely shallow. Jane Austen goes relatively deep morally, but scarcely skims the surface psychologically. All authors of stream-of-consciousness narration presumably attempt to go deep psychologically, but some of them deliberately remain shallow in the moral

---

[9] I am aware that my terminology here contrasts with Joyce's own use of the triad, *lyric, epic,* and *dramatic*. *Portrait* is dramatic in Joyce's sense, but in that sense only.

dimension.[10] We should remind ourselves that any sustained inside view, of whatever depth, temporarily turns the character whose mind is shown into a narrator; inside views are thus subject to variations in all of the qualities we have described above, and most importantly in the degree of unreliability. Generally speaking, the deeper our plunge, the more unreliability we will accept without loss of sympathy (see chap. x).

Narration is an art, not a science, but this does not mean that we are necessarily doomed to fail when we attempt to formulate principles about it. There are systematic elements in every art, and criticism of fiction can never avoid the responsibility of trying to explain technical successes and failures by reference to general principles. But we must always ask where the general principles are to be found.

It is not surprising to hear practicing novelists report that they have never had any help from critics about point of view. In dealing with point of view the novelist must always deal with the individual work: which particular character shall tell this particular story, or part of a story, with what precise degree of reliability, privilege, freedom to comment, and so on. Shall he be given dramatic vividness? Even if the novelist has decided on a narrator who will fit one of the critic's classifications—"omniscient," "first person," "limited omniscient," "objective," "roving," "effaced," or whatever—his troubles have just begun. He simply cannot find answers to his immediate, precise, practical problems by referring to

---

10 Discussion of the many devices covered by the loose term "stream-of-consciousness" has generally concentrated on their service to psychological realism, avoiding the moral effect of different degrees of depth. Even unfriendly critics—Mauriac in *Le romancier et ses personnages* (Paris, 1933), for example—have generally pointed to their amorphousness, their lack of clear control and their obvious artifice, not to their moral implications. Too often, both attack and defense have assumed that there is a single device which can be assessed as good or bad, once and for all, for such-and-such general reasons. Melvin Friedman (*Stream of Consciousness* [New Haven, Conn., 1955]) concludes that it is "almost axiomatic that no further work of the first order can be done within this tradition," since the method depended on a "certain literary mentality which died out with Joyce, Virginia Woolf, and the early Faulkner" (p. 261). But the works he treats make use of dozens of varieties of stream-of-consciousness, some of which are now an established part of the novelist's repertory. Most of them are likely to find new uses in the future.

statements such as that the "omniscient is the most flexible method," or that "the objective is the most rapid or vivid." Even the soundest of generalizations at this level will be of little use to him in his page-by-page progress through his novel.

As Henry James's detailed records show, the novelist discovers his narrative technique as he tries to achieve for his readers the potentialities of his developing idea. The majority of his choices are consequently choices of degree, not kind. To decide that your narrator shall not be omniscient decides practically nothing. The hard question is: Just how *inconscient* shall he be? Again, to decide on first-person narration settles only a part of one's problem, perhaps the easiest part. What kind of first person? How fully characterized? How much aware of himself as narrator? How reliable? How much confined to realistic inference; how far privileged to go beyond realism? At what points shall he speak truth and at what points utter no judgment or even utter falsehood? These questions can be answered only by reference to the potentialities and necessities of particular works, not by reference to fiction in general, or the novel, or rules about point of view.

There are no doubt *kinds* of effect to which the author can refer; for example, if he wants to make a scene more amusing, poignant, vivid, or ambiguous, or if he wants to make a character more sympathetic or more convincing, such-and-such practices may be indicated. But we can understand why in his search for help in his decisions, the novelist should find the practice of his peers more helpful than the abstract rules of the textbooks: the sensitive author who reads the great novels finds in them a storehouse of precise examples, of how *this* effect, as distinct from all other possible effects, was heightened by the proper narrative choice. In dealing with the types of narration, the critic must always limp behind, referring constantly to the varied practice which alone can correct his temptations to overgeneralize. In place of our modern "fourth unity," in place of abstract rules about consistency and objectivity in the use of point of view, we need more painstaking, specific accounts of how great tales are told.

We turn now to a closer view of the arts of telling.

"Sir, as you and I are in a manner perfect strangers to each other, it would not have been proper to have let you into too many circumstances relating to myself all at once.—You must have a little patience. I have undertaken, you see, to write not only my life, but my opinions also; hoping and expecting that your knowledge of my character, and of what kind of a mortal I am, by the one, would give you a better relish for the other: As you proceed further with me, the slight acquaintance which is now beginning betwixt us, will grow into familiarity; and that, unless one of us is in fault, will terminate in friendship.——O diem præclarum!——then nothing which has touched me will be thought trifling in its nature, or tedious in its telling."—*Tristram Shandy*

PART II

The Author's
Voice
in Fiction

"My reader then is not to be surprised, if, in the course of this work, he shall find some chapters very short, and others altogether as long; some that contain only the time of a single day, and others that comprise years; in a word, if my history sometimes seems to stand still, and sometimes to fly. For all which I shall not look on myself as accountable to any court of critical jurisdiction whatever; for as I am, in reality, the founder of a new province of writing, so I am at liberty to make what laws I please therein."—FIELDING, *Tom Jones*

Enter *Time, the Chorus*
                    Impute it not a crime
To me or my swift passage, that I slide
O'er sixteen years and leave the growth untried
Of that wide gap. . . . —*The Winter's Tale*

"But I see I can't go on like this, partly because some things I did not hear, others I did not notice, and others I have forgotten, but most of all because, as I have said before, I have literally no time or space to mention everything that was said and done."—*The Brothers Karamazov*

"And this, as I could not prevail on any of my actors to speak, I was obliged to declare myself."—FIELDING, *Tom Jones*

"One's poor word of honour has *had* to pass muster for the show."—HENRY JAMES, Preface to *The Wings of the Dove*

The Uses of Reliable Commentary

It is not surprising that critics have been tempted to discuss commentary—and usually to condemn it—as if it were a single thing which can be judged simply according to our general views of the novel. But it should prove worthwhile to abandon such a priori judgments and to look into some good novels to discover the effects commentary has, in fact, been used to achieve. Afterward we may still find ourselves saying that though authors have used commentary for such-and-such purposes, we wish that they had not. But at the very least we should be in a position to decide with some precision whether any of the particular achievements of the author's voice have been worth the sacrifice of whatever general qualities we hold dear.

PROVIDING THE FACTS, "PICTURE," OR SUMMARY

The most obvious task for a commentator is to tell the reader about facts that he could not easily learn otherwise. There are many kinds of facts, of course, and they can be "told" in an unlimited number of ways. Stage setting, explanation of the meaning of an action, summary of thought processes or of events too insignificant to merit being dramatized, description of physical events and details whenever such description cannot spring naturally from a character —these all occur in many different forms.

As Chaucer begins his tale of Criseyde's woes, he disposes of the fall of Troy in seven lines of summary exactly suited to the needs of his story:

> But how this town com to destruccion
> Ne falleth naught to purpos me to telle;
> For it were here a long disgression
> Fro my matere, and yow to long to dwelle.
> But the Troian gestes, as they felle,
> In Omer, or in Dares, or in Dite,
> Whoso that kan may rede hem as they write.

The "Chaucer" who here reminds us that we are reading one tale among many, that he is selecting his materials in our own interest, and that if we want other stories we can go to Homer and other authors for them, accompanies us intimately throughout *Troilus and Criseyde*. Whatever is not directly pertinent to his purposes, he summarizes.

> And if I hadde ytaken for to write
> The armes of this ilke worthi man,
> Than wolde ich of his batailles endite;
> But for that I to writen first bigan
> Of his love, I have seyd as I kan.—
> His worthi dedes, whoso list him heere,
> Rede Dares, he kan telle hem alle ifeere.[1]

He never lets us forget his presence, yet his presence cannot be said to detract from the tale he tells. He *tells* us a good deal about those aspects of the tale which, though necessary, are not entitled to the heightening that would come if they were dramatized. And yet the over-all effect is to make us feel that we have been given a better story, more carefully worked, than would have been possible if he had simply served up his materials raw.

The great narrators have always managed to find some way to make such summary interesting, as Fielding does with his ironic invitation for us to fill in the gaps in *Tom Jones*. He gives the reader, he says, "an opportunity of employing that wonderful sagacity,

---

[1] Book V, ll. 1765–71. For a discussion of the relation between this "Chaucer" and Chaucer himself, see Morton W. Bloomfield, "Distance and Predestination in 'Troilus and Criseyde,'" *PMLA*, LXXII (March, 1957), 14–26.

of which he is master, by filling up these vacant spaces of time with his own conjectures." Since he is assured that most of his readers are "upper graduates in criticism," he leaves them "a space of twelve years" in which to apply their skills (Book III, chap. i).

The provision of this kind of summary is only one of dozens of distinguishable techniques for providing facts, most of which—perhaps fortunately—have never been named. What, for example, are we to call the device of narrating by footnotes? In Marcel Aymé's *Le chemin des écoliers* (1946) the author occasionally provides in footnotes information that lies beyond the range of his characters. During the German occupation of France, Michaud watches four German soldiers "performing their tourist duties" in front of the Sacré-Cœur. He envies them, momentarily, their carefree existence. Suddenly we are given a footnote, telling us that the four soldiers were named Arnold, Eisenhart, Heinecken, and Schulz. "The first one was killed on the Russian front. The second one, wounded in the Crimea, returned home with both legs missing and was poisoned by his wife." And so on, until Schulz, the last, is described as torn to bits by an angry mob of Parisians at the time of the liberation. This factual intrusion commenting sardonically on Michaud's envy is brief, clean, effective, and entirely appropriate to the work in which it appears. If we try to think of an equally concise way to provide this ironic juxtaposition of the hero's envy with the soldiers' disastrous future, we see that it simply could not be done by anyone but the omniscient author speaking in his own person. It need not be done in a footnote, of course, although the outlandish artifice of a footnote is in this case the simplest way of showing that these facts, while necessary to the story, are strictly side issues; the characters described cannot possibly become important to the story later on. The only ready alternative would be a dramatized interpolation, shifting us forward to four episodes, swiftly giving the future of the four soldiers. But to do so would not only take much more space, it would imply importance and thus muddy the pattern of expectations for the reader.[2]

---

2 See also J. D. Salinger, "Zooey," in *The New Yorker*, May 4, 1957, p. 33, for other narrative uses of what Salinger's narrator calls "the aesthetic evil of a footnote."

This is simply one colorful recent example of the most common and most useful service that direct telling can perform. In the same way the author may provide a bit of summary between scenes, summary that could be provided by none of the characters. Or he may give facts about one character that no other character could know. "Ray saw Leopold thinking: Oh yes, an Englishman! (It should be clear that Ray looked like any of these tall Englishmen who . . .)." Thus Elizabeth Bowen's narrator enters *The House in Paris* (1935) to give us a description of Ray which Ray could *almost* achieve himself but which, coming from the author, is more useful since more certain; it is untainted with doubt about whether he is in fact giving an unbiased report.

When we remember the many cumbersome "mirror-views" in modern fiction—"What he saw in the mirror was a man of middle-height"—we see how much trouble the desire to dramatize such descriptive detail can cause. Some situations do, indeed, lend themselves to this kind of pseudodrama, particularly when what is seen in the mirror, and the fact of the character's long, self-absorbed gaze, are themselves clues to help us grasp his nature. But even when the mirror is thus truly functional, more concentrated information can often be given by maintaining a reliable narrator's voice independent of the character's subjective vision. "Though the sleepy, short-sighted countenance and rather bald head reflected in the looking-glass were of such an insignificant type that at first sight they would certainly not have attracted particular attention in any one, yet the owner of the countenance was satisfied with all that he saw in the looking-glass." Thus Dostoevski, in *The Double* (1846), writing before point of view had been much troubled about, makes his opening description largely dramatic and at the same time uses his own commentary to betray his character's egotism. By taking an omniscient position he can do in four lines what any other method would require far more to do. Anyone who tries to translate the passage into a completely objective portrayal of Golyadkin's own thoughts without losing any of the effect, including the clarity, will see how much he has sacrificed.

A major function of indisputable fact is the control of dramatic irony. The simplest form is a straight description, as in several of the above examples, of how one character misinterprets another's unspoken thoughts or motives. "After she got to be a big girl," the narrator of Faulkner's *Light in August* tells us, Lena would "ask her father to stop the wagon at the edge of town and she would get down and walk. She would not tell her father why she wanted to walk in instead of riding. He thought that it was because of the smooth streets, the sidewalks. But it was because she believed that the people who saw her . . . would believe that she lived in the town too." The fact of the misinterpretation is something only the omniscient narrator could know, since it is made up of the father's private judgment and the daughter's private motive; yet the scene would be pointless as a clue to Lena's character unless the misjudgment were made clear to us.

More obvious effects are achieved by explicitly controlling the reader's expectations, insuring that he will not travel burdened with the false hopes and fears held by the characters. Some sophisticated readers object strenuously to self-evident manipulations of this kind, yet half the fun of many novels depends on them. Even the "effaced" James found it appropriate in *The Ambassadors* (1903) to heighten our anticipations by saying such things as, "This was the very beginning with him of a condition as to which, later on, as will be seen, he found cause to pull himself up. . . ."[3]

James was the first to formulate clearly the aesthetic problem presented by bald factual summary. He did not, except in *The Awkward Age* (1899), attempt to do away with summary entirely. But he became more and more determined to find a way to make summary itself dramatic—whether as description, narration, or moral and psychological evaluation.

The details of his effort to keep "it all within my hero's compass,"[4] to push all summary back into the minds of the characters, are so important that they must be discussed at length later on. No

---

[3] New York, 1930, p. 80. For a discussion of the methods and advantages of keeping the audience better informed than the characters, see Bertrand Evans, *Shakespeare's Comedies* (Oxford, 1960).

[4] Preface to *The Ambassadors*, in *The Art of the Novel*, ed. R. P. Blackmur (New York, 1947), p. 317.

one has ever resisted with more intelligence and integrity the temptations to unassimilated information that beset every novelist. We need only look at any one of thousands of "informative" novels written before and since his time to realize the importance of his effort to make everything count. The travelogues inserted by Balzac (for example, *Les chouans* [1829]), Madame de Staël (for example, *Corinne* [1807]), and Dickens (for example, *Martin Chuzzlewit* [1843–44]), to say nothing of many modern regional novelists, are only an extreme form of a blight that can be found everywhere, from novels that are really only disguised gossip about army life or penthouse life or life in Greenwich Village to novels that do little more than catalogue the unfortunate contents of one type of mind.[5]

But we can accept James's importance without agreeing with Lubbock that James's solution to the problem of summary exacts no price. "The novelist, more free than the playwright, could of course *tell* us, if he chose, what lurks behind this agitated spirit [Strether in *The Ambassadors*]; he could step forward and explain the restless appearance of the man's thought. But if he prefers the dramatic way, admittedly the more effective, there is nothing to prevent him from taking it."[6] By following the Jamesian way the novelist surrenders none of his freedom. "That liberty . . . of standing above the story and taking a broad view of many things, of transcending the limits of the immediate scene—nothing of this is sacrificed by the author's steady advance in the direction of drama. The man's mind has become visible, phenomenal, dramatic; but in acting its part it still lends us eyes, is still an opportunity of extended vision" (p. 149).

But there is, after all, a sacrifice. When the novelist chooses to deliver his facts and summaries as though from the mind of one of his characters, he is in danger of surrendering precisely "that liberty of transcending the limits of the immediate scene"—par-

---

[5] For a discussion of the indispensable role of fact in fiction, see Mary McCarthy, "The Fact in Fiction," *Partisan Review*, XXVII (Summer, 1960), 438–58. For a discussion of the harm that can result from a confusion of sociological fact and fiction, see Geoffrey Wagner, "Sociology and Fiction," *Twentieth Century*, CLXVII (February, 1960), 108–14.

[6] *The Craft of Fiction* (London, 1921), pp. 157–58.

ticularly the limits of that character he has chosen as his mouth-piece. The consequences of this sacrifice will run thematically throughout Part III of this book. For the present, it is enough to say that a fact, when it has been given to us by the author or his unequivocal spokesman, is a very different thing from the same "fact" when given to us by a fallible character in the story. When a character speaks realistically, within the drama, the convention of absolute reliability has been destroyed, and while the gains for some fictional purposes are undeniable, the costs are undeniable too.

Whenever a fact, whenever a narrative summary, whenever a description must, or even might, serve as a clue to our interpretation of the character who provides it, it may very well lose some of its standing as fact, summary, or description. Prufrock's notion of the evening sky as etherized patient is no longer fact or description at all, if what the reader requires is knowledge about the real weather. As unreliability increases, there obviously can come a point at which such transformed information ceases to be useful even in characterization of minds, unless the author retains some method of showing what the facts are from which the speaker's interpretations characteristically diverge.

What Caliban sees of Prospero in Browning's poem can tell us all we need to know about Caliban only because we know about Prospero from another source. Much of our pleasure in the irony would be lost—though there might be compensations of another kind—if we had to spend our time puzzling whether Browning's and Caliban's views are identical.

There can be no dramatic irony, by definition, unless the author and audience can somehow share knowledge which the characters do not hold. Though reliable narration is by no means the only way of conveying to the audience the facts on which dramatic irony is based, it is a useful way, and in some works, works in which no one but the author can conceivably know what needs to be known, it may be indispensable. In much of the great comic fiction, for example, our amusement depends on the author's telling us in advance that the characters' troubles are temporary and their concern ridiculously exaggerated. Anyone who doubts the value of this kind of rhetoric should imagine himself trying to narrate *Tom Jones* without the author's voice to remind his readers that things are not as bad for Tom as they look, or *Great Expectations* without the voice of the mature Pip to heighten, on the one hand, our sense of the younger Pip's moral decline and to preserve, on the other, our sympathy for him as he goes down and our certainty that he will again rise. But dramatic irony can be equally important in more serious works. Could we ever really prefer a reading of *The Great Gatsby* cleansed of the knowledge given us in the opening? "When I came back from the East last autumn," Nick tells us, "I felt that I wanted the world to be in uniform and at a sort of moral attention forever. . . . Only Gatsby . . . was exempt from my reaction—Gatsby, who represented everything for which I have an unaffected scorn. . . . There was something gorgeous about him . . . an extraordinary gift for hope, a romantic readiness such as I have never found in any other person and which it is not likely I shall ever find again. No—Gatsby turned out all right at the end; it is what preyed on Gatsby, what foul dust floated in the wake of his dreams that temporarily closed out my interest in the abortive sorrows and short-winded elations of men." After reading this, we know a good deal that no one in the story will know as it progresses. The younger Nick as a "lucid reflector" in the James manner would be an unreliable witness to the events. As it is, the older Nick provides thoroughly reliable guidance.

"Sing, goddess, the anger of Peleus' son Achilleus / and its devastation, which put pains thousandfold upon the Achaians / . . ."—yes, *that* is the order of causation in *this* work; we know where we stand from this point on, despite the great number of lesser ambiguities. To purge the *Iliad* of this absolutism would be to destroy it. Whenever the demands of concision or clarity or dramatic irony of the most emphatic kind are more important than making the story seem to be telling itself, or giving an air of the puzzling ambiguities of life, the author will seek those devices which can maintain facts as facts and reliable judgments as reliable judgments.[7]

---

[7] "Fiction, which still has the resource of Summary undisguised, has very little excuse for employing Summary badly disguised as Scene, when it needs to 'hark back to make

MOLDING BELIEFS

If all this is true of fact, it is even more true of evaluative commentary. Indeed, most seeming facts carry, in fiction, a heavy load of evaluation. They order in some way the importance of the parts; they work on the beliefs of the reader.

As a rhetorician, an author finds that some of the beliefs on which a full appreciation of his work depends come ready-made, fully accepted by the postulated reader as he comes to the book, and some must be implanted or reinforced. We might expect to find that whatever space is devoted to overt rhetoric will be spent on questionable matters. Yet there is a surprising amount of commentary directed to reinforcing values which most readers, one would think, already take for granted. "There are two sorts of people, who, I am afraid, have already conceived some contempt for my hero on account of his behaviour to Sophia," says "Fielding" in *Tom Jones* (Book IV, chap. vi), and he then attempts, through ridicule, to persuade all of his readers to feel what most of them really must have felt in some degree before the passage began—that they are "the sort" who feel contempt only when it is really justified. But Fielding knows that mere agreement is not enough. Every reader knows, or thinks he knows, "the value of true love." But the author cannot count on such general agreement to be lively enough for his purposes. By making us laugh at those imaginary fools who do not know love's true worth, he at the same time makes us value it actively, in the precise form to be encountered in his book.

> Examine your heart, my good reader, and resolve whether you do believe these matters with me. If you do, you may now proceed to their exemplification in the following pages: if you do not, you have, I assure you, already read more than you have understood; and it would be wiser to pursue your business, or your pleasures (such as they are), than to throw away any more of your time in reading what you can neither taste nor comprehend. To treat of the effects of love to you, must be as absurd as to discourse on colours to a man born blind; . . . love probably may, in your opinion, very greatly resemble a dish of soup or a sirloin of roastbeef [Book VI, chap. i].

---

up' " (Robert Liddell, *Some Principles of Fiction* [London, 1953], p. 55). Another excellent defense of authorial summary can be found in Phyllis Bentley, *Some Observations on the Art of Narrative* (London, 1946).

In this way he often defines for us the precise ordering of values on which our judgment should depend. Tom's admirable "goodness of heart, and openness of temper," for example, are carefully balanced against his lack of prudence. Indispensable as they are, they are not enough. "Prudence and circumspection are necessary even to the best of men. They are indeed as it were a guard to Virtue, without which she can never be safe. It is not enough that your designs, nay that your actions are intrinsically good, you must take care they shall appear so. If your inside be never so beautiful, you must preserve a fair outside also" (Book III, chap. vii). Since in real life we do not agree about the precise ordering of "goodness of heart" and "prudence," we need such guidance—not for our own lives, but for our judgment on Tom Jones.[8]

Similar overt efforts to reinforce norms can be found in most fiction. In *Billy Budd* there is danger that the readers' admiration for Billy's integrity may be submerged beneath their contempt for his simplicity. So Melville tries to do something about it. "But shrewd ones may opine that it was hardly possible for Billy to refrain from going up to the afterguardsman and bluntly demanding to know his purpose. . . . Shrewd ones may also think it but natural in Billy to set about sounding some of the other impressed men of the ship in order to discover what basis, if any, there was for the emissary's obscure suggestions." The shrewd may question, but "something more, or rather, something else than mere shrewdness is perhaps needful for the due understanding of such a character as Billy Budd's."[9] Similarly, in *Thomas the Impostor* readers may confuse the values by which the various "heroes" are to be judged, and Cocteau intrudes unashamedly to set us straight: "Heroism gathered together a mixed group under the same palm. Many embryonic murderers found in war the opportunity, the excuse, and the reward of their vice, side by side with the martyrs." On the one hand,

---

[8] For the best discussion of the role of Tom's imprudence, and his resulting vulnerability, see R. S. Crane, "The Concept of Plot and the Plot of *Tom Jones*," *Critics and Criticism*, ed. R. S. Crane (Chicago, 1952), pp. 616–47. Crane's discussion of the narrator is also very helpful.

[9] "Billy Budd, Foretopman," in *Melville's Billy Budd*, ed. F. Barron Freeman (Cambridge, Mass., 1948), pp. 210–11.

there were the "criminals," the *Joyeux,* and on the other, the Zouaves and the marines, whose officers were "charming heroes. These young men, the bravest in the world and of whom not one remains alive, played at fighting without the least hatred. Alas, such games end badly."[10]

Finally, when Graham Greene senses, in *Brighton Rock* (1938), that we may apply the conventional standards of right and wrong rather than the required standards of Good and Evil, he does not hesitate to comment directly, distinguishing carefully between the pitiable but blessed "hole" where Rose lives, knowing "murder, copulation, extreme poverty, fidelity, and the love and fear of God," and the glaring, "open world outside" where people make a false claim to "experience."[11]

Though we find such reinforcing rhetoric even in works based on generally accepted norms, the need naturally increases whenever there is the likelihood of crippling disagreement with the reader. The skilful author will, of course, make his rhetoric in itself a pleasure to read; it is thus often difficult to tell whether a passage about values is present for its own sake, as ornament, or for a larger cause. "And so they fell to it," says the narrator of Balzac's "The High Constable's Wife" (*Droll Tales* [1832–37]), "in the time-honoured fashion, and in the delicious throes of that wild fever which you know of—at least, I hope you do—they became totally indifferent. . . ." And in the "Virgin of Thilhouse" he makes the point even more explicit by intruding to say that his "Droll Stories are designed rather to impart the morality of pleasure than to preach the pleasure of morality." The pleasure we take in such passages depends on their comic attack on conventional morality, and they are in this aspect self-justifying. Yet the attack is itself needed to insure the success of the dramatic portions of the stories. If the reader for a moment judges the characters by everyday standards of chastity and fidelity, the stories will be ruined. We might easily fall into the error of thinking that in this respect Balzac's readers came ready-made, but we can be sure that his work would

---

[10] Jean Cocteau, *Thomas the Impostor,* trans. Lewis Galantiere (London, 1925), p. 99.

[11] Part IV, chap. ii, conclusion (Penguin ed., 1943), p. 124.

not contain so much rhetoric in favor of licentiousness if he felt that he could count on his readers to accept licentiousness as a matter of course.

It is commonly believed that readers in the twentieth century have become tolerant about sexual matters. If we accepted this belief, we might expect that Balzac's kind of rhetoric about love or sexual behavior would disappear from our novels—especially since overt rhetoric of any kind has been in disfavor on technical grounds. But in fact we find great quantities of such rhetoric. Since the precise relationship of love to sex can never be taken for granted, each novelist is left to establish the world in which the loves of his characters take place. One of the most interesting and successful examples of this effort is the novel *La jument verte* by Marcel Aymé (1933). In this story there are two narrators, the unspecified author, suave, ironic, but reliable in his basic opinions, the other a painted portrait of a green mare, a kind of lustful goddess of love who blesses by her presence anyone who really understands the message of her fecundity. For proper enjoyment of this story of the comic battle between two very different brothers and their contrasting families, we must grant the superiority of the peasant-brother's open and loving sexuality over the "respectable" brother's secret pleasures. In Honoré's house, the narrator tells us again and again, love was something shared; though each member of the family drank the wine of love from his own glass, he found in it an intoxication which "brother recognized in brother, father in son, and which broke out everywhere in silent song." In Ferdinand's house this "unity of pleasure" was missing. "Each member of the family followed his own road of love in a direction which he alone knew." In the whole family, only the father "bothered himself with the secrets of the others, but that was only to persecute them."[12] Whatever the real beliefs of Aymé's readers, however free or constrained

---

[12] "Dans la maison d'Honoré, l'amour était comme le vin d'un clos familial; on le buvait chacun dans son verre, mais il procurait une ivresse que le frère pouvait reconnaître chez son frère, le père chez son fils, et qui se répandait en chansons du silence. . . . A Saint-Margelon, dans la maison de Ferdinand, cette solidarité dans le plaisir n'existait pas. Chacun cherchait son chemin d'amour dans une direction qu'il était seul à connaître. De toute la famille, il n'y avait que le vétérinaire à se préoccuper des secrets des autres, mais c'était pour les persécuter" (Paris, 1933), pp. 152–53.

they may be in their private behavior, he re-creates them temporarily in his own image—or rather, in the image of the "author" who
has his existence only in the book. We cannot infer Aymé's beliefs
or behavior with any certainty from the book, but we can infer
with some confidence what Aymé expects his postulated readers'
beliefs to be. And again it is clear that they do not come ready-
made. Even the most emancipated reader will not fall unaided into
the precise code of the Maison d'Honoré.

One would predict even more elaborate rhetoric when, instead
of elevating one recognized code over another, an author tries to
effect a transvaluation of all values, to go beyond this or that code
to entirely new territory, or to hold all values in abeyance. But intrusions used for these ends are not easy to find. Such radical transformations have generally been attempted only by the very authors
who were most strongly opposed to reliable narration. Gide, for
example, pretending to neutrality toward his characters and the
conflicts of values they face, rebukes his readers for their unfairness
in asking him to pass judgment.

> I intended to make this book as little an indictment as an apology
> and took care to pass no judgment. The public nowadays will not
> forgive an author who, after relating an action, does not declare
> himself either for or against it; more than this, during the very course
> of the drama they want him to take sides, pronounce in favor either
> of Alceste or Philinte, of Hamlet or Ophelia. . . . I do not indeed
> claim that neutrality (I was going to say "indecision") is the certain
> mark of a great mind; but I believe that many great minds have been
> very loath to . . . conclude—and that to state a problem clearly is
> not to suppose it solved in advance.[13]

If Gide really requires neutrality of his readers, then such a statement is helpful indeed. But for good or ill, nothing like it appears
within the book itself.

Intrusions about values and beliefs offer a special temptation to
the novelist, and we can all name works in which the philosopher-

---

[13] Commenting on *The Immoralist*, originally published in 1921. My quotation is from
the Introduction to the Knopf Vintage edition, 1954. On Gide's general rhetorical
program, see Kenneth Burke, "Thomas Mann and André Gide," *Counter-Statement*
(New York, 1931; 2d ed.; Los Altos, Calif., 1953), pp. 92–106, as reprinted in Zabel,
Literary Opinion in America (rev. ed.; New York, 1951).

manqué indulges in irrelevant pontification. But as we have seen (pp. 77 ff.), the quality of such passages depends far more on the quality of the author's mind than upon whether he chooses to push his profundities back into the mind of a dramatized character. One's attitude toward the much debated theorizing of Gavin Stevens at the end of Faulkner's *Intruder in the Dust* is not affected markedly by the fact that the ideas are not given directly by Faulkner. The question is whether Gavin's elaborate commentary is essentially related to the nephew's experience of a near-lynching and his consequent growth toward maturity. In any "truth-discovery" novel, and especially in novels which try to lead young people to the hard truths of adulthood, the problem is to make the discovery a convincing outcome of the experience. In *Intruder*, as in many such works, the attitude toward which Faulkner wants his young hero to grow is so complex that neither the boy nor the reader is likely to infer it from the experience itself. They both must therefore be preached at by the wise uncle, sometimes with little direct relevance to the drama. "The American really loves nothing but his automobile: not his wife his child nor his country nor even his bank-account first (in fact he doesn't really love that bank-account nearly as much as foreigners like to think because he will spend almost any or all of it for almost anything provided it is valueless enough) but his motorcar. Because the automobile has become our national sex symbol. . . ." And this goes on for page after page.

If we choose to join the chorus of protests against these pages, we must be very clear that we are not objecting to authorial commentary but rather to a particular kind of disharmony between idea and dramatized object. Even if Stevens' views could be shown to differ from Faulkner's, the discovery of irony would not save the work; the disharmony would remain. What is more, our objections would not be stronger if these opinions had been given in Faulkner's own name.

RELATING PARTICULARS TO THE ESTABLISHED NORMS

If novelists must work hard to establish their norms, they often must work even harder to make us judge their characters accurately in the light of those norms. After all, there is a measure of agreement among us about the relative value of generosity, say, as opposed to meanness, or kindness as opposed to brutality. Though some of the terms for the four cardinal virtues may, like the word virtue itself, be in disrepute, the virtues themselves are still in high esteem. But like Socrates' interlocutors, we do not agree about whether a particular action is wise, temperate, just, or courageous. Though our critical fashions do not favor talk about praising and blaming literary characters, many critical disputes still stem from our inability to agree on precise measures of praise and blame. Is Don Quixote a Christian saint or a lovable old fool?[14] Does Tom Jones go too far when he allows Lady Bellaston to buy him? Is Fleda Vetch's grand renunciation justified in *The Spoils of Poynton?*

Whenever we can easily infer what the author's own judgment is, such questions become questions about his merit: Is Faulkner justified in using the word "nun" to describe the heroine of *Requiem for a Nun?* If not, so much the worse for Faulkner. Can we allow Silone to compare Pietro Spina with Christ in *Bread and Wine?* Does Stephen's vocation, in Joyce's *Stephen Hero*, justify all of the narrator's explicit deification of the artist-God? It is true that an author can avoid crippling disagreements about such matters by concealing his own opinions. But whenever our concurrence is essential to the success of his work, he must take the opposite, more difficult, course of working to insure it.

The kind and amount of rhetoric required will depend on the precise relation between the detail of action or character to be judged and the nature of the whole in which it occurs. Most of the great storytellers of all periods have found it useful to employ direct judgment, whether in the form of descriptive adjectives or extended commentary. "And Aeneas, / Being a thoughtful father, speeds Achates," Vergil says, and we know as much about Aeneas' motives as if his thoughtfulness had been dramatized for us at great length. Ovid calls Jason "brilliant," Chaucer (or rather his Miller) calls

---

[14] For an excellent defense of Cervantes' own explicit judgments, see Oscar Mandel, "The Function of the Norm in *Don Quixote*," *Modern Philology*, LV (February, 1958), 154–63.

Nicholas "sleigh," Maupassant, who prided himself on writing "objectively," calls Pierre, in *Pierre and Jean*, "enthusiastic, intelligent, fickle, but obstinate, full of Utopias and philosophical notions," while Jean is "as gentle as his brother is unforgiving." When Zola introduces Hubert into *Le rêve*, he describes his sad and tender mouth. Unless the narrator is deceiving us, Hubert has been given a permanent trait of tenderness. The belief that tenderness is a sympathetic trait Zola—even Zola—of course takes for granted, just as Maupassant feels no need to argue that to be gentle is better than to be unforgiving.

We may for some purposes prefer the slight indirection introduced here by describing the character's mouth rather than his soul. Modern authors have often managed to give an acceptable air of objectivity while reaping all the benefits of commentary, simply by dealing largely with the appearances, the surfaces, while allowing themselves to comment freely, and sometimes in seemingly wild conjecture, on the meaning of those surfaces. "Upon the book Hightower's hands are folded, peaceful, benignant, almost pontifical," says the narrator of Faulkner's *Light in August*. This novel shows Faulkner as a master of the conjectural description which is really not conjectural at all. He is always saying that nobody could tell whether it was this or that, whether the motive was such-and-such or so-and-so, but *both* of the alternatives he suggests convey the evaluation he intends: they establish a broad band of possibilities within which the truth must lie. In another form, he gives such evaluation almost as the great epic poets would have given it, in the form of similes and metaphors, but using "as if" or "as though," rather than "as" or "like." On two pages one can find as many as fourteen evaluative comparisons, nine of them introduced with "as though" or "as if."[15] This device may for some readers serve general realistic demands—it is "as if" the author really shared the human condition to the extent of not knowing for sure how to evaluate these events. But morally the effect is still a rigorous control over the reader's own range of judgment.[16]

---

[15] *Light in August* (New York, 1932; Modern Library ed., 1933), pp. 317, 323–24.
[16] This particular device of objectivity, the artificial limitation of a narrator who in other respects shows himself to be omniscient, was foreshadowed in many comic works

Most novelists before James did not trouble about such disguises. "And he even began blubbering," Dostoevski's narrator says of old Karamazov. "He was sentimental. He was wicked and sentimental" (Modern Library ed., p. 24). And when Karamazov's behavior becomes equivocal, the narrator prevents any possible misinterpretation: "Our monastery never had played any great part in his life. . . . But he was so carried away by his simulated emotion, that he was for a moment almost believing it himself. He was so touched he was almost weeping" (p. 103). Such "unnecessary" attacks on the wicked can be matched by eulogies of the good. Even Alyosha's saintliness, which might seem obvious enough in itself, is heavily underscored.

> I would only beg the reader not to be in too great a hurry to laugh at my young hero's pure heart. I am far from intending to apologize for him or to justify his innocent faith on the ground of his youth, or the little progress he had made in his studies, or any such reason. I must declare, on the contrary, that I have genuine respect for the qualities of his heart. No doubt a youth who received impressions cautiously, whose love was lukewarm, and whose mind was too prudent for his age and so of little value, such a young man might, I admit, have avoided what happened to my hero. But in some cases it is really more creditable to be carried away by an emotion, however unreasonable, which springs from a great love, than to be unmoved. And this is even truer in youth, for a young man who is always sensible is to be suspected and is of little worth— that's my opinion! [p. 407].

This apology goes on for two more pages. If simple clarity were the author's goal, it is far too long. But for emotional emphasis it is all justifiable: we are made more deeply involved with Alyosha's fate

---

in the seventeenth and eighteenth centuries. See, for example, the anonymous work (plagiarizing heavily from Furetière's *Le roman bourgeois*) *The Temple Beau; or the Town Coquets* (London, 1754): "I could never learn any Thing more of their Courtship, than what I set down here in Publick, and even that I have pick'd up by Hear-say, and by the bye. And even (*not to lye*) I am sometimes forced to help out the Story, with some Guesses of my own" (pp. 29–30). "But unluckily for us, we know nothing certain of these Matters" (p. 36). See also *Scarron's City Romance, Made English* (1671).

through the combination of action and apology than could be accomplished with the action alone.[17]

If the saintly Alyosha can profit from such underlining, sinful or foolish characters who must be kept sympathetic may require a powerful apologetic indeed. When the silly Catherine Morland in *Northanger Abbey* (1798; 1818), for example, allows her judgment to be bought off by John Thorpe's obvious flattery (chap. vii), the narrator tells us that "had she been older or vainer, such attacks might have done little; but, where youth and diffidence are united, it requires uncommon steadiness of reason to resist the attraction of being called the most charming girl in the world, and being so very early engaged as a partner"—and the apology continues for half a page.

Such useful apologies occur, even in modern fiction, far more often than objective theories would lead us to expect. They may be completely or partially disguised as explanatory facts from the hero's early life, as in the following passage from Graham Greene's *This Gun for Hire* (1936). But the author can be seen as making his apology none the less clearly for that. "These thoughts were colder and more uncomfortable than the hail," Greene tells us of his vicious, pathetically lost little hero. "He wasn't used to any taste that wasn't bitter on the tongue." And almost imperceptibly we are led into a passage that might be put in the same form as Austen's: "Had he been. . . ."

> He had been made by hatred; it had constructed him into this thin, smoky, murderous figure in the rain, hunted and ugly. His mother had borne him when his father was in gaol, and six years later, she had cut her own throat with a kitchen knife. Afterwards there had been the home. He had never felt the least tenderness for anyone; he was made in this image, and he had his own odd pride in the result; he didn't want to be unmade. He had a sudden terrified conviction that he must be himself now as never before if he was to escape. It was not tenderness that made you quick on the draw.[18]

---

[17] I should point out that the narrator in *The Brothers Karamazov* is not always quite so reliable as he appears to be here. A good discussion of Dostoevski's use of narrators is given by Ralph E. Matlaw in *The Brothers Karamazov: Novelistic Technique* (The Hague, 1957), esp. pp. 36–41.

[18] *This Gun for Hire* (New York, 1955), pp. 55–56.

And we are led quickly back into the action. Though when taken out of context such treatment seems obvious and, as we say, unrealized, it is highly effective in its proper place, and it is certainly not noticed as a blot when one is reading the novel—unless one has learned that such passages are never allowed.

It is interesting to compare successful apologetics of this kind with the many failures that blot the history of fiction. Why should Jane Austen's defense seem proper, while the following defense of Fanny Seymour seems heavy, tasteless, and finally dishonest? "Should these Memoirs fall into the Hands of a Prude, or be read before a Circle of antiquated Maids, I know my Heroine will be reprobated by them. She yielded, say they; and be the Consequence ever so bad, she deserves it all for being a Strumpet. Let such Imps of Ill-nature . . . rail on. . . . But to my gentle Readers of another Cast, I would willingly apologize, and endeavour to rescue my Heroine from sharing too much of their Censure. . . . Pray imagine yourselves in her Situation." "Whatever were her Errors, a large Portion of Suffering was decreed to her."[19]

Though there are clues to the answer even in the isolated quotations, a full answer would require a careful analysis of both works. Note that the author is equally obtrusive, equally personal, equally biased, and equally unrealistic in both accounts. Most of the arguments against overt rhetoric which we considered in chapters ii through v apply as well to the one as to the other. To find grounds for choice we must abandon general rules and become precise: How does *this* comment, portrayed in *this* style, serve or fail to serve *this* structure? In chapter ix, I shall attempt this kind of precision with one of Jane Austen's works.

The need for authorial judgment increases, naturally enough, with an increasing complexity of virtues and vices within the same character.[20] The intensity of our tragic journey with the Mayor of

---

19 [John Cleland?], *The History of Fanny Seymour* (London, 1753), pp. 60, 319.

20 See Paul Goodman, *The Structure of Literature* (Chicago, 1954), p. 117: "Generally, in any poem where the comic and serious, or other ethical kinds, are mixed continually, there is required the systematic interference of the narrator to direct the reading." Goodman is the only author I have found who discusses this aspect of rhetoric at any length. See esp. pp. 75–76, 117–24, 158–60, 223.

Casterbridge, Hardy's great, impetuous, stumbling hero, depends partly upon the "old-fashioned" narrator's voice, telling us of complexities of which Henchard and his fellow characters are unaware. "That laugh was not encouraging to strangers. . . . Its producer's personal goodness, if he had any, would be of a very fitful cast—an occasional almost oppressive generosity rather than a mild and constant kindness" (chap. v). "With all domestic finesse he was hopelessly at variance. Loving a man or hating him, his diplomacy was as wrongheaded as a buffalo's" (chap. xvii). Henchard "might not inaptly be described as Faust has been described—as a vehement gloomy being who had quitted the ways of vulgar men without light to guide him on a better way" (chap. xvii).

Most great writers of fiction—and I include, of course, the authors of verse epic—have in fact worked with a rich spectrum of values. No other art, indeed, is so well suited to the portrayal of characters who are complex mixtures of good and bad, of the admirable and the contemptible. Even drama, which comes closest to rivaling fiction, must ordinarily rely on relatively simple dichotomies of heart and head. It is true that some few plays can accommodate a Hamlet or a Macbeth, but even in these most complex of dramatic characters we do not find anything so intricate as Faulkner's Ike McCaslin or as the sympathetic murderer Raskolnikov, embodying as part of his "excuse" the intellectual history of a generation. It may be that some dramatic characters are *conceived* in such complexity, but no spectator in a two-hour production can ever hope to assimilate conflict on so many planes and with so many religious, philosophical, and political overtones.

Instead of comparing fiction unfavorably with music and drama, then, why should we not expect other arts to aspire enviously to the condition of fiction? Actually, neither expectation makes good sense; though we may, in our search for aesthetic constants, find some qualities common to all art, each art thrives when it pursues its own unique possibilities. At any rate, we need not apologize for an art that can give form to moral complexities like those that the narrator helps us to see in *A Passage to India.* "A friendliness, as of dwarfs shaking hands, was in the air. Both man and woman were at the height of their powers—sensible, honest, even subtle. They spoke the same language, and held the same opinions, and the variety of age and sex did not divide them. Yet they were dissatisfied . . ." (Modern Library ed., p. 264). One is struck by the extraordinary wealth of this judgment on Fielding and Miss Quested, as compared with the relative poverty of the characters' own judgments. "As of dwarfs shaking hands"—no one in the book is capable of that simile except the narrator, the one character who sees the full value of being sensible, honest, and subtle, and yet sees that men and women may exemplify these virtues and still be only amiable dwarfs.

Where are the dramatic devices that are suited to present economically the picture which Conrad, violating the principles which Ford attributes to him, gives us of Decoud in *Nostromo* (1904): "This life, whose dreary superficiality is covered by the glitter of universal blague, like the stupid clowning of a harlequin by the spangles of a motley costume, induced in him a Frenchified—but most un-French—cosmopolitanism, in reality a mere barren indifferentism posing as intellectual superiority" (Modern Library ed., p. 168)? Or this picture of the doctor, including as it does details that no one, not even the subject himself, could know? "People believed him scornful and soured," a bit of gossip which *he* presumably does not know about. "The truth of his nature consisted in his capacity for passion and in the timidity of his temperament. What he lacked was the polished callousness of men of the world, the callousness from which springs an easy tolerance for one's self and others; the tolerance wide as poles asunder from true sympathy and human compassion. This want of callousness accounted for his sardonic turn of mind and his biting speeches" (p. 581). No reader could ever infer such an intricate judgment from the actions and speech of a man who has deceived everyone around him. Yet the judgment springs from and is adequately supported by what is shown. The telling has here revealed to us an almost inaccessible but indispensable part of the dramatic object itself.

The full importance of these first three functions can be seen most clearly in an extended example showing a work "before" and "after" revision. To be convincing, such an example must show the author himself wrestling with difficulties that are best solved by

using old-fashioned devices. Clear-cut illustrations of such complicated matters are naturally not easy to find. But fortunately most of
what we need is shown in F. Scott Fitzgerald's efforts to find the
right way to tell *Tender Is the Night*.

Just as critics have long puzzled over the comparative failure of
Fitzgerald, compared, that is, with what we might have expected
from him after the triumph of *The Great Gatsby* in 1925, so did
Fitzgerald puzzle over the comparative failure of *Tender Is the
Night*. The first edition of 1934 did not satisfy him—and not only
because public response was much slower than he had hoped. He
went on tinkering with the book almost until his death, and though
he probably never completed the revision to his satisfaction, Mal-
colm Cowley was able to issue in 1953 a version of the book which
Fitzgerald had called "final."[21]

The two versions now in print do not seem to differ radically
(though there are earlier manuscript versions that are almost unrec-
ognizable). In the first edition, we are initially confined to the
point of view of the seventeen-year-old Rosemary as an affair develops between her and the hero, Dick Diver. After one hundred
and fifty pages the reliable narrator takes over and tells us in four
pages exactly what Dick was like in his more "heroic period" eight
years before. Then, using chiefly Dick's own vision, he shows us in
a few brief episodes how the brilliant, generous, young psychiatrist
came to marry his rich patient, Nicole Warren, and thus unknow-
ingly began his long decline into the drunken obscurity with which
the novel ends.

In Fitzgerald's revision, the major difference is that the sixty
pages from the heroic youthful period are restored to the beginning
of the book. We arrive at Rosemary's view of Dick only after we
have come to know him in a more intimate view than Rosemary
ever achieves.

How does one go about deciding whether such a revision is an
improvement? Obviously we can get little help from considering

---

[21] I am entirely dependent for the facts in my account on Cowley's excellent Introduction and Notes to *Tender* in *Three Novels of F. Scott Fitzgerald* (New York, 1953).
My page references are to Cowley's text. His interpretation of the merit of the two
published versions, with which I mainly agree, has also been useful.

the general qualities of style or technique that we discussed in chapters ii–v. The versions are equally inconsistent in the use of point of view. Both versions move irregularly in and out of characters' minds, with corrective or supporting commentary freely provided by the reliable, privileged narrator. When Dick suspects Baby Warren of planning to capture him for her sister, for example, the narrator leaves Dick's point of view to say, "He was wrong; Baby Warren had no such intentions. She had looked Dick over . . . and found him wanting" (p. 49). The two versions are equally helped or harmed, in their realistic quality, by such intrusions: a four-page disquisition by the reliable narrator is as artificial when it begins on the first page as when it comes one-third of the way through.

There is one general principle of realistic narration, popular at the time, that might lead us to choose the earlier version: It is "unrealistic" to begin at the beginning and plod methodically through to the end. Under the impact of James's insistence on presenting one troubled vision through another troubled vision, and of the experiments by Conrad and others with distorted chronologies, there had by the mid-twenties developed a theory that a technique using flashbacks was more realistic than the old-fashioned, routine chronology. "It became very early evident to us," Ford had written of himself and Conrad, one year before Fitzgerald began *Tender* in 1925, "that what was the matter with the Novel, and the British novel in particular, was that it went straight forward, whereas in your gradual making acquaintanceship with your fellows you never do go straight forward." To get a vivid impression of any strong character in fiction, "you could not begin at his beginning and work his life chronologically to the end. You must first get him in with a strong impression, and then work backwards and forwards over his past."[22] A great many of the most serious young novelists were by this time not only following Ford's principle but repudiating traditional notions of plot altogether. And by 1933 when Fitzgerald was working to complete his first printed version, he had available as

---

[22] *Joseph Conrad: A Personal Remembrance* (Boston, 1924), pp. 129–30. See Joseph Warren Beach, *The Twentieth-Century Novel* (New York, 1932), pp. 359–65, for a good discussion of Conrad's transformations of chronology.

models dozens of much praised works which first got their heroes in "with a strong impression" and then filled in the chronology; most notably, he had the success of his own *The Great Gatsby*, in which the technique of the flashback had been highly effective.

We can probably never learn how far such general considerations influenced his decision in favor of the original flashback. But if they were important to him in 1934 when he published *Tender* with great hopes for its success, by December, 1938, when he proposed the restoration of chronological order to Maxwell Perkins (p. v), his attention was entirely on the special requirements of Dick Diver's story. However appropriate chronological shifts may be for Conrad or Ford or Huxley or Dos Passos, however appropriate they may be even for the story of Jay Gatsby, Dick Diver's kind of tragedy requires a different rhetoric.

Long before the publication of the first edition Fitzgerald had seen that his story was to be Dick Diver's tragedy. "The novel should do this," he wrote in 1932, "show a man who is a natural idealist, a spoiled priest, giving in for various causes to the ideas of the haute bourgeoisie, and in his rise to the top of the social world losing his idealism, his talent and turning to drink and dissipation. Background one in which the leisure class is at their truly most brilliant and glamourous" (p. x). It is true that he expressed his purpose differently at different times, and it may be, as Cowley suggests, that he could never fully harmonize the different intentions of the different drafts.[23] But once he saw clearly that his story was to be Dick Diver's tragedy, he never changed his emphasis: he wanted to show the destruction of a man, not simply give a convincing impression of this or that character or milieu. The emphasis is on Dick's "giving in" and "turning to" his moral destruction. If this is so, any technical stroke should be judged on its service in realizing Dick's tragedy.

The problem is, then, to decide in terms of detailed effects what is accomplished by the transposed section in each of its positions.

---

[23] See also Arthur Mizener, "F. Scott Fitzgerald: The Poet of Borrowed Time," *Critiques and Essays on Modern Fiction: 1920–1951*, ed. John W. Aldridge (New York, 1952), pp. 286–302, esp. pp. 297–99. The essay was first printed in *Sewanee Review*, Winter, 1946.

In both positions, it seems most clearly accounted for as performing the three functions I have described above, particularly the last two. The facts about Dick Diver and Nicole and the norms according to which the narrator judges them are described most directly in this section. The narrator describes Dick authoritatively as a brilliant, promising, twenty-six-year-old bachelor, a "fine age for a man," the "very acme of bachelorhood," a "fine age for Dick." He is charming, capable of giving and inspiring affection, "lucky," a "genius," an "idealist" but, unlike many idealists, he is aware that the good fortune that makes his "idealism" possible is itself a kind of vulnerability. He is capable of genuine love; he can give himself far more than most men. He wants desperately to be good and kind and courageous, and for the most part he succeeds, as we see again and again in this section. He is physically strong and attractive; he is expert with people, possessing exquisite tact and sensitivity. Though attracted by youth and freshness, he can see the phoniness of the American worship of Hollywood's idea of youthfulness. In short, he is so dangerously close to a caricature of all the Fitzgeraldian virtues that a skeleton account like this, unrelieved by the drama in which the virtues are exemplified, makes him sound a bit ridiculous.

Set against his near perfection are the flaws in his character and the many threats of the world surrounding him. His flaws are few, but ominous. He occasionally cannot resist striving for mere charm, as in the scene with Kaethe Gregorovius which leads him to curse himself as "like all the rest after all" (p. 23). What is more important, there is something threatening about the very approach to fulness and perfection that he makes. "He wanted to be good, he wanted to be kind, he wanted to be brave and wise, but it was all pretty difficult. He wanted to be loved, too, if he could fit it in." Most ominously, he is determined to know misfortune (how can one be perfect without it?); he feels guilty about his luck. He is, in short, ready to make some fatal mistake. As the narrator says, men and women had made much of him, and he had an intuition that this was not too good for a serious man.

The world surrounding Dick, in its empty and vicious modernity, is used both to heighten our sense of his unique value and to increase our sense of his vulnerability. Dick is, in fact, caught between two worlds: the world of his aspirations—romantic, a bit "Victorian" (p. 236), as he says, believing in "good instinct," honor, courtesy, and courage (p. 221)—and the postwar world of Baby Warren—valueless, drifting, incapable of understanding the achievement that Dick cares for, willing, in fact, to buy Dick as a husband for Nicole in the hope of using him to cure her. Much of the worst side of this world is established in other sections of the book, but the contrast itself is built firmly in this earliest period of Dick's life.

Now our intellectual picture of this man and of the two worlds he moves between is identical in the two versions. Whatever moral or social themes help to hold this work together are left unchanged from version to version. What *is* changed, radically, is the reader's emotional attachment to Dick. To begin the novel part-way down the slope, as it were, confined to the confused vision of a secondary character, is to sacrifice some of our attachment to Dick and consequently a good deal of the poignant dramatic irony as we watch him move to his doom.

It is true that we gain other effects by this costly flashback. As Cowley says, the original beginning from Rosemary's point of view is much more scintillating, exotic, mysterious. It arouses curiosity about Nicole's baffling illness and about what Violet McKisko saw in the bathroom at the Villa Diana; it mystifies us not only about how Dick initially launched himself on the path to failure but at first even about whether he is the main character. The love affair between Dick and Rosemary is, finally, much more charming in this version; we do not see it as a clear step in the destruction of a man we have come to admire.

But exoticism and mystery and charm are not qualities to be sought at all costs in all novels. *This* novel requires strong sympathy for Dick Diver. "That book is not dead," Fitzgerald wrote. "I meet people constantly who have the same exclusive attachment to it as others had to *Gatsby* . . . people who identified themselves with Dick Diver. Its great fault is that the true beginning—the young psychiatrist in Switzerland—is tucked away in the middle of the book" (p. v). If "identification" with Dick is to be one standard of this book's success, Rosemary's angle of vision is not adequate at the beginning; it cannot establish the contrast between Dick and the world that is pulling him down. Her vision of Dick is almost immediately clouded by infatuation; we cannot gather from it even whether he is genuinely attractive, since she seems to be ready to fall in love with almost any handsome man. Far less is she adequate to present the complicated picture of Dick's position midway from happy promise to failure. Seeing through her eyes, we enter the novel, as Cowley says, with uncertain focus (p. ix), and the result is that though we gradually come to care about Dick, even in this first version, we do so hesitantly and to some extent too late.

We can see this sacrifice clearly by taking a close look at any crucial episode in both versions and comparing our responses. Consider, for example, the scene in which Rosemary has learned that Nicole and Dick are to meet for love-making at four. If we read Rosemary's jealous reactions ("It was more difficult than she thought and her whole self protested as Nicole drove away") without ever having seen Dick's and Nicole's love in the early years, and without knowing anything of all the qualities besides sex that enter into that love, we can hardly avoid feeling all on the side of Rosemary: too bad about that poor man trapped by the mysterious and obviously dangerous Nicole. But in the revised version our sympathies are properly divided: we see two women fighting over the drowning man, himself a victim of both, though each is in her own way sympathetic. A fairly trivial affair has been transformed, through proper preparation, into a significant step in a moral collapse that none of the principals sees as clearly as we do.

The achievement of the revision is, in short, to correct a fault of over-distancing, a fault that springs from a method appropriate to other works at other times but not to the tragedy Fitzgerald wanted to write. His true effect could be obtained only by repudiating much of what was being said by important critics of fiction about point of view and developing a clean, direct, old-fashioned presentation of his hero's initial pre-eminence and gradual decline.

HEIGHTENING THE SIGNIFICANCE OF EVENTS

Commentary about the moral and intellectual qualities of characters always affects our view of the events in which those characters act. It consequently shades over imperceptibly into direct statements about the meaning and importance of events themselves. "Next day," Hardy tells us in "The Three Strangers," "the quest for the clever sheep-stealer became general and keen, to all appearance at least. But the intended punishment was cruelly disproportioned to the transgression, and the sympathy of a great many country-folk in that district was strongly on the side of the fugitive. Moreover, his marvelous coolness and daring . . . won their admiration. . . ." Such talk sets up explicitly an emotional interest of the kind that any dramatized injustice sets up implicitly: a strong pull toward either a restoration of justice or a tragic denouement. The same kind of commentary can be used to heighten the significance of the resolution when it comes. "Having placed my heroine in the happiest of all happy situations," says the reliable narrator, ostensibly a male, of Sarah Fielding's *History of Betty Barnes* (1753), "loving, and fondly beloved by a man of sense and virtue, dear to his relations, and caressed by all his friends, I shall now bid her adieu" (p. 298). And "he" then gives us, in a heavy-handed imitation of Sarah's brother, Henry, a point-blank description of the moral of the tale.

Direct commentary of this kind on the event is likely to seem more obtrusive than commentary about the characters; it can, indeed, be very bad when it is used as a substitute for, rather than a heightening of, the event itself. Knowing this danger, novelists very early developed methods for disguising their portents as part of the represented object. Long before the dogmas about showing rather than telling became fashionable, authors often concealed their commentary by dramatizing it as scenery or symbol. Such implicit commentary can, like the natural setting in *Wuthering Heights* or the fog in *Bleak House*, be very effective. But though seemingly more dramatic it can be fully as tiresome as the worst direct address to the reader. When every bad turn in the plot is foreshadowed by a turn in the weather, when every murder takes place at the stroke

of midnight, the effect becomes less dramatic than a simple statement by the narrator that the future is blacker than it looks. In
Manon Lescaut (1733), for example, although the Chevalier's an-
ticipatory lamentations may seem inept, a burst of gothic omens
like the rumblings of old Vesuvius in Mrs. Radcliffe's *The Italian*
(1797) would be worse. To my taste many of the symbols employed in modern fiction as a substitute for commentary are fully
as obtrusive as the most direct commentary might be. One's taste
changes in such matters, of course. At one time the invention of
the turtle, heading southwest across the highway in *The Grapes of
Wrath* (1939), paralleling in his direction, his helplessness, his determination, and his pace the Joads' hopeless, dogged lives, may
seem brilliant, while Tolstoy's interchapters seem heavy and lum-
bering and obvious. But after twenty years that turtle seems decidedly outmoded and obtrusive, and Tolstoy's commentary, nearly
a century old, has somehow taken on a new vitality. Symbolic commentary, like any other kind, must be done with genius, or at least
with craftsmanship, if it is to endure beyond the shifts in fashion.

GENERALIZING THE SIGNIFICANCE OF THE WHOLE WORK

All of these kinds of commentary serve the purpose of heightening
the intensity with which the reader experiences particular moments
in a book. Though they may do other things as well, they are primarily justified by some service they perform in molding the reader's judgment on one scale of values or another.

Many of these rhetorical tasks could have been performed,
though less economically, without explicit commentary. But as we
turn to the task of generalizing the effect of the entire work, making it seem to have a universal or at least representative quality beyond the literal facts of the case, it is not so clear that other devices can even approximately serve. "That things are not so ill with
you and me as they might have been," George Eliot tells us in
Middlemarch (1871–72), "is half owing to the number who," like
her heroine, "lived faithfully a hidden life, and rest in unvisited
tombs." It is conceivable that some responsible spokesman like
Conrad's Marlow could have been given this speech, but it could

never come with authority from any character fully involved in the action.²⁴

No character in *Tom Jones*, no character in *Bleak House*, *The Scarlet Letter*, or *War and Peace*, knows enough about the meaning of the whole to go beyond his personal problems to any general view. Since the same is true of almost all modern works, and since reliable narration is often not allowed, the task of generalization may be left entirely to the reader. No narrator's voice extends the significance of *The Sun Also Rises*—except, of course, to provide the generalizing title and epigraphs.²⁵

Still, even in modern works, most authors incorporate more direct generalizing commentary than one would think on reading the critics. In *Decline and Fall*, for example, published in the late twenties when the passion for dramatic objectivity was perhaps at its highest, Waugh allows his narrator almost no generalizing intrusions, but when he gives one at last, it is extremely important:

> For an evening at least the shadow that has flitted about this narrative under the name of Paul Pennyfeather materialized into the solid figure of an intelligent, well-educated, well-conducted young man, a man who could be trusted to use his vote at a general election with discretion and proper detachment, whose opinion on a ballet or a critical essay was rather better than most people's, who

---

24 The best defense of this kind of commentary is W. J. Harvey's "George Eliot and the Omniscient Author Convention," *Nineteenth-Century Fiction*, XIII (September, 1958), 81–108. In dealing with what he considers the misleading "post-Jamesian" critical "dogmas" of impersonal narration, Harvey makes a compelling case for George Eliot's skill in the use of commentary. He concludes his essay with a plea for a book that might go beyond his "crude" distinction between the Jamesian and non-Jamesian modes, a book that might make finer discriminations "by judicious use of literary history, by analysis of technical devices and also by a closer study of the kinds of relationship assumed or created between author, reader and novel. A study of this sort would be vast, complex and arduous; in such a perspective this essay must dwindle to the status of a footnote" (p. 108). I first read this passage when my book was almost completed; in some respects I have attempted to write the kind of book Harvey seems to have in mind. My willingness to let his fine essay "dwindle to the status of a footnote" does not mean, however, that I pretend to have given him the book he asked for.

25 It is interesting to note how much more importance titles and epigraphs take on in modern works, where they are often the only explicit commentary the reader is given: *Portrait of the Artist as a Young Man, The Sun Also Rises, Vile Bodies, A Handful of Dust, Brave New World, Antic Hay, The Sound and the Fury*—strange titles these for a literature that rises unauthored from the waves of art.

could order a dinner without embarrassment and in a creditable French accent, who could be trusted to see to luggage. . . . This was the Paul Pennyfeather who had been developing in the placid years which preceded this story. In fact, the whole of this book is really an account of the mysterious disappearance of Paul Pennyfeather, so that readers must not complain if the shadow which took his name does not amply fill the important part of hero for which he was originally cast. . . . For an evening Paul became a real person again, but next day he woke up leaving himself disembodied somewhere between Sloane Square and Onslow Square.[26]

In a satiric work of this kind such talk is fully appropriate and acceptable. The invention, later in the book, of a Professor Otto Silenus to speak wisdom at us is much less effective, however objective or dramatic it may seem.

How we feel about generalizing commentary will depend partly on the fashions of the moment but more basically on the author's skill in suiting its quality to the quality of his dramatic portions. The Vanity Fair presented in *Vile Bodies* or *Decline and Fall* could never support the narrator's loquacity in *Vanity Fair* itself. But for Thackeray's highly general, expansive kind of satire such loquacity is clearly useful. "Ah! *Vanitas Vanitatum!* Which of us is happy in this world? Which of us has his desire? or, having it, is satisfied?— Come, children, let us shut up the box and the puppets, for our play is played out." Waugh's reticence would partially ruin the conclusion to *Vanity Fair*, as it would ruin *Bleak House, Middlemarch*, and *The Egoist*. As modern novelists like Faulkner have rediscovered, the very effort of the narrator to wrestle explicitly with his world of values can make even the most insignificant characters seem of world-shaking importance. Though garrulity in narrators is as tedious as garrulity in acquaintances, though commenting narrators are, in fact, peculiarly tempted to be pompous and redundant, at their best they can yield a breadth of experience unlike that provided by any other artistic device. "The Preedy-Syson slander case at once made headlines: a minister on one side, a parson on the other, a charge of immorality with a young girl"—so far Joyce Cary's narrator in *The Captive and the Free* (1959) gives us only

---

[26] London, 1928; Penguin ed., 1937, pp. 122–23.

the facts. But in this posthumous work Cary does not follow his usual practice of leaving his opinions about the event to inference. And how fortunate that he did not.

> It had everything to stir the deepest, most primitive feelings. Those who hated the headlines, as Hooper pointed out, hated them simply because they did concern those powerful senses; those everlasting preoccupations. For the less Britons go to church, the more they are troubled by religious problems, moral issues. They are like refugees whose cities have been bombed. All at once they reveal the fundamental needs of their souls—men who thought little of a comfortable home are seen painfully cobbling a shack of a few sticks and an old blanket to give themselves and their families a habitation in the wilderness of ruin. And for this shelter the desperate owner will fight to the death.
>
> So atheists do battle for the ideal dignity of mathematics, and scientists war savagely among themselves about the moral responsibility of atomic physicists for the atom bomb. Rationalists rush from their holes at the very sight of a gaiter and positivist philosophers bark all night at the whisper of a loving couple in the back lane.
>
> For among the displaced it's every man for himself—all neighbours are enemies and all possessions are a provocation to somebody [chap. xxvii].

Anyone who thinks that he could have inferred this meaning in such poignant form from the dramatized events alone has a high opinion of his own novelistic powers. Though the Preedy-Syson slander case does in fact support the judgment, Cary confers more representative value upon his story than it would seem to have without his direct and unembarrassed aid.

MANIPULATING MOOD

So far we have considered only commentary which is about something clearly dramatized in the work. The authors have simply tried to make clear to us the nature of the dramatic object itself, by giving us the hard facts, by establishing a world of norms, by relating particulars to those norms, or by relating the story to general truths. In so doing, authors are in effect exercising careful control over the reader's degree of involvement in or distance from the events of the story, by insuring that the reader views the materials with the degree of detachment or sympathy felt by the implied author.

A different element enters when an author intrudes to address the reader's moods and emotions directly. "There are certain themes of which the interest is all-absorbing, but which are too entirely horrible for the purposes of legitimate fiction. . . . To be buried while alive is, beyond question, the most terrific of the extremes which has ever fallen to the lot of mere mortality." When Poe begins "The Premature Burial" (1844) in this way and continues for several pages with talk about the horror of premature burial, and about its frequency, we feel that something is wrong. He is addressing us directly, immediately, attempting to put us into a frame of mind *before* his story begins; it is difficult for us to resist boredom or annoyance. "Fearful indeed the suspicion [that such events occur]—but more fearful the doom! It may be asserted, without hesitation, that no event is so terribly well adapted to inspire the supremeness of bodily and of mental distress, as is burial before death." Whatever the effect of this kind of thing on Poe's original magazine readers, one can hardly believe that experienced readers have ever been very strongly moved by it.

We might at first be tempted to blame the superlatives; after all, one remembers so many other "supreme" horrors in other Poe stories. But such superlatives would be much more acceptable if reserved to describe the actual plight of the victim during his interment. Just as Melville's "Shakespearean" commentary seems ludicrously exaggerated when read in extracts from *Moby Dick* but usually seems unobjectionable and appropriate in context, so this prose, bad as it seems in isolation, might in a proper setting be acceptable. But the story provides it with no context. It is isolated rhetoric, the author in his own name and person doing what he can, with all the stops pulled, to work us into a proper mood before his story begins. "Get ready to shudder," he seems to say, and like the voice of the commentator in a bad documentary film, he is divorced from the effects of his own rhetoric.

If we compare this with the fully integrated mood-building of a better story, "The Fall of the House of Usher" (1839), we see one reason for the frequent insistence that indispensable commentary be spoken by a character in the story.

> During the whole of a dull, dark, and soundless day in the autumn of the year, when the clouds hung oppressively low in the heavens, I had been passing alone, on horseback, through a singularly dreary tract of country, and at length found myself, as the shades of the evening drew on, within view of the melancholy House of Usher. I know not how it was—but, with the first glimpse of the building, a sense of insufferable gloom pervaded my spirit. I say insufferable; for the feeling was unrelieved by any of that half-pleasurable, be- cause poetic, sentiment, with which the mind usually receives even the sternest natural images of the desolate or terrible.

By the simple expedient of creating a· character who experiences the rhetoric in his own person, it has been made less objectionable. Every adjective and detail intended to set our mood is a part of the growing mood and experience of the central character; the rhetoric now seems functional, "intrinsic." It is no longer simply directed outward—as if it were a drug that could be injected into the specta- tor on his way into the theater.

We might easily make the mistake, however, of generalizing falsely from this comparison. It does not follow either that com- mentary is always effective so long as it is spoken by a character in the story or that this story would be further improved by revealing more and more of its tone through dramatized detail and less and less through narrative statement. Caroline Gordon and Allen Tate view this story as an important step, but a step only, in the grand progress toward the mastery of "*creative, active detail* which came into this tradition of fiction with Flaubert, to be perfected later by James, Chekhov, and Joyce."[27] To them, since the story has "not one instance of dramatized detail," it is still only half-realized. What they are really asking is that *all* general commentary, unre- lieved by irony, should be eliminated. The narrator must not say "bleak walls," or "vacant eye-like windows," or "black and lurid tarn that lay in unruffled lustre." The walls and windows and tarn should be dramatically portrayed in order to be made visually alive with their bleakness and vacuity and luridness *shown* to the reader rather than merely *told*. This seems to me a demand that springs from the prejudices of an age desiring effects basically different

---

[27] *The House of Fiction* (New York, 1950), p. 116.

from Poe's. For Poe's special kind of morbid horror, a psychological detail, as conveyed by an emotionally charged adjective, is more effective than mere sensual description in any form. Whatever may be wrong with the "Fall of the House of Usher" is not to be cured by changing the technique. If I am now unable to react as Poe intended, it seems quite clear that I would not do so no matter what technique he used. Those of us who can remember a time when Poe *was* effective know how indispensable the heavy adjectives are.

We can admit that mood-setting commentary, like philosophizing, presents special difficulties, and indeed is very likely to lead the author into practices that justify attacks on commentary. It is nevertheless true that many great authors have used it and used it well. "The morning was one peculiar to that coast. Everything was mute and calm; everything grey. The sea, though undulated into long roods of swells, seemed fixed, and was sleeked at the surface like waved lead that has cooled and set in the smelter's mould. The sky seemed a grey surtout. Flights of troubled grey fowl, kith and kin with flights of troubled grey vapours among which they were mixed, skimmed low and fitfully over the waters, as swallows over meadows before storms. Shadows present, foreshadowing deeper shadows to come."

It is harder than we might think to give solid reasons why this opening to Melville's "Benito Cereno" (1855) seems so much more acceptable than the mood-building in "The Premature Burial." One certainly cannot settle the question by appeal to rules about point of view. Neither author makes any effort to disguise the source of the commentary; Melville does not try to convince us that Captain Delano himself felt the foreshadowing of deeper shadows to come. Both authors are clearly addressing us directly, rhetorically. Though Melville seems somewhat more interested than Poe in describing *things*, Poe's topic is more explicitly related to the subject of his story, and hence more nearly "intrinsic" in that respect. One must surely feel uncomfortable if he must decide that Melville's superiority lies simply in the obvious ruse of inventing a gloomy day—and anyway, Poe can match that one with a dozen equally clever and equally obvious. Finally, it may be true that part of Poe's difficulty lies in his reminding us that he is telling the story simply to horrify us. To say, "There is probably nothing more ominous than . . ." seems to suggest, "I have looked around a bit and have come up with the most ominous subject I could find." To impugn the autonomy of the action, to suggest that one can make of a story whatever one pleases, has been counted a serious crime ever since James expressed his shock at Trollope's playful, noisy meddling with his character's lives. But it is not hard to find highly successful commentary that breaks even this rule, as I shall show in the next chapter. And if I am right in this, we are left with a rule that says simply, "When you do such-and-such badly, it will be bad."

I am not at all sure that I know why I like the Melville better than the Poe. But I feel fairly confident about where to look for an answer: I must look very closely at the commentary itself, as it relates to its unique context. As I do so I am almost certain to appeal, finally, to some standards that are common to many stories. For example, the Poe commentary is "too long"; it is wasteful, uneconomical. Obviously, "economy" is a general standard, but I discover a particular economy in each story, according to which a given element is or is not "too much." (Is Shakespeare economical? He is—usually—in establishing his peculiarly rich economies.) And even a fairly inexperienced writer could be trusted, after reading "The Premature Burial" several times, to discover ways of shortening the preliminaries with no losses and some real gains. But few of us would feel comfortable attempting the same operation on the opening of "Benito Cereno"—and not simply because the introductory material is much shorter and the story itself much longer.

We could go on through other criteria, attempting to mediate between general standards that are often useful and the particular needs of each story. Is the style, for example, "fresh," "interesting," "appropriate"? Though to be acceptable a style must always be interesting in some way, there is no general quality of style—for example, "be concrete!"—that must be in all works in the same form. One could show, I think, that Melville's style does what is required of it without introducing distracting or misleading interests, while Poe's constantly reminds us that the author does not care very much about what he is doing.

The author may intrude, in short, even to work upon our emotions directly, provided he can convince us that his "intrusions" are at least as carefully wrought and as pertinent as his presented scenes.

COMMENTING DIRECTLY ON THE WORK ITSELF

If direct appeals to the reader's moods and emotions have been thought objectionable, direct appeals for his admiration should seem even more so. Not only do they have no immediate relationship to other elements in the story, but they frequently call the reader's attention explicitly to the fact that he is reading just a story. It was certainly this kind of intrusion to which James objected most strenuously, and it is perhaps the kind which has been most widely avoided in modern fiction.[28] Any kind of praise of one's work for its artistry implies, it might seem, a lack of reality in the world with which one's artistry deals. And certainly any direct self-praise by the author, however wittily disguised, is likely to suggest that he can do as he will with his characters.

But to argue in this way is again to substitute general ends for that kind of particular study which makes technical conclusions possible. There may be some fictional effects which are always ruined by any suggestion of the author's direct presence, though I can discover none. It is only certain kinds of authors who must not be present at certain kinds of events.

All successful novelists show much more care about their self-conscious commentary than one would think from reading critical attacks since Flaubert. Trollope, for example, who can indeed be unpleasantly garrulous and who does sometimes make us wish he

---

[28] There have been, it is true, many self-conscious narrators in modern fiction, but they have almost all been dramatized as unreliable characters quite distinct from their authors. The narrators of Mann's *Dr. Faustus* and *The Holy Sinners,* of Gide's *Les faux monnayeurs,* and of Huxley's *Point Counter Point,* all engage in strongly implied praise for the works they are writing, but despite their pretensions, they are writing works rather strikingly different from the actual novels of Mann, Gide, and Huxley.

would stop praising himself and get on with his story, ordinarily respects his materials fully. Only very rarely does he commit the sin, if it really is a sin, of suggesting that the events of the book can be altered to suit his pleasure. The suggestion is only that *how he tells* about the events can be altered, as in the famous intrusion into *Barchester Towers* (1857):

> But let the gentle-hearted reader be under no apprehension whatsoever. It is not destined that Eleanor shall marry Mr. Slope or Bertie Stanhope. And here, perhaps, it may be allowed to the novelist to explain his views on a very important point in the art of telling tales. He ventures to reprobate that system which goes so far to violate all proper confidence between the author and his readers, by maintaining nearly to the end of the third volume a mystery as to the fate of their favorite personage. . . .
>
> Our doctrine is, that the author and the reader should move along together in full confidence with each other. Let the personages of the drama undergo ever so complete a comedy of errors among themselves, but let the spectator never mistake the Syracusan for the Ephesian; otherwise he is one of the dupes, and the part of a dupe is never dignified [end of chap. xv].

Here the characters' lives are inviolable; what may be manipulated is only the relation of the author and reader to those lives, and the author, in praising his own mastery, heightens the comedy of these petty but representative lives which he is using for our pleasure. Most of Trollope's intrusions show precisely this attitude, even when they remind us most directly that the book is a book: "But we must go back a little, it shall be but a little, for a difficulty begins to make itself manifest in the necessity of disposing of all our friends in the small remainder of this one volume. Oh, that Mr. Longman would allow me a fourth!" (chap. xliii). To "dispose of" all our friends is not in this context to do with them as we please. The author is facing the facts of their lives, manifold and difficult, and he recruits the reader with him for the comic battle to do justice to their lives in spite of Mr. Longman, the publisher.

Intrusions discussing the book itself or its frailties can range from a "meanwhile" or explicit digression to the most elaborate burlesque of the technique of other authors. "I should have told you, gentle reader," says the narrator of *The History of Joshua Trueman*,

Esq. (1754; p. 91), and we are likely to feel that we are in clumsy hands; either he genuinely forgot to tell us something or he deliberately held something back simply for his own convenience; in either case, he was not so skilful as he might have been. Realizing this, cleverer narrators have always doctored such intrusions sufficiently to suggest that they know as much about the clichés as any reader possibly can. "We must now return, as the novelists say, and as we all wish they wouldn't, to the man from Somewhere," says one of Dickens' characters, himself telling a story, in *Our Mutual Friend* (1864–65; chap. ii). Such intrusions, half apology, half self-praise, are plentiful throughout the history of fiction. They can be delightful or annoying, depending on the genius of the writer, the taste of the reader, the fashions of the time, and the kind of work in which they occur; "qualitative" pleasures are often highly dependent on fad, and what in one decade may seem a grace will in the next be hopelessly outmoded. The following passage from *The Old Curiosity Shop* (1841) would set most modern readers' teeth on edge, but it was no doubt considered one of the graces of Dickens' work by many of his contemporaries.

> As the course of this tale requires that we should become acquainted, somewhere hereabouts, with a few particulars connected with the domestic economy of Mr. Sampson Brass, and as a more convenient place ... is not likely to occur for the purpose, the historian takes the friendly reader by the hand, and springing with him into the air, and cleaving the same at a greater rate then ever Don Cleophas Leandro Perez Zambullo and his familiar travelled through that pleasant region in company, alights, with him upon the pavement of Bevis Marks. The intrepid aeronauts alight before a small dark house, once the residence of Mr. Sampson Brass [chap. xxxiii].

Is this not mere toying while the important matters go unheeded?

Certainly in some novels the charge is unanswerable: "toying" becomes an end in itself. In *Charlotte Summers*,[29] for example, the task of changing a scene is expanded, as it is occasionally in *Tom Jones*, to a very long paragraph.

> Before I introduce my Readers into the Company of Miss *Charlotte Summers*, I must make them acquainted with some of her

---

[29] *The History of Charlotte Summers, the Fortunate Parish Girl* (London, 1749?).

Friends . . . for which Purpose, I must beg their Company as far as *Carmarthenshire*, in *Wales*. Tho' the Journey is pretty long, and, in the ordinary Way of travelling, may take up some Days, yet we Authors are always provided with an easy flying Carriage, which can waft our Readers in an Instant, much longer Journeys than this we are now setting out on: We are Masters of a Kind of Art Magic, that we have only to speak the Word, and *presto*, you are transported, in the very Position you chance to be in at the Time, to the Place where we would have you attend us. Don't you find already the magical Effect? The Journey is over, and we are just alighted at the Gate of a stately old Building, surrounded with reverend Oaks. . . . You may enter freely . . . [pp. 12–13].

Annoying as this may seem, especially out of context, most of us can accept with pleasure the same device, more elegantly managed, in *Henry V*, when the Chorus—whom we would expect to seem more intrusive in a historical drama than the narrator's voice in a novel—whisks the spectators out of "this wooden O" and "thence to France." The excursions in the two *novels* may be bad, but unless we are willing to condemn Shakespeare's Chorus as well, we can hardly argue that they are bad because they are made up of intrusive rhetoric. The difference in quality really lies, first, in the superiority of Shakespeare's style, line for line, and second, in the degree of appropriateness of the rhetoric to the context. The Chorus' flight supports the invasion, as it were. Our imaginations sweep us across the channel in the wake of Henry V's forces. The world is enlarged by his speech just as it is enlarged by Henry's exploits.

There is nothing in the action of *The Old Curiosity Shop* or *Charlotte Summers* that is similarly enhanced by imaginary flight. To be made into intrepid aeronauts does nothing for us that needs doing to insure the success of either story. And yet the two fictional flights are not even as bad as this might suggest. If our criterion is at this point appropriateness to the whole work, we are forced to ask ourselves what the "whole work" is when dozens of pages have already been devoted to commentary. We do not experience these "intrusions" as independent outbursts; they are continuing steps in our acquaintance with the narrators. In this respect, the fictional intrusions seem less like unprepared outbursts than does the speech by Shakespeare's Chorus. The "Dickens" we have come to know talks like this; even the raw edges of his unsophisticated humor are thus appropriate to a context—the context provided by the rest of his explicit narrative strategy.

But to begin to talk about such a context and the relationship it establishes between narrator and reader is to go far beyond all of the notions of function with which we have been working so far. Though the functions we have illustrated would in themselves require us to resist any general attempt to erase commentary, they do not begin to account for the profound effect achieved by the great authors when they call attention to their works as literature and to themselves as artists. We can approach justice to this effect only by looking in detail at our relationship with dramatized narrators, reliable and unreliable.

"And now Reader, let me tell you, that by what you have read hitherto, you may ghess what you are like to have for the future, this that I have written already, is an Essay of what I intend for you, by this piece of Stuff you may judge what Garment you shall have. . . . But here some waggish Readers will be apt to *measure my Corn by their Bushel*, and to judge that I had some cause to think of this story. . . . I tell thee Reader, it was no such matter, I utterly deny it."
—FRANCIS KIRKMAN, *The Unlucky Citizen* (1673)

"Here Bernard was obliged to pause [in reading this book]. His eyes were blurred. . . . Well, we must go on. All this that I have been saying is only to put a little air between the pages of this journal. Now that Bernard has got his breath back again, we will return to it."—GIDE, *The Counterfeiters* (1925)

"Well, our hero was, by chance, high—very high born. READER. What! in a garret? AUTHOR. No, bless your soul! . . . Having thus gone through the usual routine of an author . . , in giving some account of our hero's birth and parentage, we have to add that he cried, whined, plied the nipple, puked up what he had gulped down, bep—s'd and bewrayed himself, like all other children."—EATON STANNARD BARRETT, *The Miss-Led General; A Serio-Comic, Satiric, Mock-Heroic Romance* (1808)

"Thus, Gentle Reader, I have given thee a faithful History of my Travels for Sixteen Years, and above Seven Months, wherein I have not been so studious of Ornament as Truth. I could perhaps like others have astonished thee with strange improbable Tales; but I rather chose to relate plain Matter of Fact in the simplest Manner and Style, because my principal Design was to Inform, and not to amuse thee."—*Gulliver's Travels* (1726)

CHAPTER EIGHT

Telling as Showing: Dramatized Narrators, Reliable and Unreliable

RELIABLE NARRATORS AS DRAMATIZED SPOKESMEN FOR THE IMPLIED AUTHOR

What is the context into which Fielding's narrator intrudes, at the end of *Joseph Andrews*, to say of Fanny, "How, reader, shall I give thee an adequate idea of this lovely young creature! . . . to comprehend her entirely, conceive youth, health, bloom, beauty, neatness, and innocence, in her bridal bed; conceive all these in their utmost perfection, and you may place the charming Fanny's picture before your eyes"? His earlier comments obviously provide part of the context. But if this is so, how does this new context, itself made up of "intrusions," relate to the whole story? And what of that still larger context, the author's and reader's experience with previous fiction?

Obviously the notion of function with which we have been working so far must be enlarged. Though commentary has served in the ways outlined above, and though no other device could have served most of them as well, it is also true that to look at these functions is only a first step in explaining the power of the great commentators. In *Don Quixote*, for example, our delight in the comments by various narrators obviously is not fully explained by showing that such commentary serves to heighten the effect of the knight's adventures. Though Cid Hamete Benengeli's farewell to his pen parallels in comic style Don Quixote's farewell to his books and to life itself, such a parallel fails to explain the full delight of the passage. "Here shalt thou remain, hung upon this rack by this brass wire. I know not if thou beest well cut or not, O pen of mine, but here thou shalt live for long ages to come, unless some presumptuous and scoundrelly historians should take thee down to profane thee. . . . For me alone Don Quixote was born and I for him; it was for him to act, for me to write, and we two are one in spite of that Tordesillesque pretender who had, and may have, the audacity to write with a coarse and ill-trimmed ostrich quill of the deeds of my valiant knight. . . ."[1]

The effect here is made up of many elements. There is pleasure in mere ornament: the history of intruding narrators is full of sheer overflowing narrative exuberance, as if the story itself, good as it is, did not provide adequate scope for the author's genius. There is parody of previous fiction: the laying down of swords, flutes, horns, and other romantic objects was part of the tradition ridiculed in *Don Quixote*. But quite obviously the most important quality here is something else entirely: the narrator has made of himself a dramatized character to whom we react as we react to other characters.

Narrators like Cid Hamete, who can speak for the norms on which the action is based, can become companions and guides quite distinct from the wonders they have to show. Our admiration or affection or sympathy or fascination or awe—no two of these narrators affect us in precisely the same way—is more intense just because it has been made personal; the telling is itself a dramatic rendering of a relationship with the author's "second self" which in strictly impersonal fiction is often less lively because only implicit.

---

[1] Samuel Putnam translation (New York, 1949).

There has been very little critical discussion of this relationship. But it is not hard to find confessions to its effect. At the beginning of *The Catcher in the Rye* (1951), J. D. Salinger's adolescent hero says, "What really knocks me out is a book that, when you're all done reading it, you wish the author that wrote it was a terrific friend of yours and you could call him up on the phone whenever you felt like it." Many more mature readers have found themselves feeling the same way.[2] Even Henry James, in spite of his mistrust of the author's voice, cannot resist the appeal of a great loquacious author like Fielding. After describing the deficiencies of Tom Jones's mind and the partial compensation of his vitality, James says, "Besides which his author—he handsomely possessed of a mind—has such an amplitude of reflexion for him and round him that we see him through the mellow air of Fielding's fine old moralism, fine old humour and fine old style, which somehow enlarge, make every one and every thing important."[3]

It may be extreme to call this relationship one of identification, as do Paul Goodman and H. W. Leggett,[4] but there are times when we do surrender ourselves to the great authors and allow our judgments to merge completely with theirs. Our surrender need not be dramatized by giving open voice to the narrator, but it is in its service that many comments find their major justification. Much commentary that seems excessive if judged by narrow standards of

---

[2] See, for example: (1) Clayton Hamilton, *Materials and Methods of Fiction* (London, 1909): "Many readers return again and again to 'The Newcomes' not so much for the pleasure of seeing London high society as for the pleasure of seeing Thackeray see it" (p. 132): (2) G. U. Ellis, *Twilight on Parnassus: A Survey of Post-war Fiction and Pre-war Criticism* (London, 1939): "It was not mere rhetoric that made *The Times* liken him [Dickens] to a personal friend. In every book we meet him, swinging along at our side . . . till, with a sort of infection, we catch his mood. . . . When afterwards, in soberer mood, we find his world largely vivid fantasy, his own vivid presence remains with us, as someone we are personally fond of" (p. 121); and (3) Harold J. Oliver, "E. M. Forster: The Early Novels," *Critique*, I (Summer, 1957), 15–32: "The omniscient method of narration . . . may indeed be the best possible one if the author's personality is to be an important element in the whole. It is so with Forster" (p. 30).

[3] Preface to *The Princess Casamassima*, p. 68.

[4] "In novels we identify with the omniscient narrator" (Goodman, *Structure of Literature* [Chicago, 1954], p. 153). "It is indeed true that the reader of fiction identifies himself with the author of a story rather than with the characters of the story" (H. W. Leggett, *The Idea in-Fiction* [London, 1934], p. 188).

function is wholly defensible when seen as contributing to our sense of traveling with a trustworthy companion, an author who is sincerely battling to do justice to his materials. George Eliot, for example, involves us constantly in her battle to deal with the truth, even at the expense of beauty or pleasure. " 'This Rector of Broxton is little better than a pagan!' I hear one of my readers exclaim. 'How much more edifying it would have been if you had made him give Arthur some truly spiritual advice! You might have put into his mouth the most beautiful things—quite as good as reading a sermon.' " The story of *Adam Bede* (1859) stops for several pages while she gives her answer to "my fair critic." "Certainly I could, if I held it the highest vocation of the novelist to represent things as they never have been and never will be." But her "strongest effort is to avoid any such arbitrary picture, and to give a faithful account of men and things as they have mirrored themselves in my mind." Even if the mirror is "defective," she feels herself "as much bound to tell you as precisely as I can what that reflection is, as if I were in the witness-box narrating my experience on oath." Out of context such talk may sound overdone, even boastful. But in context it can be convincing. "So I am content to tell my simple story, without trying to make things seem better than they were; dreading nothing, indeed, but falsity, which, in spite of one's best efforts, there is reason to dread. Falsehood is so easy, truth so difficult."[5] Obviously, one effect of this passage is to remind us that the Rector *is* more convincing than an idealized portrait would be. But a more important effect is to involve us on the side of the

---

[5] *Adam Bede*, Book II, chap. xvii, "In Which the Story Pauses a Little." W. J. Harvey objects to this particular intrusion for its "arch brightness." The "reader is repelled by having his reactions determined for him; he feels himself, and not the characters, to be a puppet manipulated by the author" ("George Eliot and the Omniscient Author Convention," *Nineteenth-Century Fiction*, XIII [September, 1958], 88). But George Eliot clearly intends our rejection of this pious female reader (1st ed.: "one of my lady readers"). Mr. Harvey offers an excellent defense of George Eliot's usual practice: "The 'illusion of reality' aimed at in this kind of fiction is not that of a self-contained world, a fictional microcosm intact and autonomous as in the Jamesian mode, but a world coterminus with the 'real' world, the factual macrocosm. The author bridges the two worlds. . . . No sharp boundaries between real and fictional are to be drawn here; the edges are blurred, and the omniscient author allows us an easy transition from one world to the other" (p. 90).

honest, perceptive, perhaps somewhat inept, but certainly uncompromising author in the almost overwhelming effort to avoid falsehood.

Even the most clumsily worded intrusion can redeem itself by conveying this sense of how deeply the narrator cares about what he is doing. The graceless conclusion of Melville's *Billy Budd*, for example, serves to remind us of the author's very real problems and thus to make us forgive every seeming fault. "The symmetry of form attainable in pure fiction cannot so readily be achieved in a narration essentially having less to do with fable than with fact. Truth uncompromisingly told will always have its ragged edges. . . . Though properly the story ends with his life something in way of sequel will not be amiss. Three brief chapters will suffice" (p. 274, chap. xxix).

Dostoevski is frequently masterful in making his narration seem to be a part of the battle. When he says that he does "not feel very competent" to the tremendous task before him, the effect is never to make us doubt his competence. His tendency to identify himself and his weaknesses with his hero's is especially effective. In *The Double* there is a fine satirical passage about the futility of the author's desire to portray the glorious world into which his hero desires, with equal futility, to rise.[6]

"FIELDING" IN "TOM JONES"

It is frustrating to try to deal critically with such effects, because they can in no way be demonstrated to the reader who has not experienced them. No amount of quotation, no amount of plot summary, can possibly show how fully the implied author's character dominates our reactions to the whole. About all we can do is to look closely at one work, *Tom Jones*, analyzing in static terms what in any successful reading is as sequential and dynamic as the action itself.[7]

Though the dramatized Fielding does serve to pull together many

---

[6] *The Short Novels of Dostoievsky*, trans. Constance Garnett (New York, 1945), chap. iv, p. 501.

[7] Perhaps the best defense of Fielding's commentary is that of Alan D. McKillop, in *Early Masters of English Fiction* (Lawrence, Kan., 1956), esp. p. 123.

parts of *Tom Jones* that might otherwise seem disconnected, and though he serves dozens of other functions, from the standpoint of strict function he goes too far: much of his commentary relates to nothing but the reader and himself. If we really want to defend the book as art, we must somehow account for these "extraneous" elements. It is not difficult to do so, however, once we think of the effect of our intimacy on our attitude toward the book as a whole. If we read straight through all of the seemingly gratuitous appearances by the narrator, leaving out the story of Tom, we discover a running account of growing intimacy between the narrator and the reader, an account with a kind of plot of its own and a separate denouement. In the prefatory chapter to his final volume, the narrator makes this denouement explicit, suggesting a distinct interest in the "story" of his relationship with the reader. This interest certainly requires some explanation if we wish to claim that *Tom Jones* is a unified work of art and not half-novel, half-essay.

> We are now, reader, arrived at the last stage of our long journey. As we have, therefore, travelled together through so many pages, let us behave to one another like fellow-travellers in a stagecoach, who have passed several days in the company of each other; and who, notwithstanding any bickerings or little animosities which may have occurred on the road, generally make all up at last, and mount, for the last time, into their vehicle with cheerfulness and good-humour.

The farewell goes on for several paragraphs, and at times the bantering tone of much of the work is entirely abandoned. "And now, my friend, I take this opportunity (as I shall have no other) of heartily wishing thee well. If I have been an entertaining companion to thee, I promise thee it is what I have desired. If in anything I have offended, it was really without any intention."

It may be extravagant to use the term "subplot" for the story of our relationship with this narrator. Certainly the narrator's "life" and Tom Jones's life are much less closely parallel than we expect in most plots and subplots. In *Lear*, Gloucester's fate parallels and reinforces Lear's. In *Tom Jones*, the "plot" of our relationship with Fielding-as-narrator has no similarity to the story of Tom. There is no complication, not even any sequence except for the gradually increasing familiarity and intimacy leading to farewell. And much of what we admire or enjoy in the narrator is in most respects quite different from what we like or enjoy in his hero.

Yet somehow a genuine harmony of the two dramatized elements is produced. It is from the narrator's norms that Tom departs when he gets himself into trouble, yet Tom is always in harmony with his most important norms. Not only does he reassure us constantly that Tom's heart is always in the right place, his presence reassures us of both the moral and the literary rightness of Tom's existence. As we move through the novel under his guidance, watching Tom sink to the depths, losing, as it appears, Allworthy's protection, Sophia's love, and his own shaky hold on decency, we experience for him what R. S. Crane has called the "comic analogue of fear."[8] And our growing intimacy with Fielding's dramatic version of himself produces a kind of comic analogue of the true believer's reliance on a benign providence in real life. It is not just that he promises a happy ending. In a fictional world that offers no single character who is both wise and good—even Allworthy, though all worthy, is no model of perspicacity—the author is always there on his platform to remind us, through his wisdom and benevolence, of what human life ought to be and might be. What is more, his self-portrait is of a life enriched by a vast knowledge of literary culture and of a mind of great creative power—qualities which could never be so fully conveyed through simply exercising them without comment on the dramatic materials of Tom's story.

For the reader who becomes too much aware of the author's claim to superlative virtues, the effect may fail. He may seem merely to be posing. For the reader with his mind on the main business, however, the narrator becomes a rich and provocative chorus. It is his wisdom and learning and benevolence that permeate the world of the book, set its comic tone between the extremes of sentimental indulgence and scornful indignation, and in a sense redeem Tom's world of hypocrites and fools.

One can imagine, perhaps, a higher standard of virtue, wisdom, or learning than the narrator's. But for most of us he succeeds in

---

8 *Critics and Criticism*, ed. R. S. Crane (Chicago, 1952), p. 637.

being the highest possible in his world—and, at least for the nonce, in ours. He is not trying to write for any other world, but for *this* one he strikes the precise medium between too much and too little piety, benevolence, learning, and worldly wisdom.[9] When he draws to the end of his farewell, then, at a time when we know we are to lose him, and uses terms which inevitably move us across the barrier to death itself, we find, lying beneath our amusement at his playful mode of farewell, something of the same feeling we have when we lose a close friend, a friend who has given us a gift which we can never repay. The gift he leaves—his book—is himself, precisely himself. The author has created this self as he has written the book. The book and the friend are one. "For however short the period may be of my own performances, they will most probably outlive their own infirm author, and the weakly productions of his abusive contemporaries." Was Fielding literally infirm as he wrote that sentence? It matters not in the least. It is not Fielding we care about, but the narrator created to speak in his name.

IMITATORS OF FIELDING

We might think it a fairly simple matter to imitate such straightforward effects. Surely one man can play this game as well as another. But among the hundreds of attempts at similar narrators there are far more failures than successes.

The most obvious cause of failure comes when there is a gross disparity between the claims to brilliance of the author and the shoddiness of his presented story. In *Tom Jones* there is a marvelous reciprocity of boast and performance, but many imitators boasted about setting out a banquet and in fact served left-overs. The brilliant structure of Tom Jones's adventures, the plot in the full sense of the power which that story in its complete form has to

---

[9] *Ibid.*, p. 642. William Empson gives a lively and convincing defense of Fielding's code and of the moral stature of *Tom Jones* in "*Tom Jones*," *Kenyon Review*, XX (Spring, 1958), 217–49. Though Empson mars his case a bit by arriving "circuitously at what Fielding tells us plainly enough" (C. J. Rawson, "Professor Empson's *Tom Jones*," *Notes and Queries*, N.S., VI [November, 1959], 400), his statement is a valuable antidote to the oversimplifications which have been used in dismissing Fielding and his commentary.

affect us,[10] is the chief proof of the narrator's overt claims. Naturally enough, most authors who have thought it easy to copy the various intrusive devices have lacked the powers needed to back up their Olympian claims.

But there are two other kinds of failure more pertinent to the analysis of fictional rhetoric. The first is a failure of character in the implied author. An author who intrudes must somehow be interesting; he must live as a character. And in hundreds of works from Fielding to the present, dull minds have produced dull spokesmen who emphasize their dulness by claiming to be brilliant. The great narrators in this mode often look so much like gossips that mere gossips have often attempted to create great narrators.

Fielding's sister, Sarah, for example, radically shifted her narrative method under the impact of *Tom Jones*. In the works she published in the 1740's (*David Simple, The Governess*, etc.) there are few intrusions, and the implicit character of the narrator, while on the whole dull and heavy-handed, is sufficiently dim to be untroublesome. In the wake of *Tom Jones*, however, she busily experimented with new narrative techniques (for example, in *The Cry* [1754], and *The Lives of Cleopatra and Octavia* [1757]), and particularly with the intrusive manner. Though it could hardly be said that her work as a whole becomes worse, her attempts at creating effects similar to Fielding's fail miserably. The narrator's wit is clumsy, "his" wisdom unconvincing. In *The Countess of Dellwyn* (1759), in place of Fielding's compelling self-image we are given a pretentious parade of a little pointless learning. In place of the relatively short, pithy prefatory chapters of *Tom Jones*, we are given an intolerably long, diffuse preface of forty-three pages, discussing all of the literary problems Sarah Fielding apparently can think of, with extensive quotation from Le Bossu and from "An old gentleman of taste." In place of Fielding's genuinely diverting interruptions of the narrative, we are given a puerile analysis of the "Various Humours" to be found at public places (Book II, chap. vi)

10 For a full discussion of the concept of plot as intended here and of the unique plot of *Tom Jones*, see R. S. Crane, *op. cit.*, esp. pp. 616–23.

and a collection of commonplaces about literature: Literary characters "are in a great measure disliked, or approved, in proportion to the Acquaintance the Reader, or the Audience, have before had with them. My Lord *Foppington*, and Sir *Fopling Flutter*, by their Names on the Bills, could formerly, at any time, croud the Playhouse with Spectators; but that Species of Coxcombs are now as much out of Mode as the very Dresses in which they were represented." And she concludes a long paragraph on this subject with the hope that the "Character I am now about to introduce will not be in such an unfortunate Situation, as to be esteemed a Creature that *nobody knows*; but that he will be owned as an Acquaintance by some Part at least of the *World*" (Book II, chap. viii).

This claim to realism makes an interesting contrast with her brother's witty intrusions designed for the same effect. Commenting on Bridget Allworthy's sexual prudence, Fielding says, "Indeed, I have observed (tho' it may seem unaccountable to the reader) that this guard of prudence, like the trained bands, is always readiest to go on duty where there is the least danger. It often basely and cowardly deserts those paragons for whom the men are all wishing, sighing, dying, and spreading every net in their power; and constantly attends at the heels of that higher order of women, for whom the other sex have a more distant and awful respect, and whom, (from despair, I suppose, of success) they never venture to attack" (Book I, chap. ii). The boast is the same: My characters are based on accurate observation of real manners. But the voice is masterful, able to be ironic without losing its direct power.

What I am saying here may seem like mere tautology: interesting narrators are interesting. But there is much more to it than that: some interesting narrators perform a kind of function in their works that nothing else could perform. They are not simply appropriate to a context, though that is essential.[11] They originally

---

11 The "author" of Sarah Fielding's *The Governess; or, the Little Female Academy, Calculated for the Entertainment and Instruction of Young Ladies in their Education* (1749) is appropriate enough: "The Design of the following Sheets is to prove to you, that Pride, Stubbornness, Malice, Envy, and, in short, all manner of Wickedness, is the greatest Folly we can be possessed of. . . . I depend on the Goodness of all my little Readers, to acknowledge this to be true. But there is one Caution to be used, namely, That you are not led into many Inconveniencies, and even Faults, by this

succeeded and still succeed by persuading the reader to accept them as living oracles. They are reliable guides not only to the world of the novels in which they appear but also to the moral truths of the world outside the book. The commentator who fails in this mode is the one who claims omniscience and reveals stupidity and prejudice.[12]

"TRISTRAM SHANDY" AND THE PROBLEM OF FORMAL COHERENCE

The third kind of failure is both more widespread and more difficult to grapple with: a failure of formal coherence. As I have tried to show in chapter v, certain qualities pursued for their own sakes can interfere with other qualities or effects, and in the tradition of the intruding narrator, omniscient or unreliable, we find hundreds of books in which an independent interest in this intrusive style interferes with other effects. The very qualities conferred by the great narrators can, when pursued for their own sake, transform or destroy the works which the narrators are ostensibly invented to serve.

To many of its critics, *Tristram Shandy* has seemed to be one of the worst offenders in this regard. The "mad," "merely odd,"

Love and Affection: For this Disposition will naturally lead you . . . into all manner of Errors, unless you take care not to be partial to any of your Companions, only because they are agreeable, without first considering whether they are good enough to deserve your Love" (pp. ix–x).

It is impossible to know how a young lady in the eighteenth century would react to this highly appropriate commentary, but it is not hard to recognize that for anyone in the twentieth century, adult or child, it has become intolerable.

12 Just how seriously an author can undercut his effects by the wrong kind of self-portrait can be seen in the following Preface to *The History of Cleanthes, an Englishman of the highest Quality, and Celemene, the Illustrious Amazonian Princess* (1757): "The following Sheets are the Productions of a Person, who writes not for Interest, or the Desire of Applause, but merely for Amusement. My Situation is such, having no Sort of real Business, that many Hours would hang heavy upon my Hands, if I did not endeavour to find out divers Sorts of Recreation, in order to fill up that Space of Time." In case there is any reader who has not been completely discouraged by this, the heavy-footed author finishes himself off with a final blow: "At length I resolved to try my own Abilities: This I have done; and from the Mixture of Adventures in my Narration, it is plainly to be discovered, that my Reading has been both ancient and modern, as my Work is a Composition, founded upon both Plans. . . . I write not with a Design to acquire Fame; and as a Proof of it, shall subscribe no Name, hoping that I may never be even suspected of having been AN AUTHOR."

"salmagundi of odds and ends" that took England and the Continent by storm in 1760 was from the beginning seen as among other things a literary puzzle. Is it simply a scrambled comic novel, with the antics of Walter and Toby and Tristram more obscured by narrative commentary than any comic subject had ever been before? Is it a collection of playful speculative essays, like Montaigne's, but with more fictional sugar-coating than Montaigne felt necessary? Or is it a satire in the tradition of Swift's *A Tale of a Tub*, taking in, as Sterne himself put it, "everything which I find Laugh-at-able in my way"? Even the many recent critics who have granted the work its own kind of unity, making their way confidently through the windings and turnings, the seeming digressions that turn out to be "progressive," the involutions and superpositions of time schemes, have been unable to agree about what kind of work it really is.[13]

Regardless of the position from which we try to apprehend such a book, the secret of its coherence, its form, seems to reside primarily in the role played by the teller, by Tristram, the dramatized narrator. He is himself in some way the central subject holding together materials which, were it not for his scatterbrained presence, would never have seemed to be separated in the first place. His double claim—that he knows yet does not know what he is about— simply makes explicit what is self-evident in our experience from beginning to end: that in some ways he is giving us a novel like other novels, and in some ways he is not. A very large part of the whole book is made up of talk about his writing chores and his rhetorical relation to the reader.

> In less than five minutes I shall have thrown my pen into the fire . . . ——I have but half a score things to do in the time——I have a thing to name——a thing to lament——a thing to hope . . . and a thing to pray for.——This chapter, therefore, I *name* the chapter of THINGS——and my next chapter to it, that is, the first chapter of my next volume, if I live, shall be my chapter upon WHISKERS, in order to keep up some sort of connection in my works.
>
> The thing I lament is, that things have crowded in so thick upon

---

[13] The best recent summary of the problems, together with one of the sanest assessments of the formal brilliance and the historical influence of *Tristram Shandy*, is found in Alan D. McKillop, *Early Masters of English Fiction*, chap. v.

me, that I have not been able to get into that part of my work, towards which, I have all the way, looked forwards, with so much earnest desire; and that is the campaigns, but especially the amours of my uncle *Toby*, the events of which are of so singular a nature, and so Cervantick a cast, that if I can so manage it, as to convey but the same impressions to every other brain, which the occurrences themselves excite in my own——I will answer for it the book shall make its way in the world, much better than its master has done before it——Oh *Tristram! Tristram!* can this but be once brought about ——the credit, which will attend thee as an author, shall counterbalance the many evils which have befallen thee as a man. . . . No wonder I itch so much as I do, to get at these amours——They are the choicest morsel of my whole story! [Vol. IV, conclusion].

Now what kind of a work are we reading here? Is this "telling" invented as rhetoric to aid in the realization of the dramatic elements? What, in fact, is the dramatic subject in James's sense (chap. iv, above)? If we try to find an analogue in *Tristram Shandy* for the character and story of Isabel Archer, say, in *The Portrait of a Lady*, what do we find? Is it the systematic time scheme of events, starting with the wounding of my uncle Toby at the siege of Namur in 1695 and ending with—well, with what? Already we are in difficulties. Do the events end with the final date named in the work, when Tristram describes himself as sitting before his desk in a purple jerkin and yellow pair of slippers, on "this 12th day of August, 1766," "a most tragicomical completion" of his father's prediction that he should neither think nor act like any other man's child? Can we say that this is an event in the writing of the book, while the siege of Namur is an event in the "subject" treated in that writing? The final event in the "dramatic object" is—what? The breeching in volume six? Certainly not the events of the final chapter, which take place four years before Tristram's birth. The trip through Europe of the adult Tristram? But this is really a digression in the *writing* of the work, part of the same sequence of events that leads to his sitting at his desk writing the odd book that results from his character, which in turn results from his father's theories, which. . . .

The dramatized narrator has ceased here to be distinguishable from what he relates. James's ideal of a seamless web of subject and treatment has somehow been stumbled upon more than a century before its time—and in a work that gives an air of complete disorganization!

THREE FORMAL TRADITIONS: COMIC NOVEL,
COLLECTION, AND SATIRE

To decide what Tristram really is, we should look briefly at three of his ancestors. Though this book is not intended as a historical study, the history of narrators before Sterne happens to present to us, in three main literary traditions, the most crucial questions about the contrast between dramatic form and the rhetoric of narration. In a rough way the traditions correspond, as we might expect, to the three most popular hypotheses about the form of *Tristram Shandy*: the comic novel exploded; the sugar-coated collection of philosophical essays, and the miscellaneous satire.

Even if any of the novelists between 1749 and 1760 had been able to create the kind of monumental comic action Fielding had revealed, many of them would have submerged the potential comic plot with their careless extensions of his carefully controlled facetiousness. One of the most revealing works of this kind is *Charlotte Summers, the Fortunate Parish Girl*, published anonymously within a year of *Tom Jones*.[14] The narrator claims to be the "first Begotten, of the poetical Issue, of the much celebrated Biographer of *Joseph Andrews* and *Tom Jones*" (p. 3). But though he feels "under the strongest Impulse to mimic every Action of that Gentleman" (p. 4), and does indeed copy a great many of the explicit devices of *Tom Jones*, the relationship of the rhetoric to the comic plot of the parish girl is very different. The author is, in fact, exploiting a temporary fashion in intrusions, and though he does a relatively clever job of it, the result is disunity of the most radical kind: as critics used to say, the manner has begun to rival the matter.

Sometimes this drama of the telling consists of a dialogue between the "I" and a "Reader" with whom the true reader can more or

---

14 Not dated, but generally assigned to 1749 or 1750. It has been attributed, without much plausibility, to Sarah Fielding. For other works written in the fifties that either explicitly avow indebtedness to "The King of *Biographers*" or show clear signs of having been deeply impressed by his narrative manner, see Bibliography, Sec. V.

less comfortably identify. More often, it is a dialogue between the "I" and a ridiculous, hypothetical reader who is as much a comic character as any other in the book. "Beau *Thoughtless*" and "pretty Miss *Pert*" and "grayhair'd Mrs. *Sit-her-time*" and "*Dick Dapperwit*" are constantly intruding in a "passion" to complain about the story or the characters' behavior. The most curious instance of this independent drama of the telling is an audacious bit of tomfoolery concerning one pair of "readers," Miss Arabella Dimple and her Maid Polly. "Pray, Ma'am, where shall I begin, did your Ladyship fold down where you left off?——No, Fool, I did not; the Book is divided into Chapters on Purpose to prevent that ugly Custom." They struggle with their memories: "Now I think on't, the Author bid me remember, that I left off at the End of——I think it was the 6th Chapter. Turn to the 7th Chapter, and let me hear how it begins——*Polly* reads, 'Chapter the 7th,—The Death of my Lady *Fanciful's* Squirrel. . . .'" Miss Dimple interrupts: "Hold, Wench, you read too fast; and I don't understand one Word of what you are saying. . . . I must not have got so far—Look back to the End of that Chapter where the Blookhead [sic] of an Author bids us take a Nap, and remember where he left off.—O la, Ma'am, I have found it; here it is. As your Ladyship said, he says . . ." (I, 68–69). She reads the conclusion of chapter four, a passage the reader has already encountered some pages previously. She then goes on reading aloud for sixteen pages, and then the narrator intrudes: "But the Reader must remember *Polly*, Miss *Dimple's* Maid, is reading all this while. She had just come to this Length, when she looks about at her Mistress and finds her fast asleep. . . . It's time to put an end to the Chapter, when pretty Miss *Dimple* sleeps over it."[15]

Such mock readers are played off against the elaborate self-portraiture of the narrator, a half-clown, half-oracle who is only

---

[15] For other instances of this mirror-within-a-mirror effect see the quotation from Gide's *Counterfeiters* given among the epigraphs to this chapter, and Mark Harris' *The Southpaw*, in which there is one chapter, labeled "11-A," giving an account of the narrator's reading of chapter xii to his friends. They object to section after section of chapter xii, and he expunges and expunges again until only one sentence is left. This sentence then begins chapter xiii; there is no chapter xii.

remotely related to any inferable author. It is as if the author had deliberately chosen to imitate his "Father F——g" only on the capricious side, taking seriously, as Fielding does not, the "Doctrine, that an Author, in spite of all critical Authority, has an absolute Right to digress when and where he pleases, and to amuse himself and his Readers with any thing that comes uppermost in his Head, whether it has any Connection with the Subject in Hand or not" (I, 28–29). Needless to say, in pursuit of this doctrine the poor parish girl is often forgotten, as Tom Jones never really is, for dozens of pages on end. What purports to be a comic novel has been torn into bits and fragments by facetious intrusions.[16]

A very different effect is produced by a similar air of caprice in the works of a second tradition, that of the unifying rather than disruptive self-portraits best exemplified by Montaigne. In a long line of works leading up to and away from Montaigne's *Essays*, Sterne had encountered elaborate and whimsical commentary as an end in itself, more or less divorced from any other narrative interest. Montaigne's book, a rambling collection of opinions about this and that, owes whatever dramatic coherence it has to the consistently inconsistent portrait of the author himself, in his character as a writer, and the "Montaigne" who emerges is as fascinating as any fictional hero could be. Like Tristram, he tells us a great deal about his moral and physical characteristics, enough, perhaps, to justify his claim to "paint himself." But he gives us much more: a running account of the writing of the book as it is written, and thus a running portrait of his character as a writer. "I presented my self to my Self for Argument and Subject. 'Tis the only Book in the world of its kind, and of a wild and extravagant Design; there is nothing worth Remark but the Extravagancy in this Affair: for in a Subject so vain and frivolous, the best Workman in the World could not have given it a form fit to recommend it to any manner

---

[16] I have given a fuller account of this as well as other pre-Shandean comic novels of the fifties in "The Self-conscious Narrator in Comic Fiction before *Tristram Shandy*," *PMLA*, LXVII (March, 1952), 163–85.

of Esteem" (II, 85).[17] He discusses in great detail his qualifications as an unskilled man undertaking to write a book that will be truer than other men's books. His "Fancy and Judgment do but grope in the dark," and he writes "indifferently of whatever comes into my Head" (I, 214). He has "naturally a Comick, and familiar Stile; but it is a peculiar one, and not proper for Publick business, but like the Language I speak, too Compact, Irregular, Abrupt and Singular" (I, 398). Like Tristram Shandy following his pen wherever it leads, he works "without premeditation, or design, the first word begets the second, and so to the end of the Chapter" (I, 400). He defends his digressions with precisely Tristram's manner: "This medly is a little from my Subject. I go out of my way, but 'tis rather upon the account of licence than oversight. My Fancies follow one another, but sometimes at a great distance; and look towards one another, but 'tis with an oblique glance. . . . I love a Poetick March by leaps and skips . . ." (III, 348–49). He predicts, foreshadowing Tristram's prophecy of forty volumes, that he will proceed "incessantly and without labour . . . so long as there shall be Ink and Paper in the World" (III, 263). And like Tristram he argues frequently and at length with his postulated readers: "Well, but some one will say to me, this design of making a man's self the subject of his writing, were indeed excusable [only] in rare and famous Men. . . . It is most true, I confess it, and know very well, that a Tradesman will scarce lift his Eyes from his work to look at an ordinary man. . . . Others have been encourag'd to speak of themselves, because they found the Subject worthy and rich; *I*, on the contrary, am the bolder, by reason the Subject is so poor and steril, that *I* cannot be suspected of Ostentation" (II, 541, 542).

The full effect of all this discussion of his character as a new kind of writer cannot be grasped unless one rereads the book with an eye on this matter alone; it can certainly not be given by quotation. But it is important to recognize that Montaigne's only claim to formal coherence is provided by the very material which many self-respect-

---

[17] Because it was most influential on English fiction, particularly through John Dunton and Sterne, I use the Charles Cotton translation. My page numbers are to the second edition, London, 1693.

ing modern novelists would automatically reject as disruptive and inartistic. Perhaps as much as one-fifth of this work is made up of mere commentary.

It is true that it is not a novel; there is no sustained narrative in the *Essays*. But it presents for that very reason an excellent opportunity to study commentary when it has no function other than to be itself. What is more, if we look closely at the "Montaigne" who emerges from these completed pages, we cannot help rejecting any simple distinction between fiction and biography or essay. The Montaigne of the book is by no stretch of the imagination the real Montaigne, pouring himself onto the page without regard for "aesthetic distance." Despite his endlessly repeated claim to "present me to your Memory, such as I naturally am" (II, 718), we find him often confessing to self-transformations. Phrases like "as far as a respect to the public has permitted me" are to be found in almost every statement of his intention to portray himself. "In moulding this Figure upon my self, I have been so oft constrain'd to temper and compose my self in a right posture, that the Copy is truly taken, and has in some sort form'd it self. But painting for others, I represent my self in a better colouring than my own natural Complexion" (II, 543). "Now, as much as Decency permits, I here discover my Inclinations and Affections . . ." (III, 329). "And withal a man must curl, set out and adjust himself to appear in publick . . ." (II, 75). Curl and adjust himself he certainly does: we need no research into the facts of his life to know it, we who have learned to read behind the curling and adjusting of the self-conscious narrators of Proust, Gide, Huxley, and Mann.

It is this created fictional character who pulls the scattered thoughts together. Far from dispersing otherwise coherent materials, as intrusive commentary does in *Charlotte Summers*, in this work it confers unity—though still of a casual kind—on what would otherwise be intolerably diffuse. And in a long stream of works after Montaigne, Sterne could have found similar effects.[18]

The third Shandean influence, which I must treat more briefly, is to be found in innumerable satires and burlesques, from Rabelais

---

[18] See Bibliography, Sec. V, C.

through Erasmus and Swift to a host of minor folk in the decades immediately before *Tristram Shandy*. Since the rhetorical intent of these works is evident to every reader, the function of the dramatized spokesmen, whether fools, knaves, or sages, is usually quite clear; no one accuses them of mad incoherence. Yet in some respects works in this tradition come even closer than *Charlotte Summers* and the *Essays* to what we find in the "radically new" *Tristram Shandy*. While in the comic novels using a self-conscious narrator, the organization of the story itself was ordinarily independent of the narrator's intrusions, in works like *A Tale of a Tub*, the narrator is much more central: as in *Tristram Shandy*, his character alters the very design of the work, the fundamental nature of the progression from one chapter to the next. When Swift's grub-street hack "intrudes," the quality of the intrusion is radically different from anything we have seen so far; even if precisely the same words were used by the narrators of *Charlotte Summers* and *A Tale*, in the one case there would be a genuine intrusion into more fundamental matters, and in the other the "intrusions" would themselves be integral to the effect. Just as *Tristram Shandy* is the mad kind of book it seems because of the life and opinions of the man it is about, so the hack's *Tale of a Tub* (as distinct from Swift's) is the atrociously poor thing it seems because of the assumed literary opinions and intellectual habits which the book is attacking.[19] The "author" is, in fact, the chief object of the satire.

THE UNITY OF "TRISTRAM SHANDY"

When we look at *Tristram Shandy* in the light of these traditions, we see that elements from all three help to hold it together: it has a kind of comic plot, though an "exploded" one; it gives us a consistent over-all portrait of the inconsistent mind of one man; and it is the ridiculous product, in its entirety, of a capricious narrator like the grubstreet hack. In only one of these aspects is the commentary disruptive; in the other two, the dramatic presentation of the act of writing is the chief element of cohesion.

But in combining the three traditions, Sterne has created some-

---

[19] See Bibliography, Sec. V, C.

thing genuinely new: since Tristram, unlike Montaigne, is really trying to tell a story, his struggle as a writer has itself a kind of plot form impossible in Montaigne. Though this action disrupts the comic action that he pretends to be relating, the two are really interdependent, like Swift's story of the three brothers and the grub-street narrator who tells that story. And yet, unlike what we find in *A Tale of a Tub*, the action of writing a book does not seem here to be shown simply for the sake of making fun of other writers or their opinions; despite the great amount of incidental satire, the action of Tristram in writing this book seems, like the great comic actions of Tom Jones or Don Quixote, to rise above any satirical intent, to exist ultimately as something to be enjoyed in its own right: the satire is for the sake of the comic enjoyment, and not the other way round.

The complexity of this comic action can best be seen by distinguishing two aspects of Tristram's nature, the ridiculous and the sympathetic. On the one hand, since many of Tristram's difficulties are of his own making, his action is like any traditional comic action viewed by spectators who know better than the character. It produces the kind of dramatic irony that we experience when we see Tartuffe making love to Orgon's wife, knowing, as Tartuffe does not, that Orgon is under the table: that is, we laugh *at* him, and we look forward to his comic unmasking. On the other hand, since Tristram is in many respects admirable, we are on his side. He is up against insurmountable obstacles that we all face—the nature of time, the nature of our unpredictable minds, and the nature of human animality as it undercuts all of our efforts to attain to the ideal.

In the first of these aspects Tristram is a hopeless incompetent. Sterne places his bumbling forty-one-year-old hero at his desk in his study, as if on a stage, dressed in whimsical garb and flinging ink about him as he writes. His life has been hopelessly botched by the clumsiness of his begetting, the crushing of his nose at birth, the confusion of his naming, and a variety of other disasters peculiar to the Shandy household. With such a man in charge, our expectation of comic catastrophe is of course far different from that in comic novels like *Tom Jones*, or even *Charlotte Summers*. Though we hope to see ever more embarrassing disasters for the young Tristram and his uncle Toby, we expect even more to see the adult Tristram caught in ever increasing narrative difficulties. It is always highly probable that his story will not get told, his failures are so many. Yet it is also more and more probable that the story he *wants* to tell will be told, since it is obvious that from his own viewpoint he is enjoying success after success. When he concludes, we make the discovery that we half expected all along. "L—d! said my mother, what is all this story about?——A COCK and a BULL, said *Yorick*—— And one of the best of its kind, I ever heard." A pitifully comic anticlimax indeed, after all the brave promises. And yet the longer we look at his concluding volume, the more signs we see that he has succeeded very well in telling the story *he* had in mind, ridiculous as that story may be.

The telling of his story is in itself comic chiefly because there is nothing in the nature of his subject, when viewed as material for a conventional comic novel, that should require all of this complexity. The chaos is all of his own making. Sterne and the reader are always aware of the existence of a clear, simple chronology of events that could be told in a hundred pages without difficulty. We have, in fact, only two simple story threads: Tristram's conception, birth, naming, circumcision, and breeching, and uncle Toby's courtship of the Widow Wadman. The two are juggled adroitly throughout the nine volumes, and the ninth volume nicely finishes off what Tristram has told us again and again is his "choicest morsel," the story, which he has "all the time" been "hastening" to tell, of how uncle Toby got his modesty by courting the Widow.[20] The ironies that operate against Tristram depend on the contrast between this

---

[20] See Theodore Baird, "The Time-Scheme of *Tristram Shandy* and a Source," *PMLA*, LI (1936), 803–20; James A. Work's edition of *Tristram Shandy* (New York, 1940), Introduction, pp. xlviii–li; and my "Did Sterne Complete *Tristram Shandy?*" *Modern Philology*, XLVII (February, 1951), 172–83. For an intelligent expression of skepticism about my claim that Sterne had "all the time" been planning to complete his book with this "choicest morsel," see McKillop, *Early Masters*, pp. 213–14. It is true, as McKillop says, that there are "innumerable other ways of *not* telling of Tristram's life and opinions" besides telling uncle Toby's story. But my claim rests on the fact that none of these other possible ways is rhetorically heightened by repeated promises from Volume I on, and particularly by such promises given at the end of each separately published instalment.

essential simplicity and the fantastic chaos that Tristram makes of it. In the service of this contrast, it is obvious that the greater the actual simplicity and the greater the seeming complexity, the funnier Tristram's narration will seem. We have, in fact, found a work of which we can say the more commentary the better.

But there are aspects of his struggle to write his book which force the reader—perhaps especially the modern reader—to take his side. His two story-threads are simple, after all, only when they are considered as if they were material for a traditional novel. If an honest writer really tries to render, as Tristram does, the inner reality, the full truth about how his life and opinions are related to each other and to truth itself, then he is in trouble; in fact, his battle is a hopeless one from the beginning. Yet we are made to think that the effort is a meaningful one, even though hopeless. Compared with all of the artifices used in conventional novels to ignore the problem of how the fictional world relates to the real world, Tristram's effort seems a noble one; we who have learned the lessons about the supreme value of reality taught by Ford and others (chap. ii, above) may even overrate Tristram's effort and miss some of the ridicule Sterne intends. But in any case we cannot help sympathizing with him in his struggle, however humorously expressed, to get at the inner reality of events, always elusive, always just beyond the artist's grasp. If we read with sympathy Henry James's talk about these problems, how can we deny the same sympathy to Tristram? "Really, universally, relations stop nowhere, and the exquisite problem of the artist is eternally but to draw, by a geometry of his own, the circle within which they shall happily appear to do so."[21] Nobody knows what James means better than Tristram, and at times his description of his problem reads like a comic version of James. It is interesting, for example, to stand back and watch the two masters of amplification struggle with the rendering of time:

> This eternal time-question is accordingly, for the novelist, always there and always formidable; always insisting on the effect of the great lapse and passage, of the "dark backward and abysm," by the terms of truth, and on the effect of compression, of composition and form,

---

[21] Preface to *Roderick Hudson*, in *The Art of the Novel*, ed. R. P. Blackmur (New York, 1947), p. 5.

by the terms of literary arrangement. It is really a business to terrify
all but stout hearts into abject omission and mutilation, though the
terror would indeed be more general were the general consciousness
of the difficulty greater.[22]

That stout heart, Tristram, as conscious of the difficulties as James,
puts the problem somewhat more concretely:

> I am this month one whole year older than I was this time twelve-
> month; and having got, as you perceive, almost into the middle of
> my fourth volume—and no farther than to my first day's life—'tis
> demonstrative that I have three hundred and sixty-four days more
> life to write just now, than when I first set out; so that instead of
> advancing, as a common writer, in my work with what I have been
> doing at it—on the contrary, I am just thrown so many volumes
> back—was every day of my life to be as busy a day as this—And why
> not?—and the transactions and opinions of it to take up as much
> description—And for what reason should they be cut short? as at this
> rate I should just live 364 times faster than I should write—It must
> follow, an' please your worships, that the more I write, the more I
> shall have to write—and consequently, the more your worships read,
> the more your worships will have to read. . . . write as I will, and
> rush as I may into the middle of things, as *Horace* advises,—I shall
> never overtake myself—whipp'd and driven to the last pinch, at the
> worst I shall have one day the start of my pen—and one day is
> enough for two volumes—and two volumes will be enough for one
> year.—[Vol. IV, chap. xiii.]

Sterne and the reader, it is true, share this plight with Tristram
only in reduced form; part of the comedy is that even here Tristram
has chosen to go beyond what Sterne or James would think reasonable. But Sterne faces, like the reader, the world of chaos in fleeting
time as it threatens the artist's effort to be true to that world without lapsing into chaos itself. It is hardly surprising that modern
critics have tried to account for the whole book as a battle with
time, or as an effort to ascend from the world of time into a truer
world. It is more than that, but in the valiant figure of the little
eccentric we do have a prefiguring of the many modern narrators—
in Joyce, Proust, Huxley, Gide, Mann, Faulkner, among others—
who dramatize James's message by fighting the reader's hopeless
battle against time.

---

[22] *Op. cit.*, p. 14.

Obviously to talk of eliminating commentary from the narrator's arsenal as he conducts this battle would be absurd. The battle is shown *in* the commentary; telling has become showing. Every comment is an action; every digression is "progressive" in a sense more profound than Tristram intends when he boasts about getting on with his story.

SHANDEAN COMMENTARY, GOOD AND BAD

After Sterne had extended commentary in quantity and quality until it dominated the whole book and created a new kind of unity, various aspects of *Tristram Shandy* were imitated in work after work, at first in overwhelming numbers and then trailing off to a steady trickle of works on down to the great outburst of self-conscious narrators in the twentieth century.[23]

The difference between good and bad again here, as in reliable narration, cannot be easily illustrated with excerpts. A foolish intrusion in a wise work can yield its own kind of delight; a foolish intrusion in a foolish work merely compounds boredom.

Some of the intrusions of Thomas Amory's *John Buncle* (1756), for example, might not seem badly out of place in *Tristram Shandy:* "I have little right to pretend to any thing extraordinary in understanding, as my genius is slow, and such as is common in the lower classes of men of letters; yet, my application has been very great: my whole life has been spent in reading and thinking: and nevertheless, I have met with many women, in my time, who, with very little reading, have been too hard for me on several subjects" (p. 274). Throw in a dash here and some livelier diction there, and it would pass for Tristram's. But when we know from the context that this is not in any sense ironic, that it is intended as straightforward praise for the understanding of women, it becomes amusing in a sense not intended by Amory. On the other hand, many of the intrusions of Swift's grubstreet hack into *A Tale of a Tub* are in themselves stupid in the extreme. Though careful reading reveals Swift's genius at work everywhere, it would not be hard to find fairly extensive quotations which, if read straight, would be as dull as Amory's:

---

[23] See Bibliography, Sec. V, C and D.

> I hope, when this Treatise of mine shall be translated into Forein
> Languages, (as I may without Vanity affirm, That the Labor of
> collecting, the Faithfulness in recounting, and the great Usefulness
> of the Matter to the Publick, will amply deserve that Justice) that
> the worthy Members of the several *Academies* abroad, especially
> those of *France* and *Italy*, will favourably accept these humble Offers,
> for the Advancement of Universal Knowledge. . . . And so I proceed
> with great Content of Mind, upon reflecting, how much Emolu-
> ment this whole Globe of Earth is like to reap by my Labors.

The narrator here is a dull and foolish man, but the book he
"writes" is a great one partly because of the contrast between his
role and that of the implied author.

Two requirements for success are, then, appropriateness to a context and usefulness within that context.[24] But though necessary,
these will not insure success. One could name dozens of failures in
which the commentary is appropriate and functional in exactly the
same sense as in *Tristram Shandy*. In all of them a dramatized narrator pretends to give one kind of story but really gives another; in
many of them there is a good deal of comic detail about how the
hero came into the world, and about how his character determines
the kind of book he writes. All of the narrators intrude into their
ostensible stories "whenever they please" to discuss their own opinions, and all pride themselves on their wit and eccentricity. One
could write an accurate description of their mental habits that
would make them sound identical. We might then claim to have
found a true literary genre, and we could formulate rules of style for
the intruding author that all prospective commentators must follow. But what would we then do with the fact that the very words
spoken by one narrator to great effect will seem footling and inad-

---

[24] In general the successful imitations have been based on a discovery of new uses for
this kind of narrator. Diderot and Bage, for example, both succeeded with genuinely
new works. Diderot, in *Jacques le fataliste* (1796; written 1773), created a narrator
who illustrated, in the fatalistic principles that governed his writing, the fatalistic
principles which govern the book and life itself. Bage, in *Hermsprong* (1796), embodied
his satirical message, somewhat in the manner of Swift, in his narrator's imperfections.
On the other hand, when there is little reason for such narration other than fashion
(*The Man of Feeling* [1771]), or when the imitation is so patent as to seem mere
plagiarism (*Yorick's Meditations* [1760]), or when the commentary seems to serve
mainly an immature exhibitionism in the author (Hemingway's *Death in the Afternoon*) the result is of course unsatisfactory.

missible when spoken by another narrator who seems to be trying for precisely the same kind of effect? What rules can we formulate to show us which of the following three passages comes from one of the "great books"—it really is on the Chicago list—and which are from books that are almost completely and properly forgotten? I have altered a few proper nouns.

1. And, now I pray all critics existing and possible, since I have let them into the secret of my genius and humour, to muster up all the animadversions they are capable of, on the *Life* and *Opinions* I am going to write. I no more know myself yet than the man of the Moon, what sort of *Life*, and what sort of *Opinions* they are likely to turn out: but supposing (to avoid the imputation of self-sufficiency,) that they will deserve something more than a supercilious treatment from the critics, I think it proper to give them here notice, that the moment they read this paragraph, they may judge themselves, by my special permission, authorized and privileged, to prepare their arms, ordinary and extraordinary, for exterminating them, if they have power to effect it; as for their good will, I make no doubt of it. . . .

2. Upon looking back from the end of the last chapter and surveying the texture of what has been wrote, it is necessary, that upon this page and the five following, a good quantity of heterogeneous matter be inserted, to keep up that just balance betwixt wisdom and folly, without which a book would not hold together a single year: nor is it a poor creeping digression (which but for the name of, a man might continue as well going on in the king's highway) which will do the business——no; if it is to be a digression, it must be a good frisky one, and upon a frisky subject too, where neither the horse or his rider are to be caught, but by rebound. The only difficulty, is raising powers suitable to the nature of the service; FANCY is capricious ——WIT must not be searched for—and PLEASANTRY (good-natured slut as she is) will not come in at a call, was an empire to be laid at her feet.——The best way for a man, is to say his prayers——

3. *My Life is a continued Digression, from my Cradle to my Grave; was so before I was born, and will be so after I am dead and rotten—* the History of which I have been sweating at the best part of this seven Years; and having now with great Pains and Industry, charge and care render'd compleat, and ready for the Press, I first send out this *First* Volume by way of *Postilion*, to slap-dash, and spatter all about him, (if the Criticks come in his way) in order to make

Elbow-room for all the rest of his *little Brethren* that are to come after. *My Name is* TRISTRAM SHANDY, alias—'Twas just upon my Tongues end, if 'thad been out, *I'd ha' bit it off.* . . .

As great a *Coward* as I am, there may have gone I know n't how many *particles of a Lyon* into my Composition, and as *small as my Body is*, my great Grandfather might be made out of a Whale or an Elephant. You remember the Story of the *Dog that kill'd the Cat, that eat the Rat,*—for I love to Illustrate *Philosophical Problems,* with common Instances for the use of the less knowing part of the World,—why just so here . . . but I am apt to think (*between Friends*) if there be any thing in't, that most of the Lyoness Particles rambled *somewhere else,* to another *Branch* of the Family; and that more of the *Sheep,* the gentle Lamb, or such harmless innocent Creatures *Rambled* into my Composition.

Even the reader who knows Tristram's style well enough to recognize that his is the second of these three might have trouble in defending not simply its superiority over the other two, but its claim to greatness in contrast to their deserved oblivion. Yet the source of the first, *The Life and Opinions of Bertram Montfichet, Esq.* (1761), is a wretched imitation almost impossible to read for five pages on end. The third, John Dunton's *Voyage Round the World; or, a Pocket-Library* (1691), though far superior to *Montfichet,* is intolerably tedious when compared either with Montaigne's *Essays,* which it frequently copies at length, or with Sterne's work, which borrows from it heavily.

It is hard to formulate a general description of the purposes or techniques of *Tristram Shandy* that will not fit both other works precisely. Why, then, is Sterne's work so much better, not only in its over-all effect but even in the texture from line to line, from comment to comment, when we put the comments back into context? Sterne knew the answer, at least in part. "I have undertaken, you see, to write not only my life, but my opinions also; hoping and expecting that your knowledge of my character, and of what kind of a mortal I am, by the one, would give you a better relish for the other: As you proceed further with me, the slight acquaintance which is now beginning betwixt us, will grow into familiarity; and that, unless one of us is in fault, will terminate in friendship.——O *diem præclarum!*——then nothing which has touched me will be thought trifling in its nature, or tedious in its telling" (Vol. I, chap. vi).

Our knowledge of his character does, indeed, make everything that has touched him seem worth talking about. Our friendship is in one sense more complete than any friendship in real life, because we know everything there is to be known about Tristram and we see the world as he sees it. Our interests correspond with his interests, and his style is thus used in a larger context that helps to give it life; in this respect our relationship is more like identity than friendship, despite the many respects in which we "keep our distance" from him. Montfichet tries rather half-heartedly for this same effect, but with his wretched Aunt Dinah and Uncle Dick, Parson Yorrick (sic), and Doctor Rantum, he surrounds his commentary with signs that it comes from a despicable man. While "nothing that has touched" Tristram "will be thought trifling in its nature," everything that has touched Montfichet, whether his ambiguously sexed uncle or the philosophies of Descartes and Locke, is defiled; we thus find ourselves judging each detail in its own right, unillumined by any general radiance. "Don Kainophilus," Dunton's narrator, is somewhat more successful, but his character will not sustain the burden placed upon it; his wit is feeble, his wisdom often foolish, his claims to be one jump ahead of the cleverest reader often belied by our ability to predict his moves far in advance.

But Tristram is Tristram.

I wish either my father or my mother, or indeed both of them, as they were in duty both equally bound to it, had minded what they were about when they begot me; had they duly consider'd how much depended upon what they were then doing;—that not only the production of a rational Being was concern'd in it, but that possibly the happy formation and temperature of his body, perhaps his genius and the very cast of his mind;—and, for aught they knew to the contrary, even the fortunes of his whole house might take their turn from the humours and dispositions which were then uppermost:——Had they duly weighed and considered all this, and proceeded accordingly,——I am verily persuaded I should have made a quite different figure in the world, from that, in which the reader is likely to see me.——Believe me, good folks, this is not so inconsid-

erable a thing as many of you may think it;—you have all, I dare
say, heard of the animal spirits, as how they are transfused from
father to son. . . . Well, you may take my word. . . .

Take his word we do, but only part of the time, and the resulting
delightful ambiguities permanently enlarge our view of the possibilities of fiction.

But Sterne enlarges our view of its problems as well. We take his
word only part of the time; of all the many problems the reader of
Tristram Shandy shares with the reader of modern fiction, that of
the narrator's indeterminately untrustworthy judgment is most important here.

With his own confusions, he makes our path a troubled, insecure
one. The history of unreliable narrators from *Gargantua* to *Lolita* is
in fact full of traps for the unsuspecting reader, some of them not
particularly harmful but some of them crippling or even fatal.

Consider the difficulties in the following simple passage, written
by Tristram's ancestor, "Don Kainophilus, alias Evander, alias Don
John Hard-Name," in *Voyage Round the World*:

> —but *O! my Mother, O! my dearest Muz!* why did you leave me?
> Why did you go so soon, so very soon away,—Nurses are careless,
> sad careless Creatures; and alas the young *Evander* may get a knock
> in his Cradle if you dye. . . . Your Death leads me to the *House of
> weeping*;—it spoils all my *Pastimes*, dissipates all my *Remains* . . .
> persecutes me, destroys me, makes a *Martyr* of me, and sets my very
> Brains a *Rambling* agen, as much as my Feet have been:—But what
> does all this avail,—could I get all the *Irish Howlers* . . . to hoot and
> hollow over her Grave, they'd never bring her to *Life* agen,—for she
> was dead. . . . —If you ask what she was, that I'll tell you,—she was
> a *Woman*, yet no *Woman*, but an *Angel*.

Is this sentimentality intentionally comic? Perhaps. But it is hard
to be sure. There is no direct clue to guide us. The context is itself
equivocal, though the full page of panegyric that follows seems at
many points to be serious. Even if we take the trouble to look up
the biography of Dunton, and discover from his *Life and Errors*
and other sources that Evander's Mother as described in the *Voyage* corresponds point for point with Dunton's own, with dates and
characteristics matching as well as they would in an ordinary serious

autobiography, we still cannot be sure. Our problems in determining the author's distance in such a comic work are, in short, similar to our problems in reading much serious fiction since James. Once the author has decided to go away and send no letter,[25] the reader's task in trying to determine just how far away he has gone can be a troubling one indeed. Though the narrator may frequently trip himself up, the reader will know that he has done so only if his own sense of what is sane and sound is better—that is, more nearly like the departed author's—than is the narrator's. By drawing such ambiguous practices into the mainstream of fiction, Sterne developed a kind of reliance on the reader's superior judgment that had formerly been required only in esoterica and in some forms of ironic satire.[26]

The most extreme form of this new burden on the reader comes whenever there is tension between the compassionate effect of intimacy with a narrator or reflector and the distancing effect of characteristics we deplore. As we have seen in *Tristram Shandy*, whenever a narrator reveals a fault, the fault itself tends to repel us, or at least to make us laugh at him, while the act of honest self-revelation tends to attract us.

This double, and sometimes contradictory, effect is one of the major subjects of Part III. But before we turn to the modern impersonal novelists who have wrestled with it, we should look closely at one earlier triumph in the control of distance. Since it should be a work in which a self-revealing protagonist is to be loved as well as judged, Jane Austen's *Emma* is a natural choice.

---

25 Rebecca West, *Henry James* (London, 1916), p. 88.

26 See William Bragg Ewald, Jr., *The Masks of Jonathan Swift* (Cambridge, Mass., 1954): "One cannot, as in *A Tale of a Tub*, ironically condemn Homer for . . . his failure to understand the Church of England . . . unless one's readers are aware that Homer has excellences which cannot be touched by such criticism. Mistakes have been made when critics have tried to interpret Swift in the light of their own idea of a norm rather than his" (p. 188). It should be noted that the decision about this type of distance can seem less important in comic fiction than it is in satire or serious fiction. Sterne and Dunton can survive vast quantities of downright misunderstanding of their intentions, without the reader's suspecting that anything is wrong. This indeterminacy and seeming permissiveness can of course serve as a protective device for the weak author. If, for example, Sterne's grammar is weak, he needn't worry: we will surely attribute the grammatical errors to Tristram.

"Jane Austen was instinctive and charming. . . . For signal examples of what composition, distribution, arrangement can do, of how they intensify the life of a work of art, we have to go elsewhere."—HENRY JAMES

"A heroine whom no one but myself will much like."—JANE AUSTEN describing Emma

Control of Distance
in Jane Austen's "Emma"

SYMPATHY AND JUDGMENT IN "EMMA"

Henry James once described Jane Austen as an instinctive novelist whose effects, some of which are admittedly fine, can best be explained as "part of her unconsciousness." It is as if she "fell-a-musing" over her work-basket, he said, lapsed into "wool-gathering," and afterward picked up "her dropped stitches" as "little masterstrokes of imagination."[1] The amiable accusation has been repeated in various forms, most recently as a claim that Jane Austen creates

---

[1] "The Lesson of Balzac," *The Question of Our Speech* (Cambridge, 1905), p. 63. A fuller quotation can be found in R. W. Chapman's indispensable *Jane Austen: A Critical Bibliography* (Oxford, 1955). Some important Austen items published too late to be included by Chapman are: (1) Ian Watt, *The Rise of the Novel* (Berkeley, Calif., 1957); (2) Stuart M. Tave, review of Marvin Mudrick's *Jane Austen: Irony as Defense and Discovery* (Princeton, N.J., 1952) in *Philological Quarterly*, XXXII (July, 1953), 256–57; (3) Andrew H. Wright, *Jane Austen's Novels: A Study in Structure* (London, 1953), pp. 36–82; (4) Christopher Gillie, "*Sense and Sensibility:* An Assessment," *Essays in Criticism*, IX (January, 1959), 1–9, esp. 5–6; (5) Edgar F. Shannon, Jr., "*Emma:* Character and Construction," *PMLA*, LXXI (September, 1956), 637–50.

characters toward whom we cannot react as she consciously intends.[2]

Although we cannot hope to decide whether Jane Austen was entirely conscious of her own artistry, a careful look at the technique
of any of her novels reveals a rather different picture from that of
the unconscious spinster with her knitting needles. In *Emma* especially, where the chances for technical failure are great indeed, we
find at work one of the unquestionable masters of the rhetoric of
narration.

At the beginning of *Emma*, the young heroine has every requirement for deserved happiness but one. She has intelligence, wit,
beauty, wealth, and position, and she has the love of those around
her. Indeed, she thinks herself completely happy. The only threat
to her happiness, a threat of which she is unaware, is herself:
charming as she is, she can neither see her own excessive pride honestly nor resist imposing herself on the lives of others. She is deficient both in generosity and in self-knowledge. She discovers and
corrects her faults only after she has almost ruined herself and her
closest friends. But with the reform in her character, she is ready
for marriage with the man she loves, the man who throughout the
book has stood in the reader's mind for what she lacks.

It is clear that with a general plot of this kind Jane Austen gave
herself difficulties of a high order. Though Emma's faults are comic,
they constantly threaten to produce serious harm. Yet she must remain sympathetic or the reader will not wish for and delight sufficiently in her reform.

Obviously, the problem with a plot like this is to find some way
to allow the reader to laugh at the mistakes committed by the
heroine and at her punishment, without reducing the desire to see
her reform and thus earn happiness. In *Tom Jones* this double attitude is achieved, as we have seen, partly through the invention of
episodes producing sympathy and relieving any serious anxiety we
might have, and partly through the direct and sympathetic commentary. In *Emma*, since most of the episodes must illustrate the
heroine's faults and thus increase either our emotional distance or

---

[2] See, for example, Mudrick, *op. cit.*, pp. 91, 165; Frank O'Connor, *The Mirror in
the Roadway* (London, 1957), p. 30.

our anxiety, a different method is required. If we fail to see Emma's faults as revealed in the ironic texture from line to line, we cannot savor to the full the comedy as it is prepared for us. On the other hand, if we fail to love her, as Jane Austen herself predicted we would[3]—if we fail to love her more and more as the book progresses —we can neither hope for the conclusion, a happy and deserved marriage with Knightley following upon her reform, nor accept it as an honest one when it comes.[4] Any attempt to solve the problem by reducing either the love or the clear view of her faults would have been fatal.

SYMPATHY THROUGH CONTROL OF INSIDE VIEWS

The solution to the problem of maintaining sympathy despite almost crippling faults was primarily to use the heroine herself as a kind of narrator, though in third person, reporting on her own experience. So far as we know, Jane Austen never formulated any theory to cover her own practice; she invented no term like James's "central intelligence" or "lucid reflector" to describe her method of viewing the world of the book primarily through Emma's own eyes. We can thus never know for sure to what extent James's accusation of "unconsciousness" was right. But whether she was inclined to speculate about her method scarcely matters; her solution was clearly a brilliant one. By showing most of the story through Emma's eyes, the author insures that we shall travel with Emma rather than stand against her. It is not simply that Emma provides, in the unimpeachable evidence of her own conscience, proof that she has many redeeming qualities that do not appear on the surface; such evidence could be given with authorial commentary, though perhaps not with such force and conviction. Much more

---

[3] "A heroine whom no one but myself will much like" (James Edward Austen-Leigh, *Memoir of His Aunt* [London, 1870; Oxford, 1926], p. 157).

[4] The best discussion of this problem is Reginald Farrer's "Jane Austen," *Quarterly Review*, CCXXVIII (July, 1917), 1–30; reprinted in William Heath's *Discussions of Jane Austen* (Boston, 1961). For one critic the book fails because the problem was never recognized by Jane Austen herself: Mr. E. N. Hayes, in what may well be the least sympathetic discussion of *Emma* yet written, explains the whole book as the author's failure to see Emma's faults. "Evidently Jane Austen wished to protect Emma. . . . The author is therefore in the ambiguous position of both loving and scorning the heroine" ("'Emma': A Dissenting Opinion," *Nineteenth-Century Fiction*, IV [June, 1949], 18, 19).

important, the sustained inside view leads the reader to hope for good fortune for the character with whom he travels, quite independently of the qualities revealed.

Seen from the outside, Emma would be an unpleasant person, unless, like Mr. Woodhouse and Knightley, we knew her well enough to infer her true worth. Though we might easily be led to laugh at her, we could never be made to laugh sympathetically. While the final unmasking of her faults and her humiliation would make artistic sense to an unsympathetic reader, her marriage with Knightley would become irrelevant if not meaningless. Unless we desire Emma's happiness and her reform which alone can make that happiness possible, a good third of this book will seem irredeemably dull.

Yet sympathetic laughter is never easily achieved. It is much easier to set up a separate fool for comic effects and to preserve your heroine for finer things. Sympathetic laughter is especially difficult with characters whose faults do not spring from sympathetic virtues. The grasping but witty Volpone can keep us on his side so long as his victims are more grasping and less witty than he, but as soon as the innocent victims, Celia and Bonario, come on stage, the quality of the humor changes; we no longer delight unambiguously in his triumphs. In contrast to this, the great sympathetic comic heroes often are comic largely because their faults, like Uncle Toby's sentimentality, spring from an excess of some virtue. Don Quixote's madness is partly caused by an excess of idealism, an excess of loving concern for the unfortunate. Every crazy gesture he makes gives further reason for loving the well-meaning old fool, and we can thus laugh at him in somewhat the same spirit in which we laugh at our own faults—in a benign, forgiving spirit. We may be contemptible for doing so; to persons without a sense of humor such laughter often seems a wicked escape. But self-love being what it is, we laugh at ourselves in a thoroughly forgiving way, and we laugh in the same way at Don Quixote: we are convinced that his heart, like ours, is in the right place.

Nothing in Emma's comic misunderstandings can serve for the same effect. Her faults are not excesses of virtue. She attempts to manipulate Harriet not from an excess of kindness but from a de-

sire for power and admiration. She flirts with Frank Churchill out
of vanity and irresponsibility. She mistreats Jane Fairfax because of
Jane's *good* qualities. She abuses Miss Bates because of her own essential lack of "tenderness" and "good will."

We have only to think of what Emma's story would be if seen
through Jane Fairfax' or Mrs. Elton's or Robert Martin's eyes to
recognize how little our sympathy springs from any natural view,
and to see how inescapable is the decision to use Emma's mind as a
reflector of events—however beclouded her vision must be. To Jane
Fairfax, who embodies throughout the book most of the values
which Emma discovers only at the end, the early Emma is intolerable.

But Jane Austen never lets us forget that Emma is not what she
might appear to be. For every section devoted to her misdeeds—
and even they are seen for the most part through her own eyes—
there is a section devoted to her self-reproach. We see her rudeness
to poor foolish Miss Bates, and we see it vividly. But her remorse
and act of penance in visiting Miss Bates after Knightley's rebuke
are experienced even more vividly. We see her successive attempts
to mislead Harriet, but we see at great length and in high color her
self-castigation (chaps. xvi, xvii, xlviii). We see her boasting proud-
ly that she does not need marriage, boasting almost as blatantly of
her "resources" as does Mrs. Elton (chap. x). But we know her too
intimately to take her conscious thoughts at face value. And we
see her, thirty-eight chapters later, chastened to an admission of
what we have known all along to be her true human need for love.
"If all took place that might take place among the circle of her
friends, Hartfield must be comparatively deserted; and she left to
cheer her father with the spirits only of ruined happiness. The child
to be born at Randalls must be a tie there even dearer than herself;
and Mrs. Weston's heart and time would be occupied by it. . . . All
that were good would be withdrawn" (chap. xlviii).

Perhaps the most delightful effects from our sustained inside
view of a very confused and very charming young woman come
from her frequent thoughts about Knightley. She is basically right
all along about his pre-eminent wisdom and virtue, and she is our
chief authority for taking *his* authority so seriously. And yet in

every thought about him she is misled. Knightley rebukes her; the reader knows that Knightley is in the right. But Emma?

> Emma made no answer, and tried to look cheerfully unconcerned, but was really feeling uncomfortable, and wanting him very much to be gone. She did not repent what she had done; she still thought herself a better judge of such a point of female right and refinement than he could be; but yet she had a sort of habitual respect for his judgment in general, which made her dislike having it so loudly against her; and to have him sitting just opposite to her in angry state, was very disagreeable [chap. viii].

Even more striking is the lack of self-knowledge shown when Mrs. Weston suggests that Knightley might marry Jane Fairfax.

> Her objections to Mr. Knightley's marrying did not in the least subside. She could see nothing but evil in it. It would be a great disappointment to Mr. John Knightley [Knightley's brother]; consequently to Isabella. A real injury to the children—a most mortifying change, and material loss to them all;—a very great deduction from her father's daily comfort—and, as to herself, she could not at all endure the idea of Jane Fairfax at Donwell Abbey. A Mrs. Knightley for them all to give way to!—No, Mr. Knightley must never marry. Little Henry must remain the heir of Donwell [chap. xxvi].

Self-deception could hardly be carried further, at least in a person of high intelligence and sensitivity.

Yet the effect of all this is what our tolerance for our own faults produces in our own lives. While only immature readers ever really identify with any character, losing all sense of distance and hence all chance of an artistic experience, our emotional reaction to every event concerning Emma tends to become like her own. When she feels anxiety or shame, we feel analogous emotions. Our modern awareness that such "feelings" are not identical with those we feel in our own lives in similar circumstances has tended to blind us to the fact that aesthetic form can be built out of patterned emotions as well as out of other materials. It is absurd to pretend that because our emotions and desires in responding to fiction are in a very real sense disinterested, they do not or should not exist. Jane Austen, in developing the sustained use of a sympathetic inside view, has mastered one of the most successful of all devices for inducing a parallel emotional response between the deficient heroine and the reader.

Sympathy for Emma can be heightened by withholding inside views of others as well as by granting them of her. The author knew, for example, that it would be fatal to grant any extended inside view of Jane Fairfax. The inadequacies of impressionistic criticism are nowhere revealed more clearly than in the suggestion often made about such minor characters that their authors would have liked to make them vivid but didn't know how.[5] Jane Austen knew perfectly well how to make such a character vivid; Anne in *Persuasion* is a kind of Jane Fairfax turned into heroine. But in *Emma*, Emma must shine supreme. It is not only that the slightest glance inside Jane's mind would be fatal to all of the author's plans for mystification about Frank Churchill, though this is important. The major problem is that any extended view of her would reveal her as a more sympathetic person than Emma herself. Jane is superior to Emma in most respects except the stroke of good fortune that made Emma the heroine of the book. In matters of taste and ability, of head and of heart, she is Emma's superior, and Jane Austen, always in danger of losing our sympathy for Emma, cannot risk any degree of distraction. Jane could, it is true, be granted fewer virtues, and *then* made more vivid. But to do so would greatly weaken the force of Emma's mistakes of heart and head in her treatment of the almost faultless Jane.

CONTROL OF JUDGMENT

But the very effectiveness of the rhetoric designed to produce sympathy might in itself lead to a serious misreading of the book. In reducing the emotional distance, the natural tendency is to reduce —willy-nilly—moral and intellectual distance as well. In reacting to

---

[5] A. C. Bradley, for example, once argued that Jane Austen intended Jane Fairfax to be as interesting throughout as she becomes at the end, but "the moralist in Jane Austen stood for once in her way. The secret engagement is, for her, so serious an offence, that she is afraid to win our hearts for Jane until it has led to great unhappiness" ("Jane Austen," in *Essays and Studies, by Members of the English Association*, II [Oxford, 1911], 23).

Emma's faults from the inside out, as if they were our own, we may very well not only forgive them but overlook them.[6]

There is, of course, no danger that readers who persist to the end will overlook Emma's serious mistakes; since she sees and reports those mistakes herself, everything becomes crystal clear at the end. The real danger inherent in the experiment is that readers will overlook the mistakes as they are committed and thus miss much of the comedy that depends on Emma's distorted view from page to page. If readers who dislike Emma cannot enjoy the preparation for the marriage to Knightley, readers who do not recognize her faults with absolute precision cannot enjoy the details of the preparation for the comic abasement which must precede that marriage.

It might be argued that there is no real problem, since the conventions of her time allowed for reliable commentary whenever it was needed to place Emma's faults precisely. But Jane Austen is not operating according to the conventions, most of which she had long since parodied and outgrown; her technique is determined by the needs of the novel she is writing. We can see this clearly by contrasting the manner of *Emma* with that of *Persuasion*, the next, and last-completed, work. In *Emma* there are many breaks in the point of view, because Emma's beclouded mind cannot do the whole job. In *Persuasion*, where the heroine's viewpoint is faulty only in her ignorance of Captain Wentworth's love, there are very few. Anne Elliot's consciousness is sufficient, as Emma's is not, for

---

[6] I know of only one full-scale attempt to deal with the "tension between sympathy and judgment" in modern literature, Robert Langbaum's *The Poetry of Experience* (London, 1957). Langbaum argues that in the dramatic monologue, with which he is primarily concerned, the sympathy engendered by the direct portrayal of internal experience leads the reader to suspend his moral judgment. Thus, in reading Browning's portraits of moral degeneration—e.g., the duke in "My Last Duchess" or the monk in "Soliloquy of a Spanish Cloister"—our moral judgment is overwhelmed "because we prefer to participate in the duke's power and freedom, in his hard core of character fiercely loyal to itself. Moral judgment is in fact important as the thing to be suspended, as a measure of the price we pay for the privilege of appreciating to the full this extraordinary man" (p. 83). While I think that Langbaum seriously underplays the extent to which moral judgment remains even after psychological vividness has done its work, and while he perhaps defines "morality" too narrowly when he excludes from it such things as power and freedom and fierce loyalty to one's own character, his book is a stimulating introduction to the problems raised by internal portraiture of flawed characters.

most of the needs of the novel which she dominates. Once the ethical and intellectual framework has been established by the narrator's introduction, we enter Anne's consciousness and remain bound to it much more rigorously than we are bound to Emma's. It is still true that whenever something must be shown that Anne's consciousness cannot show, we move to another center; but since her consciousness can do much more for us than Emma's, there need be few departures from it.

The most notable shift for rhetorical purposes in *Persuasion* comes fairly early. When Anne first meets Captain Wentworth after their years of separation that follow her refusal to marry him, she is convinced that he is indifferent. The major movement of *Persuasion* is toward her final discovery that he still loves her; *her* suspense is thus strong and inevitable from the beginning. The reader, however, is likely to believe that Wentworth is still interested. All the conventions of art favor such a belief: the emphasis is clearly on Anne and her unhappiness; the lover has returned; we have only to wait, perhaps with some tedium, for the inevitable outcome. Anne learns (chap. vii) that he has spoken of her as so altered "he should not have known her again!" "These were words which could not but dwell with her. Yet she soon began to rejoice that she had heard them. They were of sobering tendency; they allayed agitation; they composed, and consequently must make her happier." And suddenly we enter Wentworth's mind for one time only: "Frederick Wentworth had used such words, or something like them, but without an idea that they would be carried round to her. He had thought her wretchedly altered, and, in the first moment of appeal, had spoken as he felt. He had not forgiven Anne Elliot. She had used him ill"—and so he goes on, for five more paragraphs. The necessary point, the fact that Frederick believes himself to be indifferent, has been made, and it could not have been made without some kind of shift from Anne's consciousness.

At the end of the novel, we learn that Wentworth was himself deceived in this momentary inside view: "He had meant to forget her, and believed it to be done. He had imagined himself indifferent, when he had only been angry." We may want to protest against the earlier suppression as unfair, but we can hardly believe it to be what Miss Lascelles calls "an oversight."[7] It is deliberate manipulation of inside views in order to destroy our conventional security. We are thus made ready to go along with Anne in her long and painful road to the discovery that Frederick loves her after all.

The only other important breaks in the angle of vision of *Persuasion* come at the beginning and at the end. Chapter one is an excellent example of how a skilful novelist can, by the use of his own direct voice, accomplish in a few pages what even the best novelist must take chapters to do if he uses nothing but dramatized action. Again at the conclusion the author enters with a resounding reaffirmation that the Wentworth-Elliot marriage is as good a thing as we have felt it to be from the beginning.

> Who can be in doubt of what followed? When any two young people take it into their heads to marry, they are pretty sure by perseverance to carry their point, be they ever so poor, or ever so imprudent, or ever so little likely to be necessary to each other's ultimate comfort. This may be bad morality to conclude with, but I believe it to be truth; and if such parties succeed, how should a Captain Wentworth and an Anne Elliot, with the advantage of maturity of mind, consciousness of right, and one independent fortune between them, fail of bearing down every opposition?[8]

---

[7] *Jane Austen and Her Art* (Oxford, 1939), p. 204.

[8] It seems to be difficult for some modern critics, accustomed to ferreting values out from an impersonal or ironic context without the aid of the author's voice, to make use of reliable commentary like this when it is provided. Even a highly perceptive reader like Mark Schorer, for example, finds himself doing unnecessary acrobatics with the question of style, and particularly metaphor, as clues to the norms against which the author judges her characters. In reading *Persuasion*, he finds these clues among the metaphors "from commerce and property, the counting house and the inherited estate" with which it abounds ("Fiction and the Matrix of Analogy," *Kenyon Review* [Autumn, 1949], p. 540). No one would deny that the novel is packed with such metaphors, although Schorer is somewhat overingenious in marshaling to his cause certain dead metaphors that Austen could not have avoided without awkward circumlocution (esp. p. 542). But the crucial question surely is: What precisely are these metaphors of the countinghouse doing in the novel? Whose values are they supposed to reveal? Accustomed to reading modern fiction in which the novelist very likely provides no direct assistance in answering this question, Schorer leaves it really unanswered; at times he seems almost to imply that Jane Austen is unconsciously giving herself away in her use of them (e.g., p. 543).

But the novel is really very clear about it all. The introduction, coming directly from the wholly reliable narrator, establishes unequivocally and without "analogy" the conflict between the world of the Elliots, depending for its values on selfishness, stupidity, and pride—and the world of Anne, a world where "elegance of mind and

Except for these few intrusions and one in chapter xix, Anne's own mind is sufficient in *Persuasion,* but we can never rely completely on *Emma.* It is hardly surprising that Jane Austen has provided many correctives to insure our placing her errors with precision.

The chief corrective is Knightley. His commentary on Emma's errors is a natural expression of his love; he can tell the reader and Emma at the same time precisely how she is mistaken. Thus, nothing Knightley says can be beside the point. Each affirmation of a value, each accusation of error is in itself an action in the plot. When he rebukes Emma for manipulating Harriet, when he attacks her for superficiality and false pride, when he condemns her for gossiping and flirting with Frank Churchill, and finally when he attacks her for being "insolent" and "unfeeling" in her treatment of Miss Bates, we have Jane Austen's judgment on Emma, rendered dramatically. But it has come from someone who is essentially sympathetic toward Emma, so that his judgments against her are presumed to be temporary. His sympathy reinforces ours even as he criticizes, and her respect for his opinion, shown in her self-abasement after he has criticized, is one of our main reasons for expecting her to reform.

If Henry James had tried to write a novel about Emma, and had cogitated at length on the problem of getting her story told dramatically, he could not have done better than this. It is possible, of course, to think of *Emma* without Knightley as *raisonneur,* just as it is possible to think of *The Golden Bowl,* say, without the Assinghams as *ficelles* to reflect something not seen by the Prince or Princess. But Knightley, though he receives less independent space than the Assinghams and is almost never seen in an inside view, is clearly more useful for Jane Austen's purposes than any realistically limited *ficelle* could possibly be. By combining the role of commentator with the role of hero, Jane Austen has worked more economically than James, and though economy is as dangerous as any other criterion when applied universally, even James might have profited

---

sweetness of character" are the supreme values. The commercial values stressed by Schorer are only a selection from what is actually a rich group of evils. And Anne's own expressed views again and again provide direct guidance to the reader.

from a closer study of the economies that a character like Knightley can be made to achieve. It is as if James had dared to make one of the four main characters, say the Prince, into a thoroughly good, wise, perceptive man, a thoroughly clear rather than a partly confused "reflector."

Since Knightley is established early as completely reliable, we need no views of his secret thoughts. He has no secret thoughts, except for the unacknowledged depths of his love for Emma and his jealousy of Frank Churchill. The other main characters have more to hide, and Jane Austen moves in and out of minds with great freedom, choosing for her own purposes what to reveal and what to withhold. Always the seeming violation of consistency is in the consistent service of the particular needs of Emma's story. Sometimes a shift is made simply to direct our suspense, as when Mrs. Weston suggests a possible union of Emma and Frank Churchill, at the end of her conversation with Knightley about the harmful effects of Emma's friendship with Harriet (chap. v). "Part of her meaning was to conceal some favourite thoughts of her own and Mr. Weston's on the subject, as much as possible. There were wishes at Randalls respecting Emma's destiny, but it was not desirable to have them suspected."

One objection to this selective dipping into whatever mind best serves our immediate purposes is that it suggests mere trickery and inevitably spoils the illusion of reality. If Jane Austen can tell us what Mrs. Weston is thinking, why not what Frank Churchill and Jane Fairfax are thinking? Obviously, because she chooses to build a mystery, and to do so she must refuse, arbitrarily and obtrusively, to grant the privilege of an inside view to characters whose minds would reveal too much. But is not the mystery purchased at the price of shaking the reader's faith in Jane Austen's integrity? If she simply withholds until later what she might as well relate now—if her procedure is not dictated by the very nature of her materials— why should we take her seriously?

If a natural surface were required in all fiction, then this objection would hold. But if we want to read *Emma* in its own terms, the real question about these shifts cannot be answered by an easy appeal to general principles. Every author withholds until later what he "might as well" relate now. The question is always one of desired effects, and the choice of any one effect always bans innumerable other effects. There is, indeed, a question to be raised about the use of mystery in *Emma,* but the conflict is not between an abstract end that Jane Austen never worried about and a shoddy mystification that she allowed to betray her. The conflict is between two effects both of which she cares about a good deal. On the one hand she cares about maintaining some sense of mystery as long as she can. On the other, she works at all points to heighten the reader's sense of dramatic irony, usually in the form of a contrast between what Emma knows and what the reader knows.

As in most novels, whatever steps are taken to mystify inevitably decrease the dramatic irony, and, whenever dramatic irony is increased by telling the reader secrets the characters have not yet suspected, mystery is inevitably destroyed. The longer we are in doubt about Frank Churchill, the weaker our sense of ironic contrast between Emma's views and the truth. The sooner we see through Frank Churchill's secret plot, the greater our pleasure in observing Emma's innumerable misreadings of his behavior and the less interest we have in the mere mystery of the situation. And we all find that on second reading we discover new intensities of dramatic irony resulting from the complete loss of mystery; knowing what abysses of error Emma is preparing for herself, even those of us who may on first reading have deciphered nearly all the details of the Churchill mystery find additional ironies.

But it is obvious that these ironies could have been offered even on a first reading, if Jane Austen had been willing to sacrifice her mystery. A single phrase in her own name—"his secret engagement to Jane Fairfax"—or a short inside view of either of the lovers could have made us aware of every ironic touch.

The author must, then, choose whether to purchase mystery at the expense of irony. For many of us Jane Austen's choice here is perhaps the weakest aspect of this novel. It is a commonplace of our criticism that significant literature arouses suspense not about the "what" but about the "how." Mere mystification has been mastered by so many second-rate writers that her efforts at mystification seem second-rate.

But again we must ask whether criticism can be conducted effectively by balancing one abstract quality against another. Is there a norm of dramatic irony for all works, or even for all works of a given kind? Has anyone ever formulated a "law of first and second readings" that will tell us just how many of our pleasures on page one should depend on our knowledge of what happens on page the last? We quite properly ask that the books we call great be able to stand up under repeated reading, but we need not ask that they yield identical pleasures on each reading. The modern works whose authors pride themselves on the fact that they can never be read but only re-read may be very good indeed, but they are not *made* good by the fact that their secret pleasures can only be wrested from them by repeated readings.

In any case, even if one accepted the criticism of Jane Austen's efforts at mystification, the larger service of the inside views is clear: the crosslights thrown by other minds prevent our being blinded by Emma's radiance.

The Reliable Narrator and the Norms of "Emma"

If mere intellectual clarity about Emma were the goal in this work, we should be forced to say that the manipulation of inside views and the extensive commentary of the reliable Knightley are more than is necessary. But for maximum intensity of the comedy and romance, even these are not enough. The "author herself"—not necessarily the real Jane Austen but an implied author, represented in this book by a reliable narrator—heightens the effects by directing our intellectual, moral, and emotional progress. She performs, of course, most of the functions described in chapter vii. But her most important role is to reinforce both aspects of the double vision that operates throughout the book: our inside view of Emma's worth and our objective view of her great faults.

The narrator opens *Emma* with a masterful simultaneous presentation of Emma and of the values against which she must be judged: "Emma Woodhouse, handsome, clever, and rich, with a comfortable home and happy disposition, seemed to unite some of the best blessings of existence; and had lived nearly twenty-one years in the world with very little to distress or vex her." This "seemed" is immediately reinforced by more directly stated reservations. "The real evils of Emma's situation were the power of having rather too much her own way, and a disposition to think a little too well of herself; these were the disadvantages which threatened alloy to her many enjoyments. The danger, however, was at present so unperceived, that they did not by any means rank as misfortunes with her."

None of this could have been said by Emma, and if shown through her consciousness, it could not be accepted, as it must be, without question. Like most of the first three chapters, it is non-dramatic summary, building up, through the ostensible business of getting the characters introduced, to Emma's initial blunder with Harriet and Mr. Elton. Throughout these chapters, we learn much of what we must know from the narrator, but she turns over more and more of the job of summary to Emma as she feels more and more sure of our seeing precisely to what degree Emma is to be trusted. Whenever we leave the "real evils" we have been warned against in Emma, the narrator's and Emma's views coincide: we cannot tell which of them, for example, offers the judgment on Mr. Woodhouse that "his talents could not have recommended him at any time," or the judgment on Mr. Knightley that he is "a sensible man," "always welcome" at Hartfield, or even that "Mr. Knightley, in fact, was one of the few people who could see faults in Emma Woodhouse, and the only one who ever told her of them."

But there are times when Emma and her author are far apart, and the author's direct guidance aids the reader in his own break with Emma. The beautiful irony of the first description of Harriet, given through Emma's eyes (chap. iii) could no doubt be grasped intellectually by many readers without all of the preliminary commentary. But even for the most perceptive its effect is heightened, surely, by the sense of standing with the author and observing with her precisely how Emma's judgment is going astray. Perhaps more important, we ordinary, less perceptive readers have by now been raised to a level suited to grasp the ironies. Certainly, most readers would overlook some of the barbs directed against Emma if the novel began, as a serious modern novelist might well begin it, with this description:

> [Emma] was not struck by any thing remarkably clever in Miss Smith's conversation, but she found her altogether very engaging—not inconveniently shy, not unwilling to talk—and yet so far from pushing, shewing so proper and becoming a deference, seeming so pleasantly grateful for being admitted to Hartfield, and so artlessly impressed by the appearance of every thing in so superior a style to what she had been used to, that she must have good sense and deserve encouragement. Encouragement should be given. Those soft blue eyes . . . should not be wasted on the inferior society of Highbury. . . .

And so Emma goes on, giving herself away with every word, pouring out her sense of her own beneficence and general value. Harriet's past friends, "though very good sort of people, must be doing her harm." Without knowing them, Emma knows that they "must be coarse and unpolished, and very unfit to be the intimates of a girl who wanted only a little more knowledge and elegance to be quite perfect." And she concludes with a beautiful burst of egotism: "*She* would notice her; she would improve her; she would detach her from her bad acquaintance, and introduce her into good society; she would form her opinions and her manners. It would be an interesting, and certainly a very kind undertaking; highly becoming her own situation in life, her leisure, and powers." Even the most skilful reader might not easily plot an absolutely true course through these ironies without the prior direct assistance we have been given. Emma's views are not so outlandish that they could never have been held by a female novelist writing in her time. They cannot serve effectively as signs of *her* character unless they are clearly disavowed as signs of Jane Austen's views. Emma's unconscious catalogue of her egotistical uses for Harriet, given under the pretense of listing the services *she* will perform, is thus given its full force by being framed explicitly in a world of values which Emma herself cannot discover until the conclusion of the book.

The full importance of the author's direct imposition of an elaborate scale of norms can be seen by considering that conclusion. The sequence of events is a simple one: Emma's faults and mistakes are brought home to her in a rapid and humiliating chain of rebukes from Knightley and blows from hard fact. These blows to her self-esteem produce at last a genuine reform (for example, she brings herself to apologize to Miss Bates, something she could never have done earlier in the novel). The change in her character removes the only obstacle in the way of Knightley's proposal, and the marriage follows. "The wishes, the hopes, the confidence, the predictions of the small band of true friends who witnessed the ceremony, were fully answered in the perfect happiness of the union."

It may be that if we look at Emma and Knightley as real people, this ending will seem false. G. B. Stern laments, in *Speaking of Jane Austen,* "Oh, Miss Austen, it was *not* a good solution; it was a bad solution, an unhappy ending, could we see beyond the last pages of the book." Edmund Wilson predicts that Emma will find a new protégée like Harriet, since she has not been cured of her inclination to "infatuations with women." Marvin Mudrick even more emphatically rejects Jane Austen's explicit rhetoric; he believes that Emma is still a "confirmed exploiter," and for him the ending must be read as ironic.[9]

But it is precisely because this ending is neither life itself nor a simple bit of literary irony that it can serve so well to heighten our sense of a complete and indeed perfect resolution to all that has gone before. If we look at the values that have been realized in this marriage and compare them with those realized in conventional marriage plots, we see that Jane Austen means what she says: this will be a happy marriage because there is simply nothing left to make it anything less than perfectly happy. It fulfils every value embodied in the world of the book—with the possible exception that Emma may never learn to apply herself as she ought to her reading and her piano! It is a union of intelligence: of "reason," of "sense," of "judgment." It is a union of virtue: of "good will," of generosity, of unselfishness. It is a union of feeling: of "taste," "tenderness," "love," "beauty."[10]

---

[9] The first two quotations are from Wilson's "A Long Talk about Jane Austen," *A Literary Chronicle: 1920–1950* (New York, 1952). The third is from *Jane Austen,* p. 206.

[10] It has lately been fashionable to underplay the value of tenderness and good will in Jane Austen, in reaction to an earlier generation that overdid the picture of "gentle Jane." The trend seems to have begun in earnest with D. W. Harding's "Regulated Hatred: An Aspect of the Work of Jane Austen," *Scrutiny,* VIII (March, 1940), 346–62. While I do not feel as strongly aroused against this school of readers

In a general way, then, this plot offers us an experience superficially like that offered by most tragicomedy as well as by much of the cheapest popular art: we are made to desire certain good things for certain good characters, and then our desires are gratified. If we depended on general criteria derived from our justified boredom with such works, we should reject this one. But the critical difference lies in the precise quality of the values appealed to and the precise quality of the characters who violate or realize them. All of the cheap marriage plots in the world should not lead us to be embarrassed about our pleasure in Emma and Knightley's marriage. It is more than just the marriage: it is the *rightness of this* marriage, as a conclusion to all of the comic wrongness that has gone before. The good for Emma includes both her necessary reform and the resulting marriage. Marriage to an intelligent, amiable, good, and attractive man is the best thing that can happen to this heroine, and the readers who do not experience it as such are, I am convinced, far from knowing what Jane Austen is about—whatever they may say about the "bitter spinster's" attitude toward marriage.

Our modern sensibilities are likely to be rasped by any such formulation. We do not ordinarily like to encounter perfect endings in our novels—even in the sense of "perfectedness" or completion, the sense obviously intended by Jane Austen. We refuse to accept it when we see it: witness the many attempts to deny Dostoevski's success with Alyosha and Father Zossima in *The Brothers Karamazov*. Many of us find it embarrassing to talk of emotions based on moral judgment at all, particularly when the emotions have any kind of affirmative cast. Emma herself is something of a "modern" in this regard throughout most of the book. Her self-deception about marriage is as great as about most other important matters. Emma boasts to Harriet of her indifference to marriage, at the same time unconsciously betraying her totally inadequate view of the sources of human happiness.

---

as does R. W. Chapman (see his *A Critical Bibliography*, p. 52, and his review of Mudrick's work in the *T.L.S.* [September 19, 1952]), it seems to me that another swing of the pendulum is called for: when Jane Austen praises the "relenting heart," she means that praise, though she is the same author who can lash the unrelenting heart with "regulated hatred."

If I know myself, Harriet, mine is an active, busy mind, with a great many independent resources; and I do not perceive why I should be more in want of employment at forty or fifty than one-and-twenty. Woman's usual occupations of eye and hand and mind will be as open to me then, as they are now; or with no important variation. If I draw less, I shall read more; if I give up music, I shall take to carpet-work.

Emma at carpet-work! If she knows herself indeed.

And as for objects of interest, objects for the affections, which is, in truth, the great point of inferiority, the want of which is really the great evil to be avoided in *not* marrying [a magnificent concession, this] I shall be very well off, with all the children of a sister I love so much, to care about. There will be enough of them, in all probability, to supply every sort of sensation that declining life can need. There will be enough for every hope and every fear; and though my attachment to none can equal that of a parent, it suits my ideas of comfort better than what is warmer and blinder. My nephews and nieces!—I shall often have a niece with me [chap. x].

Without growing solemn about it—it is wonderfully comic—we can recognize that the humor springs here from very deep sources indeed. It can be fully enjoyed, in fact, only by the reader who has attained to a vision of human felicity far more profound than Emma's "comfort" and "want" and "need." It is a vision that includes not simply marriage, but a kind of loving converse not based, as is Emma's here, on whether the "loved" person will serve one's irreducible needs.

The comic effect of this repudiation of marriage is considerably increased by the fact that Emma always thinks of marriage for others as *their* highest good, and in fact unconsciously encourages her friend Harriet to fall in love with the very man she herself loves without knowing it. The delightful denouement is thus what we want not only because it is a supremely good thing for Emma, but because it is a supremely comic outcome of Emma's profound misunderstanding of herself and of the human condition. In the schematic language of chapter v, it satisfies both our practical desire for Emma's well-being and our appetite for the qualities proper to these artistic materials. It is thus a more resounding resolution than either of these elements separately could provide. The other major resolution of the work—Harriet's marriage with her farmer—reinforces this interpretation. Emma's sin against Harriet has been something far worse than the mere meddling of a busybody. To destroy Harriet's chances for happiness—chances that depend entirely on her marriage—is as close to viciousness as any author could dare to take a heroine designed to be loved. We can laugh with Emma at this mistake (chap. liv) only because Harriet's chance for happiness is restored.

Other values, like money, blood, and "consequence," are real enough in *Emma*, but only as they contribute to or are mastered by good taste, good judgment, and good morality. Money alone can make a Mrs. Churchill, but a man or woman "is silly to marry without it." Consequence untouched by sense can make a very inconsequential Mr. Woodhouse; untouched by sense or virtue it can make the much more contemptible Mr. and Miss Elliot of *Persuasion*. But it is a pleasant thing to have, and it does no harm unless, like the early Emma, one takes it too seriously. Charm and elegance without sufficient moral force can make a Frank Churchill; unschooled by morality it can lead to the baseness of Henry Crawford in *Mansfield Park* or of Wickham in *Pride and Prejudice*. Even the supreme virtues are inadequate in isolation: good will alone will make a comic Miss Bates or a Mr. Weston, judgment with insufficient good will a comic Mr. John Knightley, and so on.

I am willing to risk the commonplace in such a listing because it is only thus that the full force of Jane Austen's comprehensive view can be seen. There is clearly at work here a much more detailed ordering of values than any conventional public philosophy of her time could provide. Obviously, few readers in her own time, and far fewer in our own, have ever approached this novel in full and detailed agreement with the author's norms. But they were led to join her as they read, and so are we.

EXPLICIT JUDGMENTS ON EMMA WOODHOUSE

We have said in passing almost enough of the other side of the coin—the judgment of particular actions as they relate to the general norms. But something must be said of the detailed "placing" of Emma, by direct commentary, in the hierarchy of values established by the novel. I must be convinced, for example, not only that tenderness for other people's feelings is an important trait but also that Emma's particular behavior violates the true standards of tenderness, if I am to savor to the full the episode of Emma's insult to Miss Bates and Knightley's reproach which follows. If I refuse to blame Emma, I may discover a kind of intellectual enjoyment in the episode, and I will probably think that any critic who talks of "belief" in tenderness as operating in such a context is taking things too seriously. But I can never enjoy the episode in its full intensity or grasp its formal coherence. Similarly, I must agree not only that to be dreadfully boring is a minor fault compared with the major virtue of "good will," but also that Miss Bates's exemplification of this fault and of this virtue entitle her to the respect which Emma denies. If I do not—while yet being able to laugh at Miss Bates—I can hardly understand, let alone enjoy, Emma's mistreatment of her.

But these negative judgments must be counteracted by a larger approval, and, as we would expect, the novel is full of direct apologies for Emma. Her chief fault, lack of good will or tenderness, must be read not only in relationship to the code of values provided by the book as a whole—a code which judges her as seriously deficient; it must also be judged in relationship to the harsh facts of the world around her, a world made up of human beings ranging in degree of selfishness and egotism from Knightley, who lapses from perfection when he tries to judge Frank Churchill, his rival, down to Mrs. Elton, who has most of Emma's faults and none of her virtues. In such a setting, Emma is easily forgiven. When she insults Miss Bates, for example, we remember that Miss Bates lives in a world where many others are insensitive and cruel. "Miss Bates, neither young, handsome, rich, nor married, stood in the very worst predicament in the world for having much of the public favour; and she had no intellectual superiority to make atonement to herself, or frighten those who might hate her, into outward respect." While it would be a mistake to see only this "regulated hatred" in Jane Austen's world, overlooking the tenderness and generosity, the hatred of viciousness is there, and there is enough vice in evidence to make Emma almost shine by comparison.

Often, Jane Austen makes this apology-by-comparison explicit. When Emma lies to Knightley about Harriet, very close to the end of the book, she is excused with a generalization about human nature: "Seldom, very seldom, does complete truth belong to any human disclosure; seldom can it happen that something is not a little disguised, or a little mistaken; but where, as in this case, though the conduct is mistaken, the feelings are not, it may not be very material.—Mr. Knightley could not impute to Emma a more relenting heart than she possessed, or a heart more disposed to accept of his."

The Implied Author as Friend and Guide

With all of this said about the masterful use of the narrator in *Emma*, there remain some "intrusions" unaccounted for by strict service to the story itself. "What did she say?" the narrator asks, at the crucial moment in the major love scene. "Just what she ought, of course. A lady always does.—She said enough to show there need not be despair—and to invite him to say more himself." To some readers this has seemed to demonstrate the author's inability to write a love scene, since it sacrifices "the illusion of reality."[11] But who has ever read this far in *Emma* under the delusion that he is reading a realistic portrayal which is suddenly shattered by the unnatural appearance of the narrator? If the narrator's superabundant wit is destructive of the kind of illusion proper to this work, the novel has been ruined long before.

But we should now be in a position to see precisely why the narrator's wit is not in the least out of place at the emotional climax of the novel. We have seen how the inside views of the characters and the author's commentary have been used from the beginning to get the values straight and to keep them straight and to help direct our reactions to Emma. But we also see here a beautiful case of the dramatized author as friend and guide. "Jane Austen," like "Henry Fielding," is a paragon of wit, wisdom, and virtue. She does not talk about her qualities; unlike Fielding she does not in *Emma* call direct attention to her artistic skill. But we are seldom allowed

---

[11] Edd Winfield Parks, "Exegesis in Austen's Novels," *The South Atlantic Quarterly,* I.I (January, 1952), 117.

to forget about her for all that. When we read this novel we accept her as representing everything we admire most. She is as generous and wise as Knightley; in fact, she is a shade more penetrating in her judgment. She is as subtle and witty as Emma would like to think herself. Without being sentimental she is in favor of tenderness. She is able to put an adequate but not excessive value on wealth and rank. She recognizes a fool when she sees one, but unlike Emma she knows that it is both immoral and foolish to be rude to fools. She is, in short, a perfect human being, within the concept of perfection established by the book she writes; she even recognizes that human perfection of the kind *she* exemplifies is not quite attainable in real life. The process of her domination is of course circular; her character establishes the values for us according to which her character is then found to be perfect. But this circularity does not affect the success of her endeavor; in fact it insures it.

Her "omniscience" is thus a much more remarkable thing than is ordinarily implied by the term. All good novelists know all about their characters—all that they need to know. And the question of how their narrators are to find out all that *they* need to know, the question of "authority," is a relatively simple one. The real choice is much more profound than this would imply. It is a choice of the moral, not merely the technical, angle of vision from which the story is to be told.

Unlike the central intelligences of James and his successors, "Jane Austen" has learned nothing at the end of the novel that she did not know at the beginning. She needed to learn nothing. She knew everything of importance already. We have been privileged to watch with her as she observes her favorite character climb from a considerably lower platform to join the exalted company of Knightley, "Jane Austen," and those of us readers who are wise enough, good enough, and perceptive enough to belong up there too. As Katherine Mansfield says, "the truth is that every true admirer of the novels cherishes the happy thought that he alone—reading between the lines—has become the secret friend of their author."[12] Those who love "gentle Jane" as a secret friend may undervalue the

---

[12] *Novels and Novelists,* ed. J. Middleton Murry (London, 1930), p. 304.

irony and wit; those who see her in effect as the greatest of Shaw's heroines, flashing about her with the weapons of irony, may under-value the emphasis on tenderness and good will. But only a very few can resist her.

The dramatic illusion of her presence as a character is thus fully as important as any other element in the story. When she intrudes, the illusion is not shattered. The only illusion we care about, the illusion of traveling intimately with a hardy little band of readers whose heads are screwed on tight and whose hearts are in the right place, is actually strengthened when we are refused the ro-mantic love scene. Like the author herself, we don't care about the love scene. We can find love scenes in almost any novelist's works, but only here can we find a mind and heart that can give us clarity without oversimplification, sympathy and romance without sentimentality, and biting irony without cynicism.

"At every point we are forced to ask, 'How can we believe *him?* His must be exactly the *wrong* view.' The fracture between the character of the event as we feel it to be, and the character of the narrator as he reports the event to us, is the essential irony, yet it is not in any way a simple one. . . ."
—MARK SCHORER, commenting on Ford Madox Ford's *The Good Soldier*

"It only remains for me to say, unfortunately, that 90 per cent of this strictly truthful account, given by the authoress, is not truthful at all, including even the identity of the authoress herself. In fact, the question no longer can be escaped, that is the second enigma of this work—who wrote it? Who indeed?

"Surely, not Susan . . . And certainly not Phil . . .

"Who, then? The obvious answer is angel child herself. She is the authoress in the cold-water flat, whatever the authoress says her name is. Considering the style of work, and its heathenish anti-intellectual philosophy, she is obviously the author.

"Yet one is bound to wonder . . . It would be beyond her.

"Who did write it, then? By logical deduction, only one last possibility remains—I, myself. . . . But this can be ruled out. . . . Somebody else did it. It wasn't me. Maybe the cat wrote it."—CALDER WILLINGHAM, *Natural Child*

"If I have lied to you [the reader], it is because I must show you that falsehood is truth."—JEAN CAYROL, *Les corps étrangers*

PART III

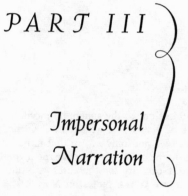

Impersonal Narration

"To lift our subject out of the sphere of anecdote and place it in the sphere of drama . . . we supply it with a large lucid reflector, which we find only . . . in that mind and soul concerned in the business that have at once the highest sensibility and the highest capacity, or that are . . . most admirably agitated."—HENRY JAMES, *Notes on Novelists*

"The action of the drama is simply the girl's 'subjective' adventure."—HENRY JAMES, Preface to "In the Cage"

The Uses of Authorial Silence

"EXIT AUTHOR" ONCE AGAIN

In *Emma* we see a very precise control over a prolonged inside view of a seriously flawed consciousness. The direction of the control is in every respect determined by the effort to realize for the reader the unique plot. In order to preserve the correct mixture of sympathy and condemnation in our view of Emma, Jane Austen has cheerfully sacrificed realistic narrative manner.

If we can imagine an *Emma* purged of the improbable wisdom of Knightley and the narrator, a novel in which the reader must infer the truth about Emma through her own beclouded vision, we will have a loose prototype for many important modern novels. *Madame Bovary* and *The Ambassadors*, *A Portrait of the Artist as a Young Man* and *Ulysses*, *The Trial* and *The Castle*, *As I Lay Dying*, *The Stranger* and *The Fall*—in each of these we are presented with the confused viewpoint of an Emma, or of a collection of Emmas, groping their way relatively unaided toward their destinies. In hundreds of other works by Woolf, Waugh, Greene, and Cary, by Mauriac, Duhamel, Sartre, and Camus, by Dos Passos, Hemingway, Faulkner, and Porter, by Eudora Welty, Wright Morris, James Baldwin, and Saul Bellow—the list might be extended indefinitely—the author and reader may meet, like Voltaire and God, but they do not speak.

They do not speak, that is, directly. The author's voice is still dominant in a dialogue that is at the heart of all experience with fiction. With commentary ruled out, hundreds of devices remain for revealing judgment and molding responses. Patterns of imagery and symbol are as effective in modern fiction as they have always been in poetry in controlling our evaluation of details.[1] Decisions about what parts of a story to dramatize and about the sequence and proportion of episodes can be as effective in *The Hamlet* as they are in *Hamlet*, as decisive in *Ulysses* as they are in the *Odyssey*.[2] In fact all of the old-fashioned dramatic devices of pace and timing can be refurbished for the purposes of a dramatic, impersonal narration.[3] And manipulation of dramatized points of view can, as hundreds of studies following upon Percy Lubbock's *Craft of Fiction* have shown, convey the author's judgment with great precision.

For logical completeness, I should at this point provide a demonstration of each of the major devices of disclosure and evaluation that have been used to replace direct statement. A full rhetoric of fiction would include a discussion of these devices. But the fact is that they have been adequately demonstrated over and over again in criticism since James. One need not show once more that symbols can be used to evaluate character or that manipulation of point of view can reveal the meaning of a work. Perhaps it is too much to expect that my readers will at this point incorporate into their view of the rhetoric of fiction their experience with the best analyses of impersonal works.[4] But I have more than enough to do

---

[1] For a discussion of the rhetorical use of imagery in poetry, see Rosemond Tuve, "The Criterion of Rhetorical Efficacy," *Elizabethan and Metaphysical Imagery* (Chicago, 1947), pp. 180–91; *Images and Themes in Five Poems by Milton* (Cambridge, Mass., 1957); and her "A Name To Resound for the Ages," *The Listener*, August 28, 1958, pp. 312–13, a discussion of "the evaluative functioning of figurative speech" in Milton.

[2] See Paul Goodman, *The Structure of Literature* (Chicago, 1954), esp. the analysis of Kafka's *The Castle*, pp. 173–83.

[3] For a brief, convincing analysis of how Joyce worked with pace and "focus," in "The Dead," to solve a problem similar to the one we have seen in *Emma*, see C. C. Loomis, Jr., "Structure and Sympathy in Joyce's 'The Dead,'" *PMLA*, LXXV (March, 1960), pp. 149–51.

[4] See Bibliography, Sec. II, B.

if I am to discuss here the uses of authorial silence and, in the remaining chapters, the new problems that this silence presents to authors and readers.

By the kind of silence he maintains, by the manner in which he leaves his characters to work out their own destinies or tell their own stories, the author can achieve effects which would be difficult or impossible if he allowed himself or a reliable spokesman to speak directly and authoritatively to us.

The most frequently discussed of these effects is, as we have seen, the air of naturalness that is thought to be given by an "authorless" work. But the realistic, limited characters whom the author gives us in his stead bring with them many additional effects not accounted for in the usual defenses of authorial effacement. A narrator chosen for the sake of objectivity may, as James says of Flaubert's reflectors, Frédéric and Emma, partially destroy other important general qualities like "interest" or "suspense." Or he may, by virtue of his helpless isolation, attract a kind of sympathy which can inadvertently strengthen or weaken a work, depending on the appropriateness of that sympathy. No narrator or central intelligence or observer is *simply* convincing: he is convincingly decent or mean, brilliant or stupid, informed, ignorant, or muddled. Since there are few such qualities that even the most tolerant of us can observe in full neutrality, we usually find our emotional and intellectual reactions to him as a character affecting our reactions to the events he relates. This effect is seen clearly in drama whenever a hero, boor, or villain is used to relate events that must take place off stage. Othello's account of how he won Desdemona by telling her his adventures leads the Duke to say, "I think this tale would win my daughter too," and it wins us in the same way; we cannot react to it dispassionately.

The same effect is unavoidable in fiction. Though it is most evident when a narrator tells the story of his own adventures, we react to all narrators as persons. We find their accounts credible or incredible, their opinions wise or foolish, their judgments just or unjust. The gradations and axes of approval or condemnation are almost as rich as those presented by life itself, but we can distinguish two radically different types of reaction, depending on whether a narrator is reliable or unreliable. At one extreme we find narrators whose every judgment is suspect (the barber in "Haircut"; Jason in *The Sound and the Fury*). At the other are narrators scarcely distinguishable from the omniscient author (Conrad's Marlow). In between lies a confused variety of more-or-less reliable narrators, many of them puzzling mixtures of sound and unsound. Though we cannot draw a sharp line between the two types with any great confidence, the distinction is not arbitrary: it is forced upon us by our recognition that we have, in fact, two different kinds of experience, depending on which kind of narrator is in charge.

Because narrators who clearly fall on the unreliable side of the line are in many respects more troublesome to deal with, we shall begin with that other, more amiable breed: the narrators who, however human and limited and bewildered, earn our basic trust and approval.

CONTROL OF SYMPATHY

Perhaps the most important effect of traveling with a narrator who is unaccompanied by a helpful author is that of decreasing emotional distance. We have seen that much traditional commentary was used to increase sympathy or to apologize for faults. When an author chooses to forgo such rhetoric, he may do so because he does not care about conventional sympathy, like Gide in *Les Caves du Vatican*. But he may also do so because his central intelligence is of the kind that will seem most sympathetic if presented as an isolated, unaided consciousness, without the support that a reliable narrator or observer would lend.

Such an effect is possible, I think, only when the reflected intelligence is so little distant, so close, in effect, to the norms of the work that no complicated deciphering of unreliability is required of the reader. So long as what the character thinks and feels can be taken directly as a reliable clue about the circumstances he faces, the reader can experience those circumstances with him even more strongly because of his moral isolation.

Such isolation can be used to create an almost unbearably poignant sense of the hero's or heroine's helplessness in a chaotic, friendless world. In "Pale Horse, Pale Rider" (1936), Katherine

Anne Porter confines the point of view strictly to what Miranda can see and know and feel. The story opens with Miranda's dream of a lonely "journey I do not mean to take." Convinced that she has "only nothing but it is enough," she wakes to find herself still alone, isolated, in a "day-to-day existence, where survival . . . had become a series of feats of sleight of hand." She is overwhelmed by the meaninglessness of the war and her own helpless isolation in a society obsessed with war. "There must be a great many of them here who think as I do, and we dare not say a word to each other of our desperation, we are speechless animals letting ourselves be destroyed, and why? Does anybody here believe the things we say to each other?"

Clearly a good deal of the poignancy of her inward cry would be lost if anyone, even an unspecified omniscient narrator, could accompany her on her desperate journey into feverish delirium and near-death. She must travel alone toward the discovery that the man she loves has died, leaving her "to put in order her disordered mind, and to set . . . once more safely in the road that would lead her again to death." Even her lover must not be fully a companion; no one is allowed to share her views of the war, no one may appear to support her in her loss or to interpret for her the meaning of her lonely discovery that rapture is forever gone from her world and that the unreal world of the living is unwittingly preparing itself, "in the dead, cold light of tomorrow," for the reality of death. In her delirium, after a moment of rapture, "the bright landscape faded, she was alone in a strange stony place of bitter cold, picking her way along a steep path of slippery snow, calling out, Oh, I must go back! But in what direction?" Recovered to consciousness, she "folded her painful body together and wept silently, shamelessly, in pity for herself and her lost rapture."

She must be alone in every respect, if this lonely experience is to have full power; she can be alone, as she reflects her story to us, because at every point throughout we are intended to feel with her. Though her mind is clouded enough in one respect, she sees clearly the full chaos for what it is; we are expected, if not to share precisely her views of the war ("Coal, oil, iron, gold, international finance, why don't you tell us about them, you little liar?"), at least to share precisely her feeling about it, and about the life it reflects to her, awake, asleep, and in delirium: "Danger, danger, danger, the voices said, and War, war, war."

In such a story, then, the isolated heroine can do for herself what no other narrator could possibly do for her. Very little heightening of her character is needed to make us unite with her against the hostile world around her; simply because she is the only sensitive person visible—even her lover has lost part of his natural sensitivity in his patriotism—she wins us irresistibly. What little heightening of her moral character is needed can be made to spring naturally from her own recollections; she can recall, in this third-person form, episodes which in a first-person account would imply conceited self-praise. "Miranda and Towney had a great deal in common, and liked each other. They had both been real reporters once, and had been sent together to 'cover' a scandalous elopement, in which no marriage had taken place, after all." Out of pity, they both suppressed the story and were demoted. "They had this in common, that neither of them could see what else they could possibly have done, and they knew they were considered fools by the rest of the staff—nice girls, but fools." One such episode of her own quixotism is sufficient—on re-reading it may even seem superfluous—to establish Miranda's moral superiority, and it of course heightens our sense of her isolation at the same time; everyone else thinks she's a fool for not being a knave.

It is difficult, in short, to think of any other way to tell this story; any reliable commentator, attempting to heighten our sympathy and pity, would probably do more harm than good—particularly since the story comes dangerously close to sentimentality even as it stands. Alone as she is, Miranda seems justified in her self-pity, and she can stand for the one supreme value of the human personality. But Miranda and any collaborating "I" would probably seem mawkish.

The peculiar intensity of such an effect depends, however, on a static character. The changes which go to make up the story are all changes in fact and circumstance and knowledge, never in the essential worth or rightness of the character herself. She must be accepted at her own estimate from the beginning, and that estimate must, for greatest effect, be as close as possible to the reader's estimate of his own importance. Whether we call this effect identification or not, it is certainly the closest that literature can come to making us feel events as if they were happening to ourselves. As we read, we know only Miranda's world and we know only her values. Our only value becomes, in a sense, her well-being, and we accept any threat to her happiness precisely as she accepts it. The slightest suggestion that she is at fault will create too much distance; the slightest sign that author and reader are observing Miranda from above rather than alongside will destroy, at least in part, the quality of our concern and hence of our final revelation. To look down on her would make us want to see her either change or be punished; either desire would diminish our pity or require a rewriting of the story to accommodate it.

This kind of near-identification can be used for innumerable effects. The success of many so-called hard-boiled detective and adventure stories written under the influence of Hemingway depends largely on the fear we feel as soon as we see danger as if through our own eyes. A motion picture can achieve this kind of thrill perhaps more easily than any other medium, but the devices of showing developed by modern fiction can do it well. In Greene's *Brighton Rock* (1938), for example, we are caught up by the opening paragraph into the hunted life of Hale. As we travel with the frightened little man, moving aimlessly and without moral support in a world where there *is* no support for anyone, we come as close to identifying with him as it is possible to come without losing our sense of his aimless, weak insignificance. "Hale rose. His hands were shaking. This was real now: the boy, the razor cut, life going out with the blood in pain; not the deck chairs and the permanent waves, the miniature cars tearing round the curve on the Palace Pier. The ground moved under his feet, and only the thought of where they might take him while he was unconscious saved him from fainting. But even then common pride, the instinct not to make a scene, remained overpoweringly strong; embarrassment had more force than terror, it prevented his crying his fear aloud, it even urged him to go quietly."

And then he is gone. He is dead, and we have experienced a personal loss, a personal blow, of a kind that would be difficult, perhaps impossible, to achieve with a technique which provided us with any clear moral or intellectual guidance about the meaning of this death. We are almost as helpless as the victim himself, and we are thus ready to fall into the emotional trap that Greene lays for us by going beyond the conventions of the murder story and involving us in the ethics of revenge. It is not, of course, simply that we have been made to hate Hale's murderers, to desire their punishment, and to accept Ida, the avenger, as our champion. That could have been done with conventional methods. But with a conventional omniscient narrator, we could only with great difficulty be made to feel personally helpless, personally in want of a champion and avenger. We accept Ida as our champion— only to find ourselves trapped into a recognition that our judgment, like hers, has been made according to conventional standards of "what's Right and Wrong"; the conclusion of the book is an attempt—I think much less successful than the beginning—to wrench us into a willingness to judge in terms of Good and Evil rather than Right and Wrong. But even the limited success of this conclusion could never have been achieved if Greene had not built from the beginning upon our immediate, involved compassion.[5]

Neither Miranda nor Hale has done anything to offend us. But even characters whose behavior would be intolerable to us in real life can be made sympathetic by means of this paralogical proof that they are human beings like ourselves. The egotism of John Marcher, for example, in Henry James's *The Beast in the Jungle* (1903), is pardoned with this strange excuse. Marcher has always been convinced that he is peculiarly marked for some great future event, an event which he thinks of as the leap of a beast in the jungle. He shares his expectation with only one person, May Bartram, and, after living for years in futile expectation of the

---

[5] This does not prevent him, of course, from employing a reliable narrator later in the book, for other purposes. See above, pp. 186–87.

leap, discovers at the end that the great event has come and passed: it was his failure to grasp May Bartram's love when it was offered him. Standing beside her grave, he sees at a neighboring grave the face of a man ravaged by genuine grief. And suddenly Marcher sees the truth of his life; he recognizes that "no passion had ever touched him," that he was doomed to be "the man of his time, the man, to whom nothing on earth was to have happened." His escape would have been to love May Bartram: "then he would have lived." But instead he had treated her "but in the chill of his egotism and the light of her use." In refusing love and life, he "had failed, with the last exactitude, of all he was to fail of." "He saw the Jungle of his life and saw the lurking Beast; then, while he looked, perceived it, as by a stir of the air, rise, huge and hideous, for the leap that was to settle him. His eyes darkened—it was close; and, instinctively turning, in his hallucination, to avoid it, he flung himself, on his face, on the tomb."

Now the true character of John Marcher, as revealed to him at the end, is not an attractive one; he is an egoist fully as monstrous as Meredith's Sir Willoughby Patterne. Viewed from outside, as in a sense he views himself for the first time at the end, he is unsympathetic in the extreme. If one were to describe his thoughts and actions apart from his own expression of them, it would be hard to believe that anyone as sensitive as May Bartram could have loved him—so chilling is his "use" of everyone and everything about him for the absorbed contemplation of his own ego.

And yet his story is very moving. We feel a deep involvement with this man even as we condemn and laugh at him. Our feelings reach a climax that includes, even though it is not exhausted by, those old war horses pity and fear. We are made to fear for him, and to pity him when his *éclaircissement* comes, rather than to detest him and rejoice in his misery, or simply to study him as an interesting realistic portrait.

It is not that we fail to judge him. His words and deeds provide a multitude of clues about his true quality from the beginning. His self-absorption is supreme from the opening moments; his thoughts are always of the "luxury" of May Bartram's sympathetic

interest, the "comfort" of having someone to go with him endlessly over the same ground. And while her interest in him develops into love, his interest in her remains completely selfish; she
is merely a sounding board for his problem.

Even so we might become too fully immersed in his own highly
plausible view of things if James did not provide secret clues behind the observer's back, commenting through the unobtrusive
style of the seemingly effaced author. The result, as many critics
have pointed out, is a kind of double vision: we have the effect of
seeing things through Marcher's eyes, but the moral vision is
James's all the while. It was "as if Marcher had been visited by
one of his *occasional* warnings against egotism. He had kept up,
he felt, and very *decently* on the whole, his consciousness of the
importance of not being selfish, and it was true that he had never
sinned in that direction without promptly enough *trying* to press
the scales the other way. He often repaired his fault, *the season
permitting*, by inviting his friend to accompany him to the opera."
With innumerable touches of the kind I have italicized, James
preserves his own insistence that we judge Marcher's deficiencies
at every step of the way.[6]

And yet we travel with him. Since we know him in a view which
in real life we never obtain of anyone but ourselves, we view his
egotism almost as we might our own: it is deplorable, but there it

---

[6] A rigorous criticism of this story in an effort to prove James's own theories can
easily meet difficulties. Gordon and Tate find that since there are "only two Short
View scenes," it slights "the scenic effect" and thus possibly violates "one of his
[James's] primary canons: the importance of rendition over statement." "There is
too much of the elaborate voice of James," even disguised as it is. "James has not . . .
made either Marcher or Miss Bartram a *visible* character." Indeed, if we "look at it
in terms of the visible material—the material *made* visible," it is "much too long."
All this may be true, if we accept these criteria. But it is hard to see then how Gordon
and Tate can conclude, without providing other evidence, that this is probably the
"greatest of the James *nouvelles*" and "one of the great stories in the language." If,
as they say, "in the long run the effect is that of tone, even of lyric meditation,"
and if that is seriously marred by his failure to make it scenic, then what is there that
is so great? I suspect that straightforward reading pleasure has here won out over
critical doctrine: the story is great because, through the mastery of sympathy and
irony, it becomes a peculiarly poignant modern tragedy of self-discovery. If there is
too much of James's voice when judged by abstract criteria about showing and telling,
there is none too much to do the job of modifying the tone of Marcher's view of
things. See Gordon and Tate, *The House of Fiction* (New York, 1950), pp. 229–31.

is. If his faults were worse—if he behaved like Faulkner's Jason—
we might have difficulty, but as it is, we can view his fate in a
sympathetic, even tragic light. By seeing the whole thing through
the isolated sufferer's vision we are forced to feel it through his
heart. And it is our sense of his isolation, of vulnerability in a
world where no one can set him straight, that contributes most to
this sympathy.

Though there are obvious limits to the usefulness of this effect,
they are hard to reach. Even extreme physical revulsion can be
overcome by it, as we see when Kafka binds our sympathies to the
man-cockroach, Gregor Samsa, in *The Metamorphosis* (1912).
Physically, Gregor is as far from human sympathy as could be, and
his redeeming qualities are by no means strong enough to cancel,
by themselves, our revulsion. Yet because we are absolutely bound
to his experience, our sympathy is entirely with him. Whether we
laugh at the story, as some critics say we should, or weep for
Gregor, we are with him against those who reject him.

> As Gregor Samsa awoke one morning from uneasy dreams he
> found himself transformed in his bed into a gigantic insect. He was
> lying on his hard, as it were armor-plated, back and when he lifted
> his head a little he could see his dome-like brown belly divided into
> stiff arched segments on top of which the bed quilt could hardly
> keep in position and was about to slide off completely. His numer-
> ous legs, which were pitifully thin compared to the rest of his bulk,
> waved helplessly before his eyes.[7]

We are caught in this scene, as Gregor himself is caught, in the
body of a repulsive animal; no other narrative device could possibly convey half so much intensity of physical revulsion without
dissociating us from the disgusting object. Since the story requires
this sense of being trapped in the disgusting, since it is, in part, a
story of how it feels to watch other men reacting to one's own
repulsiveness, the device is perfect for the story and indeed seems
inseparable from it.

This unique combination of revulsion with the kind of absolute

---

[7] *Selected Short Stories of Franz Kafka,* trans. Willa and Edwin Muir (Modern
Library ed., 1952), p. 19. ˙

forgiveness which we ordinarily accord only to our own nasty traits comes to a climax when an apple thrown by Gregor's father lands "right on his back" and sinks in, remaining embedded and forming a "serious injury" that disgusts everyone so much that no one dares to draw it out (pp. 64–65). What we feel is a disgust so combined with compassion as to be hardly recognizable as disgust at all. By confining us to Gregor's vision, Kafka has insured a more sympathetic reading than any amount of traditional rhetoric could do. The result is that when Gregor dies and the technical point of view inevitably shifts, the full effect of the various metamorphoses we see in his family, based on Gregor's unwilling sacrifice, still depends on our maintaining his moral point of view as our own. The result is one of the masterpieces in the effective use of an isolated narrator.

If granting to the hero the right to reflect his own story can insure the reader's sympathy, withholding it from him and giving it to another character can prevent too much identification. We have seen in an earlier section how the reader can be made to laugh at what happens to Tom Jones even when he is very seriously threatened—simply by maintaining the proper tone throughout. The author who is determined to keep his narrator realistic may achieve some of the same effect by choosing the proper observer.

The events in James's early success, *Daisy Miller* (1879), might seem to be naturally suited to tragic or strongly pathetic effects. An innocent young American girl tours Europe, behaving in the open, casual, uncircumspect way that comes naturally to her. Her free ways with men are misinterpreted by the sophisticated, Europeanized Americans she meets. She is gradually ostracized, forced more and more into the company of Europeans. Finally she is driven to an act of extreme rashness, which leads to her death. Only then do her observers recognize their mistake about her. Tragedy would be relatively easy to come by in telling this tale. But as James says in his Preface, he did not want tragedy. Though Daisy's story was to him necessarily associated with a "brooding tenderness" and "shy incongruous charm" though she was "pure poetry," she was not in his view a proper object for full tragedy or even pathos. She was "a Study," provided for "mere concentration," on an "object scant and superficially vulgar"; though her story included pathos, it included also a kind of ironic play with the international theme, even a certain amount of "drolling." James is as much interested in the comedy of those who misunderstand Daisy as he is in Daisy's pathetic end (pp. 268–70). Consequently, he works at reducing the pathos of Daisy's destruction. James never mentions in his own notes the chief means to this reduction, the misguided observer Winterbourne, but the drama of Winterbourne's chilly misunderstanding of her true nature is really more important in the finished tale than Daisy's own actions. Seen through his eyes she can hardly become emotionally important to us, though of course we must recognize that she is worth much more than he suspects. His slow caution and ready suspicions are admirably suited to make us aware of the pathos of Daisy, without giving our awareness too much emotional force.

Our interest is consequently centered on his belated recognition of her true quality, a recognition that is poignant enough, but "droll" as well. He learns that "she would have appreciated one's esteem," that he was indeed, as has been intimated earlier, "booked to make a mistake," and that he has, in fact, "lived too long in foreign parts"—so long that he can no longer distinguish the innocence of poor destroyed Daisy from true vulgarity or immorality.

It is difficult to imagine this story as told through any other view than his, since Daisy's drama is precisely the drama of being misunderstood. She is really, as James said, a "scant" object, in herself; her importance comes only from what she can suffer from and reveal about the more lucid but still bewildered expatriates. When Winterbourne discovers her alone with her Italian at night in the Colosseum, his "final horror is mitigated by a final relief." "It was as if a sudden clearance had taken place in the ambiguity of the poor girl's appearances and the whole riddle of her contradictions had grown easy to read. She was a young lady about the *shades* of whose perversity a foolish puzzled gentleman need no longer trouble his head or his heart." Winterbourne's loss produced by this wrong judgment is Daisy's loss as well. His faulty vision as a reflector is thus both a necessary cause in the overt action and a means of controlling the reader's interest in that action. But since it is a "droll" vision, it can soften the force of Daisy's tragedy without confusing us about the quality of it: yes, yes, it is a kind of tragedy, we admit, but we feel it as an ironic commentary on two kinds of American in Europe. Though there is a mixture of what James called "the tragedy and the comedy and the irony," it is a mixture of clearly distinguished ingredients, and the effect is masterful.

CONTROL OF CLARITY AND CONFUSION

If granting or withholding the privilege of being the central observer can control emotional distance, it can be equally effective in controlling the reader's intellectual path—often, of course, with accompanying emotional effect. Many stories require confusion in the reader, and the most effective way to achieve it is to use an observer who is himself confused.

Mystification.—Of the many uses of bewilderment, ordinary mystification without obvious contrivance is perhaps the most common. Mystery is easily enough attained in any mode, of course, but one trouble with the old-fashioned methods of *Bleak House* and *The Brothers Karamazov* is that often no reason for the mystery is provided other than the narrator's desire to mystify. *He* knows all the time what he holds back until later, and though a skilful author, like a skilful magician, can conceal his suppressions and unveilings pretty well, we are likely to feel cheated when we discover that facts were held back for no good reason. Particularly on reconsideration or on second reading such details come to seem like faults. " 'Look at me,' " Dmitri cries to Alyosha. " 'Look at me well. You see here, here—there's terrible disgrace in store for me.' (As he said 'here' Dmitri struck his chest with his fist with a strange air, as though the dishonour lay precisely on his chest, in some spot, in a pocket, perhaps, or hanging round his neck.)" What right has the narrator to tell us this much and not to tell us the remainder of what he knows—namely, that Dmitri is carrying fifteen hundred rubles? And three hundred pages later, when Dmitri is lamenting his lack of funds, is it not a gross violation of artistry for the narrator to intrude as follows? "To anticipate things: he did, perhaps, know where to get the money, knew, perhaps, where it lay at that moment. I will say no more of this here, as it will all be clear later." Why say no more here? Simply because he wants the reader to remain curious about the money. Why say so much? Because unless we are told that Dmitri is withholding *something*, our sense of dramatic irony toward the other characters will be diminished. If the author told us all about the money here, this second kind of interest or suspense would be heightened, the first destroyed.

Here is another instance of the choice we found in *Emma* between two kinds of suspense. If an air of naturalness is important to an author, and if he desires to heighten the mystery for the "first-time reader," then a consistently unprivileged narrator will be more useful than Dostoevski's highly unnatural mixture of omniscience and limitation. But of course on second reading all of his pains in this direction are canceled out anyway: unless the work gains in dramatic irony for each loss in mere mystery, second readings will be disappointing.

Note that in this respect *The Brothers Karamazov* is better on second reading than on first. Though the little touches of mystification may annoy us more and more, the essential contrast between Dmitri's secret and what appears to those around him becomes more and more interesting.

Deliberate confusion of the reader about fundamental truths.—A very different effect ensues when the narrator's bewilderment is used not simply to mystify about minor facts of the story but to break down the reader's convictions about truth itself, so that he may be ready to receive *the* truth when it is offered to him. If the reader is to desire the truth he must first be convinced that he does not already possess it. Like a well-written philosophical treatise, any work depending on this desire must raise an important question in a lively form if the reader is to care about reading on to find the answer, or to feel the importance of the answer when it comes. Whether the answer is itself unequivocal or, as in many modern novels, deliberately ambiguous is irrelevant to the basic form of such reading experiences. The claim that there is no answer is itself an answer, so far as literary effect is concerned.[8]

In this century we have seen hundreds of novels which, like Conrad's *Heart of Darkness* (1902), Mann's *The Magic Mountain* (1925), Kafka's *The Castle* (1926), and Hesse's *Siddhartha* (1922) and *Steppenwolf* (1927), depend heavily on this kind of intellectual interest. The authors of some works have thought of themselves, like Conrad, as in some way rivaling the philosopher and scientist, "bringing to light the truth,"[9] though it is never described as a truth that could be stated discursively. Others would deny the slightest suggestion of cognitive or didactic taint. But all of them bear a closer resemblance to a philosophical dialogue like *The Symposium*, or to allegories like *Pilgrim's Progress*, than would be true of *Tom Jones*, say, or of Hemingway's *A Farewell to Arms*. In all of them, a character or group of characters embark, like Christian, on a quest for an important truth, and in all of them the reader's own concern for the truth is made to play a heavy role.

There is, of course, a radical difference of effect, depending on whether the reader is made to feel from the beginning that he sees the truth toward which the character is drifting, or is forced to cast off his own moorings and travel on uncharted seas toward an unknown harbor. Bunyan did not expect his readers to learn from *Pilgrim's Progress* that they ought to seek "the everlasting prize." His readers knew from page one what they *ought* to desire for

---

[8] See Richard M. Eastman, "The Open Parable: Demonstration and Definition," *College English*, XXII (October, 1960), 15–18, for a helpful account of "the open parable," the parable which, "through a designed instability" presents a "single ethical motif with variations of indefinite number and strength." If the reader is to be kept from "closing" the parable—that is, settling upon a simplified interpretation too quickly—the author's rhetoric must be "so constructed with certain opaque, irreducible details as to block the final verification of any one hypothesis." The emotional response sought by the parable may similarly be kept open. By its balancing of sympathetic and antipathetic detail, the reader is hindered from endorsing any one character or any one theme." Eastman contrasts, as "open," Kafka's *The Trial*, Beckett's *Molloy* and *Endgame*, etc., with "closed parables" like the good Samaritan, Dickens' *A Christmas Carol*, Forster's "The Other Side of the Hedge," etc.

[9] Preface to *The Nigger of the "Narcissus,"* opening paragraph. For a discussion of Conrad's didactic manipulation of Marlow's (and the reader's) doubts and confusions, see James L. Guetti, Jr., *The Rhetoric of Joseph Conrad* ("Amherst College Honors Thesis," No. 2 [Amherst, Mass., 1960]).

Christian and for themselves; there is never any real question about whether Christian should, or even whether he in fact will, ·come "unto the gate of glory." There would be no question even if Bunyan did not map out the whole course in his introductory "Apology" and maintain complete clarity throughout with his reliable narration. To baffle the reader in this work, to make him unsure of what is sought, or of the proper path to it, would be silly, even if it were possible. Similarly, in Johnson's *Rasselas* (1759) the reader knows from the beginning precisely what the goal is, and he knows that there is no real hope of reaching it. "Ye who listen with credulity to the whispers of fancy, and persue with eagerness the phantoms of hope; who expect that age will perform the promises of youth, and that the deficiencies of the present day will be supplied by the morrow; attend to the history of Rasselas prince of Abbissinia." Attend to it, yes, but do not expect to participate in it as if it were your own search—you have been told in advance that the search is fruitless.

But the modern quest-novel usually allows for no such certainties. No one tells us in *The Castle* what K's goal is, or whether it is attainable, or whether it is a worthwhile goal in the first place. Our puzzlement is intended to be as great as K's. When Christian begins to turn aside from the unmistakably correct path, we experience unequivocal dramatic irony: we stand on a secure promontory and watch the character stumble. But when K stumbles, we stumble with him. The ironies work against us fully as much as they do against him. In such works we do not discover until the end—and very often not even then—what the true meaning of the events has been. Regardless of the point of view in the narrowest sense, the moral and intellectual point of view of the work is deliberately confusing, disconcerting, even staggering.

It is too bad that we have no careful structural study of the many kinds of quest-novels using this effect in Joyce, Proust, Mann, and Kafka, to say nothing of lesser figures like Huxley, Gide, Unamuno, Hermann Hesse, Italo Svevo, Samuel Beckett, and the crop of American novelists of spiritual quest in the fifties: William Styron, Saul Bellow, Herbert Gold, Wright Morris, J. D. Salinger, and so on. We have many discussions of these novelists' doctrines, and we have a few attempts to relate various quests to the archetypal "quest-myths." Northrop Frye has even claimed that all literary genres are derived from a single myth of the quest. But there is very little that relates doctrines to technical successes in making them seem important. I can make only a small beginning here, by illustrating the kinds of confusion such works rely upon.

1. *Deliberate confusion about the relation of art and reality.*— We have already seen something of the fun Sterne could produce by confusing the reader about the kind of book he was writing. Many modern works use the same kind of confusing, unreliable narration in a deliberate polemic against conventional notions of reality and in favor of the superior reality given by the world of the book.

Much of James Branch Cabell, for example, is designed to break down the reader's conventional notions of what is real, and an essential part of this polemic is the attempt to undermine the reader's normal trust in what the narrator says. In *The Cream of the Jest* (1917) we begin with the "author," Horvendile, attempting to conduct his romance as he would have it go. But we almost immediately shift from his weird, unreal, chivalric setting to the rough modern "reality" of Felix Kennaston, the ostensible author who imagines himself to be Horvendile.

> "I will tell you" [Horvendile says]. "There was once in a land very far away from this land—in my country—a writer of romances. And once he constructed a romance which, after the hackneyed custom of my country, he pretended to translate from an old manuscript written by an ancient clerk—called Horvendile. It told of Horvendile's part in the love-business between Sir Guiron des Rocques and La Belle Ettarre. I am that writer of romance. This room, this castle, all the broad rolling countryside without, is but a portion of my dream, and these places have no existence save in my fancies" [chap. vii].

We are given in this fashion many levels of commentary, but none of it is by any means clearly the commentary of Cabell himself or of anyone who speaks for him. We have Kennaston's thoughts about his imaginary life as Horvendile, and we have his thoughts about his book as it reflects that life. We have Horvendile's commentary on Kennaston. And we have the commentary of one "Richard Fentnor Harrowby" on all of them:

Competent critics in plenty have shrugged over Kennaston's cliché of pretending that the romance is 're-told' from an ancient manuscript. But to Kennaston the clerk Horvendile, the fictitious first writer of the chronicle and eye-witness of its events, was necessary. No doubt it handicapped the story's progress, so to contrive matters that one subsidiary character should invariably be at hand when important doings were in execution, and had to be taken more or less into everyone's confidence—but then, somehow, it made the tale seem real [chap. ix].

This might seem to be Cabell's true voice, but we can never be sure, since Harrowby often speaks unmistakably for himself alone: ". . . it may be that I am setting down his [Kennaston's] story not all in sympathy, for in perfect candor I never, quite, liked Felix Kennaston. His high-pitched voice . . . was irritating: you knew it was not his natural voice . . . there is no escaping, at times, the gloomy suspicion that fiddling with pens and ink is, after all, no fit employment for a grown man" (*ibid.*).

All this seeming byplay is strictly to the purpose of shaking our confidence in the superior reality of "real life" over artistic "dreams." In the end this polemic is made explicit, but it could never be so until then. We must experience confusion, we must taste genuine ambiguity if its resolution is to seem either convincing or worthwhile.[10]

An even more elaborate attack on ordinary reality is made by Unamuno. A work like his *Mist*[11] simply could not exist without the multiple narrative ambiguities on which it is based. The reader is deliberately kept in a state of confusion about the borderline between fiction and reality. There is a prologue, for example, by "Victor Goti," debating whether the climax of the book took place "in fact, and not merely in idea," followed by a reply given as if by Unamuno himself: "I should very much like to discuss here some of the statements of my prologist, Victor Goti, but since I am in the secret of his existence I prefer to leave to him the entire responsibility for what he says in the prologue." There are similar dialogues throughout the book, culminating in a long debate about

---

10 For another work playing with the deceptiveness of reality and the superior truth of the novelist's "lies," see Jean Cayrol's *Les corps étrangers* (Paris, 1959).

11 *Niebla* (Madrid, 1914), trans. Warner Fite (New York, 1928).

whether the hero should be killed off by having him commit suicide. The decision is to kill him, and it is carried out. "And then it occurred to me that I might bring him to life again." "Unamuno" falls asleep and dreams that the hero comes to him and explains that he cannot be brought to life again; the narrator replies, "But what if I dream you again." And then the hero turns upon "Unamuno" and says, "No one dreams the same dream twice. . . . Listen to me: . . . it is quite possible that you are an entity of fiction, one who does not really exist, who is neither living nor dead. It may easily be that you are nothing more than an excuse for spreading my story through the world, and other stories like mine; and that presently, when you are dead and gone, it is we who then keep your soul alive" (pp. 319–22).

This humorous undermining of ordinary reality in favor of the world of ideas could never succeed unless the reader were left in doubt—at least through most of the work—about which character, if any, speaks for reality. If reality is in fact not what it appears to be, if an imagined character is in fact more real than its author's "real" life outside his imaginings, then the reader must be led through a series of false inferences to an imaginative apprehension of the true reality. No reliable narrator can give him the truth, since the truth is itself beyond literal, non-imaginative formulation. The narrator, "Unamuno," does not know the truth. Even the author, Unamuno, who creates "Unamuno," presumably could never state the truth except in the form of a dialogue among his various heroes and narrators, no one of whom can speak entirely for him.

In contrast to these, Proust's *Remembrance of Things Past*, one of the greatest of the quest-novels, moves toward unequivocal illumination. The narrator, Marcel, involves the reader in his own confusions until, at the end of the book, he finally can speak with full reliability for the values on which it is based. Both narrator and reader constantly discover truths that Marcel Proust has known all along. In the end Marcel discovers the ultimate truth about art and life, the truth about memory and art as ways out of the world of time. It is this discovery that leads him, in fact, to write the book his reader has just read.

My apprehensiveness of death vanished the moment I instinctively recognised the savour of the little *madeleine*, because at that moment the person within me was a timeless person, consequently unconcerned with the vicissitudes of the future. That person had never come to me, never manifested himself, except independently of all immediate activity, all immediate enjoyment, whenever the miracle of a resemblance with things past enabled me to escape out of the present. He alone had the power to make me recapture bygone days, times past, which had always balked the efforts of my memory and my intelligence.[12]

This direct report on the discovery of what the author has known from the beginning extends for thirty-eight long pages in the English edition (II, 990–1028), with no scenic or dramatic content except a few allusions to earlier actions. Indeed most of the final chapter, "The Princesse de Guermantes Receives," is taken up with talk about the meaning of the narrator's discovery—and the chapter is about twice as long as the whole of Camus' *The Stranger!* A rather impressive exception to the claim, which we have seen now so many times, that "an essay is one kind of thing and a novel another kind of thing, that a mixture of kinds is improper."[13]

It might be argued that since the "I" differs from Proust himself, the concluding novel-length personal essay is after all "Marcel's," not the author's. But the whole point of Marcel's disquisition is that he has at last come to the truth about life and art—the truth which Proust himself holds. Though some of the striking differences between the author and his narrator remain through this final section, the intellectual differences are left behind: author, narrator, and reader must see the truth together if the chapter is to succeed as Proust intends. It does succeed, even if we refuse to accept as literally true some of Marcel's theories, because—though we cannot illustrate the success here—the timeless world he discovers *is* in its main lines compatible with our experience of life, time, memory, and art.[14]

---

[12] *Remembrance of Things Past,* trans. C. K. Scott Moncrieff (New York, 1934), II, 995.

[13] Bernard DeVoto, *The World of Fiction* (New York, 1950), p. 207.

[14] See Germaine Brée, *Marcel Proust and Deliverance from Time,* trans. C. J. Richards and A. D. Truitt (Paris, 1950; New York, 1955). The question of the difference between Proust and Marcel is discussed especially in chap. ix.

The over-all power of this work can only be explained by treating the discursive account of Marcel's discoveries as the climax, the goal, the reward that we have sought from the beginning: this is the story of how Marcel becomes a reliable narrator. The book is held together, in short, by an idea, or by the quest for an idea, and it is in the service of our ultimately clear hold on that idea that we must be misled and confused, like the narrator, until the final revelation. Even though many of the parts are themselves held together by other interests—Swann's pursuit of Odette, for example, which involves the reader in the conventional interests of a love-plot—they in turn serve Marcel as illustrative memories revealing his truth about life and art.

Remembrance of Things Past thus represents a large group of modern novels in which the search for truth is answered with the discovery that truth is found not in concepts but in the reality of artistic activity. No one seems to have discovered what it is that distinguishes the few successes in this mode from the innumerable failures. There is nothing more boring than a boring "novelist-hero" searching, for no discernible reason, for a truth which is so commonplace that the reader wonders, when he arrives, why the trip was undertaken in the first place. It may be that truths about art itself are the most difficult to make interesting in fiction. Certainly we will not become deeply involved in the confusions shown by a novelist-hero about his own artistic aims unless somehow, as in Proust, those artistic aims tell us something in return about the life of the book itself. Most readers are not novelists—though to read many modern works one would become convinced that the authors thought so—and there are few novelists with sufficient insight into life and art to make their relationship meaningful.

2. *Confusion about moral and spiritual problems.*—If art were "for art's sake" in the limited sense of existing only to give pleasure through abstract forms and patternings, one would expect that a quest for one truth would be just as good as another, that the way in which the quest is formed would be the only important distinction between good and bad. Why should James not be able to write as great a book on the theme of *The Sacred Fount* as on that of *The Ambassadors?* The quest of a male gossip for a clear picture of

the amatory pairings of a group of weekend guests is simply not as important as the quest of Strether for the meaning of life itself. Even if, by some miracle of will, James had been able to bring himself to develop *The Sacred Fount* with anything like the fulness of *The Ambassadors*, it would take another miracle of our wills to make us care about the first quest as much as the second. But the conflict between full consciousness and narrow conscience shown in *The Ambassadors* is something which everyone experiences, whether he knows it or not, and the novelist who can portray the conflict vividly will involve us in a quest close to our hearts.[15]

Strether was not the first hero to seek ethical truth that would resolve a conflict between conventional or superficial values. But he presages many works which, by removing the traditional certainties that might be provided in a play, heighten the reader's sense of the character's isolation as he faces his moral problems and thus heighten the reader's own dilemma as he reads. The reliable narrator of an older work like *Great Expectations* could provide a secure haven for the erring Pip, but there is no secure haven for Paul Morel or Stephen Dedalus. In this respect as in so many others, modern fiction has tried to move closer to life itself than was ever attempted by earlier fiction. Leave the reader to choose for himself, force him to face each decision as the hero faces it, and he will feel much more deeply the value of the truth when it is attained, or its loss if the hero fails.

It is no wonder that critics dispute whether works written in this mode are "really novels." To succeed as art they must have a strong didactic effect; the more the reader feels the moral dilemma as a personal one, the stronger will be his reaction to the work as a formed, imaginative experience. Are Kafka's novels didactic? One can only answer that if to force the reader into thought about his own moral dilemmas is to be didactic, they are. And yet it is equally

---

[15] What I am saying here is true, of course, only so long as we are talking about works the primary interest of which is the intellectual quest for some kind of truth or vision. It should go without saying that a great comedy could be written about the quest of a male gossip for a clear picture of the amatory pairings of a group of weekend guests. James at times approaches this kind of comedy in *The Sacred Fount*, but he approaches it only to shift back into something else, something that seems to be trying for profundity and that in the trying ruins itself.

easy to argue that Kafka's attempt is simply to make the reader recognize the full relevance of "K's" dilemmas—that if we are to experience fully the comic and pathetic futility of *his* blind probings we must feel them almost as if they were our own.[16]

In Albert Camus' *The Fall*,[17] for example, we see just how far an author can carry the effort to implicate the reader by confusing him. The action, if it can be called that, is pure intellectual and moral quest. The book is narrated entirely in the monologue of the hero, Clamence, who, like the ancient mariner, buttonholes a normal, middle-class auditor and arouses his curiosity about the narrator's spiritual trials—in this case about why he calls himself a judge-penitent. He gradually strips himself of all his protective pretenses to virtue, uncovering more and more of his empty, vicious pride as he goes. The details of his self-revelation, as he constructs a modern analogue of Ivan's dream of The Grand Inquisitor, are not important here. The method is important, however; it is precisely because there is no author in sight that Clamence can trick both his auditor and reader into undergoing the same spiritual collapse that he has himself experienced. "Admit anyway that you feel today less satisfied with yourself than you did five days ago?" (p. 163). But if the auditor feels less satisfied with himself after listening for five days to this moral undermining, so does the reader. The portrait Clamence has painted of himself becomes a portrait of the reader. Clamence's failure to meet his own grand moral crisis, when he once refused to go to the aid of a drowning suicide, becomes our general failure to accept moral responsibility.

In so far as we read this book properly, we are thus taken in by it, tricked by the narrator into playing a role in the action. We participate in a dialogue with him for serious moral ends, somewhat like the ironic dialogue in which we engage with Tristram Shandy for comic ends. His duplicity, like Tristram's, includes deliberate distortion. Indeed, Clamence is quite explicit about his own untruthfulness. Speaking of the possibility that men might wear "shop

---

16 For an excellent "literal" reading of the plot of *The Castle*, deliberately avoiding any effort to allegorize or impose didactic patterns, see Paul Goodman, *Structure of Literature*, pp. 173–83.

17 *La Chute* (Paris, 1956), trans. Justin O'Brien (New York, 1957).

signs" telling the ultimate truth ·about themselves, displaying their "true profession and identity," Clamence says that his sign ·would be "a double face, a charming Janus, and above it the motto of the house: 'Don't rely on it.' On my cards: 'Jean-Baptiste Clamence, play actor' " (p. 47). It is not only that he is a man of many facets: he is deliberately deceptive. Unlike most of his counterparts in modern fiction, who are simply confused or lost in their own divided identities, he embraces falsehood as a necessary part of his method.[18]

> I know what you're thinking: its very hard to disentangle the true from the false in what I'm saying. I admit you are right. . . . You see, a person I knew used to divide human beings into three categories: those who prefer having nothing to hide rather than being obliged to lie, those who prefer lying to having nothing to hide, and finally those who like both lying and the hidden. I'll let you choose the pigeon-hole that suits me.
>
> But what do I care? Don't lies eventually lead to the truth? And don't all my stories, true or false, tend toward the same conclusion? Don't they all have the same meaning? So what does it matter whether they are true or false if, in both cases, they are significant of what I have been and of what I am? Sometimes it is easier to see clearly into the liar than into the man who tells the truth. Truth, like light, blinds. Falsehood, on the contrary, is a beautiful twilight that enhances every object [pp. 119–20].

It is not only that he must deceive in order to trap his auditors and readers into judging him first so that he can then turn the judgment back upon them. The very truth about human beings which he is exploring is that they are full of duplicity: "After prolonged research on myself, I brought out the fundamental duplicity of the human being" (p. 84). Thus it is true that the destructive aspect of the message of this latter-day John the Baptist, Jean-Baptiste Clamence, could only be conveyed with unreliable, impersonal narration. Like Ivan's dream of The Grand Inquisitor, it requires a narrator who is facing an impossibly difficult question, and facing it alone. (It is noteworthy that the narrator of Dostoevski's work, so

---

[18] Cf. the Janus-faced narrator-hero of Mann's *Confessions of Felix Krull, Confidence Man* (1954). Like Clamence, he prides himself on his slippery unreality; his resemblances to Hermes, which he himself does not understand, are mainly on the side of the sly, deceptive features of that many-featured god.

garrulous at some points, absents himself completely from Ivan's and Alyosha's dialogue, including the long account of the inquisitor. Ivan and Alyosha must face their question unaided.)

The affirmative side of his author's message is something else again. It is so far buried beneath Clamence's confusions and negations that one does well to seek it outside the novel, in other works by Camus, and then import it back into the work. To say this is perhaps to describe an inherent weakness in the work, yet it is hard to say how the weakness could have been avoided. To use James's method in *The Beast*, allowing the author's style to provide a constant running commentary on Clamence's judgments, would help to provide the affirmation about the importance of freely accepting responsibility—but it would also attenuate the reader's involvement in Clamence's confusions.

We find the same problem in the first-person work, *The Stranger* (1942). The form of the work resembles in some ways that of *The Beast in the Jungle*. Meursault goes through the motions of life, like Marcher a stranger to all normal human emotions and experiences. But he discovers, unlike Marcher, that he has not been a lost man after all, that in his indifferent isolation he has figured a truth about the indifference of the whole universe, and that he has been happy all along, "and that I was happy still."[19]

It is extremely difficult to make out the relation of this affirmative point to the many negations of the work. Why, if he lays his heart open to the "benign indifference of the universe," feeling it to be "brotherly" in its indifference, should Meursault conclude as he does? "For all to be accomplished, for me to feel less lonely, all that remained was to hope that on the day of my execution there should be a huge crowd of spectators and that they should greet me with howls of execration." Why, "on the brink of freedom," should he want "howls of execration" rather than, say, expressions of "benign indifference"? A highly trained reader can, no doubt, decipher answers to such questions by reading the work itself carefully. But many critics have confessed that they require Camus' own speculations as reading aids, as given in *The Myth of Sisyphus* and *The*

---

[19] Trans. Stuart Gilbert (New York, 1954), p. 154.

Rebel. And even among these one finds a good deal of disagreement about the final meaning.[20]

In the literature of moral quest there are many works in which the quest is a failure. In some, the confusion is never resolved: the reader is intentionally left baffled about one or more questions raised by the work. The final *éclaircissement*, if one can still use this term for such dimly lit matters, is a view of total meaninglessness.

One can theoretically project a novel in which no attempt would be made to give a sense of progression toward any conclusion or final illumination. Such a work might simply convey an all-pervasive sense that no belief is possible, that all is chaos, that nobody sees his way clearly, that we are all engaged in a "journey to the end of the night." In a work of this kind, not only would the narrator and reader move together through the unanswered questions as they arise, but presumably the implied author would move with them; no one could be the wiser for having read the book. The author of such a work must leave the action unresolved: any resolution would imply a standard of values in relation to which one situation would be more nearly final than another. Only an unresolved sense of meaningless continuation could do justice to a full nihilism of this kind.

There are many "nihilisms" in fiction, from Conrad's heart of darkness to the recent programs of doom inspired by the ever-present image of that final bomb blast. All of them seem to face a common problem, a problem that falls on the borderline between aesthetics and metaphysics: Since nothingness cannot be described in itself, let alone shown dramatically, *something* or *someone* must

---

[20] When *L'Étranger* was first published, Sartre confessed that he could not make it out until he read Camus' speculative works ("Camus' *The Outsider* [*L'Étranger*]," *Literary and Philosophical Essays*, trans. Annette Michelson [London, 1955]). See also Carl A. Viggiani, "Camus' *L'Étranger*," *PMLA*, LXXI (December, 1956), 865–87, esp. 886, for a discussion of the "final meaning" of this novel, which is "incomprehensible except in the context of all his works" (p. 865). See also Alex Comfort, *The Novel and Our Time* (London, 1948), pp. 40–42, for an excellent discussion of the problems raised for the reader by this puzzling work. An interpretation that was confirmed by Camus himself—oh, lucky critic, to find a modern author willing to confirm or deny—is contained in Philip Thody's *Albert Camus: A Study of His Work* (London, 1957).

always be shown doing *something*, and if the action is to be grasped at all by the reader, it must somehow be fitted into a scheme of values that is intelligible to him (see chap. v, above). If, for example, we show a character caught in a predicament that has no meaningful solution, the very terms of our literary success require the assumption that to be caught in a meaningless predicament is a bad thing, in which case there *is* meaning, however rudimentary. To write is to affirm at the very least the superiority of *this* order over *that* order.[21] But superiority according to what code of values? Any answer will necessarily contradict complete nihilism. For the complete nihilist, suicide, not the creation of significant forms, is the only consistent gesture.

It is not surprising, then, that though we find many lost characters in hopeless situations, characters whose only discovery can be that there is nothing to discover, or whose final action is suicide or some other gesture of despair, the works in which they appear can be called nihilistic only in a loose, conventional sense.[22]

Whether I am right in this conclusion, which is not fundamen-

---

[21] The current interest in "open-ended" or eccentric literary works does not seem to me to contradict this position: see Robert M. Adams, *Strains of Discord* (Ithaca, N.Y., 1958), Introduction and chap. ix; Marius Bewley, *The Eccentric Design* (New York, 1960); Richard Eastman, *op. cit.* Even the loosest, least conclusive of works is to some degree an ordered, or at least a selected, whole. And certainly those open structures which we admire always turn out, on close inspection, to be "open" only in very limited respects; in so far as we can think of them as great works, they somehow weave their various threads into a final harmony.

[22] See Norman Podhoretz, "The New Nihilism," *Partisan Review*, XXV (Fall, 1958), 576–90. Podhoretz describes many recent novels in which "nihilism is given its full head," in which characters have looked into themselves and found nothing, yet they all show some last minute recantation, like Camus' ability to "grab the edge of the cliff with his nails and hold on by God knows what miraculous instinct to survive" (p. 585). Even Nathalie Sarraute, whose novels (e.g., *Portrait of a Man Unknown*) "represent a total submission to the meaningless[ness] of existence," is still *this* side of the "point where literally everything, including the six senses themselves, are just about to dissolve into thin air." Beyond this point there may be "nothing," but no one will ever write a novel about it. Other "nihilist" novels mentioned by Podhoretz are Frederick Buechner's *The Return of Ansel Gibbs*, George P. Elliott's *Parktilden Village* (in which "the cool judiciousness is doing something more than calling your attention to the author's subtlety and good taste: it is working to define a critical attitude toward the main character" [p. 581]), J. P. Donleavy's *The Ginger Man*, and Thomas Hinde's *Happy as Larry*. I am told by Marcel Gutwirth —too late to do anything about it here—that the novels of Maurice Blanchot come remarkably close to a thoroughgoing nihilism.

tal to our problem, it is clear that in any attempt at a "nihilistic" novel, all forms of reliable narration will be inappropriate. If the world of the book is without meaning, how can there be a reliable narrator? What is he to be reliable about? The very concept of reliability presupposes that something objectively true can be said about actions and thoughts. To call Job a "perfect and upright" man is nonsensical unless perfection and uprightness are meaningful terms in a meaningful universe. The slightest intrusion of commentary by someone not caught in the same meaningless trap in which the characters find themselves will call the reader's attention to the deceit that underlies any such work. What is more, it will diminish the reader's emotional involvement in the plight of the lost souls of the book. If there really is no light to illumine our journey, then any kind of reliable insight will reduce the impact of our wanderings.

Most so-called nihilistic works are, however, really works of active protest or even of affirmation, however impersonal the mode in which they are written; they can thus, if need be, include narrators or reflectors who are at least to some extent reliable. They confuse the reader about one group of norms, only to impose another, and reliable witnesses to this other code are almost certain to be found hiding somewhere. When Hemingway writes his "nihilistic" short story, "A Clean, Well-Lighted Place," he can create a character who speaks for him because the story is, finally, not nihilistic at all. Though we have no reason to believe that Hemingway's heart is not in the waiter's prayer to *nada*, to nothingness, we know that his heart is also with the waiter in his desire to provide a clean, well-lighted place for all the solitary wanderers who must face the bitterness of *nada*. Unlike some other of Hemingway's stories, in which characters are allowed to speak for his values without having earned, as it were, the right to do so, in this story the author's spokesman carries real power. Expressing a mood of bitterness against the darkness combined with a determination to fight the darkness with light—if only the clean, well-lighted place of art itself—the story can accommodate a dramatized spokesman of a very simple, direct kind. But if Hemingway's effort had really been to substitute *nada* for all our briefs, if he had really been writing a polemic of despair, the direct voice of the waiter, muted as it is, would have been un-acceptable. On the other hand, the poignancy of the writer's vision of *nada* would be reduced if a reliable narrator intruded to explain the rather flat, comforting points about the writer that I have just made here.

"Secret Communion" between Author and Reader

The effects of deliberate confusion require a nearly complete union of the narrator and reader in a common endeavor, with the author silent and invisible but implicitly concurring, perhaps even sharing his narrator's plight. The effects we turn to now require a secret communion of the author and reader behind the narrator's back. Few modern narrators are made up entirely of qualities at either extreme, but the predominance of one kind or another will de-termine radically different effects in the works in which they are found. In the first kind, even though the narrator may, like Mi-randa, have serious faults, we are scarcely aware of them. In the second kind, though the narrator may have some redeeming quali-ties of mind or heart, we travel with the silent author, observing as from a rear seat the humorous or disgraceful or ridiculous or vicious driving behavior of the narrator seated in front. The author may wink and nudge, but he may not speak. The reader may sympathize or deplore, but he never accepts the narrator as a reliable guide.

The inferences that such narrators require of the reader may be as simple as those in *Huckleberry Finn* or as complicated as those required to make one's way through *Ulysses* with its many different narrators, most of them unreliable but no two in the same way. And the effects are equally varied, from the deep sympathy we feel for Huck to the hostility aroused by Poe's Montresor or the narrator of Joyce's *Cyclops* episode.[23] But behind the manifold particular

---

[23] Richard Ellmann, *James Joyce* (New York, 1959), p. 367: "Joyce hit upon the . . . radical device of the undependable narrator with a style adjusted to him. He used this in several episodes of *Ulysses*, for example in *Cyclops*, where the narrator is so obviously hostile to Bloom as to stir up sympathy for him, in *Nausicaa*, where the narrator's gushiness is interrupted and counteracted by Bloom's matter-of-fact reporting, and in *Eumaeus*, where the narrator writes in a style that is constabular." Note that to be undependable in this sense is not identical with being what I have called unreliable; most unreliable narrators are dependable in the sense of being consistent.

effects that can be heightened or suppressed by using this kind of narrator, one can recognize three general pleasures that are in some degree present whenever the reader is called on to infer the author's position through the semitransparent screen erected by the narrator.

The pleasure of deciphering.—A recent story by Vladimir Nabokov, "The Vane Sisters,"[24] carries the pleasure of secret communication about as far as it can go in the direction of what might be called mere cryptography. The narrator receives, quite unconsciously and contrary to his disbelief in spiritualism, a variety of communications from the dead. The most important of these is embedded as an acrostic in his final paragraph, without his suspecting that he has unconsciously put it there. In congratulating the "first five codecrackers" who sent in for the next issue of *Encounter* their unsolicited solutions to the acrostic, Nabokov wrote, "My difficulty was to smuggle in the acrostic without the narrator's being aware that it was there, inspired to him by the phantoms. Nothing of this kind has ever been attempted by any author."[25] This claim is not likely to be challenged, but there have been other similarly subtle invitations to the decoding expert, ranging from the most solemn symbolic patternings to the playfulness of Joyce's Noel greeting, "End a muddy crushmess," or the cry of his polygamist from his "bethel of Solyman's," "Brimgem young, bringem young, bringem young!"[26]

It is obvious—at least, once we have read Joyce—that there is no limit to the number of deciphering pleasures that can be packed into a book. And clearly the challenge to the cryptographer is greatest when the explicit helps from the author, speaking in his own voice, are least. In so far as a work depends, then, on the reader's activity of deciphering, it cannot offer explicit aid.

[24] *Encounter*, March, 1959.

[25] *Encounter* (April, 1959), p. 96.

[26] *Finnegans Wake* (Compass Books ed., 1959), pp. 534, 542. The novel was first published in 1939, though fragments of *Work in Progress* appeared throughout the preceding decade. If I dropped the point here I could no doubt leave some readers convinced that I have read *Finnegans Wake*. But I must confess that I have not; I do read *in* it, from time to time, with great delight until boredom sets in. Will someone, by the way, someone who *has* read this unreadable work, tell me whether that first "m" in the first "brimgem" is a typographical error? You don't know? Or care? We are in trouble, you and I.

No one has ever claimed, however, that these rewards are in themselves very important. *Finnegans Wake* has often been attacked as merely a long crossword puzzle, but so far as I know it has never been defended as such.

The pleasure of collaboration.—The true value of forcing the reader to decipher lies in what such activity does to his attitude toward the story and its author. In his early *Atlantic Monthly* review from which I have already quoted James on the art of "making the reader," his whole emphasis is on this one aspect. "When he makes him well, that is makes him interested, then the reader does quite half the labor."[27] James is not thinking here simply of giving the reader a sense of his own cleverness. He is making his readers by forcing them onto a level of alertness that will allow for his most subtle effects.

The trouble with most talk about the good and bad of asking the reader to decipher—usually under terms like "difficulty," "obscurity," "complexity," or "allusiveness"—is that it is entirely general, as if there were some abstract law which says that this or that degree of difficulty is too much or too little. We are all familiar with innumerable badly informed attacks on the obscurity of modern fiction, seemingly based on the assumption that it is wrong to expect any knowledge in your reader whatever. There are almost as many general defenses that seem to suggest that unless literature is difficult it is bad. Writers on both sides seldom talk precisely about particular works, being far more interested in attacking the ignorance of the public or the wilfulness of poets and novelists.[28]

Yet if there is anything that should be obvious about such a matter, it is that different works will give rise to different standards in this regard, that a degree of allusiveness fatal to one kind of work might even be too straightforward for another. Most readers no doubt fail, as I did, to decipher Nabokov's acrostic, but this does not necessarily mean that it is too obscure: if there is to be this

---

[27] *The Atlantic Monthly*, October, 1866, p. 485.

[28] Two of the sanest discussions of this general quarrel are Randall Jarrell, "The Obscurity of the Poet," *Poetry and the Age* (New York, 1953), and Henri Peyre, *Writers and Their Critics: A Study of Misunderstanding* (Ithaca, N.Y., 1944), esp. pp. 183–218.

story at all, the little game with the acrostic has to be a part of it, and it may be that it cannot be used unless used obscurely. Though Nabokov no doubt excludes many of the readers of *Encounter*, the degree of difficulty may be entirely proper to the work as a whole. Only a detailed consideration of the complete tale, with an exploration of possible modes of clarification, could tell us whether enough clues were provided. What meaning would it have to say to Joyce that he has asked for "too much" cryptanalysis in *Finnegans Wake?* Too much for you and me, perhaps, and we may find ourselves ultimately repudiating, on moral grounds, an author who excludes practically everyone. But not too much for *Finnegans Wake.* Who would bother about *Finnegans Wake* at all if it were not packed with Finneganswakism?

Perhaps the most obvious misapplication of general principles to the question of difficulty comes precisely on the matter of making the reader work. It is no doubt true enough that the reader must be made to apply himself. The claim that Ewald makes about Swift, that the required hard work "doubtless accounts for much of the intellectual and emotional force his writings have,"[29] applies to many novelists, but it does not solve any problems for us. In the first place, the claim can obviously be made for any difficulty, skilfully planted or carelessly dropped. The reader's problem is that of discriminating between genuinely functional difficulty and obscurities that spring from carelessness, false pride, or plain ineptitude. To praise a difficulty—whether it makes us work or not—that results simply from the author's own failure fully to write his work is as fatal to the critic as to condemn a difficulty that is actually a necessary part of the whole.

More important, such a claim may lead us to forget that to decipher allusions and subtleties is only one form of active collaboration by the reader—and not the most important form at that. There are many things a reader can be asked to do besides guessing about who is doing what to whom or about whether it is good or bad that he does so. I must work at the height of my powers if I am to experience *King Lear.* I must make, at every step of the way,

---

[29] William Bragg Ewald, Jr., *The Masks of Jonathan Swift* (Oxford, 1954), p. 187.

extremely complicated responses to extremely complex signs; my imagination and my ethical sensibility are stretched to their utmost. But I am not required to decipher very much of anything. I know the motives of each character without retiring to my reference library. I am not asked to guess about whether Lear makes a mistake in banishing Cordelia. There is never any mystery about Edmund's intentions. And I am *told* directly in dozens of ways how I should feel about Goneril and Regan. In short, though I can of course find many elements to puzzle over, they are not the major elements, and any deciphering pleasure I may get from viewing or reading the play is subordinate to the major rewards it offers. I work at this play as I work at few artistic experiences, but my work is not that of figuring out, of calculating allusions, of unraveling intentions. It is the work of raising myself to the height required to experience the imaginative and emotional complexities of Lear's tragedy.

Secret communion, collusion, and collaboration.—All of the great uses of unreliable narration depend for their success on far more subtle effects than merely flattering the reader or making him work. Whenever an author conveys to his reader an unspoken point, he creates a sense of collusion against all those, whether in the story or out of it, who do not get that point. Irony is always thus in part a device for excluding as well as for including, and those who are included, those who happen to have the necessary information to grasp the irony, cannot but derive at least part of their pleasure from a sense that others are excluded. In the irony with which we are concerned, the speaker is himself the butt of the ironic point. The author and reader are secretly in collusion, behind the speaker's back, agreeing upon the standard by which he is found wanting.

The effect is most clearly distinguishable when the narrator shows ignorance of matters of fact. When Thurber's narrator in "You Could Look It Up" says that the two friends were like Damon and Phidias, or that "Bethlehem broke loose," most of us know the facts on which the joke is based, and we experience on the simplest possible level the kind of effect I have in mind.

Our pleasure is compounded of pride in our own knowledge, ridicule of the ignorant narrator, and a sense of collusion with the silent author who, also knowing the facts, has created the trap for his narrator and for those readers who will not catch the allusion. These three ingredients may be combined in many different ways, but they are all three present whenever we see a narrator revealing his faults in his own words, without guidance from a superior mind.

I notice, of course, only those clues which I am prepared to notice, and I am therefore usually not aware of irony as something that gives me real trouble. We always think of the *other* reader as the one who is taken in. Indeed we are likely to reject simpler forms of irony, because they are too obvious—which is to say that the number excluded from the joke is too small. Everybody knows about Damon and Pythias. It is too easy. But the fun is increased as the privacy increases. When the young athlete who narrates Mark Harris' *The Southpaw* complains that Ring Lardner's baseball stories are not very good because Lardner doesn't care enough about how the games turn out, the joke against him is in this one respect more fun than it would be if the complaint were about Shakespeare; it carries an air of privacy. Fewer people know Lardner than know Shakespeare, and those of us who think we admire Lardner's baseball stories for the right reasons have been singled out more successfully than we could have been by a corrupted version of "To be or not to be." The actual numbers are not important; even if every reader gets the joke, every reader's pleasure will include a sense of private communication: the southpaw, after all, does not get it.

Such factual errors do not account for any significant part of our literary experience. But the relationship between author and reader on which they depend, extended to more subtle deficiencies, is found in many fine modern works. It is true that narrators who unconsciously betray themselves as brutal or insensitive or mean, or simply as moving toward tragic or comic error, may not require authorial reticence for their effect. In all great classical drama the speaker's mistakes and faults are corrected for the audience by what other characters do and say. When Othello approaches Desdemona in a jealous rage, we know that he is about to make a tragic mistake; Shakespeare has used Iago and Desdemona to tell us so. We can hardly argue that the play would have been greater if Shake-speare had required us to infer Othello's mistakes from behind his own plausible account.

Yet in much modern fiction there does seem to be a positive contribution from the negative quality of authorial reticence. Just as we find our sympathy heightened as we travel with the lonely Miranda, so we find our ironic pleasure heightened as we travel with less sympathetic protagonists whose faults are never described directly.

One of the finest passages in this mode is the Jason section of *The Sound and the Fury.* Though our path through Jason's perverted moral world is clarified in many ways by what has come before, essentially it is built out of secret jokes passing between ourselves and the author. As we find ourselves viewing everything in a light contrary to that thrown by Jason's own beclouded soul, we may come to feel that any commentary will taint the pure effect:

> Once a bitch always a bitch, what I say. I says you're lucky if her playing out of school is all that worries you. . . . "I don't reckon she'd be playing out of school just to do something she could do in public," I says. . . .
> "I aint gwine let him [beat you]," Dilsey says, "Dont you worry, honey." She held to my arm. Then the belt came out and I jerked loose and flung her away. She stumbled into the table. She was so old she couldn't do any more than move hardly. But that's all right: we need somebody in the kitchen to eat up the grub the young ones can't tote off. She came hobbling between us, trying to hold me again. "Hit me, den," she says, "ef nothin else but hittin somebody wont do you. Hit me," she says.
> "You think I wont?" I says. . . .
> "Let him [the farmer] make a big crop and it wont be worth picking; let him make a small crop and he wont have enough to gin. And what for? so a bunch of damn eastern jews, I'm not talking about men of the jewish religion," I says, "I've known some jews that were fine citizens. You might be one yourself," I says.
> "No," he says, "I'm an American."
> "No offense," I says. "I give every man his due, regardless of religion or anything else. I have nothing against jews as an individual," I says. "It's just the race." . . .
> Last time I gave her forty dollars. Gave it to her. I never promise a woman anything nor let her know what I'm going to give her.

That's the only way to manage them. Always keep them guessing. If you cant think of any other way to surprise them, give them a bust in the jaw. . . .

"I reckon you'll never be a slave to any business," he says.

"Not unless it's Jason Compson's business," I says.

So when I went back and opened it [the check intended for Quentin] the only thing that surprised me was it was a money order not a check. Yes, sir. You cant trust a one of them. After all the risk I'd taken, risking Mother finding out about her coming down here once or twice a year sometimes, and me having to tell Mother lies about it. That's gratitude for you. And I wouldn't put it past her to try to notify the postoffice not to let anyone except her cash it. Giving a kid like that fifty dollars.

As we go on through this catalogue of bigotry, crime, cruelty and ignorance, few of us would ask for commentary to clarify our judgment. It is not only that we need no guide. We would positively repudiate one if he offered himself to us. We take delight in communion, and even in deep collusion, with the author behind Jason's back. Most of Jason's faults and crimes are so glaring that there would be no fun in talking about them openly. In fact, one of the frustrations of criticism is that many of the effects that require explication are of a kind that lose their savor in being made explicit. Their authors left them implicit in the first place because open discussion threatened to destroy them. To call Jason a bigot, a braggart, a thief, and a sadist offers none of the comic delight that his vicious behavior offers. But to commune with Faulkner behind Jason's back is a different matter. We watch with him while this Vice reveals himself for our contempt, our hatred, our laughter, and even—so strong is the effect of his psychological vitality—our pity. The technique enables us to skirt the thrilling regions of melodrama without embarrassment. Breathing the heady airs of irony, we can ignore how close we have come to gothic fantasy.

What all this amounts to is that on this moral level we discover a kind of collaboration which can be one of the most rewarding of all reading experiences. To collaborate with the author by providing the source of an allusion or by deciphering a pun is one thing. But to collaborate with him by providing mature moral judgment is a far more exhilarating sport. In dealing with Jason, we must help

Faulkner write his work by rising to our best, most perceptive level. When we see the compound joke of Jason's not having anything against "jews as an individual" but just against "the race," we do so only by calling to bear on the passage our linguistic experience, our logical and moral sense, and our past experience with bigots. When we have seen all that Faulkner has packed into the sentence we feel almost as if we had written it ourselves, so effectively has he demanded of us our best creative effort.

But with all of this said, a larger question remains. Why do we sometimes allow, and even require, authorial reticence and sometimes allow, and even require, authorial assistance? Why should explicit judgment be banned from *The Sound and the Fury* and allowed in "Barn Burning"? When the young son betrays his father by revealing the father's plans to burn the barn and then flees, never to return, why should we not only allow but welcome a passage like the following?

> At midnight he was sitting on the crest of a hill. He did not know it was midnight and he did not know how far he had come. But there was no glare behind him now and he sat now, his back toward what he had called home for four days anyhow, his face toward the dark woods which he would enter when breath was strong again, small, shaking steadily in the chill darkness, hugging himself into the remainder of his thin, rotten shirt, the grief and despair now no longer terror and fear but just grief and despair. *Father. My father*, he thought. "He was brave!" he cried suddenly, aloud but not loud, no more than a whisper: "He was! He was in the war! He was in Colonel Sartoris' cav'ry!" *not knowing that his father had gone to that war a private in the fine old European sense, wearing no uniform, admitting the authority of and giving fidelity to no man or army or flag, going to war as Malbrouck himself did: for booty— it meant nothing and less than nothing to him if it were enemy booty or his own* [my italics].

I cannot pretend to any very satisfactory answer to the question, but clearly it cannot be answered by looking at general rules about whether the author's voice is a flaw. We can say with some confidence that the poignancy of the boy's lonely last-ditch defense of his father is greatly increased by letting us know that even that defense is unjustified. This takes us some way toward an answer, but it leaves us with no guide in deciding when and where poignancy can legitimately be heightened in this manner. Though the purposes described in this chapter—sympathy, confusion, and the pleasures of irony—are somewhat more specific, and hence more useful in criticism, than realism, objectivity, and purity, none of them can be prescribed for all literary cases. If they are treated as panaceas, they may kill as well as cure. It is all very well to say that in this work commentary is best and in that one impersonality, but of what use is such accumulation of examples to the novelist as he tries to make decisions about technique? Surely there are *some* general rules.

I return to this problem briefly later on. But I must now lead to it through a prolonged look at the costs that may be paid, deliberately or unwittingly, by the impersonal novelist.

"If anything I have said seems sharp or gossipy, remember that it is Folly and a woman who has spoken."—ERASMUS

"I had got my Lady into such a terror about me, that when I smiled it was quite an era of happiness to her; and if I beckoned to her, she would come fawning up to me like a dog. . . . I brought my high-born wife to kiss my hand, to pull off my boots, to fetch and carry for me like a servant, and always to make it a holiday, too, when I was in good humour. I confided perhaps too much in the duration of this disciplined obedience, and forgot that the very hypocrisy which forms a part of it (all timid people are liars in their hearts) may be exerted in a way that may be far from agreeable, in order to deceive you."—THACKERAY, *Barry Lyndon*

"Oh that I could not say, that I have met with more admirers of Lovelace than of Clarissa."—SAMUEL RICHARDSON

"Note that it is Edouard who is speaking; it is not Gide."—JEAN THOMAS

"A work of art that one has to explain fails in so far, I suppose, of its mission."—HENRY JAMES on *The Awkward Age*

The Price
of Impersonal Narration, I:
Confusion of Distance

"THE TURN OF THE SCREW" AS PUZZLE

If the author who resigns his public position always left a deputy as transparent as Jason Compson, we could stop here. But we have all at one time or another been baffled by a particular combination of favorable and unfavorable qualities in a narrator or reflector. Perhaps more important, we find evidence everywhere of other readers' troubles, sometimes in the form of a public confession to bewilderment, more often in the form of disputes like the famous trial of the poor narrator of James's *The Turn of the Screw*.

". . . A great deal of unnecessary mystery has been made of the apparent ambiguity" in *The Turn of the Screw*, we are told by a critic who takes the governess' word to be generally sound.[1] James's own statements about the governess suggest that he, too, would think controversy about her unnecessary. "Of course I had, about my young woman, to take a very sharp line," he wrote to H. G.

---

[1] Robert B. Heilman, "The Freudian Reading of *The Turn of the Screw*," *Modern Language Notes*, LXII (November, 1947), 441.

Wells. "The grotesque business I had to make her picture and the childish psychology I had to make her trace and present, were, for me at least, a very difficult job, in which absolute lucidity and logic, a singleness of effect, were imperative. Therefore I had to rule out subjective complications of her own—play of tone, etc.; and keep her impersonal save for the most obvious and indispensable little note of neatness, firmness and courage—without which she wouldn't have had her data."[2] In a notebook entry he says, "The story to be told—tolerably obviously—by an outside spectator, observer."[3] And in the Preface his view is still the same. "It constitutes no little of a character indeed, in such conditions, for a young person, as she says, 'privately bred,' that she is able to make her particular credible statement of such strange matters. She has 'authority,' which is a good deal to have given her, and I couldn't have arrived at so much had I clumsily tried for more."[4] Absolute lucidity" and "singleness of effect"; no "subjective complications" or "play of tone"; an "outside observer," "impersonal," with "authority," making a "credible" statement—surely James's intentions are clear: he is attempting one of his lucid—but of course not-*too-lucid*—reflectors. Her consciousness must, like that of all of James's observers, be sufficiently "bedimmed and befooled and bewildered, anxious, restless, fallible" to connect it with the "general human exposure," in order to be "thoroughly natural," and still a "sufficiently clear medium to represent a whole."[5] She must, like

---

[2] Letter to Wells, December 9, 1898, Lubbock (ed.), *Letters* (London, 1920), I, 306. In reprinting this comment in *Henry James and H. G. Wells* (Urbana, Ill., 1958), Leon Edel and Gordon Ray dismiss its relevance as proof that James intended absolute lucidity and singleness of effect; all he is doing is "explaining to Wells how he kept his governess 'impersonal'—so that she is not even named" (p. 56). Yet surely "impersonal" in James's context means that she has no "subjective complications of her own"; there is no personal "play of tone," no constant running correction of her personal views required of the reader.

[3] Notebook references are all to *The Notebooks of Henry James*, ed. F. O. Matthiessen and Kenneth B. Murdock (New York, 1947). Page references to the notes on any story can be found readily in the excellent index under "James, Henry, writings of," pp. 421–23.

[4] *The Art of the Novel*, ed. R. P. Blackmur (London, 1934; New York, 1947), p. 174.

[5] Preface to *Roderick Hudson*, in *The Art of the Novel*, p. 16. See also p. 90. Throughout the following chapters unexplained page references in my text will be to *The Art of the Novel*.

the hero of *The Princess Casamassima,* "feel enough and 'know' enough" for the "maximum dramatic value without feeling and knowing too much"—too much, of course, being defined as whatever would destroy "minimum verisimilitude" (p. 69).

All this would seem to confirm what we have been told by some of James's critics, that he "was aiming at explicitness, never at obscurities—as if he were talking to children,"[6] that "with James the clue is very firmly held through the most blind and devious windings of the labyrinth," that "the suspicion of unsureness in his 'moral touch' . . . completely vanishes" if the reader is "alert" enough to recognize that "it is not James but his characters" who have an uncertain moral touch.[7]

The fact remains that the effects of this story on James's readers have been far from clear. On the one hand, many have found the governess completely untrustworthy—even to the point of denying the reality of the ghosts whose evil workings she reports to us. ". . . The young governess who tells the story is a neurotic case of sex repression, and the ghosts are not real ghosts at all but merely hallucinations of the governess." "When one has once been given this clue . . . , one wonders how one could ever have missed it. There is a very good reason, however, in the fact that nowhere does James unequivocally give the thing away: almost everything from beginning to end can be read equally in either of two senses." So Edmund Wilson, and he has been joined by many others. "The governess . . . subjects Flora and Miles . . . to all the vagaries of her progressively more and more deranged mind, until through sheer terror Flora goes into a delirium with brain fever, and Miles, harder pressed than Flora, is literally scared to death." They are swept "to destruction by the force of their governess's emotional cannibalism." On the other hand, from the very beginning there have been many readers who, like Rebecca West, would take the "honourable and fearless lady" at her word. Between these groups, as in all such controversies, fall those who see reasons for compromise; Leon Edel agrees that the

---

6 Ford Madox Ford, "The Old Man," in *The Question of Henry James,* ed. F. W. Dupee (New York, 1945), p. 51.

7 Joseph Warren Beach, *The Method of Henry James* (rev. ed.; Philadelphia, 1954), pp. cxii, lxxvi.

ghosts are real but agrees also that "anyone wishing to treat the governess as a psychological 'case' is offered sufficient data to permit the diagnosis that she is mentally disturbed."[8]

I may as well begin by admitting—reluctantly since all of the glamor is on the other side—that for me James's conscious intentions are fully realized: the ghosts are real, the governess sees what she says she sees. What she sees disturbs her—as well it might. She is naïve, innocent, human, decidedly *inconscient* about a lot of things she ought to be aware of; she is no paragon of wisdom or even of integrity. But she behaves about as well as we could reasonably expect of ourselves under similarly intolerable circumstances.

There is no point in repeating all of the evidence here. Most of the arguments that seem to me convincing were made by Robert Liddell as long ago as 1947, and Alexander E. Jones has recently summarized the whole dispute with admirable clarity.[9] One might think that these careful arguments would lead everyone to join the ranks of "straight" readers: Joseph Warren Beach, Carl and Mark Van Doren, F. O. Matthiessen, Kenneth Murdock, Elmer Stoll, Philip Rahv, Oliver Evans, Glenn Reed, Robert B. Heilman, Edward Wagenknecht, Katherine Anne Porter, Allen Tate, F. R. Leavis, and so on. How, then, can we account for the persistence of the hallucination theory?

The natural temptation is to attack the enemies of the poor governess, pointing to their bad logic, their wilful suppression of pertinent evidence, and their happy indifference to gross inconsistencies in their own ranks. (It *is* hard to read through the stuff

---

[8] Leon Edel, Prefatory note to Harold C. Goddard, "A Pre-Freudian Reading of *The Turn of the Screw*," *Nineteenth-Century Fiction*, XII (June, 1957), 2. Other citations are from (1) Edmund Wilson, "The Ambiguity of Henry James," *Hound and Horn*, VII (April–May, 1934), 385–406, as reprinted in *The Triple Thinkers* (New York, 1938) and in F. W. Dupee (ed.), *The Question of Henry James*, pp. 160–90; Wilson later revised his statement, claiming that unconscious motives drove James to his portrait of the effects of sexual inhibition (see below, p. 370); (2) Osborn Andreas, *Henry James and the Expanding Horizon* (Seattle, Wash., 1959), pp. 46–47; (3) Rebecca West, *Henry James* (London, 1916), p. 97.

[9] Robert Liddell, "The 'Hallucination' Theory of *The Turn of the Screw*," a *Treatise on the Novel* (London, 1947), pp. 138–45; Alexander E. Jones, "Point of View in *The Turn of the Screw*," *PMLA*, LXXIV (March, 1959), 112–22.

written on this story without wishing for more signs of respect for standards of proof.) But I can be sure that those I might accuse of galloping Freudianism will have their own epithets ready, accounting for my literal-minded reading by reference to my prudery, my lack of subtlety, or my hidebound devotion to traditional, unimaginative critical methods.

If we had only this one controversy, we might avoid the comedy of such mutual accusations by joining forces and attacking James for incompetence or unfairness. Obviously he could have made things clearer if he had wanted to. "There are a number of essential questions," says Marius Bewley in a mood which we have all no doubt known at one time or another, "that simply cannot be answered without bringing to *The Turn of the Screw* that kind of attention which a work of art ought not to require. And yet the questions are not idle ones if one assumes that a work of art has a moral value."[10]

But *The Turn of the Screw* is by no means alone. If Bewley's claim is true, it applies equally well to *The Sacred Fount* and to a dozen other stories by James. The critical disagreement revealed to anyone who compares two or three critics on any one story is a scandal.[11] And we cannot stop with James. Hundreds of modern works present the reader with precisely the same kind of problem given by *The Turn*. Though most of the potential controversies have presumably never come to light, the governess is only one of a great number of indeterminately unreliable narrators who have led readers into public controversy. In such a situation, does it any longer make sense to say, "Here the reader has gone astray, there the author"? We are *all* in these troubled waters together. Rather than join in the chorus of charges against the "stupid reader" or the "wilfully obscure author," it will be more worthwhile to try to

---

10 *The Complex Fate* (London, 1952), p. 110. For other accounts of James's obscurities see (1) Robert Cantwell, "A Little Reality," *Hound and Horn*, VII (April–May, 1934), 494–505: "Before he [James] had gone very far . . . it became almost impossible, in any single work, to determine where the irony of his comments left off . . ." (p. 501); (2) Joseph Warren Beach, *The Method of Henry James*, pp. 247–49: "And the worst of it is that, among all these competitors, the reader is at a loss to know where to invest his sympathies [in *The Awkward Age*]."

11 See Bibliography, Sec. V, B.

understand, in the next two chapters, why unintentional ambiguity of effect has been so frequent in fiction since James.

TROUBLES WITH IRONY IN EARLIER LITERATURE

Confusions of distance did not begin with modern fiction. In all periods and in many different genres we find speakers who win credence when they should be doubted, or who lead critics to dispute the precise degree of their untrustworthiness. In drama (Is the villain always trustworthy in soliloquy?), in satire (Where does Rabelais stand in his work?), in comic fiction (Is Sterne laughing at his narrator in *A Sentimental Journey?*), in the dramatic monologue (What is Browning's precise judgment upon his many vicious and foolish spokesmen?)[12]—in short, wherever explicit judgment has been unavailable, critical troubles, as well as some extraordinary delights, have ensued.

If we are to see what is distinctively troublesome about modern fiction, we should be quite clear about the causes of earlier difficulties with distance.

Lack of adequate warning that irony is at work.—Most successful irony before the modern period gave unmistakable notice, in one form or another, that the speaker could not be trusted. In Lucian's *True History*, for example (about A.D. 170), the narrator introduces himself as a liar like other historians: "When I come across a writer of this sort, I do not much mind his lying; the practice is much too well established for that. . . . I see no reason for resigning my right to that inventive freedom which others enjoy; and, as I have no truth to put on record, having lived a very humdrum life, I fall back on falsehood—but falsehood of a more consistent variety; for I now make the only true statement you are to expect—that I am a liar."[13] While such a warning does not guarantee that the ironies will be easily decipherable, it at least insures that the reader will be working on the right line.

The warning need not be a direct statement, of course. Any grotesque disparity between word and word or word and deed will

---

[12] See n. 39, p. 48.

[13] *Works*, trans. H. W. and F. G. Fowler (Oxford, 1905), II, 137.

serve. Though one might, for example, be deceived by the opening of *Jonathan Wild*, the deception does not last long.

> As it is necessary that all great and surprising events, the designs of which are laid, conducted, and brought to perfection by the utmost force of human invention and art, should be produced by great and eminent men, so the lives of such may be justly and properly styled the quintessence of history. In these, when delivered to us by sensible writers, we are not only most agreeably entertained, but most usefully instructed; for, besides the attaining hence a consummate knowledge of human nature in general; of its secret springs, various windings, and perplexed mazes; we have here before our eyes lively examples of whatever is amiable or detestable, worthy of admiration or abhorrence, and are consequently taught, in a manner infinitely more effectual than by precept, what we are eagerly to imitate or carefully to avoid.

Up to this point one has no unequivocal reason for questioning the reliability of Fielding's narrator. It is easy enough to imagine an author talking in such a way. And we are not absolutely disabused until the fifth paragraph.

> But before we enter on this great work we must endeavor to remove some errors of opinion which mankind have, by the disingenuity of writers, contracted: for these, from their fear of contradicting the obsolete and absurd doctrines of a set of simple fellows, called, in derision, sages or philosophers, have endeavoured, as much as possible, to confound the ideas of greatness and goodness; whereas no two things can possibly be more distinct from each other, for greatness consists in bringing all manner of mischief on mankind, and goodness in removing it from them.

With this passage, whatever weak suspicions have been aroused by the inflated style of the first paragraphs are turned into certainties. Unless we are willing, without irony, to allow him to divorce greatness and goodness, unless we think, with the narrator, that a man who "brings all manner of mischief on mankind" is made truly great by doing so, we are forced to move behind the overt beliefs of the narrator to the implicit beliefs of the author. By the end of the chapter, no one can believe that the author himself takes goodness in a great man to be "meanness and imperfection," or that, like his narrator, he wants the reader to "concur with us in allowing" Jonathan Wild the title of "*The Great.*"

Without such unmistakable clues, irony has always given trouble, and there is no a priori reason for assuming that the fault is the reader's. We may be tempted to laugh at the foolish Tories who were taken in by Defoe's impersonated Tory as he argued for extermination in "The Shortest Way with the Dissenters" (1702). But since Defoe gives us a realistic impersonation, without providing the evidences for his unmasking, it is hardly surprising that none of its first readers "did imagine it could be wrote by a Whigg."[14] An intelligent reader, whether high churchman or dissenter, could easily read every word without having his suspicions aroused, because Defoe's mock-Tory presents no single argument that might not have been advanced by a real fanatical Tory. A careful student of polemic would of course recognize even on first reading that the arguments are specious; but so are the arguments of much serious polemic. The dialectical route by which Defoe's speaker reaches the conclusion that true charity dictates the extermination of the dissenters is, after all, common in form with much fanatical rhetoric: " 'Tis Cruelty to kill a Snake or a Toad in cold Blood, but the Poyson of their Nature makes it a Charity to our Neighbours, to destroy those Creatures, not for any personal Injury receiv'd, but for prevention; not for the Evil they have done, but the Evil they may do." "Moses was a merciful meek Man, and yet with what Fury did he run thro' the Camp, and cut the Throats of Three and thirty thousand of his dear *Israelites*, that were fallen into Idolatry; what was the reason? 'twas Mercy to the rest to make these be Examples, to prevent the Destruction of the whole Army."[15]

To us, knowing the full story of the pamphlet, the signs of Defoe's intentions may seem obvious. How could his contemporaries

---

14 From a pamphlet published in London in 1703: *The New Association, Part II, With farther Improvements, As Another and Later Scots Presbyterian-Covenant, Besides that mention'd in the Former Part. . . . An Answer to some Objections in the Pretended D. Foe's Explication, in the Reflections upon the Shortest Way . . .* (p. 6). I owe this reference to my colleague, Leigh Gibby. For a discussion of the difference between impersonation and the kind of irony that plays fair with the reader, see Ian Watt, *The Rise of the Novel* (Berkeley, Calif., 1957), p. 126.

15 *The Shortest Way with the Dissenters* (London, 1702), pp. 18, 20. Cf. Voltaire's "pour encourager les autres."

have failed to recognize the absurdity of this argument? But if we compare Defoe's masterful impersonation with the more fully developed satire of Swift's "A Modest Proposal," we see that the argument for mass cruelty in Defoe is very different from the similarly cruel proposal in Swift. The cruelty advocated by Defoe's Tory, in the name of Mercy, is not unheard of, incredible, absolutely beyond human experience; heretics have been exterminated before, as all his readers knew, and they will be again. Thus the argument, which to any dissenter must have seemed fully as infuriating and outlandish as Swift's argument for child-cannibalism, was not incredible even to the dissenters; on the contrary, it was frightening, and thus for them the irony failed. For the Tories, on the other hand, it must have been both frightening and exhilarating; even for the moderate Tories, it would not, on first reading, seem impossible that an extreme Tory could argue in this manner.

What is even more deceptive is that the appeals to fact, if we can call them that, are not by any means outright lies. He accuses the dissenters of having been cruel, immoderate, and unjust. Most dissenters must have suspected that the charge was at least in part true. Thus the argument, *"No Gentlemen, the Time of Mercy is past, your Day of Grace is over; you shou'd have practis'd Peace, and Moderation, and Charity, if you expected any your selves"* (p. 3), is, within its own limits, perfectly sound; and unlike the "sound" arguments with which Swift begins "A Modest Proposal," it does not give way, as the pamphlet progresses, to arguments that are patently absurd to all reasonable men of both parties.

Finally, there is no statement within the pamphlet of a positive program which, if read properly, would reveal the true position of the author. Even after we are alerted to irony, we cannot discover from the pamphlet alone what Defoe's position is. Compare this method with Swift's inverted statement of his own beliefs at the conclusion of "A Modest Proposal": "Therefore let no man talk to me of other Expedients: *Of taxing our Absentees at five Shillings a Pound: of using neither Cloaths, nor Houshold Furniture except what is of our own Growth and Manufacture: of utterly rejecting . . ."*—the tabulation of Swift's true proposals, as rejected by his speaker, goes on, in full italics, for half a page. There is nothing of this sort in Defoe. If we read his pamphlet unwarned, with its absolute consistency of tone and sincerity of purpose showing on every page, we might easily make the mistake made by Defoe's contemporaries.

Now the curious thing about this comparison with Swift is that in terms of realistic consistency alone, Defoe's method might seem the better one. He maintains a dramatic, realistic impersonation throughout, and he does not engage in any of Swift's winking or rib-punching. If we judge according to abstract criteria of tone or distance, Defoe's piece is the better one. It is certainly more significant as a forerunner of modern fiction.[16] But if we are willing, as I think we must be, to judge realized intentions as revealed in total structure, Swift's work is superior in its very willingness to sacrifice consistency to satiric force.[17]

Extreme complexity, subtlety, or privacy of the norms to be inferred.—Even when the reader is properly alerted, he will always have trouble if the unspoken norms are not fairly simple and generally agreed upon. The debate about where Swift stands in the fourth book of *Gulliver's Travels* is apparently as much alive today as it ever was—not because Swift has left any doubt about the presence of irony but because it is very hard to know how much distance there is between Gulliver and Swift and precisely which of the traveler's enthusiasms for the Houyhnhnms is excessive. Whatever Swift's satirical point, it is neither sufficiently commonplace nor sufficiently simple to be easily deciphered. Does he agree with Gulliver that "these noble Houyhnhnms are endowed by nature with a general disposition to all virtues" (chap. viii), or is

---

[16] See Robert C. Rathburn, "The Makers of the British Novel," in *From Jane Austen to Joseph Conrad*, ed. Robert C. Rathburn and Martin Steinmann, Jr. (Minneapolis, Minn., 1958), pp. 3–22, esp. p. 5: "Defoe used the device of a persona so well that his satire had a doubly ironic effect in that the persons satirized took him seriously. . . . The pamphlet brought Defoe to the pillory, but it also showed his skill in writing from an assumed point of view."

[17] We might also say that our comic delight is less in Defoe, even if we know that the pamphlet is ironic, because we have fewer objects of ridicule: (1) no reader could conceivably be ridiculous for failing to understand; and (2) the speaker himself is less absurd than Swift's. The more realistic his impersonation, the less ridiculously exaggerated he will be, and the less right we will feel to laugh at him or at readers deceived by him.

Swift attacking, behind Gulliver's back, the "absurd creatures" who, in their cold rationalism, "represent the deistic presumption that mankind has no need of the specifically Christian virtues?"[18] As Professor Sherburn says, it is unlikely "that there will ever be unanimous agreement as to what Swift is doing in . . . Gulliver's fourth voyage" (p. 92). Unless there has been some permanent loss of clues to meanings which were clear to Swift's contemporaries, we must conclude either that Swift's norms are too complex or that their relations with Gulliver's opinions are too complicated.

Even if we conclude that the fourth book has been left to some degree indecipherable, we may, of course, go along with the current fashion and praise Swift for his ambiguities rather than condemn him for his inconclusiveness. But whichever side we fall on, we should be quite clear that the ambiguity we accept will be paid for by a loss of satiric force. Unless we are quite sure that Swift valued subtleties and ambiguities more than effectiveness in conveying a simpler message, we must entertain the possibility that somebody—whether author or reader—has gone astray.

Fortunately my main point here does not depend on an assessment of blame: whenever an impersonal author asks us to infer subtle differences between his narrator's norms and his own, we are likely to have trouble.

We certainly meet this difficulty in *Moll Flanders*. It would be a clever reader indeed who could be sure just how much of Moll's behavior is consciously judged and repudiated by Defoe. Ian Watt, one of the most helpful commentators, finds many passages in which he cannot decide whether the reader's judgment works against Moll alone or against Defoe as well. Moll tells her lover, for example, that she would never willingly deceive him, and adds, "Nothing that ever befell me in my life sank so deep into my heart

---

[18] Irvin Ehrenpreis, *The Personality of Jonathan Swift* (London, 1958), p. 102. A substantial bibliography of the controversy over this book can be found in Kathleen Williams, *Jonathan Swift and the Age of Compromise* (Lawrence, Kan., 1958), p. 177 n. See also William Bragg Ewald, Jr., *The Masks of Jonathan Swift* (Oxford, 1954). George Sherburn and R. S. Crane have given what seem to me sound arguments for rejecting the strongly ironic reading of the Houyhnhnms (Sherburn, "Errors concerning the Houyhnhnms," *Modern Philology*, LVI [November, 1958], 92–97; Crane, "The Houyhnhnms, the Yahoos, and the History of Ideas," in *Reason and Imagination: Studies in the History of Ideas, 1600–1800*, ed. J. A. Mazzeo [New York, 1962]). But the real point is that decision is here extremely difficult.

as this farewell. I reproached him a thousand times in my thoughts for leaving me, for I would have gone with him through the world, if I had begged my bread. I felt in my pocket, and there I found ten guineas, his gold watch, and two little rings."[19] Does Defoe intend this final sentence as Moll's unconscious self-betrayal, as I am inclined to think, or is Defoe himself betrayed by it? Watt concludes that, though Defoe *reveals* Moll's sophistries which conceal her dual allegiance here to the lover and to her own economic preservation, "he does not, strictly speaking, portray them," since he is himself their victim; "consequently *Moll Flanders* is undoubtedly an ironic object, but it is not a work of irony" (p. 130). Everyone finds some examples of intended irony in the novel; everyone finds moments when Defoe seems to be giving himself away. But there is a large tract of Moll's behavior where most of us would be hard put to decide whether the inconsistencies we are amused by were intended by Defoe.

The reader who is untroubled by such problems may argue that his opinion of the book does not depend on whether the artist was on top of its ironies. But for most of us the question is an important one: if we find ourselves laughing at the author along with his characters, our opinion of the book as art must suffer. In any case, whether we read *Moll Flanders* in Watt's manner or join those who see Defoe as a great ironist, it is clear that Moll's point of view has given us difficulties that Defoe could not have intended; the very quality of our interest in the book depends on decisions which even now, more than two hundred years after the event, cannot be made with any assurance.

Vivid psychological realism.—We have already seen, particularly in *Emma*, how strongly a prolonged intimate view of a character works against our capacity for judgment. One of our troubles in *Moll Flanders* is that this effect works on us to soften our judgment of her worst misdeeds and to confuse us about her minor faults. Trollope reported that even a character as vicious as the protagonist of Thackeray's *Barry Lyndon* (1844) produced this effect on him.

---

[19] *The Rise of the Novel*, p. 125. Watt provides a thorough discussion of recent interpretations of Defoe as a conscious ironist. For a more favorable treatment of Defoe's ironies, see Alan D. McKillop, *The Early Masters of English Fiction* (Lawrence, Kan., 1956), chap. i.

The comic villain who tells his own tale is guilty of every conceivable meanness, deliberately harming almost everyone else in the book; he engages in the most outlandish arguments in self-justification, and unlike Moll he dies unrepentant. And yet, as Trollope says, "his story is so written that it is almost impossible not to entertain something of a friendly feeling for him. . . . The reader is so carried away by his frankness and energy as almost to rejoice when he succeeds, and to grieve with him when he is brought to the ground."[20] It was not only Trollope who almost grieved; many readers were caught in the net of Barry Lyndon's rhetorical vitality. It baffled them to find themselves excusing his crimes, and they then complained about Thackeray's immorality.[21] Presented with a kind of indomitable mental reality, and presented with it at first hand, they found themselves like Thackeray himself, "filled full with those blackguards."[22]

Richardson was distressed to learn that his readers admired even that case-hardened sinner, Lovelace. But once Lovelace has been given a chance to speak for himself, as the epistolary form allows him to do, our feeling toward him even at the moment when we fear for Clarissa most intensely is likely to be doubled-edged. Unlike our response to villains presented only from the outside, our feeling is a combination of natural detestation and natural fellow feeling: bad as he is, he is made of the same stuff we are. It is not surprising that Richardson's intentions have often been counteracted by this effect.[23]

THE PROBLEM OF DISTANCE IN "A PORTRAIT
OF THE ARTIST"

Everyone recognizes that each of these three sources of difficulty is present in some modern fiction, frequently in forms much more de-

---

[20] *Thackeray* (London, 1882), p. 71. First published 1879.

[21] See Gordon N. Ray, *The Buried Life* (Cambridge, Mass., 1952), pp. 28 ff.

[22] Trollope, *Thackeray*, p. 76. For a report of similar difficulties in Smollett, see McKillop, *Early Masters*, pp. 147–50.

[23] See Watt, *The Rise of the Novel*, p. 212: "Balzac, for example, thought it appropriate in 1837 to illustrate the point that there are always two sides to a question by asking, with what was certainly meant to be a rhetorical flourish— 'Who can decide between a Clarissa and a Lovelace?' "

ceptive than anything encountered in earlier work. Any one of them alone can give trouble. And in some modern fiction all three are present. There is no warning, either explicitly or in the form of gross disparity of word and deed; the relationship of the ironic narrator to the author's norms is an extremely complex one, and the norms are themselves subtle and private; and the narrator's own mental vitality dominates the scene and wins our sympathy.

It is in the last of these three that modern fiction has gone far beyond anything experienced before Flaubert. Jane Austen's implicit apology for Emma said, in effect, "Emma's vision is your vision; therefore forgive her." But modern authors have learned how to provide this apology in much more insistent form. The deep plunges of modern inside views, the various streams-of-consciousness that attempt to give the reader an effect of living thought and sensation, are capable of blinding us to the possibility of our making judgments not shared by the narrator or reflector himself.

If a master puzzle maker had set out to give us the greatest possible difficulty, he could not have done more than has been done in some modern works in which this effect of deep involvement is combined with the implicit demand that we maintain our capacity for ironic judgment. The trouble with *Moll Flanders*, such a genius of confusion might be imagined as saying to himself, is that the obvious differences between the female heroine and the author provide too many clues. Let us then write a book that will look like the author's autobiography, using many details from his own life and opinions. But we cannot be satisfied with moral problems, which are after all much less subject to dispute than intellectual and aesthetic matters. Let us then call for the reader's precise judgment on a very elaborate set of opinions and actions in which the hero is sometimes right, sometimes slightly wrong, and sometimes absurdly astray. Just to make sure that things are not too obvious, let us finally bind the reader so tightly to the consciousness of the ambiguously misguided protagonist that nothing will interfere with his delight in inferring the precise though varying degrees of distance that operate from point to point throughout the book. We can be sure that some readers will take the book as strictly autobiographical; others will go sadly astray in overlooking ironies that are intended and in discovering ironies that are not there. But for the rare reader who can make his way through this jungle, the delight will be great indeed.

The giant whom we all must wrestle with in this regard is clearly Joyce. Except for occasional outbursts of bravado nobody has ever really claimed that Joyce is clear. In all the skeleton keys and class-room guides there is an open assumption that his later works, *Ulysses* and *Finnegans Wake*, cannot be read; they can only be studied. Joyce himself was always explicating his works, and it is clear that he saw nothing wrong with the fact that they could not be thought of as standing entirely on their own feet. The reader's problems are handled, if they are to be handled at all, by rhetoric provided outside the work.

But the difficulties with distance that are pertinent here cannot be removed by simple study. Obscure allusions can be looked up, patterns of imagery and theme can be traced; gradually over the years a good deal of lore has accumulated, and about some of it by now there is even a certain amount of agreement. But about the more fundamental matters the skeleton keys and guides are of lit-tle help, because unfortunately they do not agree, they do not agree at all. It is fine to know that in *Ulysses* Stephen stands in some way for Telemachus and Bloom for his wandering father, Ulysses. But it would also be useful to know whether the work is comic or pa-thetic or tragic, or, if it is a combination, where the elements fall. Can two readers be said to have read the same book if one thinks it ends affirmatively and the other sees the ending as pessimistic? It is really no explanation to say that Joyce has succeeded in imitating life so well that like life itself his books seem totally ambiguous, to-tally open to whatever interpretation the reader wants to place on them. Even William Empson, that perceptive and somewhat over-ly ingenious prophet of ambiguity, finds himself unable to be com-pletely permissive toward conflicting interpretations. In a long, curious essay arguing that the basic movement of *Ulysses* is toward a favorable ending, with the Blooms and Stephen united, he admits that there are difficulties, and that they spring from the kind of book it is: it "not only refuses to tell you the end of the story, it also refuses to tell you what the author thinks would have been a good end to the story." And yet almost in the same breath he can write as if he thought previous critics somehow at fault for not having come to *his* inferences about the book. "By the way, I have no patience with critics who say it is impossible ever to tell whether Joyce means a literary effect to be ironical or not; if they don't know this part isn't funny, they ought to."[24] Well, but why should they know? Who is to mediate between Empson and those he attacks, or between Lawrance Thompson, in his interpretation of the book as comedy, and those critics with whom he is "decidedly at odds," Stuart Gilbert, Edmund Wilson, Harry Levin, David Daiches, and T. S. Eliot, each of whom assumes, he says, that "Joyce's artistic mode is essentially a non-comic mode, or that comedy in *Ulysses* is an effect rather than a cause"?[25]

Can it possibly make no difference whether we laugh or do not laugh? Can we defend the book even as a realistic mixture, like life itself, unless we can state with some precision what the ingredients are that have been mixed together?

Rather than pursue such general questions about Joyce's admittedly difficult later works, it will be more useful to look closely at that earlier work for which no skeleton key has been thought necessary, *A Portrait of the Artist as a Young Man* (1916). Everyone seems by now agreed that it is a masterpiece in the modern mode. Perhaps we can accept it as that—indeed accept it as an unquestionably great work from any viewpoint—and still feel free to ask a few irreverent questions.

The structure of this "authorless" work is based on the growth of a sensitive boy to young manhood. The steps in his growth are obviously constructed with great care. Each of the first four sections ends a period of Stephen's life with what Joyce, in an earlier draft, calls an epiphany: a peculiar revelation of the inner reality of an experience, accompanied with great elation, as in a mystical religious experience. Each is followed by the opening of a new chapter on a very prosaic, even depressed level. Now here is clearly a careful

---

24 "The Theme of *Ulysses*," *Kenyon Review*, XVIII (Winter, 1956), 36, 31.
25 *A Comic Principle in Sterne—Meredith—Joyce* (Oslo, 1954), p. 22.

structural preparation—for what? For a transformation, or for a merely cyclical return? Is the final exaltation a release from the depressing features of Irish life which have tainted the earlier experiences? Or is it the fifth turn in an endless cycle? And in either case, is Stephen always to be viewed with the same deadly seriousness with which he views himself? Is it to artistic maturity that he grows? As the young man goes into exile from Ireland, goes "to encounter for the millionth time the reality of experience and to forge in the smithy" of his soul "the uncreated conscience" of his race, are we to take this, with Harry Levin, as a fully serious portrait of the artist Dedalus, praying to his namesake Daedalus, to stand him "now and ever in good stead"?[26] Or is the inflated style, as Mark Schorer tells us, Joyce's clue that the young Icarus is flying too close to the sun, with the "excessive lyric relaxation" of Stephen's final style punctuating "the illusory nature of the whole ambition"?[27] The young man views himself and his flight with unrelieved solemnity. Should we?

To see the difficulties clearly, let us consider three crucial episodes, all from the final section: his rejection of the priesthood, his exposition of what he takes to be Thomistic aesthetics, and his composition of a poem.

Is his rejection of the priesthood a triumph, a tragedy, or merely a comedy of errors? Most readers, even those who follow the new trend of reading Stephen ironically, seem to have read it as a triumph: the artist has rid himself of one of the chains that bound him. To Caroline Gordon, this is a serious misreading. "I suspect that Joyce's *Portrait* has been misread by a whole generation." She sees the rejection as "the picture of a soul that is being damned for time and eternity caught in the act of foreseeing and foreknowing its damnation," and she cites in evidence the fall of Icarus and Stephen's own statement to Cranly that he is not afraid to make a mistake, "even a great mistake, a lifelong mistake and perhaps for eternity, too."[28] Well, which *Portrait* do we choose, that of the artistic soul battling through successfully to his necessary freedom, or

---

[26] *James Joyce* (Norfolk, Va., 1941), pp. 58–62.

[27] "Technique as Discovery," *Hudson Review*, I (Spring, 1948), 79–80.

[28] *How To Read a Novel* (New York, 1957), p. 213.

that of the child of God, choosing, like Lucifer, his own damnation? No two books could be further from each other than the two we envision here. There may be a sufficient core of what is simply interesting to salvage the book as a great work of the sensibility, but unless we are willing to retreat into babbling and incommunicable relativism, we cannot believe that it is *both* a portrait of the prisoner freed *and* a portrait of the soul placing itself in chains.

Critics have had even more difficulty with Stephen's aesthetic theory, ostensibly developed from Aquinas. Is the book itself, as Grant Redford tells us,[29] an "objectification of an artistic proposition and a method announced by the central character," achieving for Joyce the "wholeness, harmony, and radiance" that Stephen celebrates in his theory? Or is it, as Father Noon says, an ironic portrait of Stephen's immature aesthetics? Joyce wanted to qualify Stephen's utterances, Father Noon tells us, "by inviting attention to his own more sophisticated literary concerns," and he stands apart from the Thomist aesthetics, watching Stephen miss the clue in his drive for an impersonal, dramatic narration. "The comparison of the artist with the God of the creation," taken "straight" by many critics, is for Father Noon "the climax of Joyce's ironic development of the Dedalus aesthetic."[30]

Finally, what of the precious villanelle? Does Joyce intend it to be taken as a serious sign of Stephen's artistry, as a sign of his genuine but amusingly pretentious precocity, or as something else entirely?

> Are you not weary of ardent ways,
> Lure of the fallen seraphim?
> Tell no more of enchanted days.
>
> Your eyes have set man's heart ablaze
> And you have had your will of him.
> Are you not weary of ardent ways? . . .

---

29 "The Role of Structure in Joyce's 'Portrait,' " *Modern Fiction Studies*, IV (Spring, 1958), 30. See also Herbert Gorman, *James Joyce* (London, 1941), p. 96, and Stuart Gilbert, *James Joyce's Ulysses* (London, 1930), pp. 20–22.

30 William T. Noon, S.J., *Joyce and Aquinas* (New Haven, Conn., 1957), pp. 34, 35, 66, 67. See also Hugh Kenner, "The *Portrait* in Perspective," *Kenyon Review*, X (Summer, 1948), 361–81.

Hardly anyone has committed himself in public about the quality of this poem. Are we to smile at Stephen or pity him in his tortured longing? Are we to marvel at his artistry, or scoff at his con-
ceit? Or are we merely to say, "How remarkable an insight into the
kind of poem that would be written by an adolescent in love, if he
were artistically inclined?" The poem, we are told, "enfolded him
like a shining cloud, enfolded him like water with a liquid life: and
like a cloud of vapour or like waters circumfluent in space the liquid
letters of speech, symbols of the element of mystery, flowed forth
over his brain." As we recall Jean Paul's formula for "romantic
irony," "hot baths of sentiment followed by cold showers of irony,"
we can only ask here which tap has been turned on. Are we to
swoon—or laugh?

Some critics will no doubt answer that all these questions are irrelevant. The villanelle is not to be judged but simply experienced;
the aesthetic theory is, within the art work, neither true nor false
but simply "true" to the art work—that is, true to Stephen's character at this point. To read modern literature properly we must refuse to ask irrelevant questions about it; we must accept the "portrait" and no more ask whether the character portrayed is good or
bad, right or wrong than we ask whether a woman painted by Pi-
casso is moral or immoral. "All facts of any kind," as Gilbert puts it,
"mental or material, sublime or ludicrous, have an equivalence of
value for the artist."[31]

This answer, which can be liberating at one stage of our development in appreciating not only modern but all art, becomes less and
less satisfactory the longer we look at it. It certainly does not seem
to have been Joyce's basic attitude, though he was often misleading
about it.[32] The creation and the enjoyment of art can never be a
completely neutral activity. Though different works of art require
different kinds of judgment for their enjoyment, the position taken
in chapters three through five must stand: no work, not even the
shortest lyric, can be written in complete moral, intellectual and

---

[31] *James Joyce's Ulysses*, p. 22.

[32] Richard Ellmann concludes that whether we know it or not, "Joyce's court is, like
Dante's or Tolstoy's, always in session" (*James Joyce* [New York, 1959], p. 3).

aesthetic neutrality. We may judge falsely, we may judge unconsciously, but we cannot even bring the book to mind without judging its elements, seeing them as shaped into a given kind of thing. Even if we denied that the sequence of events has meaning in the sense of being truly sequential, that denial would itself be a judgment on the rightness of Stephen's actions and opinions at each stage: to decide that he is not growing is as much a judgment on his actions as to decide that he is becoming more and more mature. Actually everyone reads the book as some kind of progressive sequence, and to do so we judge succeeding actions and opinions to be more or less moral, sensitive, intellectually mature, than those they follow.[33] If we felt that the question of Joyce's precise attitude toward Stephen's vocation, his aesthetics, and his villanelle were irrelevant, we would hardly dispute with each other about them. Yet I count in a recent check list at least fifteen articles and one full book disputing Joyce's attitude about the aesthetics alone.[34]

Like most modern critics, I would prefer to settle such disputes by using internal rather than external evidence. But the experts themselves give me little hope of finding answers to my three problems by re-reading *Portrait* one more time. They all clutch happily at any wisp of comment or fragmentary document that might illuminate Joyce's intentions.[35] And who can blame them?

The truth seems to be that Joyce was always a bit uncertain about his attitude toward Stephen. Anyone who reads Ellmann's masterful biography with this problem in mind cannot help being struck by the many shifts and turns Joyce took as he worked through the various versions. There is nothing especially strange in that, of course. Most "autobiographical" novelists probably encounter dif-

---

[33] Norman Friedman considers it a "tribute to Joyce's dramatic genius that a Catholic can sympathize with the portrayal of Catholic values in the novel which the hero rejects" ("Point of View in Fiction," *PMLA*, LXX [December, 1955], 11–84). But this is not to say that the Catholic readers are right, or that we need not make up our minds about the question.

[34] *Modern Fiction Studies*, IV (Spring, 1958), 72–99.

[35] See, for example, J. Mitchell Morse's defense of a fairly "straight" reading of *Ulysses*, based largely on Gorman's reading of Joyce's *Notebooks* ("Augustine, *Ayenbite*, and *Ulysses*," *PMLA*, LXX (December, 1955), 1147, n. 12.

ficulty in trying to decide just how heroic their heroes are to be. But Joyce's explorations came just at a time when the traditional devices for control of distance were being repudiated, when doctrines of objectivity were in the air, and when people were taking seriously the idea that to evoke "reality" was a sufficient aim in art; the artist need not concern himself with judging or with specifying whether the reader should approve or disapprove, laugh or cry.

Now the traditional forms *had* specified in their very conceptions a certain degree of clarity about distance. If an author chose to write comedy, for example, he knew that his characters must at least to some degree be "placed" at a distance from the spectator's norms. This predetermination did not, of course, settle all of his problems. To balance sympathy and antipathy, admiration and contempt, was still a fundamental challenge, but it was a challenge for which there was considerable guidance in the practice of previous writers of comedy. If, on the other hand, he chose to write tragedy, or satire, or elegy, or celebration odes, or whatever, he could rely to some extent on conventions to guide him and his audience to a common attitude toward his characters.

The young Joyce had none of this to rely on, but he seems never to have sensed the full danger of his position. When, in his earliest years, he recorded his brief epiphanies—those bits of dialogue or description that were supposed to reveal the inner reality of things—there was always an implied identification of the recorder's norms and the reader's; both were spectators at the revealing moment, both shared in the vision of one moment of truth. Though some of the epiphanies are funny, some sad, and some mixed, the basic effect is always the same: an overwhelming sense—when they succeed—of what Joyce liked to call the "incarnation": Artistic Meaning has come to live in the world's body. The Poet has done his work.

Even in these early epiphanies there is difficulty with distance; the author inevitably expects the reader to share in his own preconceptions and interests sufficiently to catch, from each word or gesture, the precise mood or tone that they evoke for the author himself. But since complete identification with the author is a silent precondition for the success of such moments, the basic problem of distance is never a serious one. Even if the author and reader should differ in interpretation, they can share the sense of evoked reality.

It is only when Joyce places at the center of a long work a figure who experiences epiphanies, an epiphany-producing device, as it were, who is himself used by the real author as an object ambiguously distant from the norms of the work, that the complications of distance become incalculable. If he treats the author-figure satirically, as he does in much of *Stephen Hero*, that earlier, windier version of *Portrait*,[36] then what happens to the quality of the epiphanies that *he* describes? Are they still genuine epiphanies or only what the misguided, callow youth *thinks* are epiphanies? If, as Joyce's brother Stanislaus has revealed, the word "hero" is satiric, can we take seriously that anti-hero's vision? Yet if the satirical mode is dropped, if the hero is made into a real hero, and if the reader is made to see things entirely as he sees them, what then happens to objectivity? The portrait is no longer an objective rendering of reality, looked at from a respectable aesthetic distance, but rather a mere subjective indulgence.

Joyce can be seen, in Ellmann's account, struggling with this problem throughout the revisions. Unlike writers before Flaubert, he had no guidance from convention or tradition or fellow artists. Neither Flaubert nor James had established any sure ground to stand on. Both of them had, in fact, stumbled on the same hurdles, and though each had on occasion surmounted the difficulties, Joyce was in no frame of mind to look behind their claims as realists to the actual problems and lessons that lay beneath their evocative surfaces. A supreme egoist struggling to deal artistically with his own ego, a humorist who could not escape the comic consequences of his portrait of that inflated ego, he faced, in the completed *Stephen Hero*, what he had to recognize as a hodge-podge of irreconcilables. Is Stephen a pompous ass or not? Is his name deliberately ridiculous, as Stanislaus, who invented it, says? Or is it a serious act of symbolism? The way out seems inevitable, but it seems a retreat nonetheless: simply present the "reality" and let the reader judge.

---

[36] Ed. Theodore Spencer, 1944. Only part of the MS survives.

Cut all of the author's judgments, cut all of the adjectives, produce one long, ambiguous epiphany.[37]

Purged of the author's explicit judgment, the resulting work was so brilliant and compelling, its hero's vision so scintillating, that almost all readers overlooked the satiric and ironic content—except, of course, as the satire operated against *other* characters. So far as I know no one said anything about irony against Stephen until after *Ulysses* was published in 1922, with its opening in which Icarus-Stephen is shown with his wings clipped. Ironic readings did not become popular, in fact, until after the fragment of *Stephen Hero* was published in 1944. Readers of that work found, it is true, many authoritative confirmations of their exaltation of Stephen—for the most part in a form that might confirm anyone's prejudice against commentary. ". . . When he [Stephen] wrote it was always a mature and reasoned emotion which urged him" (p. 155). "This mood of indignation which was not guiltless of a certain superficiality was undoubtedly due to the excitement of release. . . . He acknowledged to himself in honest egoism that he could not take to heart the distress of a nation, the soul of which was antipathetic to his own, so bitterly as the indignity of a bad line of verse: but at the same time he was nothing in the world so little as an amateur artist" (p. 130). "Stephen did not attach himself to art in any spirit of youthful dilettantism but strove to pierce to the significant heart of everything" (p. 25). But readers were also faced with a good many denigrations of the hero. We can agree that *Portrait* is a better work because the immature author has been effaced; Joyce may indeed have found that effacing the commentary was the only way he could obtain an air of maturity. But the fact remains that it is primarily to this immature commentary that we must go for evidence in deciphering the ironies of the later, purer work.

---

[37] See Denis Donoghue's "Joyce and the Finite Order," *Sewanee Review*, LXVIII (Spring, 1960), 256–73: "The objects [in *Portrait*] exist to provide a suitably piteous setting for Stephen as Sensitive Plant; they are meant to mark a sequence of experiences in the mode of *pathos*. . . . The lyric situation is insulated from probes, and there is far too much of this cosseting in the *Portrait*. . . . Drama or rhetoric should have warned Joyce that Stephen the aesthetic *alazon* needed nothing so urgently as a correspondingly deft *eiron*; lacking this, the book is blind in one eye" (p. 258). Joyce would no doubt reply—I think unfairly—that he intended Stephen as both *alazon* and *eiron*.

What we find in *Stephen Hero* is not a simple confirmation of any reading that we might have achieved on the basis of *Portrait* alone. Rather we find an extremely complicated view, combining irony and admiration in unpredictable mixtures. Thus the Thomist aesthetics "was in the main applied Aquinas and he set it forth plainly with a naif air of discovering novelties. This he did partly to satisfy his own taste for enigmatic roles and partly from a genuine predisposition in favour of all but the premisses of scholasticism" (p. 64). No one ever inferred, before this passage was available, anything like this precise and complex judgment on Stephen. The combination of blame and approval, we may be sure, is different in the finished *Portrait*; the implied author no doubt often repudiates the explicit judgments of the younger narrator who intrudes into *Stephen Hero*. But we can also be sure that his judgment has not become less complex. Where do we find, in any criticism of *Portrait* based entirely on internal evidence, the following kind of juxtaposition of Stephen's views with the author's superior insight? "Having by this *simple process* established the literary form of art as the most excellent *he proceeded to examine it in favour of his theory, or, as he rendered it,* to establish the relations which must subsist between the literary image, the work of art itself, and that energy which had imagined and fashioned it, that center of conscious, re-acting, particular life, the artist" (p. 65; italics mine). Can we infer, from *Portrait*, that Joyce sees Stephen as simply rationalizing in favor of his theory? Did we guess that Joyce could refer to him mockingly as a "fiery-hearted revolutionary" and a "heaven-ascending essayist"?[38]

---

[38] One reviewer of *Stephen Hero* was puzzled to notice in it that the omniscient author, not yet purged in accordance with Joyce's theories of dramatic narration, frequently expresses biting criticism of the young Stephen. The earlier work thus seemed to him "much more cynical," and "much, much farther from the principles of detached classicism that had been formulated before either book was written." How could the man who wrote *Stephen Hero* go on and write, "in a mood of enraptured fervour," a work like *Portrait?*" (*T.L.S.*, February 1, 1957, p. 64).

It is true that, once we have been alerted, signs of ironic intention come rushing to our view. Those of us who now believe that Joyce is not entirely serious in the passages on aesthetics must wonder, for example, how we ever read them "straight." What did we make out of passages like the following, in those old, benighted days before we saw what was going on? "The lore which he was believed to pass his days brooding upon so that it had rapt him from the companionship of youth was only a garner of slender sentences from Aristotle's Poetics and Psychology and a *Synopsis Philosophiæ Scho-*

In *Stephen Hero*, the author's final evaluation of the aesthetics is favorable but qualified: "Except for the eloquent and arrogant peroration Stephen's essay was a careful exposition of a carefully meditated theory of esthetic" (p. 68). Though it might be argued that in the finished book he has cut out some of the negative elements, such as the "eloquent and arrogant peroration," and has presented the pure theory in conversational form, it is clear that Joyce himself judged his hero's theory in greater detail than we could possibly infer from the final version alone.

Similar clarifications can be found in *Stephen Hero* of our other two crucial problems, his rejection of the priesthood and his poetic ability. For example, "He had swept the moment into his memory . . . and . . . had brought forth some pages of sorry verse" (p. 57). Can the hero of *Portrait* be thought of as writing "sorry verse"? One would not think so, to read much of the commentary by Joyce's critics.

But who is to blame them? Whatever intelligence Joyce postulates in his reader—let us assume the unlikely case of its being comparable to his own—will not be sufficient for precise inference of a pattern of judgments which is, after all, private to Joyce. And this will be true regardless of how much distance from his own hero we believe him to have achieved by the time he concluded his final version. We simply cannot avoid the conclusion that to some extent the book itself is at fault, regardless of its great virtues. Unless we make the absurd assumption that Joyce had in reality purged himself of all judgment by the time he completed his final draft, unless we see him as having really come to look upon all of Stephen's actions as equally wise or equally foolish, equally sensitive or equally meaningless, we must conclude that many of the refine-

---

lasticæ ad mentem divi Thomæ. His thinking was a dusk of doubt and selfmistrust, lit up at moments by the lightnings of intuition. . . ." "In those moments the world perished about his feet as if it had been [with] fire consumed: and thereafter his tongue grew heavy and he met the eyes of others with unanswering eyes for he felt that the spirit of beauty had folded him round like a mantle and that in reverie at least he had been acquainted with nobility. But, when this brief pride of silence upheld him no longer, he was glad to find himself still in the midst of common lives, passing on his way amid the squalor and noise and sloth of the city fearlessly and with a light heart" (opening pp. of chap. v). If this is not mockery, however tender, it is fustian.

ments he intended in his finished *Portrait* are, for most of us, permanently lost. Even if we were now to do our homework like dutiful students, even if we were to study all of Joyce's work, even if we were to spend the lifetime that Joyce playfully said his novels demand, presumably we should never come to as rich, as refined, and as varied a conception of the quality of Stephen's last days in Ireland as Joyce had in mind. For some of us the air of detachment and objectivity may still be worth the price, but we must never pretend that a price was not paid.

"But of whom, when it comes to the point, is the fable narrated?"—HENRY JAMES on *The Reverberator*

"It's hard in our time to be as naïve as one would like."—SAUL BELLOW

"I much doubt that any young person of our time can be impressed by a poem, a painting, or a piece of music that is not flavored with a dash of irony."—ORTEGA

CHAPTER
TWELVE

*The Price
of Impersonal Narration, II:
Henry James
and the Unreliable Narrator*

If impersonal narration had been limited to ambiguous heroes who narrate or reflect their own lives, our problems would have been great enough. But as we see in *The Turn of the Screw*, the narrative situation is often far more complex than it is in *Portrait*. Some of our greatest problems come when we are given another character as unreliable as the hero to tell his ambiguous story. All of the complications of judgment we saw in the last chapter are compounded when the author, pursuing James's desire for "gradations and superpositions of effect" that will produce "a certain fulness of truth," seeks to give us one character's "troubled vision" as "reflected in the vision, also troubled enough," of an observer.[1]

With few exceptions, James's effort in his maturity is to find for

---

[1] Preface to "The Pupil," in *The Art of the Novel*, ed. R. P. Blackmur (New York, 1947), pp. 153, 154. Unexplained page references throughout this chapter will be to this work.

each story an observer, or group of observers, who because of their sensitivity can "reflect" the story to the reader. It is "in their minds" that the story really takes place; as they experience it, the reader experiences it. But James never formulates clearly the problem produced by the dramatic role of *inconscience* itself. He thus fails to provide any theory relevant to one large segment of his own work—those stories narrated, whether in the first or third person, by a profoundly confused, basically self-deceived, or even wrong-headed or vicious reflector.

THE DEVELOPMENT FROM FLAWED REFLECTOR INTO SUBJECT

Because we have his prefaces and notebooks, it is possible to trace in many of James's stories a process undoubtedly frequent in other modern authors but usually more deeply hidden: the transformation of a "subject," through the development of a "reflector" not important in the original conception, into something quite different. My interest here is in that surprisingly large body of works into which observers, and particularly unreliable observers, are imported *after* the original conception of the subject has been formulated.

In many of James's initial notebook entries about a story he includes a general description of how it is to be told. With such stories we can never be sure whether there was ever a prior version, unrecorded, existing in his mind as separated from any narrative manner, but it is clear that the manner has very early been seen as inseparable from the "subject."[2] "And I suppose the observer, as usual, must tell the tale" (*The Golden Bowl*). "Can't I see my *biais* here, don't I see my solution, in my usual third person: the observer, the *knower*, the confidant of either the 2 women or the 2 men?" ("The Given Case"). "It comes to me that the thing might be related by the 3d person, according to my wont when I want something—as I always do want it—intensely objective" ("The Friends of the Friends").

Sometimes his conception of this observer remains unchanged

---

2 All notebook references are again in this chapter to *The Notebooks of Henry James*, ed. Matthiessen and Murdock (New York, 1947). Page references can be found quickly in the excellent index under "James, Henry, writings of."

from original notebook entry to finished story. But often he gradually develops the reflector until the original subject is rivaled or
even overshadowed. It is fascinating to watch James as he trans-
forms a subject into a story of how it affects or is affected by an observer. One can see a new heroine emerging, for example, as he
plans "The Impressions of a Cousin."

> The "Cousin" of the title is a young woman who relates the
> story (in the form of a journal), living with her kinswoman as a
> companion, observing these events [the original idea] and guessing
> the secret. It is only in her journal that the secret "transpires."
> She herself of course to be a "type." I thought of infusing a little
> American local colour into it by making the story take place in New
> York and representing the Cousin as a Bostonian, with the Boston
> moral tone, etc. But that would be pale.

He did finally make the cousin an American woman, and she becomes, like so many of James's narrators, the most vivid agent in
the story. Instead of merely observing and recording, she acts. The
original idea is completely transformed by having one of the key
characters fall in love with the narrator who was originally conceived as a mere reflector.

A clearer instance of his conscious battle with the problem of the
narrator who seems to take over a subject is shown in his comments
on "The Friends of the Friends." At first his "I" is largely an observer. "I've spoken to them of each other—it's through me, mainly,
that they know of each other. I mustn't be too much of an *entre-
metteur* or an *entremetteuse*." He is clearly aware, then, of his
temptations, but observe what happens: "I may even have been a
little reluctant or suspicious, a little jealous, even, if the mediator is
a woman. If a woman tells the story she may have this jealousy of
her dead friend after the latter's death." But a reflector whose own
jealousy affects the action is no longer a mere reflector. The story
itself is changing under our eyes as the mode of narration is ex-
plored.

> Or if I don't have the "3d person" narrator, what effect would one
> get from the impersonal form—what peculiar and characteristic,
> what compensating, effect *might* one get from it? I should have in
> this case—shouldn't I?—to represent the *post-mortem* interview?

Yes—but not necessarily. I might "impersonally" include the 3d person and his (or her) feelings—tell the thing even so from his, or her, point of view. Probably it would have to be longer so. . . .

And suddenly James begins to see his way and grows excited. "The LAST *empéchement* to the little meeting, the supreme one, the one that caps the climax and makes the thing 'past a joke,' 'trop fort,' and all the rest of it, is the result of *my own act*." His "lucid reflector" is becoming less lucid and less of a mere reflector by the moment. "I prevent it, because I become conscious of a burning jealousy. . . ." And from this point on, the true subject of what is by now a new tale is clear.

> [The young man] and the narrator became engaged. . . . What do I do? I write to my fiancé not to come [to meet her, the "friend," for the first time]—that *she* can't. . . . I don't tell *her* what I have done; but, that evening, I tell *him*. I'm ashamed of it—I'm ashamed and I make that reparation. . . . The effect of this view [of the death and subsequent visitations] upon *me*. From here to the end, the attitude, on the subject, is mine: the return of my jealousy . . . the final rupture that comes entirely from ME and from my imputations and suspicions. I am jealous of the dead; I feel, or imagine I feel, his detachment, his alienation, his coldness.

In the finished tale the first-person narrator is thus both self-deceived and deceiving. She never realizes her own perfidy, and the reader is left to infer it from her own almost unconscious admissions. There is no question but that the tale has become entirely "mine."

The notebook entries for "The Next Time" show that James was sometimes aware of the transforming effect of cracking his mirror's surface. He begins as usual.

> Mightn't one oppose to him [he says of his novelist who is trying to write a best seller by becoming vulgar], some contrasted figure of another type—the creature who, dimly conscious of deep-seated vulgarity, is always trying to be refined, which doesn't in the least prevent him—or her—from succeeding. Say it's a woman. *She* succeeds— and she *thinks* she's fine! Mightn't *she* be the narrator, with a fine grotesque *inconscience*? So that the whole thing becomes a masterpiece of close and finished irony?

One would expect an author to recognize that a misguided narrator would necessarily attract much of the reader's interest and thus transform the story, at least to some degree. James does not ordinarily take this effect into account. Here he does, though the discussion is brief and cryptic. "There may be a difficulty in that— I seem to see it: so that the necessity may be for the narrator to be *conscient*, OR SEMI-CONSCIENT, perhaps, to get the full force of certain effects. The narrator at any rate, a person in the little drama who is trying bewilderedly the opposite line—working helplessly for fineness."

Unable to resolve his problem, James puts the story aside, only to return to it later.

> In my former note of this I seemed to catch hold of the tail of a dim idea that my narrator might be made the ironic portrait of a deluded vulgarian (of letters too), some striving *confrère* who has all the success my hero hasn't, who *can* do exactly the thing he can't, and who, vaguely, mistily conscious that he hasn't the suffrages of the *raffinés*, the people who count, is trying to do something distinguished. . . . Is this person the narrator—and do I simplify and compress by making him so?

Precisely the point, but the answer would seem self-evident: if his real interests were in simplification and compression, he would not embark on this kind of pursuit in the first place. As he was later to write in the Preface to *The Princess Casamassima*, as soon as he pursues his main interest—his "appreciation" of his story—"simplification is imperilled" (p. 65).

Shifting to a different concept of irony in his pursuit of the proper way to tell "The Next Time," James next decides that his narrator ought to be "fully and richly, must be ironically, *conscient*"— he must, that is, recognize the ironies of the whole story if he is to convey them to the reader with simplicity and compression. "That is, mustn't he? Can I take such a person and make him—or her— narrate my little drama *naïvement*? I don't think so—especially with so short a chance: I risk wasting my material and missing my effect." He does, indeed. His tale requires, as he goes on to say, his "real ironic painter"—ironic not as victim of the ironies but as master of them. Since the vulgar, best-selling author will not do, the problem is to discover a more suitable observer.

"*I* become the narrator, either impersonally or in my unnamed, unspecified personality. Say I chose the latter line, as in the *Death of the Lion*, the *Coxon Fund*, etc." But as usual James cannot for a moment rest contented with a mere observer. "I am a critic who doesn't sell, i.e., whose writing is too good—attracts no attention whatever. *My* distinguished writing fairly damages *his* [the original protagonist's] distinguished—by the good it tries to do for him. To keep me *quiet* about him becomes one of his needs—one of the features of his struggle, that struggle to manage to do once or twice, remuneratively, the thing that will be popular, the exhibition of which (pathetic little vain effort) is the essence of my subject. I try not to write about him—in order to help him. This attitude of mine is a part of the story."

A part of what story? Not, surely, a necessary part of the original "essence" he has just been talking about. The original hero's effort to write a potboiler recedes from the foreground just to the extent that this new narrator's effort "not to write about him" moves forward.

James embraces at this point what is in fact a new subject: "I seem to myself to want my denouement to be that in a final case I *do* speak—I uncontrollably break out (without his knowing I'm going to: I keep it secret, risk it); with the consequence that I just, after all, dish him." Who is the protagonist of *this* story? It becomes difficult to say, but it is not difficult to say that the narrator has become the primary agent, if it is his "breaking out" that "dishes" the novelist. The denouement is his; the interest is in his action and its effects, not primarily in those of the original hero.

Here we see, in short, the full force of James's drive for a realistic narrative technique. He creates and rejects one unreliable narrator, only to find himself creating another "I" who immediately becomes involved in the action so deeply that he produces the catastrophe.[3]

---

[3] Once one is alerted to this kind of shift of subject, it is astonishing how many of James's tales fit the pattern. See among others the notebook entries for *The Wings of the Dove, The Bostonians,* "The Figure in the Carpet," "The Tree of Knowledge," *The Sacred Fount,* "The Lesson of the Master," "The Marriages," "The Death of the Lion," "Four Meetings," "The Solution," "The Glasses," "The Tone of Time," "The Beldonald Holbein," "The Two Faces," "The Chaperon," "The Patagonia," "Pandora," "In the Cage," and "The Path of Duty."

His account in the *Notebooks* of the transformation of *The Spoils of Poynton* resulting from the use of Fleda Vetch as reflector is the most complete we have of this process. The original idea for this fine novel centered in a squabble between a mother and son over the inheritance "of a large place filled with valuable things." But in his search for a "centre" James discovers Fleda Vetch, who, just because she is a person of character, becomes a "main agent"; it is, as he says in the Preface, her "concentrated feeling" about everything which is his final "subject"; "the affirmation and the penetration" of her "understanding" is what makes his final "action," his "story."

He often leaves a curious ambiguity in his own description of the "subject." He will begin, as in the Preface to *Roderick Hudson*, defining the subject as a particular adventure, in this case the degeneration of Roderick himself. Soon, however, it defines itself "as not directly, in the least, my young sculptor's adventure. This it had been but indirectly, being all the while in essence and in final effect another man's, his friend's and patron's, view and experience of him" (p. 15). A moment later he is describing this other man, Rowland Mallet, not as the subject, but again as the "centre" from which "the subject has been treated"; but immediately he describes the totality of the work as "the sum of what 'happened' " to Rowland, "or in other words his total adventure; but as what happened to him was above all to feel certain things happening to others . . . so the beauty of the constructional game was to preserve in everything its especial value for *him*" (p. 16).[4]

The use of narrators who run away, in effect, with the original subject, transmuting one idea into another very different though related idea, has been so common since James that we tend to take

---

[4] Though James can be confusing about the two kinds of subject—subject as generating idea and subject as the culminating form of an observer's experience—he is quite clear about judging finished works according to the subject-as-realized, not the subject as initial material. When, for example, he rebukes Wells for not having given his "Subject, so to speak, as determined or constituted," even while seeming to praise him for achieving a "bloody little chunk of life," he is saying that art consists precisely in transforming bloody chunks of given "subjects" in order to achieve a *constituted* subject (Letter to Wells, June 17th, 1900). See also René Wellek, "Henry James's Literary Theory and Criticism," *American Literature*, XXX (November, 1958), 293–321, esp. 316.

the results for granted. This is how a novelist works, we tell ourselves, and we can point to an unlimited number of novels to prove
it. Is *The Great Gatsby* the same novel it would have been if, in
place of the deeply involved Nick, it were narrated by an omniscient narrator? As it stands it can be described as either Nick's experience of Gatsby or as Gatsby's life seen by Nick. The seamless
web of observation and experience creates a unity which we accept
—but which we can be very sure must have developed in a process
similar to that of James's exploration into possible observers. Is
"Heart of Darkness" the story of Kurtz or the story of Marlow's
experience of Kurtz? Was Marlow invented as a rhetorical device
for heightening the meaning of Kurtz's moral collapse, or was
Kurtz invented in order to provide Marlow with the core of his experience of the Congo? Again a seamless web, and we tell ourselves
that the old-fashioned question, "Who is the protagonist?" is a
meaningless one. The convincing texture of the whole, the impression of life as experienced by an observer, is in itself surely what the
true artist seeks.

Yet the controversies over stories like *The Turn of the Screw*
suggest that for most of us it is not enough. Though no one will
deny to James his right to develop his original ideas as he discovers
new complexities in his narrators, few of us feel happy with a situation in which we cannot decide whether the subject is two evil
children as seen by a naïve but well-meaning governess or two innocent children as seen by a hysterical, destructive governess.
Whatever James's final view of his subject in such stories, we can
only conclude that the relationship between his developing narrators and the original subjects was often more complex than his own
critical talk recognizes. Some of his stories present, in fact, a double
focus that seems to spring from an incomplete fusion of original
subject with the new subject that develops once a seriously flawed
narrator has been created to reflect the original. We can never know
how much of our difficulty James foresaw. But we can at least discover, in looking at two of his more troublesome stories, some of
the sources of our perplexity in dealing with unreliable narrators
since his time.

THE TWO LIARS IN "THE LIAR"

"The Liar" (1888) is a revealing instance of James's tendency to develop an observer far beyond his original function. It is not simply that "the story of one's story" has become more important than the original idea; that in itself would not necessarily cause trouble. But the reflector, in becoming *inconscient* about his own motives and about the reality around him, becomes a vicious agent in the story, and his viciousness and his unconscious distortions come to play a role far beyond anything James described in writing about observers.

In the original conception, as recorded in the *Notebooks*, the center of interest was the wife of an inveterate liar, Colonel Capadose. James's subject was the gradually corrupting effect upon the wife of having to pretend that her marriage is a success, that her husband's lying does not trouble her. "But there comes a day when he [the Colonel] tells a very big lie which she has . . . to adopt, to reinforce. To save him from exposure, in a word, she has to lie herself. The struggle, etc.; she lies—but after that she hates him." In James's subsequent discussion, in the Preface, he again centers on his initial vision of Capadose and his wife. There is never any mention of involving an observer as a prime agent in the action. The story is to be quite simply that of a woman corrupted into dishonesty by a lying husband. What James tells, however, is a story far more complex, the story of his observer's relationship with Mrs. Capadose. It is clear that as he developed his observer, his ironic bent gained control, transforming Lyon into a highly equivocal protagonist—indeed into something of a villain.

The kind of complex irony that results can best be seen by contrasting the two views of what takes place, Lyon's and the reader's. One is tempted, at a time like this, to fall into the pattern established by other recent explicators of Jamesian ironies: "A generation of readers has misread. . . ." But I am too much impressed by the difficulties to offer the following as anything more than a careful attempt at what may be an impossible task. Here is Lyon's view of the events (in the story it is given in the third person) followed by my own view as reader:

After twelve years I meet again with the woman who once refused to marry me because she did not know then that one day I would be famous. She is even lovelier than ever, and I am horrified to discover that she has married an inveterate liar.

Actually she refused the narrator because she knew that happiness would be impossible with any man as self-centered as he. He is not so much horrified by the lying as jealous; he finds, in short, that he is still in love with her, and the discovery that her husband is a liar only contributes to his unconscious jealousy.

How can she endure living with such a "monstrous foible"? And how can she avoid being herself morally destroyed by contact with such a contemptible man? I admit that Capadose is not—as yet—a "malignant liar," that he is strictly disinterested, that he has indeed a kind of code of honor in his lying. I also must admit that I, too, "lie," in a sense, when I lay on my colours as a painter. At the same time it seems to me a tragedy that a lovely creature like her should be tied to a man of no integrity.

He is really sure that she must regret having married a contemptible man, when she might have had someone like himself. His own lying is strictly "interested," and he has far less integrity than Capadose.

I decide to force her to admit that she is distressed by her husband's lies.

He really decides to make her show signs of regret about having chosen wrongly.

Using methods of a subtlety that almost makes me blush, I persuade them to allow me to paint Capadose's portrait, determined to paint it in such a way as to reveal the depths of his deceptive heart.

Lying to them about his motives, he persuades them to allow him to paint the husband's portrait, determined to paint it in such a way as to expunge all the good traits of the Colonel, whom everyone else in the story likes, and allow only the dishonesty to show, thus creating a monster out of what is actually, as James himself describes him in a letter, "a charming man, in spite of his little weakness."

When she sees what I have revealed, surely she will give some sign that her basic integrity has not been shattered.

Surely she will show some sign that she regrets her marriage, that she could imagine her happiness with her husband "more unqualified."

I paint the portrait as planned; it is a masterpiece of truth.

It is a masterpiece of the power of caricature.

The Liar stands revealed upon my canvas in his true colours.

The Liar, stripped of all his redeeming human qualities, stands betrayed upon the canvas.

But the Capadoses discover the portrait when they think I am away; actually I happen upon the scene and am forced to eavesdrop to protect my interests.

Having sneaked back without any announcement, he deliberately eavesdrops.

Mrs. Capadose is shattered by the vision, seeing it truly; Capadose, somewhat more slowly seeing what I have revealed, slashes the portrait to bits.

Lyon is really delighted to see her horror when she discovers the cruel "truth" of the portrait, and even more delighted to see Capadose slash the portrait to bits.

I do not try to stop him; rather I am glad that now, at last, I shall get her to admit regrets about her unfortunate marriage.

Now at last she is ashamed of her husband, and Lyon has made her so; but he has made her even more horrified by his own brutality.

But instead she supports her husband in the falsehood he invents about how the portrait must have been destroyed, and she reveals unmistakably to me that she *has* been totally corrupted by her husband. The Liar has triumphed, and I have lost my vision of the incorruptible woman. "Her hypocrisy" is revolting.

In supporting her husband she reveals unmistakably that she still loves the better man and is willing to lie for him. The vicious Liar—Lyon—has been caught in his own trap.

One would hesitate to belabor what may seem obvious, if critics did not seem generally to take Lyon pretty much at his own word; since James never warns us in any of his own discussions that the story finally became Lyon-as-liar even more than Capadose-as-liar, they have read it as if it had been written according to plan. Ray B. West, Jr., and Robert W. Stallman, for example, see Lyon as "inspired by the Muse of Truth," both as artist and as man. "It is *his* moral being, not hers [Mrs. Capadose's] that suffers the disillusioning shock. . . . He dares to pry beneath [the surface of her character] because his faith in her purity supports him. Call it the faith of a romantic, or call it the faith of an artist. She represents for Lyon, as artist, that Truth which is Beauty, that Beauty which is Truth."[5] And though the authors think that he deserves his punishment at the end, he deserves it because he "has committed an offence against society [by insisting on the truth]. . . . His stripping of the social mask, we are made to feel, constitutes a breach of the mores, a betrayal of the social codes whose mechanism must be preserved even though it produces hypocrisies and grinds out falsities instead of truths." And his desire to wring a confession from her is a desire to redeem her: "Redemption begins in deep abasement."

It seems likely, to judge from the first notebook entry, that something not too far from this may have been James's original idea. But when we consider some of the lies inspired in Lyon by the Muse of Truth, we are forced to admit that James's conception changed. "Then he spoke to her of her husband, praised his appearance, his talent for conversation, professed to have felt a quick friendship for him, and asked, with an amount of 'cheek' for which he almost blushed, what manner of man he was." He pursues what he calls his "legitimate treachery" of Capadose with a relentlessness that makes him "almost wince" at his own success. He lies about his portrait of the Colonel's daughter, in order to pursue his unacknowledged courtship of the wife. It was a "matter of conscience with him sometimes to take his servants unawares." He lies to them whenever it is useful to do so, yet thinks of himself as a man who "cultivated frankness of intercourse with his domestics." But if one were to detail all of his lies, the whole story would be retold, because it consists largely of them.

What are we to make of the following signs of motive, if he is probing "because his faith in her purity supports him"? "Lyon guessed him [Capadose] capable on occasion of defending his position with violence. . . . Such moments as those would test his wife's

---

[5] Ray B. West, Jr., and R. W. Stallman, *The Art of Modern Fiction* (New York, 1949), pp. 213–15.

philosophy—Lyon would have liked to see her there." "Oh to hear that woman's voice in that deep abasement. . . . He even imagined the hour when, with a burning face, she might ask *him* not to take the question up. Then he should be almost consoled—he would be magnanimous." When Mrs. Capadose cries, "It's cruel—oh it's too cruel!"—after first seeing the portrait—the man inspired by the Muse of Truth reacts characteristically: "The strangest part of all was . . . that Oliver Lyon lifted neither voice nor hand to save his picture [from Capadose's slashings]. The point is that he didn't feel as if he were losing it or didn't care if he were, so much more was he conscious of gaining a certitude. His old friend *was* ashamed of her husband, and he had made her so, and he had scored a great success, even at the sacrifice of his precious labour. . . . He trembled with his happy agitation."

In much of his lying there is an element of cruelty. Indeed, as the story progresses, Lyon's interest in his art is perverted more and more into an interest in the most blatant kind of attack upon the Colonel. In the service of this attack, his whole nature is coarsened. While at the beginning he seems interested in artistic subtlety, he later becomes troubled by the "idea that when he should send his picture to the Academy he shouldn't be able to inscribe it in the catalogue under the simple rubric to which all propriety pointed. He couldn't in short send in the title as 'The Liar'—more was the pity. However, this little mattered, for he had now determined to stamp that sense on it as legibly—and to the meanest intelligence— as it was stamped for his own vision on the living face. As he saw nothing else in the Colonel today, so he gave himself up to the joy of 'rendering' nothing else." It is impossible to reconcile this picture of the artist's task with any notion James ever espoused; it is, in fact, James's portrait of what happens to art when it is made to serve "interested," or practical ends. It is not for the sake of art that Lyon "lashed his victim on when he flagged."

Finally, one notes that all of the unequivocal intrusions by the reliable narrator—I count four and those very brief—are used to underline the difference between Lyon's picture of himself and the true picture; he acts not from artistic motives, nor from a mistaken commitment to an ideal, but rather from the motives of a disappointed lover. All the rest is rationalization, presented convincingly enough as Lyon "speaks" it or thinks it, but intended to be seen as rationalization by the discerning reader.

If this is an approximate picture of the ironies James intended to cluster about Lyon's picture of himself and his fellow liar, how do we account for the fact that only Marius Bewley, of those who have written about the story, has seen it from something like this point of view?[6]

It is customary in critical controversy over James's meanings to attribute such differences to the stupidity or carelessness of all readers except those who see the "true" interpretation. But in dealing with such a story mutual accusations are likely to be pointless. No amount of care, no amount of intelligence, no amount of background reading, can yield the kind of security about "The Liar" that all readers can feel about "The Beast in the Jungle." Though the two strikingly disparate views of the events, the observer's and the author's, may seem unmistakable in my schematic presentation, in the story itself they are surrounded by complexities which make one feel unsure of any interpretation.

In the first place, the difference between Lyon's voice and James's voice, speaking behind and through the style, is usually not so great as in the passages I have quoted; sometimes, indeed, there is no discernible difference whatever. Much of what Lyon sees about Capadose is true. His opinion of himself as a great artist is justified; we have Mrs. Capadose's reluctant testimonial to that. And in the second place, to read the story properly we must combat our natural tendency to agree with the reflector. He wins our confidence simply by being the reflector, because in life the only mind we know as we know Lyon's is our own. Yet it is this very appeal which makes him dangerous: his touch will be fatal to certain effects.

Thus in "The Liar," even when we have been alerted to Lyon's unreliability, we are still faced, after the most careful reading, with some inevitable ambiguities, ambiguities which James almost certainly did not intend. Granted that some of Lyon's opinions are unreliable and that some are not, what about the great middle group

---

[6] *The Complex Fate: Hawthorne, Henry James and Some Other American Writers* (London, 1952), pp. 84–87.

which are plausible from one point of view, implausible from another? He feels sorry for himself; he feels betrayed, lost. Does James intend us merely to scoff, or to sympathize? Are the final lies of Mrs. Capadose contemptible, as Lyon thinks, or noble, or a little of both? On the one hand, she is possibly endangering an innocent third party, but on the other she is defending a relatively harmless man from a predator. We are lost in wonder at the complexity of life—and this is part of what James undoubtedly intends. But it is at the same time clear that a story can hold together only if such perplexities are kept within certain boundaries—wide as those boundaries may be. Our very recognition of complexity depends upon the clarity of our vision of the elements which go to make it up. The mixture of good and evil in the characters of this story will be overlooked or misapprehended unless we grasp clearly which elements are good and which bad. If Lyon is read as the noble artist struggling for truth against a philistine culture, the story is a very weak one indeed; nine-tenths of the concentrated wit and irony is lost. Yet if he is not, it is still partially unrealized; the story of the liar, Lyon, is only half-developed.

If we had only the evidence I have given so far, I might be accused of doing to "The Liar" what I have accused other critics of doing to *The Turn of the Screw*: seeing more distance between author and narrator than the story justifies. But fortunately we have an unmistakable corroboration from James in the kind of revision he undertook when preparing this story for the New York edition of the collected works (1907–9). Much has been written about the complexities James introduced in revising his earlier stories, but in "The Liar" we find an attempt to *reduce* the moral complexity by heightening the interpretation I have given. Where the first version read, "Lyon put into practice that idea of drawing him [Capadose] out which he had been nursing for so many weeks," the revision says that "Lyon applied without mercy his own gift of provocation." Where the original says that "Lyon lashed him on," the revision says that he "lashed his victim on."[7] The many changes of this

---

[7] There are many other changes working to the same effect: (1) The revision heightens the favorable features of Capadose. Instead of being a "thumping liar," he "pulls the long bow." We are told that in contrast to the selfish "interest" of Lyon, Capadose's

kind take us toward a clearer view of the artist caught by his own machinations. But even in the final version, after all of the changes, we are still left baffled at some points where James cannot profit from our bafflement. Regardless of where we choose to settle in our final interpretation, with the near-nobility seen by West and Stallman or the near-villainy which I see, the reader cannot be expected to infer with certainty whether a particular fact reported by Lyon has been distorted to reflect his own character or reported accurately to give what really happened to Mrs. Capadose.

"The Purloining of the Aspern Papers" or "The Evocation of Venice"?

The effect of an incompletely resolved double focus gives us even more difficulty in a better-known story, "The Aspern Papers," published in the same year as "The Liar" (1888). In contrast with the other tales I have discussed, this one seems to have been conceived from the beginning as a story about the narrator. Though James's original notation of the possibilities of a story about his "publishing scoundrel" did not picture the full "immorality" which he finally portrays, from the beginning James clearly had in mind the comic and ironic excitement of the antiquarian's quest. "The interest would be in some price that the man has to pay—that the old woman—or the survivor—sets upon the papers. His hesitations—his struggle—for he really would give almost anything"—this is clearly moving in the direction of the narrator's statement in the finished story, "I'm sorry for it, but there's no baseness I wouldn't commit for Jeffrey Aspern's sake."

The astonishing thing is that in this first notebook entry there is only the barest suggestion of the "picture" of the romantic past that James described many years later as so important to the story. The closest James comes to it here is "the picture of the two faded,

---

lying is "quite disinterested." Instead of being "everything that's good and kind," he becomes "everything that's good and true and kind." (2) Similarly Lyon is worsened in our eyes: "Lyon was too scrupulous" is changed to "Lyon was at once too discreet and too fond of his own intimate inductions"; "with an inward audacity at which he trembled a little" is changed to "an amount of cheek for which he almost blushed"; etc. Also we are alerted with at least one additional warning to the fact that Lyon is painting his own picture: "Don't you suppose Vandyke's things tell a lot about him?"

queer, poor and discredited old English women—living on into a strange generation, in their musty corner of a foreign town'—with these illustrious letters their most precious possession." The primary interest is in the plotting "of the Shelley fanatic" against these two romantic figures.

When in the Preface he comes to remember his idea years later, however, the plot of the Shelley fanatic is passed over completely in favor of a discussion of his own effort to realize the "palpable imaginable *visitable* past." It is all talk about atmosphere and atmospheric contrasts, the delight in rendering "my old Venice" and "the still earlier one of Jeffrey Aspern"; it is all about the "romance" of his effort to evoke "a final scene of the rich dim Shelley drama played out in the very theatre of our own 'modernity.'" Except to indicate that the original "Shelleyite" whose adventure suggested the story is not to the slightest extent reflected in the finished story, James does not even mention the protagonist.

We have here, then, two neatly distinct subjects. There is a plot, the narrator's unscrupulous quest for the papers and his ultimate frustration; it is a plot that requires an agent of a particularly insensitive kind. There is, secondly, a "picture," an air or an atmosphere, a past to be visited and recorded with all the poetic artistry at James's command. So far so good; there is nothing inherently incompatible about these two subjects. On the contrary, the notion of a "visitable past" being in effect violated by a modern antiquarian who hasn't the slightest idea of how the past can be effectively visited seems on the face of it a good one. But unfortunately there is a general principle in accordance with which James feels constrained to write his stories. "Picture" must not come from the author in his own voice. It should be pushed back into the consciousness of a large, *lucid* reflector. And who should that reflector be—who can it be in this case but the antiquarian himself? Unless Mrs. Prest—already rather shamelessly present as a mere *ficelle* to give him an excuse to tell of his plans—unless she is to be expanded into what would surely be a rather incredible observer, the only mind available with a sufficient grasp of what is going on is the mind of the antiquarian. He it is who must visit and evoke the past. And yet he must "pounce on" the possessions of the poet's aging mistress and violate the naïve spirit of the dying woman's niece.

The completed story is a good one, but to me it has paid a price for the mode of narration. Foolhardy as it may seem to tamper with the procedures of the great master, one cannot help concluding that the narrator as realized, though well-suited for the jilting of Tina Bordereau, was not adequate to the task of evoking the poetry of the visitable past.

All of the motive power, all of the sense of direction in the plot is concentrated on the narrator's efforts to get the Aspern papers, and particularly on the use he makes of Tina's affection. In his immorality, though not in the precise details of his quest, he is half-brother to other "publishing scoundrels" in James's fiction, like Mathias Pardon in *The Bostonians*, George Flack in *The Reverberator*, or the reporter in "The Papers." He is also half-brother to Morris Townsend, in *Washington Square*, who plays upon an innocent woman's affections for his own selfish ends. We have passed through a time when fidelity and honor have meant so little, in terms of literary convention, that it is easy to overlook what it meant still to James. But if one applies to the narrator of this tale the standards of integrity and honor that figure in, say, *The Spoils of Poynton*, if one judges the narrator, in short, by the standards of any one of James's really *lucid* reflectors, the antiquarian's immorality can only be seen as central to the effect. Our attention from first to last cannot help being centered on the comedy of the biter bit, the man of light character who manipulates others so cleverly that he "destroys" himself.

Again here, as in "The Liar," the New York revision moves in the direction of our sharper awareness of the narrator's immorality. Anyone who doubts that James's final attention was primarily on the narrator should re-read the tale in the New York revision, checking against the original those passages that show him cheating, stealing, lying, or admitting to shame. In revising *The Portrait of a Lady*, as Matthiessen pointed out, James tried to make Osmond's moral degeneracy clearer, so that "the mystification is only Isabel's, the ambiguity is all in what Osmond concealed, not in any doubts that James entertained about him." James changed Osmond's view of Isabel, for example, from "as bright and soft as an April cloud" to "as smooth to his general need of her as handled ivory to the palm."[8] The same kind of revision is performed in this story. The following examples are only some of the more extreme instances of James's efforts to prevent, in revision, the kind of identification with the narrator which, even in this "obvious" story, might easily result from the narrator's position of command. The italics have been added.

Original	Revised
I'm sorry for it, but for Jeffrey Aspern's sake I would do worse *still*.	I'm sorry for it, but there's no *baseness* I wouldn't commit for Jeffrey Aspern's sake.
"You are very extravagant . . . ," said my companion. "Certainly you are prepared to *go far!*"	"You're very extravagant—it adds to your *immorality*."
She would die next week, she would die tomorrow—then I could *seize her papers*.	. . . then I could *pounce on her possessions and ransack her drawers*.
. . . for the first, the last, the only time I beheld her extraordinary eyes. They glared at me, they made me horribly ashamed.	. . . They glared at me; *they were like the sudden drench, for a caught burglar, of a flood of gaslight;* they made me horribly ashamed.
I had said to Mrs. Prest that I would make love to her [the daughter]; but it had been a joke without consequence and I had never said it to *Tita* Bordereau [note that "Tita" is revised to the more attractive "Tina"].	. . . I had never said it to *my victim*.
How could she, since I had not come back before night to contradict, even as a simple form, such an idea [Miss Tina's idea that he has recoiled in horror from her offer of love]?	. . . to contradict, even as a simple form, *even as an act of common humanity*, such an idea?

---

8 F. O. Matthiessen, *Henry James: The Major Phase* (Oxford, 1944), p. 167.

These isolated quotations give, of course, only a fraction of the emphasis one finds, in both versions, on the moral deterioration and ultimate baseness of James's narrator.[9] The effect of these and the other changes is in no case to make him worse *in fact;* his actions remain objectively the same in both versions. Rather they worsen only his picture of himself and thus increase our awareness that the drama is that of his unprincipled relationship with Miss Tina. They thus lessen the burden on the reader by making this aspect of the story less subtle and ambiguous than it originally was.

The story, then, consists simply of this unscrupulous man's quest for the Aspern papers, his discovery that his best way to get to them is to make love to the owner's unattractive niece, Tina, his further discovery that marriage is to be the price of full possession, his temporary withdrawal in the face of such a conflict and—but he should tell the climax in his own words. Observe how he betrays himself when he next encounters the undesirable woman he must learn to accept if he wants the papers. As he comes into the room, he recognizes that she has understood his involuntary recoil when she offered herself in exchange for the papers the day before.

> . . . I also saw something which had not been in my forecast. Poor Miss Tina's sense of her failure had produced a rare alteration in her, but I had been too full of stratagems and spoils to think of that. Now I took it in; I can scarcely tell how it startled me. She stood in the middle of the room with a face of mildness bent upon me, and her look of forgiveness, of absolution, made her angelic. It beautified her; she was younger; she was not a ridiculous old woman. This trick of her expression, this magic of her spirit, transfigured her, and while I still noted it I heard a whisper somewhere in the

---

9 For a clear-headed reading of the narrator's wide-ranging perfidies, see Sam S. Baskett, "The Sense of the Present in *The Aspern Papers,*" *Papers of the Michigan Academy of Science, Arts, and Letters,* XLIV (1959), 381–88. Baskett recognizes that the narrator's vision of the past is far from a reliable one and that in fact the ironies of the story are based on an implied contrast between his "sense of the past" and the reader's and author's sense. He is willing to make use of the past for his present "base" ends. The past he evokes is tainted—though Baskett does not stress this point—by his mode of evocation. Another prosecution of the narrator is conducted by William Bysshe Stein in "*The Aspern Papers:* A Comedy of Masks," *Nineteenth-Century Fiction,* XIV (September, 1959), 172–78. Stein deals more fully with the narrator's aesthetic deficiencies; his view of the past is tainted, and the past he evokes is largely an absurd one—as we see in the absurdities of Juliana, the last living remnant of that past.

depths of my conscience: "Why not, after all—why not?" It seemed to me I *could* pay the price.

This is *his* idea of the voice of *conscience.* If he is so unreliable about that, what of his notion that her countenance has actually changed? Is the change simply his subjective interpretation? James increases our suspicions at once: "Still more distinctly however than the whisper I heard Miss Tina's own voice" saying that the papers have been destroyed and with them, of course, all reason for "paying the price."

"The room seemed to go round me as she said this and a real darkness for a moment descended on my eyes. When it passed, Miss Tina was there still, but the transfiguration was over and she had changed back to a plain dingy elderly person." Because of the narrative method, we are forever barred from knowing whether Miss Tina was, in fact, capable of forgiveness, whether she was, in fact, transformed, whether she was, in fact, a dingy elderly person in the first place. We are confined to the drama of the narrator's own scheming, and when he concludes by regretting his loss—"I mean of the precious papers"—we are left permanently in doubt as to whether he has any suspicion of suffering a more serious loss, whether we think of that loss as of his honor or as of Miss Tina herself. What we do know is, however, sufficient to make this aspect of the story highly successful: the schemer has shown himself as the chief victim of his own elaborate scheming.

But where has that other subject, as described in the Preface, been all this while? What has happened to the "visitable past"? Well, the poor blind narrator has been periodically struggling to bring himself back up to the level of sensitivity necessary to record, with the reader's unequivocal concurrence, the romantic atmosphere of Venice and particularly of this one corner of the past, the Bordereau's villa. Here is the comic schemer in his other role, as poetic celebrant: "There could be no Venetian business without patience, and since I adored the place I was much more in the spirit of it for having laid in a large provision. That spirit kept me perpetual company and seemed to look out at me from the revived immortal face—in which all his genius shone—of the great poet who was my prompter. I had invoked him and he had come." Surely this is no ridiculous schemer; this is the worthy disciple of the great poet, speaking in the voice that James himself uses in describing *his* feelings about Venice and his imagined Aspern. And the narrator carries on in this voice at some length. In the long passage concluding section four, which contains the narrator's opinions about Aspern, about America, and about American art, surely he is intended to be reliable as a spokesman for James's theme: "That was originally what I had prized him for: that at a period when our native land was nude and crude and provincial, when the famous 'atmosphere' it is supposed to lack was not even missed, when literature was lonely there and art and form almost impossible, he had found means to live and write like one of the first; to be free and general and not at all afraid; to feel, understand and express everything."

This can scarcely be considered as the same person at all. And there is a third tone of voice when the first two openly conflict.

> It was as if his [Aspern's] bright ghost had returned to earth to assure me he regarded the affair as his own no less than as mine and that we should see it fraternally and fondly to a conclusion. . . . My eccentric private errand became a part of the general romance and the general glory—I felt even a mystic companionship, a moral fraternity with all those who in the past had been in the service of art. They had worked for beauty, for a devotion; and what else was I doing? That element was in everything that Jeffrey Aspern had written, and I was only bringing it to light.

There can be little doubt that James has deliberately planted clues here to make us see that the narrator is rationalizing his conduct. In the service of art? *Only* bringing beauty to light? And what of Aspern's own conduct? "We were glad to think at least that in all our promulgations acquitting Aspern conscientiously of any grossness—some people now consider I believe that we have overdone them—we had only touched in passing and in the most discreet manner on Miss Bordereau's connexion. Oddly enough, even if we had had the material . . . this would have been the most difficult episode to handle." Aspern is, then, also tainted with the immorality shown by the narrator? Again, debating whether Aspern had "betrayed" Juliana in his works, "had given her away, as we say nowadays, to posterity," the antiquarian exonerates Aspern, in what must be another instance of his "overdone promulgations": "Moreover was not any fame fair enough that was so sure of duration and was associated with works immortal through their beauty?" Was James so naïve as to allow his narrator to get away with blurring the distinction between this kind of betrayal, without which romantic poetry could not exist at all, and the personal betrayals of the narrator in his antiquarian quest? Again and again in the story one is forced to throw up his hands and decide that James simply has provided insufficient clues for the judgments which he still quite clearly expects us to be able to make.

We have, then, three distinct narrative voices in this story: the narrator's self-betrayals, evident to any careful reader; his efforts at straightforward evocation of the past, which taken out of context might be indistinguishable from James's own voice; and the passages of mumbling, as it were, that lie between. There are so many good things in the story that it seems almost ungrateful of us to ask whether the three narrative voices are ever really harmonized. Critics have generally followed James himself in steering clear of such questions. It is so much easier to "dislike James" for his obscurities—without troubling very much to say what we mean—or to idolize him for his subtle ambiguities. Both positions are wholly safe, backed by troops in rank on rank, with traditions of honorable battle going back several decades. What is hard is to look squarely at the master and decide—without idolatry or iconoclasm—whether he has done, after all, as well as he might have.[10]

---

[10] For a similar effort with other modern masters, see Graham Hough, *Image and Experience: Studies in a Literary Revolution* (London, 1960), e.g.: "I cannot think that the problems raised by the structure of *The Waste Land* have been faced. They have been a party matter, a matter of polemic or defence; . . . to accept this sort of technique was at one time a sort of touchstone for participation in modern poetry. . . . While the poem was still capable of causing bewilderment it established itself. The brilliance of the imagery, the auditory and incantatory grandeur of its best passages, stole into the consciousness and became a part of our poetical property; it became ungrateful, almost indecent to ask of what sort of continuum these fragments were a part. And we became satisfied with a level of coherence that we should never have found sufficient in any earlier poem. . . . But the questions remain—above all the question of what really makes the poem a totality, if it is one at all" (pp. 21–22).

It is time, then, to ask that final hard question about this story, even if we feel no great confidence about being able to answer it: Was James wrong to "give" the story to a single narrator, a narrator used on the one hand to reveal his own deficiencies with unconscious irony and on the other to praise praiseworthy things? There is no doubt that James showed himself to be experimental, advanced, sincere, objective, impersonal, difficult, but with all this said we still do not know whether his choice was the right one. To what extent did his choice of technique aid or hinder him in his effort to realize the inherent possibilities of this work?

This is not, I need hardly say again, a question that can be settled by constructing another general rule to replace those I have discussed earlier: "No narrator can be expected to do contradictory tasks." Huckleberry Finn performs contradictory tasks quite admirably, evoking the poetry of the Mississippi one minute and betraying abysmal ignorance the next. Nor is it inherently wrong to present a character who goes astray through his misunderstanding of values which are in themselves admirable. It is, in fact, one of the glories of fiction that it can encompass precisely the kind of complexity attempted here by James, without loss of clarity or intensity. But that complexity can be intense only if the elements that make it up are made to be intense, each one in its own way.

It seems clear that James always thought of this story as an effort to realize both of the elements he himself describes: the ironic comedy and the romantic evocation as background and contrast. He cannot have thought of either the publishing scoundrel or the evoked past as independent subjects with independent effects; the stronger the evocation of the true romance of Venice and its past, the greater the ironic comedy of the misled antiquarian who violates that past. And on the contrary, the more clearly his modern baseness is made to stand out, the more effective should be the contrasting genuine passion for beauty of the romantics. Far from being truly contradictory, the two effects could easily be seen as complementary; the deeper the ironic bite the sharper the contrast with what is not treated ironically. But it is evident from the published criticism of this story that most readers have fallen to one side or the other of this true complexity—not mere haze and muddlement —that the story implicitly seems to be striving for.

Some literary failures show themselves by producing the same result in all readers—boredom, disgust, or whatever. But from the nature of this story, it follows that the direction of the failure will show itself differently in different readers. Until recently most readers, to judge from printed commentary, apparently missed a good deal of the irony and comedy as a result of succumbing to the narrator's poetic talk about Venice. I find myself at the opposite extreme—unable to read the talk about Venice with anything like the effect James seems to have desired, because the narrator's voice rings false in my ears. And there must be a third group who, delighting in the very ambiguity which I am troubled by, overlook the clarities that James intended in both his condemnation of the narrator and his adulatory visitation of the past. But this is as serious a loss as the others: not the greatest ironic ambiguity but lucidity within complexity is James's goal; he always delights in "the comedy and the tragedy" fully as much as "the irony," and he would have been distressed to learn that anyone could read "The Aspern Papers" as a vague, realistic, unjudged blur.

We might, of course, imagine a reader so flexible and so thoroughly attuned to James's own values that he could shift nimbly from stance to stance, allowing the narrator to shift his character from moment to moment. But James has surrendered the very conventions which, in earlier fiction and drama, made such shifts easily acceptable. One has no difficulty when Shakespeare forces some of his characters, particularly in soliloquy, into narrative and evaluative statements that go far beyond any realistic assessment of their true capabilities within the world of the action. Shakespeare has made no claim that his manner will be realistically consistent. But James reminds us constantly, page by page, that he is attempting a new realistic intensity of narrative manner. How can I, then, excuse him when I find his narrator to be one kind of man in one paragraph and another kind of man in the next? Only by surrendering my responsibilities as a reader and saying that just because it is by James it is perfect. Good as it is, "The Aspern Papers" is not as good as James might have made it if he had preserved for a reliable voice the right to evoke the true visitable past and used the present narrator only on jobs for which he is qualified.

The attenuation of effect that must result for any reader who takes the work seriously as a whole can be seen by looking at any passage in which the narrator must do both of his jobs simultaneously. A good example is the concluding sentence: "When I look at it"—the portrait of Jeffrey Aspern—"I can scarcely bear my loss—I mean of the precious papers." In the original this read simply, "When I look at it my chagrin at the loss of the letters becomes almost intolerable." But it is not, as James well knew, really the letters that the narrator has lost, and he quite appropriately revised to introduce a shadow of doubt, a shadow of self-awareness of the price he has paid, in loss of human decency. But what happens, through this revision, to the evocation of the visitable past? Are the papers precious? Of course, one would say, of course they are precious. But they have been made to seem less so—indeed they become almost contemptible—as the result of a revision which beautifully reminds us of what the narrator has really lost.

In discussing what happens when Shakespeare's moral maxims come to us through an "unreliable spokesman," Alfred Harbage says that the effect is to "throw the maxims a little out of focus, to blur them somewhat, to rob them of finality."[11] The effect in James is similar: some—though by no means all—of the narrator's usefulness in evoking the romance of Shelley's Italy has been blurred and robbed of finality.

"DEEP READERS OF THE WORLD, BEWARE!"

I have no doubt that this reading of "The Aspern Papers" will seem as much an over-interpretation to some of my readers as the Freudian interpretation of *The Turn* seems to me. But I hope that even so my point will stand: Although mere ease of reading can never be a final test of the quality of a work, to dramatize one troubled vision of another troubled vision, or of troubled waters, can produce

---

11 "The Unreliable Spokesman," *As They Liked It: An Essay on Shakespeare and Morality* (New York, 1947), p. 106.

a kind of difficulty that is incompatible with some kinds of literary effect.

If I could only finish on that safe and sane note, my problems would be relatively simple. I could simply knock off a few—a very few—points from the master's total and go about my business. But all this while that governess and her Freudian interpreters are waiting in the wings, waiting to be explained or explained away. And they are not alone. One finds suspicions being cast on the reliability of more and more of James's reflectors; critics are in public dispute about many of them. Fleda Vetch, that lovely, sensitive creature, is suspected or directly "accused" by Mark Van Doren, Robert Cantwell, and others; Isabel Archer by William Troy; the Ververs (father and daughter) by F. O. Matthiessen; Strether (even Strether) by Van Wyck Brooks; Maisie by Stephen Spender; Merton Densher ("the villain") by H. R. Hays; Gilbert Long by Leon Edel; Bernard Longueville by Edmund Wilson; the narrator of "Four Meetings" by Ford; and so on.[12] These denigrations and the resulting controversies spring up faster than one can keep track of them. Most recently it has been the turn of poor Pemberton, the tutor in "The Pupil." A couple of winters ago Terence Martin called him the "villain" of the piece; as soon as the slow machinery of the literary quarterlies would permit, John Hagopian leapt to his defense: he is only a villain in the existentialist sense, making a tragic decision like that of Captain Vere in *Billy Budd*. William Bysshe Stein replied with a different charge: he is a "prude" who causes the pupil's tragedy by his failure to outgrow his Puritan morality. At this point the critic unlucky enough to have his head full of such matters is likely to remember dimly a somewhat different, earlier claim: Pemberton is really a homosexual who is contrasted with the "vulgarly heterosexual" parents of the pupil. The pupil dies, in this account, "because of his sudden joy on learning that he is at last free to go away with Pemberton—presumably to a lovers'

---

[12] A good beginning in such treacherous waters can be made in F. W. Dupee (ed.), *The Question of Henry James* (New York, 1945). But the size of the bibliography increases geometrically year by year.

relationship."[13] But before one has time to read "The Pupil" once again to see what has gone wrong, a new candidate for controversy comes forward. We have, it seems, been much too much inclined to see things simply as Christopher Newman sees them in *The American*. John A. Clair now sets us straight about Newman's "incorrigible lack of insight and his impetuous judgments which keep him ignorant of the real situation"—the real situation, one that is discernible only to "one reader out of a hundred"—being that Claire de Cintre is the illegitimate daughter of Mrs. Bread![14]

Surely James is not to be blamed for all of this. Though some of the stories are unintentionally ambiguous, the ambiguities are certainly not so broad as to allow the same narrator to be a villainous prude and a heroic homosexual. Yet if we exonerate James, must we not blame the critics? Or repudiate criticism itself as wholly capricious?

A full answer would probably lead into large social questions about the relations of artist and public and the history of those relations in the twentieth century—questions with which I do not feel competent to deal. But surely one part of the answer lies precisely within the domain of a rhetorical study: an author's success or failure with particular readers depends in part on their conventional expectations. And the last several decades have produced— for whatever reasons—an audience that has been thrown off balance by a barrage of ironic works.

The first readers of *The Turn* never questioned the governess' integrity. Their habitual experience of narrative testimony led them to expect reliability unless unreliability were clearly proved. By the

---

13 Martin, Hagopian, and Stein are in *Modern Fiction Studies*, IV (Winter, 1958–59), 335–45, and V (Summer, 1959), 169–71, and in the *Arizona Quarterly*, XV (Spring, 1959), 13–22. The explanation by homosexuality is in the anthology, *Short Novels of the Masters*, ed. Charles Nieder (New York, 1948), p. 15.

14 "The American: A Reinterpretation," *PMLA*, LXXIV (December, 1959), 613–18. As I write this footnote, in mid-January of 1961, I know of no attempts to reply to Clair's thesis. But I can be quite sure that replies and alternative hypotheses have already appeared, somewhere. No doubt at this moment a controversy is brewing, or is already at full boil, on the matter, and it is equally certain that other controversial readings will make those I have recorded seem old-fashioned by the time my book reaches print. But I must stop somewhere or I shall begin to sound like Tristram Shandy living his material faster than he can write it down.

nineteen-twenties, however, when the theory was first advanced that the ghosts are the governess' hallucinations,[15] readers had already experienced two decades of extreme unreliability. They knew what it was to be taken in by plausible but vicious witnesses like Lyon or to be confused by Stephen Dedalus. As experience with such deceptive folk grew, readers became more and more sensitive about their oversights and suspicious of all claims to reliability. Most of us saw little distance between Joyce and Stephen on first reading *A Portrait*; we have learned our mistake—and we now look for distance everywhere. We have been caught once too often; and the result is that the rhetorical situation of the governess and her fellow-reflectors has shifted radically.

Their first readers were most likely to commit the fault of overlooking distance when it was plain before them; inexperienced readers in 1961 are in the same position still, as we see in every year's crop of freshmen who identify authors literally with their narrators. But many of us are now in exactly the opposite condition: we can't accept a straight and simple statement when we read one.

The result is that few of us are immune to the kind of error Edmund Wilson made in reading Henry Miller's *Tropic* books. Wilson praised Miller for his skilful ironic portrait of a particular kind of "vaporing" poseur, for making his hero really live, "and not merely in his vaporings or his poses. He gives us the genuine American bum come to lead the beautiful life in Paris; and he lays him away forever in his dope of Pernod and dreams." To all of this praise for irony, Miller replied, "The theme is myself, and the narrator, or the hero, as your critic puts it, is also myself. . . . If he means the narrator, then it is me. . . . I don't use 'heroes,' incidentally, nor do I write novels. I am the hero, and the book is myself."[16]

Equally indignant, Mary McCarthy reports the search by a Freshman English class for hidden meanings in a story of hers, when in actuality "the whole point of this 'story' was that it really hap-

---

[15] See Alexander E. Jones, "Point of View in *The Turn of the Screw*," *PMLA*, LXXIV (March, 1959), 113.

[16] Wilson himself reports the exchange in *The Shores of Light* (New York and London, 1952), pp. 708–9. The exchange took place in 1938.

pened; it is written in the first person; I speak of myself in my own name, McCarthy. . . . The chief interest, I felt, lay in the fact that it happened, in real life, last summer, to the writer herself. . . ."[17] One is tempted to join in Miss McCarthy's amusing attack on the misguided professor of that class. The hunt for hidden symbols and ironies has been carried too far. But when we consider more closely the professor's plight, and particularly what Miss McCarthy herself adds about the nature of her purposes in the story, the situation is not quite so clear. The event, she tells us, happened "to the writer herself, who was a good deal at fault in the incident. I wanted to embarrass myself, and, if possible, the reader too." An interesting new twist on the artist's goal: she writes not to express herself but to embarrass herself. Since she intends to embarrass the reader, too, presumably she requires that he identify with her in her faults, that he see in her faults a reflection of his own. Fine. But meanwhile here are the poor professor and his students back in the classroom, reading this story along with some Kafka and James, some Hemingway and some Joyce, or even perhaps along with certain other of Miss McCarthy's own stories, where the ironies are piled thick and deep. It is hard to think of many important modern works they *could* come from, as they approach Miss McCarthy's story, without being led into difficulty. And even now that we know her own attitude toward the story, it is no easy task to infer which of the traits in her narrator she thinks reveal her as "a good deal at fault" and which she thinks are so sympathetic that they will lead the reader to identify with her in her embarrassment.[18]

---

17 "Settling the Colonel's Hash," *Harper's*, CCVIII (February, 1954), 68–75.

18 One can sympathize with a British reviewer of Mary McCarthy: "Time and again the reader, disliking a character heartily, and assuming that the author is with him, is suddenly brought up short by the horrid doubt (which the author has no business to leave him room for) whether he is not in fact alone" (Hilary Corke, "Lack of Confidence," *Encounter* [July, 1956], p. 76). For a similar protest against another writer, see Charles Child Walcutt, reviewing James T. Farrell's *Bernard Clare* in *Accent* (Summer, 1946), p. 267: "I believe Farrell plays fast and loose with this almost universal convention of characterization. Hence the ambiguity: for with reference to the convention Bernard is despicable, whereas with reference to actuality he is 'better' than the average pious citizen. And thus Farrell . . . can demand credit for fearless truthfulness because he reveals so much of the hog and the snake in Bernard and in the next breath can accuse of hypocrisy anyone who presumes to consider Bernard an inferior person."

Making a somewhat similar point, Saul Bellow warns us against "deep reading."[19] "Perhaps the deepest readers are those who are least sure of themselves. An even more disturbing suspicion is that they prefer meaning to feeling." But the warning cannot take us very far when, as Bellow says, "the best novelists and poets of the century have done much to promote" the kind of deep reading he deplores. Bellow's own novels all require great subtlety in the reader; their narrators are all only partially reliable. Who is to say with certainty to what degree Augie or Henderson or Leventhal speaks for Bellow's norms?

Thus even if we take McCarthy's and Bellow's advice and abandon symbol-hunting, the equally pervasive irony-hunt will go on. Once on this road we cannot turn back; we cannot pretend that things are as simple as they once seemed. We may commit absurdities, questioning not only the honest little governess, but moving on up the scale of intended reliability to take in Nelly Dean (the newly discovered "villainess" of *Wuthering Heights*), Clarissa (not quite the angelic creature she once seemed), and even the most obviously omniscient and reliable narrators. We are not stopped by the most explicit rhetoric. When Cervantes labors to place his woeful knight as a blind (though lovable) fool, we simply ignore him: the Don is really a Christian Saint, a great Ironic Hero whom Cervantes himself does not fully understand.[20]

One of the worst results of all this is that it becomes more and more difficult to rely, in our criticism, on the old standards of proof; evidence from the book can never be decisive. Have we proved that James included *in the story*, and not simply in his statements of intentions in the notebooks, unequivocal evidence that the ghosts are really there, turning that screw? All right, then, the critic simply shifts our attention from the governess' psyche to James's: it is James, rather than the governess, who has lost his "grasp of reality."

---

[19] "Deep Readers of the World, Beware!" *New York Times Book Review* (February 15, 1959), pp. 1, 34.

[20] James Hafley, "The Villain in *Wuthering Heights*," *Nineteenth-Century Fiction*, XIII (December, 1958), 199–215; Norman Rabkin, "*Clarissa*: A Study in the Nature of Convention," *ELH*, XXIII (September, 1956), 204–17; W. H. Auden, "The Ironic Hero," *Horizon*, XX (August, 1949), 86–93. For discussions concerning the unreliability of other narrators see Bibliography, Sec. V, A and B.

"The doubts that some readers feel," says Edmund Wilson, "as to the soundness of the governess's story are, I believe, the reflection of James's doubts, communicated unconsciously by James himself." We can conclude, quite happily, that "not merely is the governess self-deceived, but that James is self-deceived about her."[21] Once we decide that against their conscious aims authors work their wonders, no critical hypothesis, however far from the author's provable intentions inside the work or out, can be refuted; this in turn means that nothing can be proved, since no evidence is more relevant than any other. The critic with the greatest persuasive power—and for some readers this means simply the critic who can find the most ambiguities or ironies—wins. How would one go about arguing for or against the irresponsible imaginings contained in the latest contribution to the controversy about *The Turn*—except to call them names like "irresponsible"?

> Is it possible, then, that Douglas [the employer] is Miles [the haunted boy]? That the governess, in love with Miles (Douglas), and unable to act in the situation, herself wrote a story, a fiction? And, finally, that Douglas as a child, as well as a young man down from Trinity, was in love with the governess?[22]

What can the word "possible" mean in such a question? Is the critic's job that of conducting a story conference to decide how the author *might* have written?

> But even if there is an understated connection between Douglas and the governess, the interpretations developed by various critics are not necessarily invalidated. For the essential fact remains that the story told by the governess needs to be read at varying levels. This is all the more true if we say that her story is, in effect, a fiction. . . . We may still maintain that her manuscript is not a true story at all, that it is a work of fiction she had already committed to paper before relating orally to Douglas. Or she may have made it up as she went along and then written it down.

21 From Wilson's postscript, added in the 1948 edition of *The Triple Thinkers*, as reprinted in *The Story: A Critical Anthology*, ed. Mark Schorer (Englewood Cliffs, N.J., 1950), pp. 583–85. Not long ago Wilson reversed himself again.

22 Introduction to *A Casebook on Henry James's "The Turn of the Screw,"* ed. Gerald Willen (New York, 1960).

Or, one "might" add, she "may" have copied it out of a long lost medieval manuscript. So long as no one is asked to provide any evidence, we can go on like this forever. Yet if the author's explicit rhetoric, embodied in the work, is not taken as relevant, where do we turn for evidence?

It is sometimes suggested that anyone who deplores the resulting critical Babel is really imposing a literal-minded building code on what should be the multileveled house of fiction. Henry James could still believe that a work of art that must be explained has to some extent failed; our motto seems to be, "the more explanation called for, the better." When Edmund Wilson overinterprets James or Henry Miller, when he admits that he could not have "divined," without extraneous assistance, the "complicated scheme" of "Homeric parallels in Joyce's *Ulysses*," and that "the result is sometimes baffling and confusing,"[23] or that "*The Sacred Fount* is mystifying, even maddening," it does not lead him to mitigate his praise for the "strict objective method, in which the author must not comment on the action." Though Erich Auerbach finds that he cannot decipher "the purpose and meaning of the work itself" in reading many impersonal authors, particularly those that use a "multiplicity of consciousnesses" as reflectors, still these really give an "accurate" reflection of what life itself *is* for us as we constantly endeavor "to give meaning and order to our lives," and the potential fault is fully redeemed (*Mimesis*, pp. 485–86). And finally—to choose only one more from innumerable statements of the same kind—when Lionel Trilling confessed recently his inability to decide, in reading Nabokov's controversial *Lolita*, whether the narrator's final indictment of his own immorality is to be taken seriously or ironically, he hastened to explain that this ambiguity made the novel better, not worse. "Indeed, for me one of the attractions of *Lolita*," he says, "is its ambiguity of tone . . . and its ambiguity of intention, its ability to arouse uneasiness, to throw the reader off balance" and, by urging "moral mobility," to represent peculiarly

---

[23] "James Joyce," *Axel's Castle* (New York and London, 1931), sec. iii. esp. p. 213.

well "certain aspects of American life."[24] The argument is clear. Our life is morally ambiguous; this book makes it seem even more so—it throws us even more off balance, presumably, than we were before—and hence its very lack of clarity is a virtue.

In short, we have looked for so long at foggy landscapes reflected in misty mirrors that we have come to like fog. Clarity and simplicity are suspect; irony reigns supreme. To those general qualities we discussed in chapters ii–v, we have added irony as something which in itself is desirable. In a recent book on irony in the drama, we read that because Fielding was a "greater ironist," he is probably a greater novelist than Richardson.[25] Though no responsible critic has ever argued that all ambiguities resulting from irony are good ambiguities, it is astonishing to see how reluctant we have become to discriminate, to point to this or that particular difficulty springing from irony and say, "This is a fault." After all, we say, it is only the enemies of literature who ask that its effects be handed to the reader on a platter.

And yet we all know that our lines of communication have been fouled, and that this is not a good thing. The harried reviewer knows it, trying to infer the core of a book without having a lifetime to spend on it. "*Coup de Grâce* is, for myself at any rate, a distinctly horrifying performance. The question is, how far is this deliberate? Without question, it is predominantly so. But is the snobbery purely Erik's, or does not Mme Yourcenar too a little feel that counts are more intrinsically worth while than accountants? Is the cruelty purely his? . . . Is she altogether aware of the vapidity and bogusity of Erik's interminable 'reflections,' and (if she is)

---

24 Lionel Trilling, "The Last Lover," *Encounter*, XI (October, 1958), 19.

25 Robert Boies Sharpe, *Irony in the Drama* (Chapel Hill, N.C., 1959), p. 45. The context makes clear that "irony" here refers to the audience's sense of a contrast between life and art—a very different thing from the "irony" that recent critics have sought in Richardson by looking for signs of distance between him and his heroines. Like the other general terms we have dealt with, irony has so many different meanings that one gains nothing by declaring himself for or against it. For two basic texts in the modern debate about irony in poetry, see Cleanth Brooks, *The Well Wrought Urn* (New York, 1947), and "Irony and 'Ironic' Poetry," *College English*, IX (1948), 231–37; R. S. Crane, "The Critical Monism of Cleanth Brooks," *Critics and Criticism*, ed. R. S. Crane (Chicago, 1952), pp. 83–107.

how can she bear to inflict on us so many of them?"[26] The critics
know it, as they find themselves forced to do recondite research to
discover whether to laugh or cry, or dream or wonder, at a given
beautiful stroke.[27] And finally the author knows it, sitting before
his desk wondering which of his secret ironies will be overlooked,
which of his straightforward judgments read as irony. He may succumb to his mistrust of the unsophisticated reader and issue a
warning against identification, like William Gerhardi prefacing
Futility with "The 'I' of this work is not me,"[28] or Vladimir Nabokov with his postscript to *Lolita*: "My creature Humbert is a for-
eigner and an anarchist, and there are many things, besides nymph-
ets, in which I disagree with him."[29] Or, if he has more to fear
from the sophisticated reader inclined to resist emotional effects,
he may plead for something other than the cool, detached, ironic
reading demanded by many works. "The man here depicted," François Mauriac says in a prefatory note about the miser who relates
Knot of Vipers (1932) in the form of a diary, "was the enemy of
his own flesh and blood. His heart was eaten up by hatred and by
avarice. Yet, I would have you, in spite of his baseness, feel pity,
and be moved by his predicament. . . ."[30] Or he may show no pub-

---

[26] Hilary Corke, "New Novels," *The Listener* (November 7, 1957), p. 755.

[27] In addition to all of the confessions to bafflement and accusations of obscurity cited
elsewhere, the following two sources are useful as going beyond confession or attack to
intelligent analysis of the problem: (1) David Daiches, *Virginia Woolf* (Norfolk,
Conn., 1942): "Is the contrast between the bourgeois solidity of Mrs. Dalloway's environment and the nature of her own consciousness meant to be part of the effect?"
"Virginia Woolf seems to have felt, after *To the Lighthouse*, that in her attempt to
present the 'tranparent envelope' of experience . . . the distinction between the thought
process of the author and those of the characters [was not] made sufficiently clear" (pp.
77, 104); (2) B. F. Bart, "Aesthetic Distance in *Madame Bovary*," *PMLA*, LXIX
(December, 1954), 1112–26. Bart is one of the few sensitive readers of Flaubert
who confesses to difficulty that might be attributable to Flaubert himself; for him,
Flaubert never solved the problem of how to shift the "aesthetic distance" from point
to point, with the result that the reader is not always sure whether to sympathize with
Emma or condemn her.

[28] Collected edition (London, 1947), facing p. 1.

[29] "On a Book Entitled *Lolita*," *Lolita* (New York, n.d. [1958]), p. 317.

[30] Trans. Gerard Hopkins (London, 1952), p. vii.

lic signs of his worries at all. But unless he is more protected by egotism than most authors manage to be, he will be aware that he sends his work to a confused and confusing reception. Even if he should return to the older devices of explicit control, as a great many serious authors have done, he faces problems that writers before Henry James could ignore.

"A poet's function—do not be startled by this remark—is not to experience the poetic state: that is a private affair. His function is to create it in others." "The man of genius is the one who infuses genius into me."—VALÉRY

"The writer needs a causal connection with his society, some sense that his work does something to make everyone's privacy a privilege rather than a burden."—HERBERT GOLD

CHAPTER
THIRTEEN

The Morality
of Impersonal Narration

MORALITY AND TECHNIQUE

So far I have assumed that the purposes of the individual work should dictate the standards by which it is judged. We have no right to impose *Nightwood* on *Emma* or Kafka on Fielding.[1] It may, in fact, seem to some readers that in talking of the dangers of impersonal narration in the last two chapters, I have come close to committing the very fault I have deplored. When I say that impersonal narration may lead to confusion or unintentional ambiguity, am I not imposing on modern fiction standards of clarity or emotional intensity derived from earlier fiction? I can only say that what I have tried to do, so far, is to preserve with some rigor the structure of hypothetical argument which I find most common in effective practical critics, from Aristotle to the present: *If* an author wants

---

[1] This is not the place to attempt a reconciliation between the half-truth that all good works are *sui generis* and the undeniable fact that we cannot engage in practical criticism at all without grouping works according to *kinds* of effect. Readers who are troubled by the suspicion that I have sneaked general criteria in the back door while denouncing them from the front stoop may find some reassurance in the discussions of poetic kinds by Crane and Olson in *Critics and Criticism*, ed. R. S. Crane (Chicago, 1952), pp. 12–24, 546–66, 646–47. Also see pp. 124–25 above.

intense sympathy for characters who do not have strong virtues to recommend them, *then* the psychic vividness of prolonged and deep inside views will help him. *If* an author wants to earn the reader's confusion, *then* unreliable narration may help him. On the other hand, if a work requires an effect like intense dramatic irony, whether comic or tragic, the author may find new uses for direct reliable narration. Let each work do what it "wants" to do; let its author discover its inherent powers and gauge his techniques to the realization of those powers.

But is there no choosing among effects? Must we always grant the author what James calls his "subject" and deal only with his success in realizing that subject? Is there no disputing of taste in literary species? Is a fully realized comedy of the *Emma* kind the exact equivalent of a fully realized comedy of the very different *Ambassadors* kind or of the fully realized but unnamed mixture of effects of the *Castle* kind?

In so far as the critic wants to be of practical help to the artist or reader, I am convinced that he must follow James's advice and avoid such questions. The critic's chances of saying anything to Kafka that might help him improve his work are low enough in any case; they disappear entirely if he begins by telling Kafka that he shouldn't have tried to write like *that* at all. Yet in so far as we are men who react to each literary work with our whole being, we will inevitably follow James's practice and bring to bear, however surreptitiously, judgments of ends as well as means.

Of all the criteria one might, for some purposes, employ in such judgment—social, psychological, sexual, historical, political, religious, or whatever—only one is so strongly forced upon me by the nature of my subject that I cannot pass it by: impersonal narration has raised moral difficulties too often for us to dismiss moral questions as irrelevant to technique.

We have seen that inside views can build sympathy even for the most vicious character. When properly used, this effect can be of immeasurable value in forcing us to see the human worth of a character whose actions, objectively considered, we would deplore; the latest triumph in this mode is Faulkner's Mink Snopes, in *The*

Mansion (1959). But it is hardly surprising that works in which this effect is used have often led to moral confusion. Perhaps a majority of all charges against the immorality of serious modern fiction can be traced to this one device. One can recognize the irrelevance and wrongheadedness of many such charges and still attempt to deal honestly with the problems presented by the seductive rogues who narrate much modern fiction.[2]

THE SEDUCTIVE POINT OF VIEW: CÉLINE AS EXAMPLE

Let us imagine a non-professional reader, intelligent and well-read, approaching for the first time Céline's work, *Journey to the End of the Night* (1932). He chooses it, let us say, from the drugstore reprint rack.[3] He has a dim memory that Céline is "good," or "important," he sees on the cover that this is "one of the Major Novels of the 20th Century," and he buys it and takes it home. He reads on the flyleaf that Céline has been hailed by "American critics" as "an authentic new writing voice—an author with the compelling quality of an almost unbearable urgency in his work." He reads a commendation from André Gide. Then he reads, since he is a careful reader, Céline's own epigraph:

---

[2] The most recent full-scale attack on the immorality of modern fiction is *Man in Modern Fiction*, by Edmund Fuller (New York, 1958). Fuller accuses modern writers of abandoning the "Judeo-Christian tradition," and of forgetting that man "inhabits an orderly universe," that "his fundamental laws are commands of his Creator," and that he is "individual, responsible, guilty, redeemable." See also Harold C. Gardiner, *Norms for the Novel* (New York, 1953), and Martin Jarrett-Kerr, C.R., *Studies in Literature and Belief* (London, 1954). Counterattacks on such efforts are sometimes virulent. See, for example, Irving Howe on Edmund Fuller, *The New Republic* (June 23, 1958). Without accepting Fuller's case, we can wonder whether the moral question is as irrelevant to the critical enterprise as Howe suggests. He concludes his review with a reference to Wallace Stevens' "A High-Toned Old Christian Woman" as a "deeply serious reflection upon the relation between art and morality": "Fictive things / Wink as they will. Wink most when widows wince." It is a nice touch. Who wants to be a wincing widow like poor Fuller? Yet once we stop calling names and examine concepts, we can hardly take seriously the claim that art is invariably best when it makes the conventional most uncomfortable. We may not want to go as far as Eliot, who once said that though some modern writers can be improving, "contemporary literature as a whole," including possibly even his own work, "tends to be degrading" ("Religion and Literature," 1935, reprinted in *Literary Opinion in America*, ed. M. D. Zabel [rev. ed.; New York, 1951], p. 623). But we cannot pretend that *whether* it is degrading is irrelevant to its value.

[3] Trans. John H. J. Marks (London, 1950; New York, n.d.).

Travel is a good thing; it stimulates the imagination. Everything else is a snare and a delusion. Our own journey is entirely imaginative. Therein lies its strength.

It leads from life to death. Men, beasts, cities, everything in it is imaginary. It's a novel, only a made-up story. The dictionary says so and it's never wrong.

Besides, every one can go and do likewise. Shut your eyes, that's all that is necessary.

There you have life seen from the other side.

What our reader then discovers is an appalling problem. A first-person narrator, a modern picaresque hero, takes him through a sequence of sordid adventures. It is all, of course, completely "objective": Céline is never undeniably there, even in the long-winded commentary. But he is never undeniably dissociated, either, and therein lies the problem. The reader cannot help wondering whether Ferdinand's moralizing, of which there is a great deal, is to be taken seriously or not. Is this Céline's view? Should it be mine, at least temporarily, so that I can go along sympathetically with this hero? Or is it simply "life seen from the other side," as the epigraph has promised? Even assuming that the reader knows nothing of Céline's personal life, he must find it hard to believe, after a hundred or so pages of the following kind of thing, that Céline is merely dramatizing a narrator who is completely dissociated from him:

You don't lose anything much when your landlord's house is burnt down.

Another landlord always comes along, if it isn't always the same one—a German or a Frenchman or an Englishman or a Chinaman— and you get your bill just the same. . . . Whether you pay in marks or francs, it doesn't much matter.

Morals, in fact, were a dirty business . . . [p. 48].

A great part of one's youth is lost in trial and error. It was obvious that the girl I loved was going to throw me over, and that before very long. I hadn't yet learnt that there are two human races on this earth, the rich and the poor, and that they aren't at all the same. It's taken me, as it's taken so many people, twenty years and the war to learn to stick to my own group and to ask the price of things and people before laying hands on them, and especially before setting any store by them [p. 74].

> When one's been able to escape alive from a mad international shambles, it says something after all for one's tact and discretion [p. 102].

> It was then that one saw the whole of the white man's revolting nature displayed in freedom from all constraint, under provocation and untrammelled; his real self as you saw it in war. . . . reality, heavy-smelling pools of slime, the crabs, the carcasses and scum [p. 103].

Are these Céline's views? If not, what do they tell us about Bardamu? If his view of the white man's "real nature" is incorrect, we have no clues from Céline about the correct alternative.

Our reader will find it no easier to assess what is intended by Bardamu's judgments of character. Whether he is judging his predecessor in an African post as an "out-and-out rotter" (p. 154) or saying of Alcide, without the slightest touch of irony, "Here was a fellow who hobnobbed with the angels and you would never have guessed it. . . . he had given these years . . . to a little girl . . . with no interest except that of his own good heart" (p. 148), the reader uninstructed in Céline must be lost—even in the unlikely case that his own judgments correspond with Bardamu's in all instances. At one moment Bardamu feels guilty for his participation in life itself, corrupt as it is (p. 301), and in the next he exonerates himself thus: "It's easy enough to say I was double-crossing. Even so, it's a question of when and how. Double-crossing is like opening a window in a prison. Everyone wants to, but it isn't often you get the chance." One moment he is playing Mickey Spillane: "As long as I can remember, I had always wanted to clout a face possessed by anger, as hers was, just to see what happens to an angry face if you do. . . . She started to smile. . . . Biff! Bang! . . . I had seen nothing. It hadn't been any good" (pp. 428–29). The next moment he is moralizing about himself as the reader might moralize about him, analyzing his deficiency in "a love for the life of others," his lack of "pity" (p. 454), his "aimless pilgrimage" in the attempt to "lose my way" (p. 457).

If the reader thinks about Bardamu's style—and since he has read a good deal of modern fiction he is likely to—he will be equally confused about its intended quality. Are the repetitious sewage metaphors intended to be signs of his—and thus of Céline's—poetic insight, or of poetic insight gone to seed in a way that will characterize the narrator in contrast to Céline? Is the heavy-handed symbolism of "journey into the night" made to be heavy-handed by Céline, in order to characterize his narrator? But how account then for the fact that sometimes the style *is*, as the cover promises, "astonishingly" gifted?

If our puzzled reader became articulate and expressed his bewilderment, he might receive the reply, "But you are insisting on value judgments where value judgments are inappropriate. The very point of the book is that the man is lost and confused." But the book insists on value judgment, from the first page. When the narrator judges, how is the reader to avoid judging? To argue that the work simply intends to present a "vivid picture" is meaningless, when the vivid picture consists of acts and statements which cannot be seen for what they are except in a setting of values. If Bardamu's attacks on civilization's values are not *attacks*, and seen as such, they are nothing.

It is true, of course, that with a little effort in sources outside the book, and with careful re-reading, one can come to a fairly convincing discrimination between those of Bardamu's appalling beliefs which Céline shares and those which he does not. Like the authors of other quest novels we have considered (chap. x), Céline takes his vicious hero to a moment of revelation which is intended to show him and us what might have been.

> There was I, standing by Léon's side so as to be of help to him, and never have I felt so awkward. I couldn't manage it. . . . And he couldn't find me. . . . He must have been looking for some other Ferdinand, one of course much greater than me, so as to die, or rather, for me to help him to die, more quietly. . . . There was nobody but me, really me, just me, by his side,—a quite real Ferdinand who lacked what might make a man greater than his own trivial life, a love for the life of others.

Yes, this would have been salvation, we begin to tell ourselves. Poor man. "I hadn't any of that, or truly so little of it that it wasn't worth showing what I had. I wasn't death's equal." Ah, yes, which of us can say that he is? "I was far too small for it. I had no great conception of humanity. I would even, I believe, have more easily felt sorry for a dog dying than for Robinson, because a dog's not sly; whereas, whatever one may say, Léon was just a bit sly. I was sly too; we were all sly" (p. 454). Yes, yes, we all are sly. What a pigsty we all live in, after all. Who can blame poor Bardamu, and poor Céline, whose contempt for man, and for particular races of man, matches poor Bardamu's? This sordid world of ours has made them what they are, and Céline has expressed—and in such beautiful style and such an honest, impersonal manner, everything dramatized, no authorial intrusions—what we all know to be our real lost world. As Charles Berard says, "His reserves of compassion are limitless."

And then we draw back. At least if we are lucky enough not to be entirely vulnerable to this kind of rhetoric, we draw back and repudiate what we have been told. It is not an honest picture, it is not a realized picture at all. These things have not been "judged and given each its appointed place in the whole scheme," and as Katherine Mansfield said about Dorothy Richardson's unjudged accumulations of detail, "they have no meaning in the world of art."[4] That it includes a vision of sordidness no more makes it honest than if the sentimental identification with the hero were based on a complete denial of evil.

Yet regardless of how much we may reason about it, we have, in the course of our reading of this book, been caught. Caught in the trap of a suffering consciousness, we are led to succumb morally as well as visually. The trap which we saw Thackeray's Barry Lyndon springing on Trollope, in spite of all Thackeray could do to make his own rejection of Barry's immorality clear, has here been sprung by a thoroughly unscrupulous man. Though Céline has attempted the traditional excuse—remember, it is my character speaking and not I—we cannot excuse him for writing a book which, if taken seriously by the reader, must corrupt him. The better it is understood, the more immoral it looks. It is immoral not only in the sense that Céline cheats, though that is important: the world he portrays as

---

[4] *Novels and Novelists*, ed. J. Middleton Murry (London, 1930), p. 4 (written April 4, 1919). See also pp. 40–41 for another complaint about faulty ordering of values.

reality contains no conceivable explanation of how anyone in that world could bring himself to write a book—even this book. More important, if the reader takes its blandishments seriously, without providing a judgment radically different from Céline's, the result of reading the book must be not only to obscure his sense of what is wrong with such an action as clouting a woman's face just to see how it feels but finally to weaken his will to live as effectively as possible. Taken seriously, the book would make life itself meaningless except as a series of self-centered forays into the lives of others.

Whether or not I am too hard on Céline, I think we all encounter works that bring us up short in this way by insisting on something more than a technical judgment. And yet we go on talking as if technical triumphs had no relation to the value of what they achieve. The thoroughgoing confusion that threatens us in these matters is shown in almost frightening form by the jacket blurb for the Grove Press edition of Robbe-Grillet's novel, *The Voyeur*.[5]

> Robbe-Grillet's theory of fiction—that the surface of things is more meaningful than the depth of human beings—is brilliantly executed in this tense and shocking novel. . . . Through the accumulated detail of objective description . . . —Robbe-Grillet, without the traditional novel's inner probing, obtains a reader participation that is unprecedented in previous fiction. Our attention is invaded until inevitably we realize we are inside the mind of Mathias—accomplices of a homicidal maniac.

Curious praise, this, once we think about it. The book is a brilliant culmination of more than a hundred years of experimentation with inside views and the sympathetic identification they can yield. It does, indeed, lead us to experience intensely the sensations and emotions of a homicidal maniac. But is this really what we go to literature for? Quite aside from the question of how such a book might affect readers who already have homicidal tendencies, is there no limit to what we will praise, provided it is done with skill?

To answer this question properly would no doubt lead to a different kind of book entirely, based on careful definitions of good and evil and comparisons with other media like the movies and television that show a similar power to win our sympathy for evil.

---

[5] *Le Voyeur* (Paris, 1955), trans. Richard Howard (New York, 1958).

To pass a moral judgment without somehow providing an answer to prevailing neutralist theories is probably futile. In reply to moral criticism, the author has only to say, "But I do not intend to be improving. You are imposing your general standard." It may be finally impossible to deal in rational argument with such a position. It is like trying to dissuade a friend from suicide: Where do you find your major premise? If an author really does not care whether his works leave his readers in some sense better for having read them, if he feels no connection at all between his artistic motives and some improvement in the quality of the lives led by his readers, attempts to prove such a connection will be futile. And it is quite conceivable that a society might become so demoralized that most artists would feel driven to use their art for destructive ends.

But I am convinced that most novelists today—at least those writing in English—feel an inseparable connection between art and morality, quite apart from what it is popular to say about morality; their artistic vision consists, in part, of a judgment on what they see, and they would ask us to share that judgment as part of the vision.[6] In any case, it is only to such novelists—whatever their number—that one can have anything to say about the morality of technique. Retiring in defeat from the examination of works in which the central intent is morally questionable, we must turn to those in which an author's moral judgment is misread because of the powerful blandishments of his immoral narrator.

The Author's Moral Judgment Obscured

Impersonal works are not of course alone in risking inadvertent harm. If we were to do away with all works that might harm someone who misread them, we should probably follow Plato and ban all literature except hymns of praise and philosophical dialogues.

---

[6] It is precisely on this point that some of our most highly moralistic critics are tragically misleading. When Leslie Fiedler calls on the novelist to shout "No" in order to fulfil the "essential function of art, the negative one of provocation and scandal," he implicitly accepts the moral function of art. But he puts his charge in a way that makes no distinction between those who say "No" and give their reasons in intelligible form and those who say "No" simply by retreating into privacy and irresponsibility (Leslie Fiedler, "No, in Thunder," Esquire [September, 1960], pp. 78 ff.).

Hardy's reply, when critics said that *Tess of the D'Urbervilles* might harm inexperienced readers, seems a fair one:

> Of the effects of such sincere presentation on weak minds, when the courses of the characters are not exemplary and the rewards and punishments ill adjusted to deserts, it is not our duty to consider too closely. A novel which does mortal injury to a dozen imbeciles, and has bracing results upon intellects of normal vigor, can justify its existence; and probably a novel was never written by the purest-minded author for which there could not be found some moral invalid or other whom it was capable of harming.[7]

Robert Penn Warren uses this quotation in defense of the morality of Hemingway's *A Farewell to Arms.* For him, if the book has "meaning," if it deals "seriously with a moral and philosophical issue which, for better or worse, does exist in the modern world in substantially the terms presented by Hemingway," it is exonerated; its harmful effect on the weak is irrelevant.

But does not this balancing of the number mortally injured against the number "braced" imply a utilitarian counting of heads that we cannot really accept as a defense of the morality of literature? What do we say of a work which is "bracing" to a very few, perhaps only one, but harmful to many? More important, to show that an author's intentions are serious and that his subjects are vital or real says very little about his artistic success. To deal with a subject that is in some way important may be a necessary step toward writing well, but it is certainly not sufficient. To defend the moral intent of the author is in itself no more conclusive than to show that he wanted to write a masterpiece. In this matter, curiously enough, the "intentional fallacy" is committed by many critics who avoid it otherwise: if a novelist's intentions are "serious" rather than "commercial," or if he has set out to reveal filth rather than to celebrate nobility, many seem to feel that they should give his work at least some credit, however slovenly its technique may be.

The moral question is really whether an author has an obligation to write well in the sense of making his moral orderings clear, and if so, clear to whom. Ian Watt has suggested recently that the novel

---

[7] As quoted by Robert Penn Warren, "Hemingway," in *Literary Opinion in America,* p. 461. First printed in *Kenyon Review,* IX (Winter, 1947), 1–28.

is essentially an ambiguous form; the rise of the novel is itself a reflection of "the transition from the objective, social and public orientation of the classical world to the subjective, individualist and private orientation" of modern life and literature.[8] As the novel sought what he calls "realism of presentation," in a world in which reality itself came to seem more and more ambiguous, relativistic, and mobile, it inevitably sacrificed something of the "realism of assessment" of other genres.

There is certainly something to this claim. A play is likely to depend for its success on a consensus established immediately and without reflection; without some sort of community gathered together in one spot, the theater cannot survive, and even the most disturbing plays are almost always built upon easily grasped, commonly accepted norms, in contrast with the complex and troubling values of much fiction. What is more, any unintentional ambiguities the playwright may leave in his play are to some extent removed by a good production; each director imposes his interpretation by defining, with his innumerable devices of production, the potentially ambiguous elements. Though *Richard III* may be ambiguous in the sense of permitting both sympathetic and unsympathetic readings of King Richard, any particular production tends to follow one line or the other. But in the novel, every reader is his own producer.

This does not mean, however, that novels should or must be ambiguous. Nor does it mean that failures in communication between novelist and reader should be treated as if successful communication is an accident of personality. When communication fails, Leon Edel says, it "may sometimes be the fault of the artist," but "generally it must be recognized rather as a failure of the two consciousnesses involved to establish a harmonious relationship. This happens often enough in life; there is no reason why we may not expect it to happen sometimes in our relationship to certain novels that we read."[9] This is true enough, so far as it goes; there are no doubt good readers and good authors who somehow cannot meet on com-

---

[8] *The Rise of the Novel* (Berkeley, Calif., 1957), pp. 176, 206, and *passim*.

[9] *The Psychological Novel* (London, 1955), p. 139.

mon ground, and few readers are ever sufficiently careful to catch the clues that are provided. But we might equally well conclude from the potential ambiguity of fiction that the novelist must work harder at providing, *within his work*, the kind of definition of his elements that a good production gives to a play.

It is at precisely this point that the morality of "writing well" is so often misunderstood. "You are highly blamable," Zola said, "when you write badly. That is the only crime which I can admit in literature. I do not see where they can put morality, if they pretend to put it elsewhere. A well-made phrase is a good action."[10] Zola's credo has been accepted by perhaps a majority of important authors since his time, but it is obviously only a half-truth for all of that. If it means simply that to do anything well is a moral act because excellence is worth pursuing, it says nothing about art that it does not also say about aiming an atomic bomb or keeping a neat and efficient gas chamber or abattoir. If writing well were simply creating a well-turned phrase, the statement could mean only that. But when we say that the morality in art rests in "writing well," we silently import into our claim the concept of the realization of a worthwhile purpose. A well-made phrase can serve the rhetorical purposes of a Hitler as well as the literary purposes of a Zola. But in fiction the concept of writing well must include the successful ordering of your reader's view of a fictional world. The "well-made phrase" in fiction must be much more than "beautiful"; it must serve larger ends, and the artist has a moral obligation, contained as an essential part of his aesthetic obligation to "write well," to do all that is possible in any given instance to realize his world as he intends it.

From this standpoint there is a moral dimension in the author's choice of impersonal, noncommittal techniques. As we have seen, objective narration, particularly when conducted through a highly unreliable narrator, offers special temptations to the reader to go astray. Even when it presents characters whose conduct the author deeply deplores, it presents them through the seductive medium of

---

10 Zola, *The Experimental Novel, and Other Essays*, trans. Belle M. Sherman (New York, 1893), p. 365.

their own self-defending rhetoric. It is consequently not surprising that reactions to such works have been marked with confusion and false accusations.

Graham Greene's Catholic readers have often reproached him for making his evil characters too sympathetic, for making evil itself attractive. Such readers, presumably, have not themselves been harmed; at least they always speak only of the potential harm to other readers. But we can infer that the really harmful misreading, the most tragic false identifications of the reader with the vicious centers of consciousness, never are discussed in print. Even the great satires, in which the moral issues would seem to be crystal clear, often lead naïve students astray in this regard. How much more often must the naïve reader be led into disastrous conclusions by overlooking the subtle condemnations embedded in the works of Greene?

An intelligent friend of mine has admitted to using the works of Huxley throughout his adolescence as a steady source of pornography. The orgies satirized in *Brave New World* were for him genuinely orgiastic, with no comic or satiric crosslights; his failure to see the satirical point was of course unchallenged by any direct hint from the author. Most of us, especially if we read widely when young without guidance from more experienced readers, can recall misreadings of this kind. They can range all the way from sadistic pleasure in scenes intended to rouse horror or revulsion to the acceptance of intellectual positions that the author intended to satirize.

Such misreadings prove little, perhaps, except that there are misreadings. Certainly Hardy's answer still holds. And yet, difficult as it is to argue, and with all of the complications carefully noted, one must say that an author has an obligation to be as clear about his moral position as he possibly can be. There will come a time for many authors when there will be an open conflict between the obligation to seem dispassionate and objective and the obligation to heighten other effects by making the moral basis of the work unequivocally clear. No one can make an author's choices for him, but it is foolish to pretend that the artistic choice is always in the direction of purity and objectivity.

We should be very clear that the failures we are talking about do not come from any inherent condition of the novel or from any natural incompatibility between author and reader. They come from the reader's inability to dissociate himself from a vicious center of consciousness presented to him with all of the seductive self-justification of skilful rhetoric. Can we really be surprised that readers have overlooked Nabokov's ironies in *Lolita*, when Humbert Humbert is given full and unlimited control of the rhetorical resources? "I do not intend to convey the impression that I did not manage to be happy. Reader must understand that in the possession and thralldom of a nymphet the enchanted traveler stands, as it were, *beyond happiness*. For there is no other bliss on earth comparable to that of fondling a nymphet. It is *hors concours*, that bliss, it belongs to another class, another plane of sensitivity." This sounds very good, indeed. "Despite our tiffs, despite her nastiness, despite all the fuss and faces she made, and the vulgarity, and the danger, and the horrible hopelessness of it all, I still dwelled deep in my elected paradise—a paradise whose skies were the color of hell-flames—but still a 'paradise' " (p. 168). All for love. Just like Antony and Cleopatra, or any of the other great lovers! We have already seen that Lionel Trilling cannot accept Humbert's later self-castigation as genuine after all this lively self-defense. And who is to blame him? The "paradise" is dramatized and described and praised at length; the repentance is merely expounded—though it is expounded powerfully: "Unless it can be proven to me—to me as I am now, today, with my heart and my beard, and my putrefaction —that in the infinite run it does not matter a jot that a North American girl-child named Dolores Haze had been deprived of her childhood by a maniac, unless this can be proven (and if it can, then life is a joke), I see nothing for the treatment of my misery but the melancholy and very local palliative of articulate art" (p. 285). Nabokov means what he makes Humbert say here, and one can understand his feeling that he has done all that anyone but an "illiterate juvenile delinquent" could possibly need to prevent misunderstanding (p. 318). But the laws of art are against him. His most skilful and mature readers, it is true, will have repudiated Humbert's blandishments from the beginning; the clues are numerous, the style is a dead giveaway throughout—*if* one happens to see it as such. One of the major delights of this delightful, profound book is that of watching Humbert *almost* make a case for himself. But Nabokov has insured that many, perhaps most, of his readers will be unsuccessful, in that they will identify Humbert with the author more than Nabokov intends. And for them, no amount of final recantation will cancel out the vividness of the earlier scenes.[11]

As Kenneth Burke once said of André Gide's Lafcadio, that casual and charming criminal who murders to express his—and Gide's —freedom, such fiction assumes "a sophistication on the part of the reader whereby the reader would not attempt too slavishly to become the acting disciple of his author's speculations." It is written for "pious" readers, "not for poisoners and forgers."[12] But is not the notion that one's readers will be morally sound rather naïve? Readers will be human beings with all their sins upon their heads; it is more likely that they will yield to a comfortable identification with Lafcadio's morality—since Gide "insists" upon our sympathizing with him—than that they will be jarred by the inconsistencies in his portrayal into the precise degree of distance that Gide intends.

THE MORALITY OF ELITISM

We have noted that many of the works in the unreliable mode depend for their effects on ironic collusion between the author and his readers. The line between such effects legitimately pursued and the pleasures of snobbery is difficult to draw, but impersonal, ironic narration lends itself neatly, far too neatly, to disguised expressions of snobbery which would never be tolerated if expressed openly in commentary. Chesterton once attributed part of the decline of Dickens' popularity to "that basest of all artistic indul-

---

11 The editor of *The New Republic*, paying more attention to various ecstatic and irresponsible public misreadings of *Lolita* than to the book itself, attacked it as if it were fundamentally a defense of Humbert Humbert's behavior (October 27, 1958, p. 3). He was wrong about the book, but I wish I could think he was wrong about its likely effect on most readers.

12 *Counter-Statement* (New York, 1931; 2d ed.; Los Altos, 1953), p. 104. The whole essay on Mann and Gide is pertinent to our problem.

gences (certainly far baser than the pleasure of absinthe or the pleasure of opium), the pleasure of appreciating works of art which ordinary men cannot appreciate."[13] Even baser would be the pleasure of writing works so *that* only the select few can understand. The author who sets out to appeal by his impersonality to "the most alert young people of two successive generations—in Berlin, Paris, London, New York, Rome, Madrid," regardless of the needs of the work in hand, is as inartistic as the author who plants irrelevant appeals to the prejudices of the buying public.

We do not judge the finished work, of course, according to the motives of the author. But the prohibition works both ways: If I cannot condemn a work simply because I know that its author was a snob, neither can I praise it simply because its author refused to be commercial, or condemn another because its author set out to write a best seller. The work itself must be our standard, and if the reader can see no reason for its difficulties except that critical fashion dictates an anti-commercial pose, he is bound to condemn it fully as much as he would if he discovered cheap appeals to temporary prejudices in a popular audience. In both cases the test is whether everything has been done that ought to be done—nothing more, nothing less—to make the work fundamentally accessible, realized in the basic etymological sense of being made into a thing that has its own existence, no longer tied to the author's ego. And if it was the peculiar temptation of Victorian novelists to give a false air of sentimental comradeship through their commentary, impersonal novelists are strongly tempted to give the reader less help than they know they should, in order to make sure that they are seen to be "serious."

A frequent explanation of the snobbish air that sometimes results is that there is no serious audience left for art except the precious, saving remnant. Virginia Woolf, for example, was haunted by the sense that older writers could depend upon an audience with public norms, while she must construct her private values as she went, and then impose them, without seeming to do so, on the reader. Neither Austen nor Scott, she says, has much to say about

---

[13] Introduction to Everyman edition of *Bleak House* (n.d.), p. ix.

the matter of judgment of conduct outright, "but everything depends on it. . . . To believe that your impressions hold good for others is to be released from the cramp and confinement of personality."[14] We are told again and again that the novelist could not help turning inward to his own private world of values because there was no outer world left to which he could appeal.[15] But even if consensus has declined—something in itself hard to prove, in spite of our ready clichés about it—surely artists must accept some of the responsibility for the decline themselves. If the loss of consensus forced them into private value systems, private myths, it hardly could be said to have forced them into the kind of private techniques I have discussed in the latter part of this book. One possible reaction to a fragmented society may be to retreat to a private world of values, but another might well be to build works of art that themselves help to mold a new consensus.[16]

There have been philosophical and psychological obstacles to

---

[14] Virginia Woolf, The Common Reader (London, 1925), pp. 301–2.

[15] Robert Liddell talks of the same contrast between the chaotic present and the ordered past. "People are not [at the present time] necessarily less moral, but there is no universal standard of Moral Taste—even among Principled persons—to which a writer can appeal" (Some Principles of Fiction [London, 1953], p. 110). Alex Comfort, contrasting the traditional drama and the nineteenth-century novel, on the one hand, with the modern novel on the other, says that the latter "can make no assumptions about [the reader's] beliefs or activities comparable with those which the early nineteenth-century novel, addressed to a section of society, could make. . . . An entire world has to be created and peopled separately in each book which is written." "For the first time in recent history we have a totally fragmented society" (The Novel and Our Time [London, 1948], pp. 13, 11).

[16] For a persuasive statement of a less hopeful view of the possibilities open to the novelist, see Earl H. Rovit, "The Ambiguous Modern Novel," The Yale Review (Spring, 1960), pp. 413–24: "The modern novelist . . . seems to have no choice between simplicity and directness on the one hand and complexity and ambiguity on the other. If he tries to deal honestly with the fearful intangibilities of his own experience and the chaos of the twentieth-century human condition, he must, in some sense, invent his own peculiar form. If he attempts to employ the traditional story-telling forms . . . he will run an overwhelming danger of accepting some of the sureties of the past inherent in the form, and, consequently, of dissipating into the mood of sentimentality and the mode of melodrama. The serious modern novelist is thus obliged to plunge into the abyss of value-creation, and his resultant novel, if successful, will necessarily communicate reflexively and symbolically [that is, without direct authorial statement of the values on which the work depends]. And if he is successful in crystallizing his alienation in an aesthetically satisfying metaphor, the chances are excellent that his work will be politely ignored by the mass audience" (p. 424).

facing the presumed decline of consensus in this positive way. The philosophical obstacle at its most destructive is nihilism, with the temptations to subjectivism or even solipsism that it always brings in its train. If the novelist really believes that there is no objective meaning to existence, then his only motive for writing is that he wants to write—a motive that is no better and no worse in the ultimate scheme than would be the motive of a Hitler, or, let us say, of a scrawler of graffiti. To worry about the reader would be absurd in a genuinely absurd universe.

Most so-called nihilisms stop far short, however, of this complete negation; almost all writers think there is some meaning, at least in the act of artistic creation. The more common philosophical assumption of unphilosophical writers since Kant has been a kind of subjective art-ism: there is value, but it is only what the artist creates out of the chaos.

Now it is possible, I think, to derive even from such a position inescapable arguments in favor of the artist's making an effort to communicate his vision. But often enough it has been used in defense of an aesthetic solipsism almost as radical as would be dictated by nihilism. Dujardin, whom Joyce claimed as the father of stream-of-consciousness technique, said that "the whole of reality consists in the clear or confused consciousness one has of it." And he quotes Joyce with approval as saying that "the soul, in one sense, is all there is."[17]

Even this position might be extended to require of the author that he do everything possible to make his consciousness of reality clear, not simply to "himself" but to that part of himself which lives in relation to a public; if a work is really clear to the author-as-reader, we might argue, it will be accessible to his proper public. But in practice it has tended to produce a pose of indifference to all readers. We need not be philistines to believe that even the purest of artists can be victimized by human pride, and we must be blind devotees of modern literature indeed to ignore the destructive, though often amusing, cultism that has marked discussions of certain novelists since Joyce.

---

[17] Edouard Dujardin, *Le monologue intérieur. Son apparition. Ses origines. Sa place dans l'œuvre de James Joyce* (Paris, 1931), p. 99.

It is hard to see how anything can be done about such a situation short of rejecting the subjectivism on which it is based. Though I cannot argue the case philosophically here, it seems clear that this one aspect of our rhetorical difficulties cannot be corrected simply by working for more intelligent discrimination in readers. The author himself must achieve a kind of objectivity far more difficult and far more profound than the "objectivity" of surface hailed in many discussions of technique. He must first plumb to universal values about which his readers can really care. But it is not enough, I suspect, that he operate on some kind of eternal ground, as recommended by our religious critics.[18] He must be sufficiently humble to seek for ways to help the reader to accept his view of that ground. The artist must in this sense be willing to be both a seer and a revelator; though he need not attempt to discover new truths in the manner of the prophet-novelists like Mann and Kafka, and though he certainly need not include explicit statement of the norms on which his work is based, he must know how to transform his private vision, made up as it often is of ego-ridden private symbols, into something that is essentially public.

It is at this point that the philosophical problem becomes a psychological problem. The artist must, like all men, wrestle constantly with the temptation of false pride. Hard as it may be for him to accept the fact, his private vision of things is not great art simply through being his. It is made into great art, if at all, only by being given an objective existence of its own—that is, by being made accessible to a public.

But of course as soon as the vision is made accessible, it subjects itself to being judged; one of the nicest of ironies is that of the writer who loses more and more stature the better we understand him, because the better we understand him the more of his egotistical weakness we see untransformed in the work.

In short, the writer should worry less about whether his *narrators* are realistic than about whether the *image he creates of himself,* his implied author, is one that his most intelligent and perceptive readers can admire. Nothing will so certainly consign a work to ultimate

[18] See Edwin Muir, "The Decline of the Novel," *Essays on Literature and Society* (London, 1949), pp. 144–50.

oblivion as an implied author who detests his readers[19] or who thinks that his work is better than it is. And nothing is so certain to lead an author into creating such a picture of himself as the effort to appear brighter, more esoteric, less commercial than he really is. The convenient but ultimately ridiculous notions that all concessions to the public are equally base, that the public itself is base, and that the author himself is not a member of "the public," can be as harmful as the desire to become a best seller at all costs.

The ultimate problem in the rhetoric of fiction is, then, that of deciding for whom the author should write. We saw earlier that to answer, "He writes for himself," makes sense only if we assume that the self he writes for is a kind of public self, subject to the limitations that other men are subject to when they come to his books. Another answer often given is that he writes for his peers. True enough. The hack is, by definition, the man who asks for responses he cannot himself respect. But no one is ever the peer of any author in the sense of needing no help in viewing the author's world. If the novelist waits passively on his pedestal for the occasional peer whose perceptions are already in harmony with his own, then it is hard to see why he should not leave everything to such readers. Why bother to write at all? If the reader were really the artist's peer in this sense, he would not need the book. In a world made up of such readers, we could stop worrying about the problem of communication entirely and simply write each his own books. But if such a world is recognized as ridiculous, however close it may seem

---

[19] The case of Henry de Montherlant is one of the most interesting in this regard. The aristocratic "ethic of quality," the "virtue of contempt," that his novels seem to advocate has led to widespread protest. Whether Montherlant himself really stands for what his characters advocate is hard to determine, but it is clear that to the extent he does so, our admiration for his work suffers. As a recent reviewer said, we cannot believe that a character like Pierre Costals in *Les jeunes filles* is intended to be sympathetic and at the same time fully respect the author. "Might it not be better," he suggests, "for M. de Montherlant's reputation as an intelligent writer if Pierre Costals were looked upon as a character who has as little of his author's complete approval as Georges Carrion, Alissa, or Jean-Baptiste Clamence?" (*T.L.S.*, January 6, 1961, p. 8). Surely it would be better. But must we not ask of *the novels themselves* whether they will justify the exoneration? In any case, the novelist's stature will rise and fall depending on what they tell us.

to some of the facts of our present one, then the novelist cannot be excused from providing the judgment upon his own materials which alone can lift them from being what Faulkner has called the mere "record of man" and turn them into the "pillars" that can help him be fully man. We may scoff at the southern gentleman's rhetoric in the Stockholm address, but the greatest living novelist means—for once—what he says.

Since the war we have seen many pleas for a return to the older, pre-Flaubertian models, not only in the matter of point of view but in the general structure and interests built into the novel.[20] The false restrictions imposed by various forms of objectivity have been attacked frequently, sometimes with great acumen based on personal experience in writing novels. But it would be a serious mistake to think that what we need is a return to Balzac, or to the English nineteenth century, or to Fielding and Jane Austen. We can be sure that traditional techniques will find new uses, just as the epistolary technique, declared dead many times over, has been revived to excellent effect again and again.[21] But what is needed is not any simple restoration of previous models, but a repudiation of all arbitrary distinctions among "pure form," "moral content," and the rhetorical means of realizing for the reader the union of form and matter. When human actions are formed to make an art work, the form that is made can never be divorced from the human meanings, including the moral judgments, that are implicit whenever human beings act. And nothing the writer does can be finally understood in isolation from his effort to make it all accessible to someone else —his peers, himself as imagined reader, his audience. The novel comes into existence *as* something communicable, and the means of communication are not shameful intrusions unless they are made with shameful ineptitude.

The author makes his readers. If he makes them badly—that is,

---

[20] See, for example, Angus Wilson, *The Observer*, April 7, 1957, p. 16: "Balzac . . . is once again one of the great masters of the traditional form to which novelists are returning. . . ."

[21] The most recent is Mark Harris' delightful comic novel, *Wake Up, Stupid* (New York, 1959).

if he simply waits, in all purity, for the occasional reader whose perceptions and norms happen to match his own, then his conception must be lofty indeed if we are to forgive him for his bad craftsmanship. But if he makes them well—that is, makes them see what they have never seen before, moves them into a new order of perception and experience altogether—he finds his reward in the peers he has created.

Bibliography

The purpose of this bibliography is neither to repeat faithfully the titles of works referred to in the text—the Index will serve for that—nor to reflect fully my own additional reading. It is rather to give some help, however incomplete, to those who want to pursue further a few of the problems that I raise. Since the study of rhetoric, as I have defined it, lies on the borderline between several disciplines, a complete bibliography might well include almost everything worthwhile ever written about fiction: about any literary technique, about the diverse human values reflected in fiction, about the shifting public norms to which different works appeal, and so on. My five sections to some extent lead outward to the many areas I cannot cover, but even so I have a strong sense of the radical incompleteness of my listings.

The Bibliography is divided into five parts: (I) "General"; (II) "Technique as Rhetoric" (A. The Telling-Showing Distinction; B. Alternatives to Reliable Narration; C. Realism and Technique); (III) "The Author's Objectivity and the 'Second Self'"; (IV) "Artistic Purity, Rhetoric, and the Audience"; and (V) "Narrative Irony and Unreliable Narrators."

I. GENERAL

1. ALDRIDGE, JOHN W. (ed.). *Critiques and Essays on Modern Fiction: 1920–1951. Representing the Achievement of Modern American and British Critics.* New York, 1952.
    Includes an indispensable bibliography.
2. ALLEN, WALTER. *The English Novel: A Short Critical History.* London, 1954. New York, 1955.
3. ———. *Reading a Novel.* London and New York, 1949.
4. ALLOTT, MIRIAM. *Novelists on the Novel.* New York, 1959.
5. ALTICK, RICHARD D. *The English Common Reader: A Social History of the Mass Reading Public, 1800–1900.* Chicago, 1957.

6. ANDERSON, SHERWOOD. *Sherwood Anderson's Notebook*. New York, 1926.

7. AUERBACH, ERICH. *Mimesis: The Representation of Reality in Western Literature*. Translated by WILLARD TRASK. Princeton, 1953. Anchor ed., Garden City, N.Y., 1957. Orig. Berne, 1946.
   A major work.

8. BAKER, ERNEST. *The History of the English Novel*. 9 vols. London, 1924–38.

9. BEACH, JOSEPH WARREN. *American Fiction: 1920–1940*. New York, 1941, 1948.

10. ———. *The Comic Spirit in George Meredith: An Interpretation*. New York, 1911.

11. ———. *The Method of Henry James*. New Haven, 1918. Enlarged ed., Philadelphia, 1954.

12. ———. *The Twentieth-Century Novel: Studies in Technique*. New York, 1932.

13. BLACKMUR, R. P. *The Lion and the Honeycomb: Essays in Solicitude and Critique*. New York, 1955. London, 1956.
   See esp. chaps. xi, xvi, and xvii. Chap. xvii, "Between the Numen and the Moha: Notes toward a Theory of Literature" (originally in *Sewanee Review*, LXII [Winter, 1954], 1–23), attempts to deal with the incalculable, inspired, "numenous" aspects of literature that I have had to slight in this book.

14. BOOTH, BRADFORD A. "The Novel," in *Contemporary Literary Scholarship*, ed. LEWIS LEARY. New York, 1958.

15. BOWEN, ELIZABETH. *Collected Impressions*. London, 1950.

16. BRICKELL, HERSCHEL (ed.). *Writers on Writing*. New York, 1949.

17. BROOKS, CLEANTH, and WARREN, ROBERT PENN. *Understanding Fiction*. New York, 1943.

18. BROWN, ROLLO WALTER (ed.). *The Writer's Art by Those Who Have Practiced It*. Cambridge, Mass., 1921.

19. COMFORT, ALEX. *The Novel and Our Time*. London, 1948.

20. COOK, ALBERT. *The Meaning of Fiction*. Detroit, 1960.

21. CRANE, RONALD S. (ed.). *Critics and Criticism: Ancient and Modern*. Chicago, 1952.

22. ———. *The Languages of Criticism and the Structure of Poetry*. Toronto, 1953.
   Though the "Chicago critics" have not written much specifically about fiction, their development of Aristotle's method, as one among many valid approaches to criticism, provides what is to me the most helpful, least limiting view of character and event—those tough realities that have never submitted happily

to merely verbal analyses. For other statements of the non-verbal basis of fictional effects, see Nos. 13, 58, 65, and 261.

23. DAICHES, DAVID. "Problems for Modern Novelists," in *Accent Anthology*. New York, 1946.

24. ———. *The Novel and the Modern World*. Chicago, 1939. Rev. ed., 1960.

25. DUHAMEL, GEORGES. *Essai sur le roman*. Paris, 1925.
   An intelligent, non-technical work, containing one of the best statements (pp. 40–41) of the danger, which threatens all "rhetorical" criticism, of reducing literary success to mere rhetorical impact or "pleasure."

26. ———. "Remarques sur les mémoires imaginaires," *Mercure de France*, Vol. XXVI (1934).

27. EDEL, LEON. *The Psychological Novel, 1900–1950*. London and Philadelphia, 1955.

28. EDEL, LEON, and RAY, GORDON. *Henry James and H. G. Wells: A Record of Their Friendship, Their Debate on the Art of Fiction, and Their Quarrel*. Urbana, 1958.

29. EDGAR, PELHAM. *The Art of the Novel: From 1700 to the Present Time*. New York, 1933.

30. FORSTER, E. M. *Aspects of the Novel*. London, 1927.

31. FRANK, JOSEPH. "Spatial Form in Modern Literature," *Sewanee Review*, LIII (Spring, Summer, and Autumn, 1945), partly reprinted as "Spatial Form in the Modern Novel" in No. 1.
   A highly influential, intelligent account of the decline of interest in temporal sequence in modern fiction; misleading, I think, in its suggestion that temporal interests are somehow inferior aesthetically to "spatial" or "architectural" interests.

32. FRIEDMAN, NORMAN. "Forms of the Plot," *Journal of General Education*, VIII (July, 1955), 241–53.

33. FRYE, NORTHROP. *The Anatomy of Criticism*. Princeton, 1957.

34. GALLISHAW, JOHN. *Advanced Problems of the Fiction Writer*. New York and London, 1931.
   The shrewdest of the how-to-write-fiction books, full of the kind of commercial calculation that leads serious authors to repudiate any concern with rhetoric. A distressing book to one who would write responsibly of the rhetoric of fiction.

35. GOODMAN, PAUL. *The Structure of Literature*. Chicago, 1954.
   Deserves much more attention than it has received.

36. GRANT, DOUGLAS. "The Novel and Its Critical Terms," *Essays in Criticism*, I (October, 1951), 421–29.

37. HAMILTON, CLAYTON. *Materials and Methods of Fiction.* Norwood, Mass., and London, 1909.

> A thoroughgoing "rhetoric of fiction" which deserves reconsideration. It includes a good catalogue of the major technical devices and an excellent discussion of what I have called unreliable narration (in an analysis of Sir Willoughby Patterne of *The Egoist*).

38. HARDY, BARBARA. *The Novels of George Eliot.* London, 1959.

39. HICKS, GRANVILLE (ed.). *The Living Novel.* New York, 1957.

> Essays by ten contemporary American novelists, exhibiting an extremely wide range of attitudes toward the rhetoric of fiction.

40. JAMES, HENRY. *The Art of Fiction and Other Essays,* ed. MORRIS ROBERTS. New York, 1948. See Nos. 1, 43, 50, and 324–38.

41. JOHNSON, R. BRIMLEY (ed.). *Novelists on Novels: From the Duchess of Newcastle to George Eliot.* London, 1928.

42. KENNEDY, MARGARET. *The Outlaws on Parnassus.* London, 1958.

43. LEAVIS, F. R. *The Great Tradition.* London, 1948.

> Excellent readings of Jane Austen, George Eliot, Henry James, and Joseph Conrad, but seriously marred by the desire to elevate one kind of fiction above all others.

44. LEAVIS, Q. D. *Fiction and the Reading Public.* London, 1932.

45. LEGGETT, H. W. *The Idea in Fiction.* London, 1934.

> Brief but invaluable treatment of the relation of a novel's values —the author's "code"—to technique, to the reader's comprehension, and to the novelist's final achievement.

46. LERNER, LAURENCE D. *The Truest Poetry.* London, 1959.

47. LEVIN, HARRY. "The Novel," in *Dictionary of World Literature,* ed. JOSEPH SHIPLEY. New York, 1943.

48. LEWIS, R. W. B. *The Picaresque Saint: Representative Figures in Contemporary Fiction.* New York, 1959.

49. LIDDELL, ROBERT. *A Treatise on the Novel.* London, 1947.

50. LUBBOCK, PERCY. *The Craft of Fiction.* London, 1921.

> The best introduction to James and his influence on technique.

51. LUKÁCS, GYÖRGY. *Studies in European Realism: A Sociological Survey of the Writings of Balzac, Stendhal, Zola, Tolstoy, Gorki, and Others.* Translated by EDITH BONE. London, 1950.

52. MCCARTHY, MARY. "The Fact in Fiction," *Partisan Review,* XXVII (Summer, 1960), 438–58.

> The true novel, defined as a long prose work telling a story of "real life," depends on facts. It began with the *Decameron* and is now probably dying.

53. McKEON, RICHARD. "The Philosophic Bases of Art and Criticism," in No. 21. First published, *Modern Philology*, XLI–XLII (November, 1943, and February, 1944).

The fullest statement of the critical pluralism on which this book is based.

54. McKILLOP, ALAN DUGALD. *The Early Masters of English Fiction.* Lawrence (Kan.), 1956.

The best single account of the great eighteenth-century novelists.

55. MANSFIELD, KATHERINE. *The Journal of Katherine Mansfield*, ed. J. MIDDLETON MURRY. New York and London, 1927. "Definitive Edition," 1954.

56. ———. *Novels and Novelists*, ed. J. MIDDLETON MURRY. London, 1930.

57. MENDILOW, A. A. *Time and the Novel.* London and New York, 1952.

58. MUDRICK, MARVIN. "Character and Event in Fiction," *Yale Review,* L (Winter, 1961), 202–18.

"The unit of fiction is the event," not the word or poetic phrase.

59. MUIR, EDWIN. *The Structure of the Novel.* London, 1928. New York, 1929.

60. MULLER, H. J. *Modern Fiction: A Study of Values.* New York, 1937.

Worthwhile insights about values, thrown to waste, as it were, for lack of a method for dealing with the techniques and ironies of modern fiction.

61. O'CONNOR, WILLIAM VAN (ed.). *Forms of Modern Fiction: Essays Collected in Honor of Joseph Warren Beach.* Minneapolis, 1948.

62. PERKINS, MAXWELL E. *Editor to Author: The Letters of Maxwell E. Perkins*, ed. JOHN HALL WHEELOCK. New York and London, 1950.

63. PEYRE, HENRI. *Writers and Their Critics: A Study of Misunderstanding.* Ithaca, N.Y., 1944.

64. RADER, MELVIN (ed.). *A Modern Book of Aesthetics.* Rev. ed., New York, 1952.

On problem of aesthetic distance, see selections by Munsterberg, Bullough, Ortega y Gasset, Worringer, and Vernon Lee.

65. RAHV, PHILIP. "Fiction and the Criticism of Fiction," *Kenyon Review*, XVIII (Spring, 1956), 276–99.

66. RANSOM, JOHN CROWE. "The Understanding of Fiction," *Kenyon Review*, XII (Spring, 1950), 189–218.

67. RATHBURN, ROBERT C., and STEINMANN, MARTIN, JR. (eds.). *From Jane Austen to Joseph Conrad.* Minneapolis, 1958.

68. RICKWORD, C. H. "A Note on Fiction," in No. 61, pp. 294–305.

69. SIMON, IRÈNE. *Formes du roman anglais de Dickens à Joyce.* ("Bi-

bliothèque de la Faculté de Philosophie et Lettres de l'Université de Liège," Fascicule CXVIII), 1949.

Three forms distinguished: epic (Fielding, Dickens), dramatic (Eliot, James), and lyric (Joyce, Woolf), the triumph of the latter being a triumph of subjectivism, relativism, and irrationality. Good bibliography.

70. SNOW, C. P. "Science, Politics, and the Novelist," *Kenyon Review*, XXIII (Winter, 1961), 1–17.

Another voice in the mounting chorus of protests against arbitrary restrictions imposed upon the novel.

71. STANG, RICHARD. *The Theory of the Novel in England, 1850–1870.* New York, 1959.

A systematic, impressive study uncovering "modern" doctrines about fiction in forgotten publications before James.

72. TILLYARD, E. M. W. *The Epic Strain in the English Novel.* London, 1958.

A defense of the reality of genres—particularly the epic—and of their usefulness to criticism. The method of definition, based on one quality only, leads to some awkward acrobatics.

73. WARREN, AUSTIN, and WELLEK, RENÉ. *Theory of Literature.* New York, 1949.

See esp. "The Nature and Modes of Fiction" and Bibliography.

74. WATT, IAN. *The Rise of the Novel: Studies in Defoe, Richardson and Fielding.* Berkeley, 1957.

75. WEST, RAY B., JR., and STALLMAN, R. W. *The Art of Modern Fiction.* New York, 1949.

See also *College English*, XII (1951), 193–203.

76. WHARTON, EDITH. *The Writing of Fiction.* New York and London, 1925.

77. WINTERS, YVOR. "Problems for the Modern Critic of Literature," *Hudson Review*, IX (Autumn, 1956), 325–86.

Some fundamental questions about the effect of various types of literary structure on the quality of what a given character can be allowed to speak at a given moment.

78. *Writers at Work: The Paris Review Interview.* London, 1958.

Wonderfully diverse statements, by Forster, Mauriac, Cary, Faulkner, and twelve other novelists, on the nature, purpose, and techniques of fiction. No agreement about proper attitude toward audience or about artistic status of rhetoric.

79. ZABEL, M. D. *Craft and Character: Texts, Methods, and Vocation in Modern Fiction.* New York, 1957.

80. ZOLA, ÉMILE. *The Experimental Novel, and Other Essays.* Translated by BELLE M. SHERMAN. New York, 1893.

II. TECHNIQUE AS RHETORIC

A. THE TELLING-SHOWING DISTINCTION, THE AUTHOR'S VOICE AND RELIABLE NARRATION

In addition to the following, see Nos. 1, 4, 7 (pp. 484–85), 8 (Vol. VIII, chaps. vii–ix), 11, 12, 35, 37 (pp. 131 ff.), 41 (entries on Mac-Kenzie, Defoe, Richardson, Fielding, and Scott), 50, 54, 67, and 71 (pp. 91–111). The best bibliography is in No. 113. By far the most important single body of theory is contained in criticism by and about Henry James (see Nos. 40, 43, 50, and 324–38). Recent discussions that have given me most help are Nos. 113, 124, 157, and 165.

81. AMES, VAN METER. *Aesthetics of the Novel.* Chicago, 1928, pp. 177–93.

> "*The Nigger of the 'Narcissus'* . . . seems more true . . . because in writing it Conrad . . . abandoned the method of the omniscient author for that of the personal author."

82. ANON. "Orley Farm," *National Review*, XVI (January, 1863), 27–40. Cited in Stang, No. 71, pp. 95–96.

> Thackeray compared unfavorably with Trollope, who more consistently obeys "the wholesome rule of impersonality"; "the author is for the most part kept well out of sight. . . ." Thackeray does not "scruple to stop at every convenient point . . . to indulge in a few personal confidences, and enunciate . . . views about . . . the world in general."

83. ANON. "Novels by the Authoress of John Halifax," *North British Review*, XXIX (November, 1858), 466–80. In No. 71, p. 95.

> "There can be no doubt that the interest is more intense, where the tale does not in any way introduce the writer's thoughts or comments upon it."

84. ANON. "Two New Novels," *Spectator*, XXXV (Dec. 27, 1862), 1447–48. In No. 71, p. 96.

> The author should make "his *dramatis personae* develop their own characters in a legitimate and effective manner in the course of the story." Many similar quotations from periodicals published between 1850 and 1870 can be found in Stang.

85. ARISTOTLE. *Poetics.* Chaps. xiv, xviii, and xxiv.
86. ARNOLD, MATTHEW. "Preface" to *Poems* (1st ed., 1853).
87. BENNETT, JOAN. *George Eliot: Her Mind and Her Art.* London, 1948. Esp. p. 106.

88. BENTLEY, PHYLLIS. *Some Observations on the Art of Narrative.* London, 1946.

An excellent little book. The art of narrative consists of the proper combination of three techniques: scene, description, and summary. Woolf, Joyce, and Richardson destroyed the previously maintained combination of these three. But summary will necessarily come back into its own.

89. BLACKMUR, R. P. "The Loose and Baggy Monsters of Henry James," in No. 13.

90. BOOTH, BRADFORD. *Anthony Trollope: Aspects of His Life and Art.* Bloomington, 1958. Esp. p. 178.

91. ———. "Form and Technique in the Novel," in *The Reinterpretation of Victorian Literature,* ed. JOSEPH E. BAKER. Princeton, 1950. Esp. pp. 79, 95.

92. BOWEN, ELIZABETH. *Collected Impressions.* London, 1950. Esp. "Notes on Writing a Novel," pp. 249–63.

93. BROOKE-ROSE, CHRISTINE. "The Vanishing Author," *Observer* (Feb. 12, 1961), p. 26.

An interview with Marguerite Duras, Alain Robbe-Grillet, and Nathalie Sarraute shows them agreed only on the aim to eliminate the author. Sarraute: "No author's intervention, however slight, should break the continuity of these *tropismes....*"

94. BROWN, E. K. "Two Formulas for Fiction: Henry James and H. G. Wells," *College English,* VIII (1946), 7–17.

95. [BULWER-LYTTON, EDWARD GEORGE]. "Caxtoniana." *Blackwood's Edinburgh Magazine,* XCIII (May, 1863), 558. Cited in No. 71, p. 123.

Attacks use of "rules drawn from the drama," in the name of "freedom of the novel."

96. [CHAPMAN, R. W.]. "Jane Austen's Methods," *TLS* (Feb. 9, 1922), pp. 81–82.

97. COLERIDGE, SAMUEL TAYLOR. *Essays and Lectures on Shakspeare.* London (Everyman ed.), [1907].

"The characters of the *dramatis personae,* like those in real life, are to be inferred by the reader;—they are not told to him. And . . . Shakspeare's characters, like those in real life, are very commonly misunderstood, and almost always understood by different persons in different ways" ("Recapitulation and Summary of the Characteristics of Shakspeare's Dramas," p. 55). See also "Notes on *Othello,*" pp. 172–74, and "Notes on *Tom Jones,*" p. 363.

98. COOPER, WILLIAM. "The Technique of the Novel," in *The Author*

and His Public: Problems in Communication, ed. C. V. WEDG-
WOOD. London, 1957.

99. DEL RIO, ANGEL. Introduction to Three Exemplary Novels by Unamuno. New York, 1956.

Somewhat naïvely sees Unamuno's "distinctive feature" as his
refusal to use direct, reliable commentary (p. 29).

100. DeVOTO, BERNARD. "The Invisible Novelist," Pacific Spectator, IV
(Winter, 1950), 30–45.

101. ———. The World of Fiction. New York, 1950.

The master secret of technique is authorial invisibility, which
is a royal road to the one effect all good fiction achieves: the
intense illusion of reality.

102. DICKENS, CHARLES. The Letters of Charles Dickens, ed. WALTER
DEXTER. 3 vols. London, 1938.

". . . you constantly hurry your narrative . . . by telling it . . . in
your own person, when the people should tell it and act it
for themselves" (III, 461). See also II, 436, 624, 685; III, 138,
145. Cited in Stang, No. 71.

103. DIFFENÉ, PATRICIA I. Henry James: Versuch einer Würdigung
seiner Eigenart. [Bochum, Germany], 1939.

The most thoroughgoing collection of James's pronouncements
on the value of dramatizing lucid reflectors rather than telling
directly.

104. DREW, ELIZABETH. The Modern Novel: Some Aspects of Contemporary Fiction. New York, 1926. Esp. pp. 243–62.

105. DRYDEN, JOHN. An Essay of Dramatic Poesy, London, 1668.

106. ———. "A Letter to the Honorable Sir Robert Howard," prefacing
Annus Mirabilis (1666).

It is true that Ovid achieves superior "concernment" for his
characters, by dramatizing them rather than narrating about
them in his own person. "But when action or persons are to be
described, when any such image is to be set before us, how bold,
how masterly, are the strokes of Virgil! We see the objects he
presents us with in their native figures, in their proper motions;
but so we see them as our own eyes could never have beheld
them so beautiful in themselves. We see the soul of the poet,
like that universal one of which he speaks, informing and moving through all his pictures. . . ."

107. EDEL, LEON. "Introduction," Henry James: Selected Fiction. New
York, 1953.

James's "most important innovation was to free the novel, and
the short story, of the traditionally ubiquitous and often gar-

rulous narrator who used to interpose his own personality and preachments between the story and the reader" (p. xii).

108. EMPSON, WILLIAM. "Tom Jones," *Kenyon Review*, XX (Spring, 1958), 217–49. See No. 144, below.

109. FORD, FORD MADOX. *The English Novel: From the Earliest Days to the Death of Joseph Conrad*. London, 1930.

110. ———. *Joseph Conrad: A Personal Remembrance*. London and Boston, 1924.

111. ———. "Techniques," *Southern Review*, I (July, 1935), 20–35.

112. FRIEDEMANN, KÄTE. *Die Rolle des Erzählers in der Epik*. Leipzig, 1910.
    Includes a defense of "telling."

113. FRIEDMAN, NORMAN. "Point of View in Fiction: The Development of a Critical Concept," *PMLA*, LXX (December, 1955), 1160–84.

114. GARDINER, HAROLD C. *Norms for the Novel*. New York, 1953.
    The troubles experienced by Graham Greene and by Mauriac with their Catholic readers clearly indicate that misunderstandings between authors and readers are not simply the result of decline of consensus. Authors and critics face a problem of tension between the said (or the not-said) and the shown.

115. GEROULD, GORDON HALL. *How To Read Fiction*. Princeton, 1937.
    A highly sane guide, though the "old-fashioned" critical vocabulary is sure to conceal the usefulness from some readers. See especially pp. 110, 114, 116.

116. GIBSON, WILLIAM M., and EDEL, LEON. *Howells and James, a Double Billing*. New York, 1958.

117. GORDON, CAROLINE. *How To Read a Novel*. New York, 1957.

118. GORDON, CAROLINE, and TATE, ALLEN. *The House of Fiction*. New York, 1950.
    A fine anthology, organized to present a sustained argument for the superiority of dramatic, objective techniques.

119. GRABO, CARL H. *The Technique of the Novel*. New York, 1928.
    Defends omniscient method (pp. 78, 101, etc.) while attacking its abuses, as he sees them, in Thackeray (p. 59), Eliot (p. 98–99), and others. "The philosophizing author I had begun to think old-fashioned until I happened upon it in so ultra-modern a work as Mrs. Woolf's *Jacob's Room*." A work worth reviving.

120. GREEN, HENRY. "Interview" in *Paris Review*, XIX (Summer, 1958), 60–77.
    "But if you are trying to write something . . . which is alive, of course the author must keep completely out of the picture" (p. 72).

121. GUETTI, JAMES L., JR. The Rhetoric of Joseph Conrad. ("Amherst College Honors Thesis," No. 2.) Amherst, 1960.

122. HALLIDAY, E. M. "Narrative Perspective in Pride and Prejudice," Nineteenth-Century Fiction, XV (June, 1960), 65–71.

123. HARRIS, MARK. "Easy Does It Not," in No. 39.

124. HARVEY, W. J. "George Eliot and the Omniscient Author Convention," Nineteenth-Century Fiction, XIII (September, 1958), 81–108.

125. HOGARTH, BASIL. The Technique of Novel Writing: A Practical Guide for New Authors. London, 1934.
       "Do not under any circumstances appeal to the reader, and avoid writing anything that will remind him that he is only reading a novel" (p. 70).

126. JARRETT-KERR, MARTIN. François Mauriac. Cambridge, 1954.
       "In addition to the serious flaw of 'author's intrusion' . . ." (p. 166).

127. KNIGHT, KOBOLD. A Guide to Fiction-Writing. London, 1936.

128. [LEWES, G. H.]. "The Novels of Jane Austen," Blackwood's Edinburgh Magazine, LXXXVI (July, 1859), 101–5.
       Jane Austen "seldom describes anything. . . . But instead of description, the common and easy resource of novelists, she has the rare and difficult art of dramatic presentation: instead of telling us what her characters are, and what they feel, she presents the people, and they reveal themselves" (No. 71, p. 94).

129. LIDDELL, ROBERT. Some Principles of Fiction. London, 1953. See esp. "Summary," pp. 53–69.

130. MACCARTHY, DESMOND. Criticism. London and New York, 1932. Esp. pp. 230–34.

131. MANDEL, OSCAR. "The Function of the Norm in Don Quixote," Modern Philology, LV (February, 1958), 154–63.
       Readers should make use of the author's explicit evaluation of Don Quixote.

132. MATLAW, RALPH E. The Brothers Karamazov: Novelistic Technique. The Hague, 1957.

133. MAUGHAM, W. SOMERSET. Introduction to The History of Tom Jones. Toronto, 1948.
       Maugham solves the problem of "intrusions" by the simple device of expurgation. See p. xxv.

134. MEREDITH, GEORGE. "Belles Lettres," Westminster Review, LXVII (April, 1857), 615–16.

135. MONTAGUE, C. E. A Writer's Notes on His Trade. London, 1930.

136. MORRISSETTE, BRUCE. "New Structure in the Novel: Jealousy, by

Alan Robbe-Grillet," *Evergreen Review*, No. 10 (November–December, 1959), pp. 103–7, 164–90.

"Corrupted by their reading of analytical novels, some readers will always insist that the novelist *explain* to them . . ." (p. 178).

137. MYERS, WALTER L. *The Later Realism: A Study of Characterization in the British Novel*. Chicago, 1927.

See esp. chap. v, "The Less Imageal Elements": ". . . Shall the narrative be impersonal or personal; shall the reader be left to make his own interpretation . . . or shall the author specify what the reader should feel and think?" (p. 153). ". . . This method [block comment] cannot . . . satisfy the conscientious artist . . ." (p. 154).

138. OLIVER, HAROLD J. "E. M. Forster: The Early Novels," *Critique*, I (Summer, 1957), 15–32.

139. ORTEGA Y GASSET, JOSÉ. *The Dehumanization of Art*. Translated by WILLARD TRASK. Princeton, 1948. Anchor ed., Garden City, N.Y., 1956.

"Any reference, allusion, narration only emphasizes the absence of what it alludes to" (p. 58).

140. PARKS, EDD WINFIELD. "Trollope and the Defense of Exegesis," *Nineteenth-Century Fiction*, VII (March, 1953), 265–71.

141. ———. "Exegesis in Austen's Novels," *South Atlantic Quarterly*, LI (January, 1952), 102–19.

142. PETER, JOHN. "Joyce and the Novel," *Kenyon Review*, XVIII (Autumn, 1956), 619–32.

One of the most intelligent arguments for the importance of the author's disappearance in the drive for a "developed style." Avoids some of the simple-minded reductions I have described.

143. PLATO. *The Republic* Book iii. secs. 392D–394C.

144. RAWSON, C. J. "Professor Empson's *Tom Jones*," *Notes and Queries*, N.S. VI (November, 1959), 400–404.

145. ROVIT, EARL H. "The Ambiguous Modern Novel," *Yale Review* (Spring, 1960), pp. 413–24.

146. SAINTSBURY, GEORGE. "Technique," *Dial*, LXXX (April, 1926), 273–78.

147. SARTRE, JEAN PAUL. *Literary and Philosophical Essays*. [Extracts from "Situations I and III."] Translated by ANNETTE MICHELSON. London, 1955. Esp. "François Mauriac and Freedom," originally published as a review of Mauriac's *La fin de la nuit*, in *Nouvelle Revue Française* (February, 1939).

148. ———. *What Is Literature?* [An extract from "Situations II."] Translated by BERNARD FRECHTMAN. London, 1950.

149. SCHORER, MARK. "Technique as Discovery," *Hudson Review*, I (Spring, 1948), 67–87.
Reprinted widely (e.g., in Nos. 1 and 61).

150. SCRUTTON, MARY. "Addiction to Fiction," *The Twentieth Century*, CLIX (April, 1956), 363–73.

151. SENIOR, NASSAU. "Thackeray's Works," *Edinburgh Review*, XCIX (January, 1854), 196–243. Cited in No. 71, p. 96.

152. SHANNON, EDGAR F., JR. "*Emma*: Character and Construction," *PMLA*, LXXI (September, 1956), 637–50.

153. SHERWOOD, IRMA Z. "The Novelists as Commentators," in *The Age of Johnson: Essays Presented to Chauncey Brewster Tinker*, ed. by F. W. HILLES. New Haven, 1949.

154. SOSNOSKY, THEODOR VON. "Wie man Romane schriebt," *Die Gegenwart* (Berlin), LIX (June 1, 1901), 345–48.

155. STANZEL, FRANZ. *Die Typischen Erzählsituationen im Roman, dargestellt an Tom Jones, Moby-Dick, The Ambassadors, Ulysses, u.a.* Vienna, 1955.
Attempts a "*Typologie des Romans*," with specified narrative manners for each type. Unfortunately the classification is much too simple, with three types and three manners: "*auktorial*," "*ich-Roman*," and "*personale Roman*."

156. STEINER, F. G. "A Preface to *Middlemarch*," *Nineteenth-Century Fiction*, IX (1955), 262–79.
Sees a "total lack of technique on George Eliot's part. . . . By interfering constantly in the narration George Eliot attempts to persuade us of what should be artistically evident. . . . It should be noted that omniscience is an author's most lazy approach and that personal interference in the action must be compared to what occurs in a Chinese theatre where the manager comes on during the play to change props" (271–75).

157. STEINMANN, MARTIN, JR. "The Old Novel and the New," in No. 67.
Though I did not read this article until after my main draft was completed, I could happily incorporate most of it as preface or summary.

158. STEPHEN, LESLIE. *Hours in a Library*. New York, 1904.
"We are indeed told dogmatically that a novelist should never indulge in little asides to the reader. Why not? One main advantage of the novel is precisely that it leaves room for a freedom in such matters. . . . A child . . . dislikes to have the illusion broken. . . . But the attempt to produce such illusions is really unworthy of work intended for full-grown readers" (Vol. IV, pp. 150–52). Cited in No. 71, pp. 97–98.

159. STERN, RICHARD G. "Proust and Joyce Underway: Jean Santeuil and Stephen Hero," *Kenyon Review*, XVIII (Summer, 1956), 486–96.

160. STEVENSON, ROBERT LOUIS. "A Humble Remonstrance," in *Memories and Portraits*. London and New York, 1887, pp. 275–99.

161. TATE, ALLEN. "The Post of Observation in Fiction," *Maryland Quarterly*, II (1944), 61–64.

162. ———. "Techniques of Fiction," *Sewanee Review*, LII (1944), 210–25. Reprinted in Nos. 1 and 61; also in Tate's *On the Limits of Poetry*. New York, 1948.

163. THACKERAY, WILLIAM MAKEPEACE. "De Finibus," *Cornhill Magazine* (August, 1862). Reprinted in No. 18, pp. 263–74.

 "Among the sins of commission which novel-writers not seldom perpetrate, is the sin of grandiloquence, or tall-talking. . . . Nay . . . perhaps of all the novel-spinners now extant, the present speaker is the most addicted to preaching. Does he not stop perpetually in his story and begin to preach to you? When he ought to be engaged with business, is he not forever taking the Muse by the sleeve, and plaguing her with some of his cynical sermons? . . . I tell you I would like to be able to write a story which should show no egotism whatever—in which there should be no reflections, no cynicism, no vulgarity (and so forth), but an incident in every other page, a villain, a battle, a mystery in every chapter" (p. 271).

164. TILFORD, JOHN E., JR. "James the Old Intruder," *Modern Fiction Studies*, IV (Summer, 1958), 157–64.

165. TILLOTSON, KATHLEEN. *The Tale and the Teller*. London, 1959.

166. TINDALL, WILLIAM YORK. "Apology for Marlow," in No. 67.

167. VAN GHENT, DOROTHY. *The English Novel, Form and Function*. New York, 1953.

168. WALZEL, OSKAR. *Das Wortkunstwerk: Mittelseiner Erforschung*. Leipzig, 1926.

 As early as 1915, Walzel dealt fully with the arguments for objective narration, and his defense of the author's voice has never, it seems to me, been answered, or even honestly confronted. See, in this volume, "*Objektive Erzählung*" (pp. 182–206), esp. the "Afterword" (1925) on Thomas Mann's narrative methods; also "*Von 'erlebter Rede'*" and "*Die Kunstform der Novelle*" in same volume. Walzel cites two works by Spielhagen that I have been unable to consult: "Neuen Beiträge zur Theorie und Technik der Epik und Dramatik" (Leipzig, 1898) and "Beiträgen zur Theorie und Technik des Romans," (Leipzig, 1883). It is interesting that at a time when James was laboring objective theories based in part on analogies with painting, Spielhagen and other Germans were saying, "Bilde, Künstler, rede nicht!"

169. ———. *Ricarda Huch: Ein Wort über Kunst des Erzählens.* Leipzig, 1916. See esp. chap. i: "Bekennertum und künstlerische Objektivität."

170. WELLEK, RENÉ. "Henry James's Literary Theory and Criticism," *American Literature,* XXX (November, 1958), 293–321. See also No. 73.

171. WILLIAMS, RAYMOND. *Reading and Criticism.* London, 1950.

172. WRIGHT, ANDREW H. *Jane Austen's Novels: A Study in Structure.* New York and London, 1953.

B. SOME ALTERNATIVES TO RELIABLE TELLING

For works on symbolism, see No. 1, pp. 570–72. For discussions of point of view as evaluation, good places to start are No. 113 (esp. footnotes 9, 11, and 12) and No. 71, pp. 107–11. Most of the works listed above which attack reliable narration or commentary have something to say about the uses of controlled point of view. It is probably true that most of the discussions of technique in this century have been mainly concerned with this one important but partial subject; see, for example, the bibliography in No. 1, pp. 567–69. In general I give only the affirmative analyses here, saving the complaints and disputes for Section V, B, below on unreliable narration. Works dealing mainly with point of view as a road to realism I save for II, C.

173. ADAMS, HAZARD. "Joyce Cary's Three Speakers," *Modern Fiction Studies,* V (Summer, 1959), 108–20.

174. BECK, WARREN. "Conception and Technique," *College English,* XI (March, 1950), 308–17.

175. BLACK, F. G. *The Technique of Letter Fiction in English: 1740–1800.* Cambridge, Mass., 1933.

176. ———. *The Epistolary Novel in the Late Eighteenth Century.* Eugene, Ore., 1940.

177. BOWLING, LAWRENCE EDWARD. "What Is the Stream of Consciousness Technique?" *PMLA,* LXV (June, 1950), 333–45.

178. BROWN, E. K. *Rhythm in the Novel.* Toronto, 1950.

179. DUJARDIN, ÉDOUARD. *Le monologue intérieur. Son apparition. Ses origines. Sa place dans l'œuvre de James Joyce.* Paris, 1931.

180. FORSTREUTER, KURT. *Die deutsche Icherzählung: Eine Studie zu ihrer Geschichte und Technik.* Berlin, 1924.
　　Useful collection of first-person effects, in spite of naïve identification of authors with narrators: "Die Icherzählung ist . . .

eine epische Dichtung, in welcher der Erzähler eigene Erlebnisse vorträgt" (p. 40).

181. FRIEDMAN, MELVIN. *Stream of Consciousness: A Study in Literary Method.* New Haven, 1955.

182. GREEN, HENRY. "Interview," *Paris Review,* No. 19 (Summer, 1958), pp. 60–77.

"What one writes has to be all things to all men. If one isn't enough to enough readers they stop reading" (p. 67). "What after all is one to do with oneself in print? Does the reader feel a dread of anything? Do they all feel a dread for different things? Do they all love differently? Surely the only way to cover all these readers is to use what is called symbolism" (p. 75).

183. HATCHER, ANNA GRANVILLE. "Voir as a Modern Novelistic Device," *Philological Quarterly,* XXIII (October, 1944), 354–74.

184. HOLLOWAY, JOHN. *The Victorian Sage: Studies in Argument.* London, 1953.

For students of fiction, the title is misleading; the book is in part a study of argument in narrative, and some of the best points are about the rhetoric of such "sages" as George Eliot. An important work, in every respect.

185. HUMPHREY, ROBERT. *Stream of Consciousness in the Modern Novel.* Berkeley, 1954.

186. KERR, ELIZABETH M. "Joyce Cary's Second Trilogy," *University of Toronto Quarterly,* XXIX (April, 1960), 310–25.

187. LOOMIS, C. C., JR. "Structure and Sympathy in Joyce's 'The Dead,' " *PMLA,* LXXV (March, 1960), 149–51.

188. MARTIN, HAROLD C. (ed.). *Style in Prose Fiction* ("English Institute Essays," 1958.) New York, 1959.

189. MATLAW, RALPH E. "Structure and Integration in *Notes from Underground.*" *PMLA,* LXXIII (March, 1958), 101–9.

190. NEUBERT, ALBRECHT. *Die Stilformen der "erlebten Rede" im neueren englischen Roman.* Halle, 1957.

Contains a good bibliography.

191. POUILLON, JEAN. "Les règles du je," *Temps Modernes,* XII (April, 1957), 1591–98.

192. ROPER, ALAN H. "The Moral and Metaphorical Meaning of *The Spoils of Poynton,*" *American Literature,* XXXII (May, 1960), 182–96.

The novel can be deciphered through three patterns of imagery: battle, storm, and flight.

193. SCHORER, MARK. "Fiction and the 'Analogical Matrix,' " in No. 1.

194. SINGER, GODFREY FRANK. *The Epistolary Novel: Its Origin, Development, Decline, and Residuary Influence.* Philadelphia, 1933.

195. SOSNOSKY, THEODOR VON. "Der 'Ich' im Roman," in No. 154, pp. 347–48.

196. STEINMANN, MARTIN, JR. "The Symbolism of T. F. Powys," *Critique,* I (Summer, 1957), 49–63.

197. STONE, HARRY. "Dickens and Interior Monologue," *Philological Quarterly,* XXXVIII (January, 1959), 52–65.

198. STRUVE, GLEB. "Monologue intérieur: The Origins of the Formula and the First Statement of Its Possibilities," *PMLA,* LXIX (December, 1954), 1101–11.
    Tolstoy was the first author to use the technique consciously; Chernyshevski's appreciation of Tolstoy's use was the first critical notice given to the device.

199. TUVE, ROSEMOND. *Elizabethan and Metaphysical Imagery: Renaissance Poetic and Twentieth-Century Critics.* Chicago, 1947.

200. ———. *Images and Themes in Five Poems by Milton.* Cambridge, Mass., and London, 1957.

201. ———. "A Name To Resound for Ages," *Listener* (Aug. 28, 1958), pp. 312–13.
    On "the evaluative functioning of figurative speech."

202. VICKERY, OLGA W. "*The Sound and the Fury:* A Study in Perspective," *PMLA,* LXIX (December, 1954), 1017–37.
    "To use Dilsey as a point of view character would be to destroy her efficacy as the ethical norm, for that would give us but one more splinter of the truth confined and conditioned by the mind which grasped it" (p. 1020).

203. WEATHERHEAD, A. KINGSLEY. "Structure and Texture in Henry Green's Latest Novels," *Accent,* XIX (Spring, 1959), 112–22.

204. WENGER, JARED. "Speed as Technique in the Novels of Balzac," *PMLA,* LV (1940), 241–52.

205. WEST, RAY B., JR. "Katherine Anne Porter: Symbol and Theme in 'Flowering Judas,'" in No. 1. Originally published in *Accent,* (Spring, 1947).

206. WICKARDT, WOLFGANG. *Die Formen der Perspektive in Charles Dickens Romanen: ihr sprachlicher Ausdruck und ihre strukturelle Bedeutung.* Berlin, 1933.

207. ZELLER, HILDEGARD. *Die Ich-Erzählung im englischen Roman.* Breslau, 1933.
    Full of useful information; unfortunately, the facts are never adequately related to artistic function.

C. Realism, Distance from the Real, and Technique

No. 1 has a brief bibliography of "Realism and Naturalism," pp. 569–70. No. 71 lists, in chap. iv, a great many mid-Victorian discussions. No. 209 lists and discusses some of the important French statements on realism before 1850. A full bibliography of "realism and technique" would no doubt cover the whole history of criticism. The following are a few titles which, along with Nos. 7, 12, 51, 52, 74, 100, 109, 113, 124, 137, 139, 145, 147, 148, 260, 324, and 325, I have found most helpful or significant.

208. BECKER, GEORGE J. "Realism: An Essay in Definition," *Modern Language Quarterly*, X (June, 1949), 184–97.

209. BORGERHOFF, E. B. O. "*Réalisme* and Kindred Words: Their Use as Terms of Literary Criticism in the First Half of the Nineteenth Century," *PMLA*, LIII (September, 1938), 837–43.

210. BRISSENDEN, R. F. *Samuel Richardson* ("Writers and Their Work," No. 101). London, 1958.
    Contains a good discussion of Richardson's theories of epistolary technique as a road to vivid realistic immediacy.

211. BROD, MAX. "Flaubert und die Methoden des Realismus," *Die Neue Rundschau*, LXI (1950), 603–12.

212. BULLOUGH, EDWARD. " 'Psychical Distance' as a Factor in Art and an Aesthetic Principle," *British Journal of Psychology*, V (1912–13), 87–118. Reprinted in No. 64.

213. CARY, JOYCE. *Art and Reality*. Cambridge, 1958.

214. CONRAD, JOSEPH. Preface to *The Nigger of the "Narcissus."* Widely reprinted; e.g., in *Conrad's Prefaces to His Work*, ed. EDWARD GARNETT. London, 1937.

215. COOK, ALBERT. "The Beginning of Fiction: Cervantes," *Journal of Aesthetics and Art Criticism*, XVII (June, 1959), 463–72.
    Just as Watt finds the beginning of "the novel" in Defoe on the basis of an approach to reality, Cook finds the beginning of "fiction" in Cervantes because Cervantes for the first time sees reality as not fixed but in process.

216. CURTIS, JEAN-LOUIS. *Haute École*. Paris, 1950.
    Indispensable.

217. DAVIS, ROBERT GORHAM. "The Sense of the Real in English Fiction," in No. 224.

218. DECKER, CLARENCE R. "The Aesthetic Revolt against Naturalism in Victorian Criticism," *PMLA*, LIII (September, 1938), 844–56.

219. FLAUBERT, GUSTAVE. See No. 239 for excellent bibliography of Flaubert's varying attitudes toward realism. A carefully selected

bibliography is included in No. 235: No. 7 is helpful on Flaubert's realism, especially in chap. xviii. See also James, No. 221, and the "critical introduction" James wrote for the William Heinemann edition of *Madame Bovary* (1902, 1923, etc.).

220. HYDE, WILLIAM J. "George Eliot and the Climate of Realism," *PMLA*, LXXII (March, 1957), 147–64.

221. JAMES, HENRY. *French Poets and Novelists*. London, 1884.
Almost anything James wrote about fiction could be listed here, but the essay on "Gustave Flaubert" in this volume is perhaps most representative.

222. JOHNSON, SAMUEL. "Preface to Shakespeare." 1766.
Indispensable on dramatic illusion, its values and limitations.

223. KRIEGER, MURRAY. *The New Apologists for Poetry*. Minneapolis, 1956.

224. LEVIN, HARRY (ed.). "A Symposium on Realism," *Comparative Literature*, Vol. III (Summer, 1951).

225. ———. "What Is Realism?" *Ibid.*, pp. 193–99.

226. MCKEON, RICHARD. "The Concept of Imitation in Antiquity," in No. 21.

227. O'CONNOR, FRANK. *The Mirror in the Roadway*. London, 1957.

228. PATTERSON, CHARLES I. "Coleridge's Conception of Dramatic Illusion in the Novel," *ELH*, XVIII (June, 1951), 123–37.
Sees Coleridge as on the side of modern truth and light, since his basic judgment would be that all good novels must produce "dramatic illusion."

229. REYNOLDS, SIR JOSHUA. "*Discourse XIII*" (December, 1786).
On the limits of the "natural" in representation. "The true test . . . is not solely whether the production is a true copy of nature but whether it answers the end of art, which is to produce a pleasing effect upon the mind."

230. RICHARDSON, SAMUEL. See No. 210.

231. ROBINSON, E. ARTHUR. "Meredith's Literary Theory and Science: Realism versus the Comic Spirit," *PMLA*, LIII (September, 1938), 857–68.

232. SALVAN, ALBERT J. "L'Essence du réalisme français," in No. 224, pp. 218–33.

233. SINCLAIR, MAY. Introduction to *Pointed Roofs* by Dorothy Richardson. London, 1919.
"Obviously, she must not interfere; she must not analyse or comment or explain. Rather less obviously, she must not tell a story, or handle a situation or set a scene; she must avoid drama as she avoids narration. . . . She must be Miriam Henderson.

> She must not know or divine anything that Miriam does not know or divine. . . . They [the characters] are presented to us in the same vivid but fragmentary way in which they appeared to Miriam, the fragmentary way in which people appear to most of us" (pp. viii–ix).

234. STOLL, ELMER EDGAR. *From Shakespeare to Joyce. Authors and Critics; Literature and Life.* New York, 1944.

235. THORLBY, ANTHONY. *Gustave Flaubert and the Art of Realism.* London, 1956.

236. WOOLF, VIRGINIA. *The Common Reader.* London, 1925.

237. ———. *The Second Common Reader.* London, 1932.

238. YOUNG, EDWARD. *Conjectures on Original Composition, In a Letter to the Author of* Sir Charles Grandison. London, 1759.

> "In the theatre, as in life, delusion is the charm; and we are undelighted, the first moment we are undeceived."

III. THE AUTHOR'S OBJECTIVITY AND THE "SECOND SELF"

In addition to the following, see Nos. 4, 26, 27, 37, 39, 45, 55, 78, 149, 165, 169, 216, 219.

239. BONWIT, MARIANNE. *Gustave Flaubert et le principe d'impassibilité.* ("University of California Publications in Modern Philology," Vol. XXXIII, No. 4, pp. 263–420). Berkeley, 1950.

> An invaluable study, with helpful bibliography.

240. CHEKHOV, ANTON. *Letters on the Short Story, the Drama and Other Literary Topics.* Selected and edited by LOUIS S. FRIEDLAND. New York, 1924.

241. COLEY, WILLIAM B. "The Background of Fielding's Laughter," *ELH,* XXVI (June, 1959), 229–52.

> Includes a good analysis of the changes in Fielding's narrators from book to book.

242. CRUTTWELL, PATRICK. "Makers and Persons," *Hudson Review,* XII (Winter, 1959–60), 487–507.

243. ELLMANN, RICHARD. *Yeats: The Man and the Masks.* New York, 1948. London, 1949.

244. ———. *James Joyce.* New York, 1959.

245. EWALD, WILLIAM BRAGG, JR. *The Masks of Jonathan Swift.* Oxford and Cambridge, Mass., 1954.

246. FARBER, MARJORIE. "Subjectivity in Modern Fiction," *Kenyon Review,* VII (Autumn, 1945), 645–52.

247. GIBSON, WALKER. "Authors, Speakers, Readers, and Mock Readers," *College English,* XI (February, 1950), 265–69.

248. KAHNERT, WALTER. *Objektivismus: Gedanken über einen neuen Literaturstil.* Berlin, 1946.

249. KEATS, JOHN. *The Poetical Works and Other Writings of John Keats,* ed. H. BUXTON FORMAN. Vol. VII. New York, 1939.
Keats is a major source of talk about objectivity and "negative capability." His letters and essays have been quoted again and again in support of modern theories of fiction.

250. KINGSLEY, CHARLES. *His Letters and Memories of His Life,* ed. by his Wife. 4 vols. London, 1902. First published, 1877.
"Of course it is very easy for a reviewer who disagrees with this doctrine to call it an obtrusion of the author's self; but the author's business is to see that it is just not that—to speak, if he can, the thoughts of many hearts, to put into words for his readers what they would have said for themselves if they could" (Vol. III, p. 41). Cited in No. 71, p. 99.

251. MAUPASSANT, GUY DE. "The Novel," in No. 18, pp. 198–201.
The essay from which this section on objectivity is taken was originally the Introduction to *Pierre et Jean.*

252. PACEY, DESMOND. "Flaubert and His Victorian Critics," *University of Toronto Quarterly,* XVI (October, 1946), 74–84.
A good source of early discussions of Flaubert's objectivity.

253. RAY, GORDON N. *The Buried Life: A Study of the Relation Between Thackeray's Fiction and his Personal History.* Cambridge, Mass., 1952.

254. SCHLEGEL, A. W. VON. "Shakspeare," from "Lecture XXIII," in *Lectures on Dramatic Art and Literature* (1809–11). Translated by JOHN BLACK, 1815. Revised by A. J. W. MORRISON, London, 1861.

255. SCHORER, MARK. "The Good Novelist in 'The Good Soldier,'" *Horizon,* XX (August, 1949), 132–38.

256. STOCK, IRVIN. "A View of *Wilhelm Meister's Apprenticeship,*" *PMLA,* LXXII (March, 1957), 84–103.
"Beside detachment like his [Goethe's] the famous 'objectivity' of Flaubert is a mere literary device, and a device in the service of the most transparently passionate involvement. Beside irony like his that of Flaubert seems the angry disappointment of a persistently youthful mind" (p. 100).

257. TOYNBEE, PHILIP. "The Living Dead—III: Thoughts on André Gide," *The London Magazine,* III (October, 1956), 46–53.
Attacks Gide for "gross and prejudiced intrusion" into *The Counterfeiters,* making it "simply a piece of the Journal which

lacks the Journal's truth, sincerity, and charm." Interesting example of oversimplified identification of author and narrator: "Gide is Edouard" (p. 48).

258. WEST, JESSAMYN. "The Slave Cast Out," in No. 39.

IV. ARTISTIC PURITY, RHETORIC, AND THE AUDIENCE

In addition to the following, see Nos. 5, 19, 22, 23, 24, 31, 44, 45, 46, 63, 64, 85, 98, 123, 139, 212, 219, 324, and 325.

259. ABRAMS, M. H. (ed.). *Literature and Belief*. ("English Institute Essays," 1957), New York, 1958.

260. ———. *The Mirror and the Lamp*. New York, 1953.
   The best study of the relation of neoclassical theories of poetry (i.e., imaginative literature) as imitation or rhetoric to romantic and modern theories of poetry as expression.

261. BAKER, JOSEPH E. "Aesthetic Surface in the Novel," *The Trollopian*, II (September, 1947), 91–106.
   The "aesthetic surface" of fiction is found, not in words, but in the "world" of character, event, and value "concretely represented and temporally arranged" (p. 100). Good on the false analogy of fiction with music and drama.

262. BELLOW, SAUL. "The Writer and the Audience," *Perspectives*, IX (Autumn, 1954), 99–102.

263. BURKE, KENNETH. *Counter-Statement*. Los Altos, 1953. First published, 1931. Esp. "Psychology and Form" and "Lexicon Rhetoricae."

264. ———. *The Philosophy of Literary Form*. Rev. ed., New York, 1957. First published, 1941.
   "I wonder how long it has been since a poet has asked himself: '. . . Suppose I did not simply wish to load upon the broad shoulders of the public medium my own ungainly appetites and ambition? Suppose that, gnarled as I am, I did not consider it enough simply to seek payment for my gnarledness, the establishment of communion through evils held in common? . . . How should I go about it . . . not merely to bring us most poignantly *into* hell, but also *out* again? . . . Must there not, for every flight, be also a return, before my work can be called complete as a moral act?' " (pp. 138–39).

265. COLERIDGE, SAMUEL TAYLOR. "Greek Drama," in No. 97, pp. 13–19.

266. COLLINGWOOD, R. G. *The Principles of Art*. New York, 1958. First published, 1938.

267. CROCE, BENEDETTO. *Aesthetic.* Translated by D. AINSLIE. 2d ed., London, 1922.

> One main source of attacks on rhetoric, and a cogent one indeed. Too many defenses of traditional techniques have ignored the powerful appeal of the expression theories of Collingwood and Croce.

268. ELIOT, T. S. "Hamlet and His Problems," *Athenaeum*, Sept. 26, 1919, pp. 940–41. Reprinted widely.

269. ELLISON, RALPH. "Society, Morality, and the Novel," in No. 39.

270. KEENE, DONALD. *Japanese Literature.* London, 1953. Esp. chap. iii.

271. KENNER, HUGH. *The Art of Poetry.* New York, 1959.

272. PATER, WALTER. *The Renaissance.* London, 1888.

273. POTTLE, FREDERICK A. *The Idiom of Poetry.* Ithaca, N.Y., 1941.

> The chap., "Pure Poetry in Theory and Practice," is the best treatment I know of the subject. "What kind of prosaism is acceptable and what is not? That appears to me at the moment the hardest question in theory of poetry" (p. 99). While accepting the modern achievements in "pure" poetry, Pottle destroys the notion of purity as a useful general noun in poetic criticism and concludes that the great ages in literature "are the impure ones" (p. 100).

274. POUND, EZRA. *Make It New.* London, 1934. New Haven, 1936.

275. STYRON, WILLIAM. "Interview," in No. 78.

> "Faulkner doesn't give enough help to the reader" (p. 246). "Look, there's only one person a writer should listen to, pay any attention to . . . the reader. The writer must criticize his own work as a reader. Every day I pick up the story . . . and read it through. If I enjoy it as a reader I know I'm getting along all right" (p. 249).

276. THIBAUDET, ALBERT. *Le liseur de romans.* Paris, 1925.

277. VALÉRY, PAUL. *The Art of Poetry.* Translated by DENISE FOLLIOT. New York, 1958. Esp. the chap. entitled "Pure Poetry."

278. VIVAS, ELISEO. "The Objective Correlative of T. S. Eliot," *American Bookman*, I (Winter, 1944), 7–18. Reprinted in STALLMAN, R. W. (ed.). *Critiques and Essays in Criticism: 1920–48.* New York, 1949.

279. WARREN, ROBERT PENN. "Pure and Impure Poetry," *Kenyon Review*, V (Summer, 1943), 228–54. Reprinted in STALLMAN, *op. cit.*

280. WEINBERG, BERNARD. "Robertello on the *Poetics*," in No. 21.

281. WIMSATT, W. K. *The Verbal Icon.* Lexington, Ky., 1954.

> Contains useful analyses of rhetoric of various kinds. The chap. on the "affective fallacy" (with Monroe C. Beardsley) raises

the right questions about the reader's emotions, but the conclusions offered have, like the label itself, tended to obscure a highly complicated issue.

V. NARRATIVE IRONY AND UNRELIABLE NARRATORS

A. General Discussions of Irony, Ambiguity, and Obscurity

In addition to the following, see Nos. 1, 7, 12, 17, 24, 27, 35, 37, 74, 114, 139, 145, 221, 223, 245, 255, 335, and 336.

282. Anon. "The Ethic of Quality," *TLS*, Jan. 6, 1961, p. 8.

283. Bart, B. F. "Aesthetic Distance in *Madame Bovary*," *PMLA*, LXIX (December, 1954), 1112–26.

284. Brooks, Cleanth. "Irony as a Principle of Structure," in Zabel, Morton, Dauwen. *Literary Opinion in America*. Rev. ed., New York, 1951.

285. Burke, Kenneth. "Thomas Mann and André Gide," *Bookman*, LXXI (June, 1930), 257–64. Reprinted in No. 263.

286. Crane, Ronald S. "Cleanth Brooks; or, The Bankruptcy of Critical Monism," *Modern Philology*, XLV (May, 1948), 226–45. Reprinted in No. 21.

287. Harbage, Alfred. *As They Liked It: An Essay on Shakespeare and Morality*. New York, 1947.

288. Hough, Graham. *Image and Experience: Reflections on a Literary Revolution*. London, 1960.

289. Jankélévitch, Vladimir. *L'Ironie*. Paris, 1936.
    Includes an especially useful discussion of "ironic traps."

290. Jarrell, Randall. *Poetry and the Age*. New York, 1953.

291. Knight, G. Wilson. *The Wheel of Fire*. Rev. ed., London, 1949.
    Perhaps the most influential effort to invert traditional interpretations by setting to one side explicit authorial rhetoric.

292. Knights, L. C. "Henry James and the Trapped Spectator," *Explorations: Essays in Criticism Mainly on the Literature of the Seventeenth Century*. London, 1946.

293. Langbaum, Robert. *The Poetry of Experience*. London, 1957.
    Excellent on tension between irony and sympathy in the dramatic monologue.

294. Sarton, May. "The Shield of Irony," *Nation*, April 14, 1956, pp. 314–16.

295. Sedgewick, G. G. *Of Irony, Especially in Drama*. Toronto, 1935.
    Includes a useful classification of types of irony.

296. SHARPE, ROBERT BOIES. *Irony in the Drama: An Essay on Imper-sonation, Shock, and Catharsis.* Chapel Hill, N.C., 1959.

297. SPENDER, STEPHEN. *The Creative Element: A Study of Vision, Despair and Orthodoxy among Some Modern Writers.* London, 1953.

298. THOMPSON, ALAN R. *The Dry Mock: A Study of Irony in Drama.* Berkeley, 1948.

299. TURPIN, A. R. "Jane Austen: Limitations or Defects?" *The English Review,* LXIV (January, 1937), 53–68.
     "Structural surprise" as against dramatic irony: an important essay that, to my mind, underrates Jane Austen while raising general questions that are too often ignored.

B. SOME TROUBLES WITH UNRELIABILITY: DISPUTES, REVALUATIONS, AND CONFESSIONS

Sherwood Anderson

300. RINGE, DONALD A. "Point of View and Theme in 'I Want To Know Why,' " *Critique,* III (Spring–Fall, 1959), 24–29.
     Brooks and Warren are seriously mistaken in taking the boy's judgments as "true and valid ones" (p. 24).

Jane Austen

301. HARDING, D. W. "Regulated Hatred: An Aspect of the Work of Jane Austen," *Scrutiny,* VIII (June, 1939–March, 1940), 346–62.

Emily Brontë

302. BRICK, ALLAN R. "*Wuthering Heights:* Narrators, Audience, and Message," *College English,* XXI (November, 1959), 80–86. See also No. 149.

303. HAFLEY, JAMES. "The Villain in *Wuthering Heights,*" *Nineteenth-Century Fiction,* XIII (December, 1958), 199–215.

Albert Camus

304. BRÉE, GERMAINE. *Camus.* New Brunswick, N.J., 1959.

305. VIGGIANI, CARL A. "Camus' *L'Étranger,*" *PMLA,* LXXI (December, 1956), 865–87.

Cervantes

306. AUDEN, W. H. "The Ironic Hero: Some Reflections on *Don Quix-ote,*" *Horizon,* XX (August, 1949), 86–93. See also No. 131.

Chaucer

307. BLOOMFIELD, MORTON W. "Distance and Predestination in 'Troilus and Criseyde,'" *PMLA*, LXXII (March, 1957), 14–26.
308. DONALDSON, E. TALBOT. "Chaucer the Pilgrim," *PMLA*, LXIX (September, 1954), 928–36.
    Chaucer belongs to "a very old—and very new—tradition of the fallible first person singular."
309. MAJOR, JOHN M. "The Personality of Chaucer the Pilgrim," *PMLA*, LXXV (June, 1960), 160–62.
    A reply to Donaldson.
310. WOOLF, ROSEMARY. "Chaucer as a Satirist in the General Prologue to the *Canterbury Tales*," *Critical Quarterly*, I (Summer, 1959), 150–57.

Joseph Conrad

311. TINDALL, WILLIAM YORK. "Apology for Marlow," in No. 67.

Fëdor Dostoevski

312. FRANK, JOSEPH. "Nihilism and *Notes from Underground*," *Sewanee Review*, LXIX (January–March, 1961), 1–33.

James T. Farrell

313. WALCUTT, CHARLES CHILD. "Review" of *Bernard Clare*, *Accent* (Summer, 1946), p. 267.

William Faulkner

314. FREY, LEONARD H. "Irony and Point of View in 'That Evening Sun,'" *Faulkner Studies*, II (Autumn, 1953), 33–40.
315. WASIOLEK, EDWARD. "*As I Lay Dying*: Distortion in the Slow Eddy of Current Opinion," *Critique*, III (Spring–Fall, 1959), 15–23.

Ford Madox Ford

316. HAFLEY, JAMES. "The Moral Structure of 'The Good Soldier,'" *Modern Fiction Studies*, V (Summer, 1959), 121–28.
317. SCHORER, MARK. "The Good Novelist in 'The Good Soldier,'" *Horizon*, XX (August, 1949), 132–38.
    "In every case the 'fact' is somewhere between the mere social convention and that different order of convention which the distorted understanding of the narrator imposes upon them" (p. 135).

Henry Green

318. LABOR, EARLE. "Henry Green's Web of Loving," Critique, IV (Fall–Winter, 1960–61), 29–40.

Nathaniel Hawthorne

319. CREWS, FREDERICK C. "A New Reading of The Blithedale Romance," American Literature, XXIX (May, 1957), 147–70.
320. DAVIDSON, FRANK. "Toward a Re-evaluation of The Blithedale Romance," New England Quarterly, XXV (September, 1952), 374–83.
321. HEDGES, WILLIAM L. "Hawthorne's Blithedale: The Function of the Narrator," Nineteenth-Century Fiction, XIV (March, 1960), 303–16.
322. WAGGONER, HYATT H. Hawthorne. Cambridge, Mass., 1955.

Ernest Hemingway

323. BECK, WARREN. "The Shorter Happy Life of Mrs. Macomber," Modern Fiction Studies, I (November, 1955), 28–37.
   One of many studies debating the reliability of the guide (Wilson) as witness of Macomber's shooting.

Henry James

James is the fountainhead—of this as of so many of our achievements and problems. The whole subject of unreliability can hardly be approached except in the context of his Prefaces and Notebooks.

324. BLACKMUR, R. P. (ed.). The Art of the Novel: Critical Prefaces of Henry James. New York, 1934.
325. MATTHIESSEN, F. O., and MURDOCK, KENNETH B. (eds.). The Notebooks of Henry James. Oxford, 1947.

General bibliography on James can be found in No. 1, pp. 592–99, and in Nos. 326 and 327.

326. RICHARDSON, LYON. "Bibliography of Henry James," in No. 328.
327. SPILLER, ROBERT, et al. Literary History of the United States. New York, 1948. III, 584–90.

Good sources of disagreement about James's narrators are:

328. DUPEE, F. W. (ed.). The Question of Henry James. New York, 1945.
329. Hound and Horn, Vol. VII, No. 3 (April–May, 1934), "Homage to Henry James."
   A special number.

330. *Kenyon Review*, V (Autumn, 1943), "The Henry James Number."

On *The American:*

331. CLAIR, JOHN A. "*The American:* A Reinterpretation," *PMLA*, LXXIV (December, 1959), 613–18.

On *The Aspern Papers:*

332. BASKETT, SAM S. "The Sense of the Present in *The Aspern Papers*" ("Papers of the Michigan Academy of Science, Arts, and Letters," Vol. XLIV, 1959), pp. 381–88.

333. STEIN, WILLIAM BYSSHE. "*The Aspern Papers:* A Comedy of Masks," *Nineteenth-Century Fiction*, XIV (September, 1959), 172–78.

On "The Author of Beltraffio":

334. MATTHIESSEN, F. O. (ed.). *Stories of Writers and Artists, by Henry James.* New York, n.d.

> "And increasing this unreality is the fact that he set himself to dramatize the aesthetic gospel of the eighties without quite indicating, perhaps without being quite sure at this stage of his development, exactly how much of it he accepted for himself" (p. 2).

On *The Awkward Age:*

> "And the worst of it is that, among all these competitors, the reader is at a loss to know where to invest his sympathies. This is an almost fatal oversight in a novel . . ." (in No. 11, enlarged ed., p. 247).

On *Confidence:*

335. WILSON, EDMUND. "The Ambiguity of Henry James," in No. 328.

> "Is the fishy Bernard Longueville . . . really intended for a sensitive and interesting young man or is he a prig in the manner of Jane Austen?" (p. 168).

On "The Liar":

336. BEWLEY, MARIUS. *The Complex Fate: Hawthorne, Henry James and Some Other American Writers.* London, 1952.

On "The Pupil":

> See pp. 365–66, above.

On *The Sacred Fount:*

337. EDEL, LEON (ed.). "Introductory Essay," in *The Sacred Fount.* New York, 1953.

> "And James' attitude is one of complete *neutrality*. So neutral is he that he leaves a wide imaginative margin for the reader who, if he is not careful, will be adding material from his own mind to the story" (p. xxv). See also No. 335 (pp. 80–81).

On *The Tragic Muse:*
338. CARGILL, OSCAR. "Gabriel Nash—Somewhat Less than Angel?"
     Nineteenth-Century Fiction, XIV (December, 1959), 231–39.
   On *The Turn of the Screw:*
     See above, pp. 311–15, 370.
   On *The Wings of the Dove:*
     Leavis (No. 43) attacks those who, like Van Wyck Brooks and
     H. R. Hays, see Merton Densher as a "villain."

When one puts together these and the many other conflicting claims
about James's characters, he finds himself with an almost maddening
chorus of charges and countercharges: "Mr. Leavis does not 'get' James.
. . . One is quite at a loss to understand how this enlightened critic should
so resolutely decline to read what is written in capitals on every page of
The Ambassadors. . . ." Pound "betrays the fact that he never did really
'get' James" (Beach, in No. 11). "No critic seems to have gotten down
into the depths of James's irony; most of them have taken him at his
word . . ." (Robert Cantwell, in No. 239). "It has recently been assumed
that James believed entirely in the rightness" of Isabel Archer's conduct
in the *Portrait of a Lady.* "But that is to misread not merely the ending,
but all of James's own 'characteristic characterization' of Isabel" (F. O.
Matthiessen, in *Henry James: The Major Phase*). James "could never
have known how we should feel about the gibbering disembowelled crew
who hover around one another with sordid shadowy designs" in *The
Awkward Age* (Wilson, in No. 335). "Actually, the various ways in which
we are to feel about the various characters [in *The Awkward Age*] are
delicately but surely defined" (Leavis, in No. 43). "Not one commentator
has shown signs of understanding the design James has so clearly presented
in *The Princess Casamassima*" (Louise Bogan, in No. 328). "Spender's
. . . outlandish claim that 'there is something particularly obscene about
What Maisie Knew'" (Leavis, in No. 43)—thus on and on.

James Joyce

For a general bibliography of Joyce, see *Modern Fiction Studies,* IV
(Spring, 1958), 72–99. See also No. 187.

339. BURKE, KENNETH. "Three Definitions," *Kenyon Review,* XIII
     (Spring, 1951), 173–92.
       "Even though we may partly smile, we take each stage of his
       [Stephen's] development 'seriously'" (p. 182).
340. DONOGHUE, DENIS. "Joyce and the Finite Order," *Sewanee Review,*
     LXVIII (Spring, 1960), 256–73.

341. EMPSON, WILLIAM. "The Theme of Ulysses," *Kenyon Review*, XVIII (Winter, 1956), 26–52.

342. GOLDBERG, S. L. *The Classical Temper: A Study of James Joyce's Ulysses*. London, 1961.
   Chap. iv, "The Modes of Irony in *Ulysses*," is an especially valuable discussion of the distance between Joyce and his two main characters.

343. ———. "Joyce and the Artist's Fingernails," *A Review of English Literature*, II (April, 1961), 59–73.

344. KAIN, RICHARD M. "Joyce: Aquinas or Dedalus?" *Sewanee Review*, LXIV (Autumn, 1956), 675–83.

345. KENNER, HUGH. *Dublin's Joyce*. Bloomington, Ind., 1956.

346. ———. "The *Portrait* in Perspective," *Kenyon Review*, X (Summer, 1948), 361–81.

347. NOON, WILLIAM T., S.J. *Joyce and Aquinas*. New Haven, 1957.
   Takes issue with Gorman, Gilbert, and others who have read Stephen's ideas as Joyce's own.

348. REDFORD, GRANT. "The Role of Structure in Joyce's 'Portrait,'" *Modern Fiction Studies*, IV (Spring, 1958), 21–30.
   Sees the book as the "objectification of an artistic proposition and a method" pronounced by Stephen.

349. THOMPSON, FRANCIS I. "A Portrait of the Artist Asleep," *Western Review*, XIV (1950), 245–53.
   All previous interpretations of *Finnegans Wake* have mistaken Joyce's intentions with his main character, the narrator-dreamer. He is the son, Jerry (Shem), not HCE!

350. THOMPSON, LAWRANCE. *A Comic Principle in Sterne—Meredith—Joyce*. Oslo, 1954.

Mary McCarthy

351. CORKE, HILARY. "Lack of Confidence," *Encounter*, VII (July, 1956), 75–78.
   "But whose belief is it [in *A Charmed Life*]? Martha's? The ex-husband's? Miss McCarthy's? We simply do not know, and I entirely doubt whether Miss McCarthy does either" (p. 77).

Herman Melville

352. BOWEN, MERLIN. "*Redburn* and the Angle of Vision," *Modern Philology*, LII (November, 1954), 100–109.

353. SCHIFFMAN, JOSEPH. "Melville's Final Stage, Irony: A Re-examination of *Billy Budd* Criticism," *American Literature*, XXII (1950), 128–36.

Billy's last words are not Melville's own "testament of acceptance."

John Milton

354. EMPSON, WILLIAM. "A Defense of Delilah," *Sewanee Review,*
LXVIII (Spring, 1960), 240–55.

Marcel Proust

355. BRÉE, GERMAINE. *Marcel Proust and Deliverance from Time.* Translated by C. J. RICHARDS and A. D. TRUITT. New York, 1955; London, 1956.
356. SAMUEL, MAURICE. "The Concealments of Marcel: Proust's Jewish-
ness," *Commentary* (January, 1960), 8–28.

Samuel Richardson

357. BOYCE, BENJAMIN. Review of Ian Watt's *The Rise of the Novel,*
Philological Quarterly, XXXVII (July, 1958), 304–6.
   Sees some intentional irony in portrayal of Pamela; *Pamela*
   "need not be read as if it were totally naïve."
358. RABKIN, NORMAN. "*Clarissa:* A Study in the Nature of Convention,"
ELH, XXIII (September, 1956), 204–17.

Jonathan Swift

359. SHERBURN, GEORGE. "Errors concerning the Houyhnhnms," *Modern Philology,* LVI (November, 1958), 92–97.
360. WILLIAMS, KATHLEEN. *Jonathan Swift and the Age of Compromise.*
Lawrence, Kan., 1958.

Robert Penn Warren

361. GIRAULT, NORTON R. "The Narrator's Mind as Symbol: An Analysis of *All the King's Men,*" *Accent* (Summer, 1947). Reprinted
in No. 1.

C. SOME SOURCES OF THE MODERN UNRELIABLE NARRATOR

1. *Examples of self-conscious narration used as ornament in comic
fiction before Sterne:* (a) Cervantes, *Don Quixote* (1605); (b) [T.
Durfey?], *Zelinda: An Excellent New Romance* (1676); (c) Marivaux,
Pharsamon (1712?); translated as *Pharsamond* by J. Lockman (1750);
(d) Fielding, *Joseph Andrews* (1742) and *Tom Jones* (1749); (e) *The
History of Charlotte Summers, the Fortunate Parish Girl* (1749?); (f)
Green, G. S., *The Life of Mr. John Van, a Clergyman's Son* (n.d.); (g)
The Adventures of Mr. Loveill . . . (1750); (h) *The Adventures of Cap-*

tain *Greenland, Written in Imitation of All Those Wise, Learned, Witty, and Humorous Authors Who Either Already Have, or Hereafter May Write in the Same Stile and Manner* (1752); (i) [Kidgell, John], *The Card* (1755); (j) *The Life and Memoirs of Mr. Ephraim Tristram Bates, Commonly Called Corporal Bates, a Broken-Hearted Soldier* (1756). For a much fuller listing on this and the following topics, see Nos. 362 and 363.

362. BOOTH, WAYNE C. "Tristram Shandy and Its Precursors: The Self-Conscious Narrator." Ph.D. diss., University of Chicago, 1950.

363. ———. "The Self-Conscious Narrator in Comic Fiction before Tristram Shandy," *PMLA*, LXVII (1952), 163–85.
        A less complete listing.

   2. Examples of works (before 1760) held together by the self-conscious portrait of the commentator: (a) Montaigne, *Essays*; (b) Bouchet, *Serées* (*Les Serées de Guillaume Bouchet, Sieur de Brocourt*), ed. C. E. Roybet [Paris, 1873–1882], first published 1584–1598; (c) [Béroalde de Verville], *Le Moyen de Parvenir/œuvre contenant la raison de tout ce qui esté, est, et sera avec demonstrations certaines et necessaires selon la rencontre des effetcs [sic] de vertu Et adviendra que ceux qui auront nez à porter lunettes s'en serviront, ainsi qu'il est escrit au Dictionnaire a Dormir en toutes langues . . .* (1610); (d) Bruscambille, *Discours Facetieux et tres-recreatifs, pour oster des esprits d'un chacun, tout ennuy & inquietude . . .* (1609); (e) Burton, *The Anatomy of Melancholy* (1621); (f) Francis Kirkman, *The Unlucky Citizen Experimentally described in the various Misfortunes of an Unlucky Londoner, Calculated for the Meridian of this City but may serve by way of Advice to all the Cominalty of England, but more perticularly to Parents and Children / Masters and Servants / Husbands and Wives / Intermixed with severall Choice Novels. Stored with variety of Examples and advice / President and Precept* (1673); (g) John Dunton, *A Voyage Round the World: or, a Pocket-Library, Divided into several Volumes. The First of which contains the Rare Adventures of Don Kainophilus, From his Cradle to his 15th Year. The Like Discoveries in such a Method never made by any Rambler before. The whole Work intermixt with Essays, Historical, Moral and Divine; and all other kinds of Learning. Done into English by a Lover of Travels. Recommended by the Wits of both Universities* (1691); (h) *Farrago*, by "Pilgrim Plowden" (1733); (i) *Vitulus Aureus: The Golden Calf; or, A Supplement to Apuleius's Golden Ass. An Enquirey Physico-Critico-Patheologico-Moral into the Nature and Efficacy of Gold. . . . With the Wonders of the Psychoptic Looking-Glass, Lately Invented by the Author—Joakim Philander, M.A.* (1749). There were many other works of this kind between Montaigne and Sterne, to say

nothing of the innumerable collections of jests, periodical essays, brief tales, etc., held together by the character of the dramatized "editor"; it is known that Sterne was acquainted with a great number of them. For a detailed discussion of this tradition, see No. 362, pp. 169–231.

3. *Examples of satires using unreliable and self-conscious narration:* see No. 362, pp. 134–50, for a discussion, among others, of (a) *The Praise of Folly* (1509); (b) *Gargantua and Pantagruel* (1537); (c) *A History of the Ridiculous Extravagancies of Monsieur Oufle . . .* (1711); (d) [Thomas D'Urfey?], *An Essay Towards the Theory of the Intelligible World. Intuitively Considered. Designed for Forty-nine Parts. Part III. Consisting of a Preface, a Post-script, and a little something between. By Gabriel John. Enriched with a Faithful Account of his Ideal Voyage, and Illustrated with Poems by several Hands, as likewise with other strange things not insufferably Clever, nor furiously to the Purpose. The Archetypally Second Edition . . . . Printed in the Year One Thousand Seven Hundred, &c.* (n.d.); (e) *Like will to Like, as the Scabby Squire Said to the Mangy Viscount . . .* (1728); (f) John Arbuthnot (and others?), *Memoirs of the Extraordinary Life, Works and Discoveries of Martinus Scriblerus* (1741).

4. *Examples of imitations of Tristram Shandy and other works influenced by Sterne:* (a) [George Alexander Stevens], *The History of Tom Fool* (1760); (b) *Yorick's Meditations upon various Interesting and Important Subjects. Viz. Upon Nothing. Upon Something. Upon the Thing . . .* (1760); (c) [John Carr], *The Life and Opinions of Tristram Shandy, Gentleman* (1760); (d) *Explanatory Remarks upon the Life and Opinions of Tristram Shandy. . . . By Jeremiah Kunastrokius, M.D.* (1760); (e) *The Life and Opinions of Miss Sukey Shandy of Bow Street, Gentlewoman . . .* (1760); (f) *The Life and Opinions of Bertram Montfichet, Esq.* (1760); (g) *A Funeral Discourse, Occasioned by the much lamented Death of Mr. Yorick, Prebendary of Y–K . . . . By Christopher Flagellan* (1761); (h) *The Life, Travels, and Adventures, of Christopher Wagstaff, Gentleman, Grandfather to Tristram Shandy . . .* written in the OUT-OF-THE-WAY WAY (1762)—actually a very witty satire, accusing Sterne of plagiarism from John Dunton's *Voyage Round the World*, this work is often listed as an "imitation"; (i) [Richard Griffith], *The Triumvirate or the Authentic Memoirs of A. B. and C.* (1764); (j) *The Peregrination of Jeremiah Grant, Esq. . . .* (1763); (k) [Francis Gentleman], *A Trip to the Moon . . . . By Sir Humphrey Lunatic, Bart.* (York, 1764–65); (l) [Samuel Paterson], *Another Traveller! . . . By Coriat, Jr.* (1767); (m) *Sentimental Lucubrations, by Peter Pennyless* (1770); (n) [Richard Griffith], *The Koran: or, the Life, Character, and Sentiments of Tria. Juncta in Uno, M.N.A. or Master of No Arts. The Posthumous Works*

of a late Celebrated Genius, Deceased (1770); (o) Herbert Lawrence, *The Contemplative Man; or, The History of Christopher Crab, Esq.* (1771); (p) [Henry Mackenzie], *The Man of Feeling* (Edinburgh, 1771); (q) [Richard Graves], *The Spiritual Quixote* (1773); (r) *Yorick's Skull; or, College Oscitations. With some remarks on the Writings on Sterne, and a Specimen of the Shandean Stile* (1777); (s) [George Keate], *Sketches from Nature; taken and coloured, in a Journey to Margate* (1779); (t) *Continuation of Yorick's Sentimental Journey* (1788); (u) *Flight of Inflatus: or, the Sallies, Stories, and Adventures of a Wild-Goose Philosopher. By the author of the Trivler* (1791); (v) *The Observant Pedestrian* (1795); (w) William Beckford, *Modern Novel Writing, or the Elegant Enthusiast . . . A Rhapsodical Romance . . .* (1796).

After 1800 perhaps a majority of all novels have some "Shandean" intrusion, and there are still many works that are obviously imitative throughout, e.g., (x) [Eaton Stannard Barrett], *The Miss-Led General; a Serio-Comic, Satiric, Mock-Heroic Romance* (1808); (y) John Galt, *The Provost* (1822); (z) [W. H. Pyne], *Wine and Walnuts; or, After Dinner Chit-Chat, by Ephraim Hardcastle, Citizen and Dry-Salter* (1823); (zz) *Duodecimo, or The Scribbler's Progress. An Autobiography, Written by an Insignificant Little Volume, and Published Likewise by Itself* (1849). See also the many Shandean devices in better-known authors: in Thackeray, especially his contributions to *The Snob* as an undergraduate at Cambridge; in Balzac (e.g., *Le peau de chagrin*); in Poe (see especially the short story, "Lionizing," which even has a treatise on Nosology); in Dickens, in Melville, and of course in Trollope. Needless to say, this listing is radically incomplete. For a good, though somewhat inaccurate, bibliography of Sterne's influence in France, see F. B. Barton, *Étude sur l'influence de Laurence Sterne en France au dix-huitième siècle* (Paris, 1911), especially the bibliography reprinted from Pigoreau, pp. 154–57. For additional imitations and burlesques, see Wilbur L. Cross, *The Life and Times of Laurence Sterne* (New Haven, 1929), pp. 230–231, 271, 282–85.

D. A GALLERY OF UNRELIABLE NARRATORS AND REFLECTORS

In general I have excluded works discussed in the text. Though I have weighted the list, for obvious reasons, toward the more difficult kinds of unreliability, the presence of works like "The Spectacles" should remind the reader that the kind of irony I have called unreliability can range all the way from unstated but palpable brutality or stupidity to the baffling mixtures of some contemporary fiction. I should add that, although the presence or absence of unreliability says nothing about literary quality, my list is in part based on judgments of merit: I have excluded many shoddy imitations of Sterne in the nineteenth century and almost as many novels about novelists in the twentieth. To save space I must list only one work for each author, though most of them have succumbed again and again to the heady wines of secret communication. For further titles especially from recent years, see *Cumulated Fiction Index: 1945–60*, ed. G. B. Cotton and Alan Glencross (London, 1960); most of the novels listed as "First Person Stories" (pp. 198–217) and "Experimental Novels" (pp. 178–79) provide examples of unreliable narration.

Kingsley Amis, *Lucky Jim*. Sherwood Anderson, "The Egg." Jane Austen, *Lady Susan*. Robert Bage, *Hermsprong*. James Baldwin, *Go Tell It on the Mountain*. Djuna Barnes, *Nightwood*. Samuel Beckett, *Molloy*. Saul Bellow, *The Victim*. Stella Benson, "Story Coldly Told." Emily Brontë, *Wuthering Heights*. Michel Butor, *L'emploi du temps*, Erskine Caldwell, *Journeyman*. Albert Camus, *The Plague*. Joyce Cary, *The Horse's Mouth*. Jean Cayrol, *On vous parle*. Jacques Chardonne, *Eva*. John Cheever, "Torch Song." Anton Chekhov, "Wild Gooseberries." Ivy Compton-Burnett, *A Heritage and Its History*. Joseph Conrad, *Heart of Darkness*. Walter de la Mare, *Memoirs of a Midget*. Defoe, *Robinson Crusoe*. Dos Passos, *USA*. Dostoevski, "The Dream of a Ridiculous Man." Georges Duhamel, *Cry out of the Depths*. Marguerite Duras, *Le square*. Lawrence Durrell, *Mountolive*. Maria Edgeworth, *Castle Rackrent*. Hans Fallada, *Little Man What Now?* Faulkner, *The Wild Palms*. Gide, *Les Caves du Vatican*. William Golding, *Lord of the Flies*. Henry Green, *Loving*. Graham Greene, *The Quiet American*. Albert J. Guerard, *The Bystander*. Mark Harris, *The Southpaw*. Hemingway, *The Sun Also Rises*. Joseph Hergesheimer, *Java Head*. Hermann Hesse, *Steppenwolf*. Thomas Hinde, *Happy as Larry*. Aldous Huxley, *Point Counter Point*. Henry James (see chap. xii). James Joyce (see chap. xi). Valery Larbaud, *A. O. Barnabooth: His Diary*. Ring Lardner, "A Caddy's Diary." Wyndham Lewis, *The Childermass*. Mary McCarthy, *Cast a Cold Eye*. Carson McCullers, *The Ballad of the Sad Café*. Thomas Mann, *Dr. Faustus*. Katherine Mansfield, "A Dill Pickle." J. P. Marquand, *The Late George Apley*. Herman Melville, *The Confidence Man*. Henry de Montherlant, *Les jeunes filles*. Wright Morris, *Love among the Cannibals*. Vladimir Nabokov, *The Real Life of Sebastian Knight*. Flannery O'Connor, "The Geranium." Frank O'Connor, "Mac's Masterpiece." Edgar Allan Poe, "The Spectacles." Katherine Anne Porter, "That Tree." J. D. Salinger, *The Catcher in the Rye*. Jean-Paul Sartre, *La nausée*. Irwin Shaw, "The Eighty-Yard Run." Alan Sillitoe, "The Loneliness of the Long Distance Runner." Tobias Smollett, *Humphry Clinker*. Robert Louis Stevenson, *The Master of Ballantrae*. Italo Svevo (Ettore Schmitz), *Confessions of Zeno*. Frank Swinnerton, *A Month in Gordon Square*. Elizabeth

Taylor, "A Red-Letter Day." Jim Thompson, *Nothing More than Murder* (one of innumerable mystery and murder tales using impersonal techniques—proof, in its mediocrity, that impersonality in itself is nothing). James Thurber, "You Could Look It Up." Lionel Trilling, "Of This Time, Of That Place." Mark Twain, *Huckleberry Finn.* Miguel de Unamuno, *The Life of Don Quixote and Sancho according to Miguel de Cervantes Saavedra, Expounded with Comment, by Unamuno.* Eudora Welty, "Put Me in the Sky!" Calder Willingham, *Natural Child.* Virginia Woolf, *Mrs. Dalloway.* Marguerite Yourcenar, *Coup de grâce.*

Index

435

The Bibliography, which includes some authors and titles not mentioned in the text, is not indexed here.